Consumer Politics in Postwar Japan

STUDIES OF THE EAST ASIAN INSTITUTE

STUDIES OF THE EAST ASIAN INSTITUTE
Columbia University

The East Asian Institute is Columbia University's center for research, publication, and teaching on modern East Asia. The Studies of the East Asian Institute were inaugurated in 1962 to bring to a wider public the results of significant new research on modern and contemporary East Asia.

Consumer Politics in Postwar Japan

*The Institutional Boundaries
of Citizen Activism*

Patricia L. Maclachlan

COLUMBIA   UNIVERSITY   PRESS   NEW   YORK

COLUMBIA UNIVERSITY PRESS
Publishers Since 1893
New York   Chichester, West Sussex
Copyright © 2002 Columbia University Press
All rights reserved

Library of Congress Cataloging-in-Publication Data

Maclachlan, Patricia L.
    Consumer politics in Postwar Japan : the institutional boundaries of
citizen activism / Patricia L. Maclachlan.
        p. cm. — (Studies of the East Asian Institute, Columbia University)
    Includes bibliographical references and index.
    ISBN 0–231–12346–9 (cloth : alk. paper) — ISBN 0–231–12347–7 (pbk.
: alk. paper)
        1. Consumer protection—Japan—History.   2. Consumer
protection—History.   I. title.
    HC465.C63 M28 2001
    381.3′4′095209045—dc21   2001032521

c   10   9   8   7   6   5   4   3   2   1
p   10   9   8   7   6   5   4   3   2   1

To my parents, Mae and "Mac" Maclachlan

Contents

Acknowledgments

Several years ago, when this book was nothing but an idea and a boxful of notes, I wrote the first draft of my acknowledgments. I embarked on the exercise to help myself overcome a bad case of writer's block. By the time I was finished, the writer's block still lingered, but I had acquired a keen awareness of just how dependent we academics are on a diverse array of friends, mentors, and informants as we go about our business. As the book expanded from dissertation form into its current state, so, too, did the number of persons who contributed in some form to its development. I am indebted to them all.

This project began over lunch at the Columbia University Faculty Club with my adviser, Gerald Curtis, who was determined to find me a dissertation topic by the end of the meal. I had long been toying with the idea of researching the Japanese consumer movement, but since no one knew much about the topic at that time, I didn't mention it. After discussing my interest in questions of political participation and citizen mobilization, Professor Curtis—with no prompting from me—immediately suggested Japanese consumerism as a case study. I took this as a positive sign and ran with the topic.

I would like to begin by thanking the members of my dissertation committee (Gerald Curtis, James Morley, Hugh Patrick, Frank Upham, and Robert Uriu), all of whom gave me excellent advice and support. In Japan, I am grateful to Professor Kaneko Akira of the law faculty of Keio University, who gave me a home base during the early research phase of this project and introduced me to many of my informants and written sources. Staff members of the Iidabashi branch of the Tōkyō Consumer Center and Hosokawa Kōichi, the librarians, and other staff members of the Japan Consumer Information Center (Kokumin seikatsu sentaa), also provided me with invaluable assistance in my research.

Special thanks go to the many Japanese consumer advocates who granted me interviews and allowed me to observe their meetings, rallies, and demonstrations. I am particularly grateful to Andō Kyōji, Hara Sanae, Itō Yasue, Miyamoto Kazuko, Ohta Yoshiyasu, Shimizu Hatoko, and Takada Yuri for their extra help, attention, and, in some cases, friendship. These remarkable people made researching the Japanese consumer movement a pleasure.

This project would not have advanced very far had it not been for generous assistance from the following sources. Grants from the Mombushō (Japanese Ministry of Education), the SSHRC (Social Science and Humanities Research Council of Canada), and the Sanyo Bank of Japan facilitated both the research and writing stages of the dissertation. I am also very grateful to the Program on U.S.-Japan Relations at Harvard University, which supported me for one year as a postdoctoral research associate and enabled me to begin revising my thesis. Finally, I thank the Association for Asian Studies and the Mitsubishi Foundation of Houston for financing my more recent research trips to Japan and the East Asian Institute of Columbia University for including my book in its series.

A number of individuals took time out of their very hectic schedules to critique previous drafts of this manuscript. James Morley and Steven Vogel patiently plowed through several of those drafts, offering excellent advice each time. T. J. Pempel and Margarita Estevez-Abe helped me position my subject matter in a broader political science context, as did John Campbell, who commented on an article that incorporates many of the arguments of this book. Sheldon Garon, who tackled parts of the manuscript while sitting in the "pit" awaiting jury duty, helped me fine-tune the historical chapters. Frank Trentmann, one of the organizers of the recent "Beyond Markets" conference at Princeton University, gave me invaluable feedback on my treatment of British consumerism. Finally, Jonathan Bloch, Robert Pekkanen, and two anonymous reviewers offered a number of eye-opening suggestions. My thanks to all for your patience, insights, and encouragement.

Thanks also to those who inspired, pushed, and cajoled me through various stages of this project. Madge Huntington, a dear friend who also runs the East Asian Institute series, guided me through the publication process. Sheila Smith, my "dissertation mate," has been a friend in every sense of the word since this project began. Margarita Estevez-Abe and Sheldon Garon both inspired me with their wisdom, creativity, and friendship. Last, heartfelt thanks to my best friend and husband, Zoltan Barany. Zoltan—a fellow political scientist—and I happily agreed some time ago that we would keep our noses out of each other's academic affairs. While we both kept to our word, Zoltan's matter-of-fact approach to the writing process, strong work ethic, and wicked sense of humor helped me maintain my perspective when my self-doubts and overly active sense of perfectionism threatened to shut this project down. I wonder how far this book would have progressed had he not been around.

To conclude, I wish to acknowledge my parents, "Mac" and Mae Maclachlan, for their unfaltering support—both financial and psychological— throughout my graduate and professional careers. As I write this, my mother is across the hall painting what will soon become a baby nursery, and my father is outside surveying our sorry excuse for a lawn. I thank them for all they have done and continue to do for me. It is to them that I lovingly dedicate this book.

Consumer Politics in Postwar Japan

Introduction

Since the early postwar period, the hopes and frustrations of Japanese consumer organizations have been conveyed through rich and revealing metaphors drawn from Japanese history. In one of the oldest and most colorful examples, housewives in their consuming capacity are compared with the distressed wives of feudal times who would seek refuge from their oppressive husbands and await divorces at special Buddhist temples known as *kakekomidera*.[1] Like the hapless wives of old who had been abused by their spouses, early postwar consumers frequently fell victim to the unscrupulous practices of powerful business interests. Unlike their historical counterparts, however, disgruntled consumers lacked a place where they could "run to" (*kakekomu*) for refuge.

The establishment of a consumer *kakekomidera* at the national governmental level[2] that would address the specific concerns of consumers while giving them routinized access to the policymaking system was one of the primary political objectives of early postwar consumer organizations. After a few halfhearted attempts to address their demands during the early 1960s, the government finally responded in 1968 with the institutionalization of a comprehensive system of consumer protection policymaking and administration that accorded consumer advocates opportunities to articulate the consumer interest at the national level. Advocates, however, roundly criticized the new system for being biased toward producers and providing consumers with little more than symbolic representation in the policy process. For all intents and purposes, they argued, consumers had been "turned away at the gate" (*monzenbarai*) of the national political system.

Although one must always discount the possibility of poetic license in such metaphorical appraisals of the political, it is well known that Japanese consumer representatives lack both direct inroads into the national policy-making system and the financial and political resources needed to open those inroads. It is also common knowledge—thanks in part to the laments of American trade officials intent on opening Japanese domestic markets to more foreign imports and investment—that consumers' economic interests have often been overlooked by the country's pro-producer political system. Consider Japan's inefficient distribution system, its notoriously high consumer and land prices, and, in many sectors, the high incidence of cartels, to cite just a few examples.

With evidence like this, it is small wonder that private consumer advocates often portray both themselves and their constituents as victims of businesses and their political and bureaucratic allies. Popular analysts of Japanese consumerism, meanwhile, have taken these views one step further by depicting the movement as beholden to producers. Karel van Wolferen, for example, argues in *The Enigma of Japanese Power* that consumer organizations operate against consumers' economic interests by "zealously working to keep food prices high and to limit consumer choice to domestic produce" in accordance with postwar state goals (1990:52–53). George Fields, a veteran Japan watcher and long-time Tōkyō resident, echoes these sentiments in *Gucci on the Ginza* by marveling at the absence of protest against high consumer prices and asking rhetorically, "Japanese consumer advocates, where are you?" (1989:134).

Japanese nationals, as well, are prone to movement bashing. In a *Chūō kōron* article, one critic likens consumer organizations to a bunch of clowns (*piero*), bumbling representatives of an otherwise sophisticated consuming public (Domon 1989). Even the country's leading politicians have been known to comment on the alleged failure of private consumer advocates to act on the best interests of their constituents, as I discovered for myself a few years ago at a meeting in New York between a top-ranking Liberal Democratic Party (LDP) politician and a group of scholars. In a discussion on regulatory reform, this well-known conservative leader asserted that deregulation was proceeding slowly because consumer representatives had failed to openly support the process! "I invited consumer advocates to contact and work with the government on this issue," he remarked to the group while shaking his head in disbelief, "but nobody came!"

Clearly, the stereotypical view of Japanese consumer advocates is that they are either victims or handmaidens of powerful producers and politically incapable of representing the consuming public in national political processes. Like all stereotypes, this one contains a few grains of truth. Japanese advocates do, for instance, behave in ways that appear downright inimical to the economic interests of consumers, as American critics are quick to point out. At the same time, however, these stereotypes blind us to the fact that consumer organizations have achieved some of their policy-related goals *despite* their resource deficiencies, limited presence in national policymaking circles, and idiosyncratic behavior. Over the past three decades, for instance, advocates were instrumental in tightening the country's antitrust regulations, introducing some of the world's most stringent food safety standards, and enacting a product liability law. If consumer representatives have indeed been victimized or co-opted by producers and "turned away at the gate" of the national policy process, how can we account for these policy-related achievements?

Consumers in Politics: The Literature

The literature on Japanese public-interest policymaking offers us few clues to this puzzle. Chalmers Johnson's "developmental state" model (1982), for example, dismisses societal interests as significant political actors in Japan by portraying an economic policy process in which pro-producer bureaucrats are firmly in control. According to this argument, we should expect the consumer policy process to be governed by prescient bureaucrats acting in the long-term best interests of the economy. While recognizing the leading role played by bureaucrats in the consumer policymaking system, I challenge this point of view with evidence that consumer policy is occasionally introduced *against* the wishes of some of Japan's economic bureaucrats and in ways that inflict costs—albeit modest—on producers.

Scholars who accord a greater role for politicians in the policy process also contribute to misunderstandings about consumer protection policymaking. Kent Calder (1988), for example, argues that public-interest policies are granted as concessions by LDP politicians during periods of political and economic crisis, whereas routine policymaking is dominated by private interests like industry. Although it is certainly true that Japanese politicians are more likely to give in to consumer and other societal demands when the political going gets rough, this model overlooks the fact that some consumer-related policy is introduced during periods of relative political stability and with significant input from consumer representatives.

Margaret McKean (1993), finally, contends that public-interest policies are the product of a pro-producer corporatist system consisting of bureaucrats, conservative politicians, and organized private interests. As a result of long-term time horizons and electoral and other incentives, these actors anticipate the demands of poorly organized societal groups by introducing policies that serve the long-term interests of those groups. While this model explains a great deal about who participates directly in the consumer policy process and why, it underestimates the extent of indirect consumer participation in the policy process, levels of conflict between consumer organizations and mainstream policymakers in that process, and the degree to which the politically "weak" can influence decision making.

The literature on the Japanese consumer movement also underestimates the role and impact of consumer advocates in the national consumer policy process. In a 1992 study of consumer-producer relations and their implication for Japan's external trade ties, for example, David Vogel notes that consumer representatives have allied with producers to promote agricultural protectionism at the expense of more competitive consumer prices at home. By arguing that "Japanese consumer organizations do not represent an important political challenge to the interests of . . . Japanese producers" and that "a disproportionate amount of their criticisms of business are criticisms of the practices of foreign businesses," Vogel ignores those many occasions when consumer representatives held domestic businesses to the very same product safety standards that were recently imposed on foreign producers (D. Vogel 1992:146). Put simply, consumer organizations may be much more willing to cooperate with business representatives than American organizations usually are, but they are not nearly as beholden to producers as David Vogel would have us believe.

Other studies of the movement make important contributions to our knowledge of Japanese consumerism while raising questions for further research. My own work (Maclachlan 1995) and Steven Vogel's 1999 study of the implications of movement behavior for rational-choice theories, for example, attack many of the stereotypes that shroud our understanding of Japanese consumer activism by showing that the movement's support for agricultural protectionism and the retention of regulatory controls over the economy are perfectly rational responses (S. Vogel 1999) to the movement's historical trajectories and alliances with other actors in the polity (Maclachlan 1995; Vogel 1999). Vogel also points out that in areas like food and product safety, consumer representatives have made substantial gains in the policy realm. He does not, however, explain exactly how those gains were made.

Other authors highlight the implications of consumer activism for grass-roots citizen participation in politics. Maurine A. Kirkpatrick, for instance, correctly identifies the upsurge in consumer activism during the 1960s and early 1970s as a manifestation of a burgeoning political assertiveness among Japanese citizens and, by implication, a reflection of the general public's growing intolerance of the government's overwhelmingly pro-business policies (Kirkpatrick 1975). Kirkpatrick's work challenges the stereotypical view that consumer organizations do not reflect the wishes of the broader consuming public while complementing the research of scholars who have explored Japanese social movements as alternative channels of interest articulation for ordinary citizens (see Broadbent 1998; Huddle and Reich 1987; Krauss and Simcock 1980; McKean 1981; Upham, 1987). Kirkpatrick does not, however, explore the myriad ways in which the consumer movement articulates grassroots interests or, for that matter, influences national policymaking.

The subject of citizen participation in politics also permeates recent studies by Robin M. LeBlanc (1999) and Joyce Gelb and Margarita Estevez-Abe (1998) on the Seikatsu Club Cooperative, one of the most progressive local consumer cooperatives and politically active citizen movements in Japan. These works are among the first to examine this wing of the consumer cooperative movement and are fascinating contributions to the study of women in Japanese politics. Neither study, however, explains how consumer-oriented organs compete with mainstream interest groups in their efforts to influence government policy.

Whereas the Kirkpatrick, Gelb and Estevez-Abe, and LeBlanc studies concentrate on consumer organizations at the grassroots level, Sheldon Garon (1997) takes a more systemic view of Japanese consumerism. Garon analyzes the cooperation of both prewar and early postwar women's/consumer organizations with government authorities in order to abolish legal prostitution and to promote rational consumption patterns, high savings rates, and other state goals. By showing persuasively how consumer organizations have functioned as vehicles of social control by the state, Garon provides new and compelling insights into that gray area between state and society that has long intrigued Japan scholars. It is important to note, however, another dimension to the consumer story that falls outside the purview of Garon's research paradigm, a dimension marked by open and sustained conflict between representative organizations and state authorities when their goals diverge. The details of that dimension, I contend, are integral to understanding the contemporary consumer protection policymaking process and the movement's influence over that process.

The Argument in Brief

If the popular and academic literature proves any one thing in common, it is that we still know very little about the nature of consumer movement activism in the policy process and the impact of constituent organizations on policies relating to the consumer. What, for example, do consumer activists do in order to influence policymakers, and why do they do it? Under what circumstances can consumer activists expect to wring concessions from a policy process that is clearly biased in favor of producers? When, in other words, do consumer strategies fail, and when do they succeed?

The key to both questions, I believe, lies not so much in access by movement leaders to financial and political resources as in the nature of political institutions at both the national and local levels. Strategically, consumer representatives have learned to compensate for their resource deficiencies and lack of direct influence over national policymaking by forging alternative, nonelectoral channels of interest articulation at the local level, where institutional opportunities for political participation are more numerous. Movement representatives activate these channels at various stages of the national policymaking process to mobilize public opinion behind specific policy options and then direct the indicators of that opinion to the center in an effort to sway national policymakers. As such, the localities can be viewed as modern-day "temples for seeking refuge" (*kakekomidera*) that serve as political and bureaucratic havens for disgruntled consumers who have been "turned away at the gate" (*monzenbarai*) of national officialdom, as well as back channels to national corridors of decision-making power.

When the political conditions are right, mobilizing public opinion through local institutions can have a positive impact on national policy outputs. Put simply, movement strategies succeed in the face of political opposition when the alliance of conservative politicians, bureaucrats, and business representatives—the movers and shakers of Japanese consumer protection policymaking—is diffuse and fraught with dissension. But when that alliance is limited in size and based on consensus, consumer representatives fail in their objectives no matter how well endowed in political and financial resources they may be. While the long-term configurations of both local and national institutions may shape the strategies adopted by consumer organizations, in other words, the overall effectiveness of those strategies is ultimately a function of short-term changes in those configurations at the national level.

The story of consumer politics in postwar Japan is replete with examples of how the politically disadvantaged can leverage small but significant concessions from state and economic interests, that is, how diffuse societal interests are incorporated into Japan's pro-producer polity. Accordingly, this study identifies new and innovative ways in which those interests can influence the outcomes of Japan's policymaking process, paying particular attention to local opportunities for citizen activism. In the process, it depicts a style of public-interest policymaking that, though rooted in corporatist arrangements encompassing state and economic interests, is more vulnerable to pluralist pressures from below than previously thought.

The Plan of the Book

For purposes of analysis and simplicity, I have divided the chapters of this book into two parts, the first of which explores the sources and evolution of Japanese consumer movement strategies from institutional, comparative, and historical perspectives. In chapter 1, I critique both the resource mobilization and the political opportunity structure approaches to social movements on the grounds that neither gives us enough analytical tools to assess the behavior and influence of consumer advocates in policymaking systems. I then combine aspects of these two approaches with insights gleaned from historical institutionalism to fashion an inductive analytical framework through which I address the major questions of this study and illuminate the rich details of postwar Japanese consumer advocacy. This approach assesses the behavior and impact of consumer movement organizations in the policy process largely—but not exclusively—from the perspective of the institutions making up that process. More specifically, it views institutions as filters through which socioeconomic and political developments and policy change can affect the resource configurations and hence strategies and policy-related impact of consumer organizations. This approach also assumes that institutional configurations are themselves subject to changes—changes that in turn can influence a movement's access to resources and its subsequent behavior in the policy process. Chapter 2 applies this framework to the American and British consumer movements and, in the process, proposes two contending models of consumer protection policymaking that serve as points of comparison for the Japan-specific chapters that follow.

In keeping with the historical focus of my analytical framework, chapters 3 and 4 trace the early postwar evolution of Japanese consumer organizations and show how shifting institutional contexts have influenced the resources at the movement's disposal and hence the nature of consumer participation in both national and local politics. I also use this opportunity to explore Japan's distinctive consumer identity and to explain some of the idiosyncratic features of the organized movement that have intrigued Japan watchers over the years, including the predominance of women, the willingness of con- sumer activists to cooperate with both government and producer groups, the movement's support of agricultural protectionism, and opposition to dereg- ulation, to cite just a few examples. The section ends with a chapter on the post-1968 consumer protection policymaking process and a detailed outline of the strategies employed by consumer representatives over the past three decades in their efforts to influence the direction of national policy. These strategies focus primarily on the activation or manipulation of public opinion through the institutions of local government. Throughout these last three chapters, I measure movement developments against broader trends in Jap- anese politics and compare them with those of consumer movements abroad and environmental organizations at home.

Before progressing, an important caveat is in order. With more than 4,600 consumer organs at the national and local levels and almost 1,200 consumer cooperatives (Keizaikikakuchō 1997:3), the contemporary consumer move- ment is an extremely large and varied network of consumer groups and organizations.[3] Since my purpose in this book is to assess the behavior and impact of consumer *advocates*[4] in the national policy process, I concentrate on the activities of private national and prefectural organizations that regu- larly participate in policy processes and legislative campaigns. Although I offer a few snapshots of local and other types of consumer organs, this book does not systematically address this vibrant and eclectic dimension of the organized movement except when national organizations link up with those organs in pursuit of common goals.

Whereas part 1 explores the evolution of consumer movement strategies in the political sphere, part 2 explains variations in the impact of post-1968 strategies on national policymaking. To that end, chapters 6 through 8 show how the strategies outlined at the end of chapter 5 were applied in the following issue-specific cases: the revision of the Antimonopoly Law during the mid-1970s, the 1983 deregulation of safety standards governing synthetic food additives, and the 1994 enactment of a product liability law based on the concept of strict liability. I chose these cases for several reasons. First, since each is characterized by open and protracted conflict between consumer organizations and business interests over how best to fulfill the consumer interest,[5] they serve as ideal laboratories for studying the circumstances in which private consumer organizations can wrest concessions from powerful business and government actors.[6] Second, since the cases involve variations in both access to movement resources and political power alignments at the national level, they enable us to test the proposition that politics in specific institutional contexts, rather than access to resources, ultimately determines the impact of movement organizations on policymaking. In the product liability and antimonopoly movements, for example, consumer organizations mobilized much smaller movements than they did in the anti-deregulation movement, yet they managed to accomplish considerably more in terms of policy outputs. To repeat, the key to this divergence in outcomes lies in the level of cohesiveness in pro-business power alliances: in the antitrust and product liability cases, the decision-making processes were diffuse and disorganized and hence vulnerable to outside influence in the form of movement-activated public opinion, whereas in the deregulation case, power was concentrated in a relatively small group of like-minded policymakers who were able to control the procedures and outcomes of the decision-making process despite the onslaught of public opposition.

Finally, these cases speak volumes about the structure of the consumer protection policymaking process and the quality of democratic participation in that process. In keeping with this latter point, and as befits a movement that places great store in political symbolism, consumer organizations have been careful to package all their political campaigns in the language of five universal consumer rights: the right to safety, the right to choose, the right to be informed, the right to redress, and the right to be heard. The campaigns chronicled here are a representative cross section of those rights, each of which has been overlooked—if not blatantly abused—by industry and governmental officials at specific points during the postwar period. The antitrust case, for example, involved movement efforts to enhance the right to a range of product choice at competitive prices in the marketplace, and the anti-deregulation and product liability cases addressed the right to product safety. The right to redress was a key objective in the product liability campaign, while the right to be informed was upheld to varying degrees in all three cases.

Last but not least, advocates in each of these cases pursued an objective that many regarded as a precondition for all other consumer rights: the institutionalization of the right to be heard in both business and governmental circles. In every case, consumer organizations articulated their demands with reference to the virtues of participatory democracy and chastised their national government for colluding with business interests during decision-making processes and excluding private representatives of the consumer interest from the corridors of national power. In this way, the politics of consumer protection in Japan is as much a normative statement on the condition of the political process itself and the representation of diffuse societal interests in that system as it is competition between consumer organizations and their business-oriented opponents for policy-related concessions.

And with this, we return full circle to the opening theme of this chapter. The significant postwar accomplishments of the organized consumer movement notwithstanding, advocates and their allies are still frustrated by the manner in which the interests of consumers are reflected in the Japanese public policy process. Accordingly, advocates continue to demand the introduction of a more responsive consumer-oriented bureaucratic space in the preexisting public policy process—a *kakekomidera*, in other words, that would guarantee consumer representatives direct access to decision-making processes. As I argue in the ninth and concluding chapter, at the turn of the century there are signs that a few of the movement's demands are finally being met, a development that bodes well not only for the future representation of consumers in the Japanese political system but for other diffuse societal interests as well.

Part 1

Japanese Consumer Advocacy
from Theoretical, Comparative,
and Historical Perspectives

1 Toward a Framework for the Study of Consumer Advocacy

Consumers are the bedrock of modern capitalist systems. By spending and saving, they provide both the demand according to which goods and services are supplied and the resources needed to fuel the production process. As such, consumers have significant power, for to ignore their basic wishes is to invite a drop in profits or, in the case of governments, defeat at the polls.

Consumers are not interested only in spending and saving, however. Many are also concerned about the impact of the production and consumption processes on the environment and the health and welfare of their families; how economic and political authorities respond to their grievances; the ways in which their voices are incorporated into business and government decision-making processes; and the incidence of corruption in government and business circles. In today's capitalist economies, in other words, consumers recognize that consumption has moral, social, and political ramifications as well as economic ones.

Unfortunately for consumers, producers and their governmental allies are not always willing to acknowledge all their economic and "quality-of-life" concerns, particularly those without an immediate bearing on the profitability of firms or the outcomes of elections. In response, consumers in many advanced industrial democracies have sought power through association in both the marketplace and the political system in order to pressure the economic and political powers that be into addressing their grievances. To that end, consumer activists have met with mixed results, both longitudinally and across national settings. In the United States, for example, consumer organizations spent years on the periphery of the political system before the mid-1960s, at which time they exploded onto the national political scene and oversaw the introduction of a spate of regulatory controls that brought corporate America virtually to its knees. In Britain and Japan, by contrast, consumer movement gains have been more modest.

The ultimate aim of this chapter is to devise an analytical framework for explaining variations in the strategies and policy-related impact of consumer advocacy organizations both over time and across countries. By way of introduction, I begin with an overview of the features that distinguish those organizations from other political actors and, more important, that handicap them as players in the political process. I then draw on the social movement and historical institutionalism literatures to identify factors that explain the behavior and influence of consumer movements. I conclude with a brief recipe for analyzing consumer advocacy that will be applied in later chapters.

Features of Consumer Advocacy Organizations

No matter what their country of origin, consumer movement organizations that systematically perform political advocacy functions are characterized by a number of features that distinguish them from both other types of social movement organizations and well-established economic-interest groups. These features are particularly important for our purposes because they tend to weaken consumer advocates relative to many other actors in the policymaking process.

First a definition of terms. According to one school of thought, a *social movement* is "a collectivity acting with some continuity to promote or resist a change in the society or organization of which it is a part" (Turner 1981:1). This definition facilitates the analysis of movement impact on political systems by roughly equating movements with the goals and activities of organized groups or subgroups in a society. Definitional utility, however, is achieved at the price of oversimplification, for many social movements are characterized by specific sets of ideas and beliefs that are by no means confined to their representative organizations. It may therefore be more appropriate to define a social movement as "a set of opinions and beliefs in a population which represents preferences for changing some elements of the social structure and/or reward distribution of a society" (McCarthy and Zald 1977:1218). This definition allows for the possibility that social movements may not be represented by organized groups (p. 1218, n.) and that the ideas and opinions of a movement writ large and of the representative organizations of that movement may not always converge.

A consumer movement (or "consumerism")[1] is a social movement characterized by beliefs and opinions that favor the promotion and protection of the "consumer interest" in a society. A highly subjective term often used indiscriminately (Mayer and Brobeck 1997:153) by public personages to enhance the legitimacy of their particular political objectives, the consumer interest is difficult to define.[2] That said, advocates in advanced industrial democracies—including Japan—tend to equate the consumer interest during much of the postwar period with five internationally recognized consumer rights, the first four of which were proclaimed by President John F. Kennedy in 1963: the right to product safety, the right to a range of product choice at competitive prices, the right to consumer-related information, the right to be heard as a consumer by both industry and government, and the right to consumer redress. This list was recently expanded by Consumers International[3] to include the rights to life, to a consumer-related education, and to a healthy environment—a move that reflected the shifting interests of consumers at the end of the twentieth century.

Depending on the particular mix of historical, political, legal, economic, and cultural factors, different countries emphasize different rights over others. Many American consumers, for instance, value low prices and product choice over safety concerns, whereas the reverse is true in Japan, where a cultural premium is placed on safety and cleanliness, particularly for food products. Consumer organizations also uphold additional rights that reflect problems specific to their particular geographical environment. In Japan, for example, advocates in Tōkyō successfully demanded the enactment of a consumer ordinance in 1975 that recognized the right to be free from unreasonable business practices—a reflection of consumer problems that were particularly prevalent in Japan's large metropolitan areas. Finally, even in a specific country or locality, consumer organizations may conflict with other actors in society over which rights are most important and how those rights should be fulfilled. Not surprisingly, those disagreements are most likely to occur between movement activists and business interests. Moreover, they are particularly intense in Japan, where the interests of producers are deeply entrenched in the political system and popular awareness of individual rights is still comparatively weak. The consumer interest is not, in other words, a uniform and static concept; rather, much depends on how it is defined by representative consumer organizations in specific social, political, cultural, and economic settings—assuming, of course, that such organizations exist at all—and how contending political and economic actors challenge those definitions in their quests to fulfill alternative political, economic, and social agendas.

The consumer interest in advanced industrial democracies is generally represented by three organizational types. *Consumer cooperatives* are economic organizations that combat the negative side effects of market forces by circumventing normal market relations, that is, by providing their members/consumers with opportunities to control aspects of the manufacturing, distribution, and retail processes. *Educational consumer organs*, by contrast, focus on informing their members or a particular population about rational consumption and consumer-related problems in the marketplace. Product-testing organizations fall under this category. Both types of organs vary in terms of size, geographic orientation, and degree of organizational fluidity. This study concentrates on *consumer advocacy organizations*, which represent the consumer interest in the political sphere. Some advocacy organizations, like Britain's Consumers' Association and the United States's Consumers Union, are organized from above by political entrepreneurs.[4] Others, including many Japanese advocacy organizations, begin as more mass-based, grassroots organizations and assume advocacy functions over time. These three types of consumer organs can, of course, overlap. Some consumer cooperatives, for example, assume educational and/or advocacy functions, while many advocacy organs, like Consumers Union and Shufuren in Japan, provide educational services for their members and/or the general population.

Consumer advocacy organizations resemble the environmental, human rights, feminist, and other "new" social movements insofar as they espouse both democratic values and quality-of-life issues that transcend socioeconomic boundaries. Unlike new social movement organizations, however, with their decentralized and democratic modes of decision making, consumer advocacy organizations tend to become centralized and bureaucratized with time. These organizational traits can be explained as follows.

First, consumer advocacy organs tend to have more trouble attracting members than do many new social movement organizations. Consumer constituencies in advanced industrial democracies are extremely large and diffuse[5] and are characterized by very low levels of solidarity (Nadel 1971:64–65). In the feminist and civil rights movements, groups of individuals set apart from the rest of society on the basis of some social, economic, or political characteristic organize and engage in collective action in response to a collective perception that those lines of differentiation are unjust. In the case of consumerism, it is unlikely that the issues in question will stimulate comparable levels of group solidarity, since the burdens of consumer "injustices" such as high prices and defective products often transcend social, economic, and political divisions to affect all citizens to varying degrees. Except in rare circumstances when problems like inflation and product shortages become acute or affect a particular socioeconomic class disproportionately, consumer grievances do not often motivate individuals to join advocacy organizations.[6]

These mobilizational challenges are further compounded by free-rider problems faced by all social movement organizations involved in political advocacy (see Mayer 1989:6–7). Since consumer advocacy organizations seek the provision of public goods like product safety regulations—regulations that benefit members and nonmembers alike—individuals engaged in rational calculations of costs and benefits have few incentives to join those organizations (Olson 1965). The provision of consumer-related literature and consultation services to individual members may increase overall membership levels, but these increases are likely to be insignificant to organizations that provide those incentives to nonmembers as well.

Free-rider problems can be particularly intense in the consumer case because of the nature of conflicting identities at the individual level. More specifically, even though all individuals are consumers, many are also producers or dependents of producers,[7] and the history of consumerism in advanced industrial democracies indicates that when the two conflict, one's interests as a producer usually prevail.[8]

To compensate for their weak mass memberships, consumer advocacy organizations tend to delegate the tasks of representing the consumer interest to professional advocates like Ralph Nader, who are motivated by a commitment to public service rather than by rational calculations of individual costs and benefits. The need for professional leaders is further strengthened by the nature of the political goals pursued by these organizations. Most consumer advocacy organizations seek the protection of consumer rights from infringements by firms, a goal often achieved through the regulation of industry standards (Bloom and Greyser 1981:131).[9] The introduction of governmental regulation often requires lobbying by individuals with specialized knowledge of the political, economic, and legal systems, resources that are most easily acquired by groups of full-time, well-coordinated professionals rather than part-time rank-and-file members.

As consumer advocacy organizations professionalize and bureaucratize, divisions often develop between leaders and rank-and-file members (Berry 1977:186–87).[10] This can be particularly problematic for organizations that engage in protest, a tactic that is most effective when carried out by large groups of consumers. Some advocacy organizations compensate for this weakness by eschewing protest and focusing on lobbying and other tactics pursued by well-established economic-interest groups in the policy process, but this approach has limitations as well. First, consumer organizations lack the political clout of economic-interest groups. Whereas labor, business, and professional groups have the power to sanction political decisions by withholding their labor, capital, or services, the only comparable weapon that consumer organs have at their disposal is the product boycott, which is an extremely difficult tactic to carry out given the diffuseness of their constituencies, the relative weakness of consumer grievances, and the resulting collective-action problems encountered while mobilizing supporters.[11]

The fact that consumer organizations do not normally function as vehicles for mobilizing voters[12] weakens their political clout even further. Electoral mobilization is often impossible for these organizations, given the size and diffuseness of the consumer constituency, conflicting political preferences in that constituency, and the fact that consumer issues do not often achieve priority positions on the electoral platforms of individual politicians. This is not to suggest that consumers are not important during electoral campaigns; to the contrary, a politician who ignores the basic wishes of the broad consuming public does so at his or her peril. I simply wish to emphasize that consumer advocacy organizations are more poorly positioned than are business and labor groups, with their well-endowed coffers and their tightly knit memberships, to establish enduring alliances with key policymakers and influence political processes by mobilizing the electorate.

In sum, consumer advocacy organizations are inherently disadvantaged relative to many other pressure groups as a result of (1) the absence of large, politically active memberships that would enhance the effectiveness of the protest tactics common to many other social movement organizations and (2) a shortage of political weapons that would enable them to compete on equal footing with economic-interest groups and to extract concessions from the powers that be from within routine political processes. As a result of these features, consumer advocacy organizations in all advanced industrial democracies function almost by definition from the fringes of the established political system, applying a mixture of strategies that range from institutional to extrainstitutional, confrontational to cooperative, in their attempts to fulfill their policy-related goals. Although consumer organizations around the world adopt each kind of strategy to varying degrees, their exact mixture and overall impact on policy varies, a phenomenon that in turn depends less on the nature of consumerism as an issue area than on political variables external to movement organizations.

The Resource Mobilization Approach to Social Movements

One explanation for the particular bundle of strategies adopted by an organized consumer movement and the overall effectiveness of those strategies on policy rests on the movement's access to resources.

Political scientists interested in the formation and impact of social movements owe an enormous debt to the so-called resource mobilization perspective[13] formulated by sociologists during the 1970s. Originally devised as a critique of social-psychological or "classical" models, which view the formation of social movements as products of mass discontent,[14] resource mobilization theorists base their arguments on the premise that grievances cannot beget effective social movements without "organization": the mobilization of economic and political resources by rational movement leaders. No matter how intense their members' grievances may be, in other words, social movement organizations will not last long unless their leaders have access to financial support, specialized knowledge of the specifics of the political and legal systems and of pertinent issue areas, and allies elsewhere in the political system (see McCarthy and Zald 1977). With its practical and prescriptive overtones, the model serves almost as a blueprint for movement leaders on how to overcome the problems of collective action and identify the objective conditions for political effectiveness (see, e.g., Freeman 1979). The ultimate message, moreover, is similar to one long held by interest-group theorists: without money, expertise, and connections, societal groups are doomed to political obscurity—assuming, of course, that they have managed to form at all.[15]

While it is now universally acknowledged that social movements cannot survive without organizational support, knowledge, money, and friends, the resource mobilization perspective is not without theoretical ambiguities. How, for example, does one decide whether a particular resource is necessary for a specific movement organization? What are the criteria for assessing the relative contributions of different resources on a movement's influence? More to the point, what is the exact operational definition of a "resource"? As Doug McAdam points out, some analysts use the term to refer to such diverse intangibles as moral commitment and trust, as well as more identifiable factors like money and political alliances (McAdam 1982:32). Definitions like these may very well be the product of *ex post facto* speculation and are so all-encompassing and arbitrary as to weaken the overall usefulness of the model.

More important to our purposes, the resource mobilization approach may be useful for explaining the mobilization of social movement organizations, but it does not tell us much about variations in the strategies and policy impact of either a particular type of social movement organization (SMO) across multiple country settings or different (but comparable) SMOs in the same national context. As students of feminist movements in the United States and Europe have shown, for example, there is no direct correlation between the size and wealth of women's organizations and the progressiveness of national feminist policies (see, e.g., Katzenstein and Mueller 1987). Herbert Kitschelt's cross-national research on antinuclear movements also reveals a lack of fit between the level of movement organization and the movement's impact on policy (Kitschelt 1986:73–74). In the case of Japan, the resource mobilization perspective does not adequately explain why environmental and consumer organizations pursued different strategies in the past, even though they shared members and alliance networks and faced similar financial problems. Clearly, organization may be a necessary component of particular movement strategies and a prerequisite for movement success, but it is not a sufficient one.

The Political Opportunity Structure Perspective

The missing link between a movement's resources and its particular strategies and policy-related impact, many social movement theorists now argue, is the nature of the movement's "political opportunity structure" (POS): vari-

ables specific to an SMO's external environment that function as filters between movement resources and the ultimate impact of those resources on
the social and political environment (Kitschelt 1986:59).

While theorists working in this genre acknowledge that political opportunity structures are complex, multivariate entities, they differ on which
variables should be included under the concept. Sidney Tarrow defines a
POS as "consistent—but not necessarily formal, permanent, or national—
signals to social or political actors which either encourage or discourage
them to use their internal resources to form social movements" (Tarrow
1996:54). He identifies four such signals: the opening of access points into
the political system; the development of unstable political alignments caused
by such factors as electoral instability; the appearance of influential allies;
and divisions in elites (pp. 54–56). McAdam, McCarthy, and Zald opera-
tionalize opportunity structures in a similar fashion save for one important
difference. Instead of "divisions in elites," a variable that seems to be subsumed under the notion of "elite alignments," the authors highlight "the
state's capacity and propensity for repression" (McAdam et al. 1996b:10).
Finally, Kitschelt offers an even broader definition by including "historical
precedents for social mobilization"[16] alongside "specific configurations of
resources" and "institutional arrangements" (Kitschelt 1986:58, 62).

Kitschelt's analysis of antinuclear movements in Western Europe differs
from that of many other studies of the POS genre in that it is mainly concerned with the policy effects of social movement activism, as opposed to
the initial formation and subsequent lifecycles of movement organizations.
Accordingly, Kitschelt devotes much of his study to analyzing the institutional arrangements that influence both the strategies available to social
movement organizations and the impact of those strategies on the broad
political environment. Paying particular attention to the number and nature
of access points into the political system and to the capacity of states to
control the implementation of policy, he hypothesizes that social movement
organizations are most influential in open and strong political systems, as
opposed to closed and weak ones. He also argues that both the degree of
permeability and the strength of the state in terms of its ability to implement
policies determine whether social movement organizations choose to operate inside or outside established channels of interest articulation (Kitschelt
1986:63–67).

Differences in political opportunity structures as defined by Kitschelt go
a long way in explaining cross-national variations in the political behavior

and impact of social movement organizations—why some European feminist organizations, for example, often achieve more progressive policy outcomes than do their American counterparts, even though they are comparatively less well endowed with resources (Katzenstein and Mueller 1987). The approach also helps explain changes in a particular movement's behavior over time. Broadbent, for example (1998), points out shifts in the political opportunity structure to explain the evolution and impact of the postwar Japanese environmental movement.

The positive contributions of Kitschelt and other POS theorists to the study of social movements notwithstanding, the concept of political opportunity structures is open to criticism as a deductive analytical device. First, analysts working in this perspective run the risk of losing their theoretical persuasiveness by incorporating too many variables under the conceptual heading of "opportunity structure." As Gamson and Meyer argue, the notion of opportunity structure "threatens to become an all-encompassing fudge factor for all the conditions and circumstances that form the context for collective action" (Gamson and Meyer 1996:275). In a similar vein, McAdam notes that analytical problems arise when resources are subsumed under the category of political opportunity structures, a practice that often leads to treating political opportunities as "just another resource" (McAdam 1996:26).

These criticisms pose a challenge to the study of social movements. On the one hand, locating and analyzing social movement organizations in a broad political context in order to explain these organizations' particular strategic choices and policy-related impact is intuitively very appealing. If we are to acknowledge the inherent complexity of social movement activism, moreover, it is reasonable to include as many variables as possible in the analysis in order to make sense of that complexity. At the same time, however, it may be counterproductive to apply the language of political opportunity structures to concrete social movement organizations when we are still uncertain about exactly how those structures should be defined from a comparative, cross-national perspective. The process of theory application becomes particularly problematic when we apply the concept to our empirical analyses in a deductive fashion, thereby running the risk of neglecting important empirical details or unanticipated variables that play a role in some political contexts or time periods but not others.

How, then, can we explain the strategies and policy impact of social movements in a way that incorporates such variables of the POS approach as resources, institutions, political alignments, and historical forces while preserving the analytical distinctions among those variables? How, moreover, can we accommodate additional variables that may crop up unexpectedly in our empirical work without losing the analytical persuasiveness of our research methods?

Insights from the Historical Institutional Approach

One way to meet some of these analytical and methodological challenges is to disaggregate the concept of "political opportunity structure" and extract political institutions as an analytical lens through which we can observe the workings and dynamic interrelationships of the numerous variables that affect the strategies and political influence of social movement organizations operating in policymaking processes. The literature on historical institutionalism can give us some insights into how we can accomplish that task.[17]

Before progressing, we should define exactly what we mean by the term *institution*. Although institutions occupy an important position in the POS literature, theorists working in this genre are not as precise as institutionalists are in defining the term. That said, there are a few differences in the definitions employed by historical institutional theorists as well.[18] Some scholars, like Peter Hall, define the concept largely in terms of rules and norms: "institutions are the formal rules, compliance procedures, and standard operating practices that structure the relationship between individuals in various units of the polity and the economy" (Hall 1986:19).

Others, like Robert Putnam, include concrete organizational structures as well as abstract rules and norms in their definitions (Putnam 1993:8). As noted later on, this study combines elements of both definitions by distinguishing among structural, formal, and informal institutions and recognizing the capacity of each to shape "the relationship between individuals in various units of the polity." These distinctions can help us explain (1) variations in movement behavior across countries that may look very similar structurally and (2) idiosyncrasies in movement behavior in a particular political context that cannot be explained simply by referring to that system's organizational structure.

Social movement scholars have yet to compare the similarities of and differences between the political opportunity structure approach and the historical institutionalism perspective,[19] both of which developed contemporaneously but largely independently of each other during the 1980s and

1990s. Some of the differences are simply a matter of degree but are nevertheless significant for the purposes of this study.

To begin, both the political opportunity and historical institutional perspectives share the following two assumptions regarding the impact of institutions on societal actors. First, and in marked contrast to the resource mobilization approach, the two perspectives recognize the capacity of state institutions to influence the distribution of resources among contending interests and to control the degree of access into decision-making fora by nonstate actors over time. That is, the state is treated as an important determinant of who gets what in terms of political perks and spoils, as well as who gets a hearing in the policy process.[20]

Second, students of both approaches posit that institutions—state or otherwise—shape societal group behavior over the long term by rendering some political strategies more viable than others. The short-term effectiveness of those strategies in the policy process is in turn ascribed to strategic openings in the political system that enable certain interests to influence policy outcomes. Some of those openings occur as a matter of course, but others may arise unexpectedly in response to the denouement of a particular policy-making process.

These basic similarities notwithstanding, the POS and historical institutional approaches differ both analytically and methodologically. One such difference pertains to the actual objects of academic inquiry. While the analytical tools devised by theorists of the POS approach were primarily intended to explain the emergence and subsequent life cycles of social movements,[21] the historical institutional perspective was largely fashioned to explain a phenomenon that is central to this study, namely, the relationship between political actors and public policy (Cammack 1992:402).

Accordingly, the two approaches differ in their research methods. Much of the recent research on political opportunity structures suggests that theorists working in this tradition aspire to perfect a deductive theory that can be applied across social movement types and national contexts. Historical institutionalists, on the other hand, "generally develop their hypotheses more inductively, in the course of interpreting the empirical material" (Steinmo, Thelen, and Longstreth 1992:12)[22] on a case-by-case basis and from a broad historical perspective. Furthermore, particular institutions are subjected to analysis in response to the political outcomes that are to be explained (Steinmo et al. 1992:6). Historical institutionalism is, in sum, problem driven rather than theory driven.

The analytical implications of this methodological focus are significant. First, the issue-specific, long-term historical perspective of historical institutionalism enables us to incorporate, systematically and effectively, the phenomenon of institutional change into our analysis. This is especially important to the comparative study of social movements over time, since changes in the structural, formal, and informal institutional setting of a particular country can have a profound effect on the resource configurations, strategies, and ultimate policy impact of constituent organizations.

Second, the inductive focus of the historical institutional perspective makes it less deterministic than the POS approach. To quote Immergut, "Institutions tell us what courses of action are likely to bring success or failure, but they do not predict the final choices made by [political] actors" (Immergut 1992b:85). To restate the argument from the perspective of consumer movement activism in the policy sphere, institutions condition the menu of strategic choices available to advocates but do not necessarily determine it, nor do they tell us how advocates will choose from among those strategies.

The nondeterministic nature of the historical institutional perspective makes it flexible enough to accommodate other variables that condition the boundaries of social movement activism and influence in the policy realm. One such variable that is particularly important to the study of consumer movements in all national contexts is policy change, a phenomenon that can have both a direct and an indirect impact on a movement's behavior and ultimate effectiveness.[23]

Paul Pierson (1993) argues along these lines with reference to interest groups.[24] According to him, public policies are important to the study of both institutions and interest mobilization because they "establish rules and create constraints that shape [the] behavior" of political actors (p. 608). More specifically, the outputs or "spoils" of many public policies can motivate interest groups to mobilize either for or against the maintenance or expansion of those policies (pp. 599–600). Public policies can also influence the activities of interest groups by altering access points into the political system or enhancing the availability of such resources as funding and political allies (p. 601). Finally, public policies can shape many of the political conditions that make some interest-group strategies more politically feasible than others (p. 598). In short, "policies create politics" by arming organized interests with disproportionate levels of power, by rendering certain goals and strategies more viable than others, and by opening or closing institutional arenas for conflict resolution.

Studying the effects of institutions *and* policy change on the activism of social movement organizations has several analytical benefits. First, by tracing policy developments and their impact on institutions, we are in a better position to explain the phenomenon of institutional change and its long-term effects on movement activism. Second, and in keeping with the key research interests of social movement theorists, attention to policy change can enhance our understanding of the historical trajectories of organized social movements. As Pierson contends, the impact of policy on mass publics is "likely to be most consequential in issue-areas . . . where interest group activity is not yet well established" (p. 602). It is particularly fruitful, therefore, to establish the connection between institutions and public policies and the creation of specific configurations of movement resources and political strategies at "critical junctures" or "formative moments" in a movement's development (p. 602).[25]

Together, institutions and policy change can explain a great deal about the strategic menus available to consumer activists in the policy process and the impact of strategies on actual policy outcomes, but they do not explain everything. They do not, for example, tell us why consumer representatives champion some issues over others at particular times. This is a phenomenon, I believe, that has more to do with stages of economic development, prevailing ideas about how best to articulate and fulfill the consumer interest, and even cultural considerations. Nor do institutional configurations and policy change explain why consumer organizations choose some strategies over others from their menus of strategic options. To explain such choices, we would have to analyze the personal histories and proclivities of both the organizations in question and the individuals who run those organizations. In this regard, cultural considerations can be particularly important insofar as they help shape notions of consumer identity, notions that in turn can influence what consumer activists want from the political system and with whom they are willing to ally in order to get it. As I argue in chapter 3, notions of consumer identity are particularly important in the Japanese case.

In sum, the political opportunity structure and historical institutional perspectives complement each other in terms of the importance attached to the role of political institutions in shaping the nature and consequences of political participation by societal interests. They differ, however, in their research objectives, methodologies, and the range of variables incorporated into the analysis. While the POS perspective tends to employ a deductive methodology and a relatively small number of variables to explain the origins and evolution of social movements, historical institutionalism tends to be an inductive perspective that, while focusing on the pivotal role of institutions, encompasses a larger palette of variables in order to highlight the complex and evolving relationship between political actors and the public policy process. As the following section shows, the framework of analysis used in this study accepts the points of commonality between the two approaches while incorporating the methodological perspective (and hence theoretical flexibility) of historical institutionalism.

Toward a Composite Framework of Analysis

To explain differences in the strategic behavior and policy impact of consumer advocacy organizations both cross-nationally and over time in Japan, I adopt a methodology of inductive historical analysis and in-depth case studies that rests on the following interrelated assumptions and propositions.

First, I assume that consumer advocacy organizations are distinctive forms of social movement organizations that are politically weaker than most economic-interest groups and even some mass-based social movement organizations. This is largely because advocacy organizations lack the inherent ability to leverage concessions from governmental policymakers and, therefore, to compete on more or less equal footing with other interests on the demand side of the policymaking process.

Since consumer advocacy organizations are intrinsically handicapped within the policy process, we should expect them to score few policy-related victories. Why, then, do these organizations occasionally manage to wrest concessions from pro-business policymakers? Why are they more successful in this regard in some countries and time periods but not others? Finally, how can we explain variations in the strategic behavior of these organizations both longitudinally and across national settings?

Part of the answer to these questions lies in movement access to resources. While it is impossible to predict with precision which resources are necessary ones for consumer organizations, I believe it reasonable to assume that like all politically active social movement organizations and interest groups, these organizations require money, legal and political expertise, and allies in the political system. We can also assume that in order to compensate for their membership deficiencies and inability to effectively sanction the decisions of powerful policymakers, advocates are more dependent on media attention and broad public support than are, say, economic-interest groups. Finally, we can expect consumer organizations that, for one reason or another, have adequate access to financial and informational resources and allies in the system to be more likely—ceteris paribus—to emphasize assimilative (or "insider") strategies like lobbying and litigation. Those lacking such resources are more apt to lean on media attention, public opinion, protest, and other extrainstitutional channels of interest articulation. No matter what their strategic choices are, however, even the best-endowed organizations will be politically powerless if the relevant political institutions are closed to effective consumer participation.

As we observed earlier, the resources and strategic choices available to consumer advocates are influenced by the nature of the institutional configurations of the consumer policymaking process. To clarify this point, it is helpful to distinguish among three types of institution: institutional structures, formal rules, and informal norms and conventions.

Examples of institutional structures—the most straightforward of the three—are the legislative, executive, and judicial branches of government. How these three branches are balanced against one another can have a major impact on the strategies of consumer advocates. As chapter 2 illustrates, for example, American advocates have access to a much broader menu of strategic options—as a result of the institutional separation of powers and availability of multiple access points into the policy process—than they do in the British and Japanese parliamentary systems, where policymaking is far more centralized.

Formal rules, which are superimposed on these structures and subject to enforcement according to prescribed procedures, include electoral rules and the codified operating procedures of bureaucratic advisory councils that deliberate on consumer issues. As the Japanese case shows, electoral rules can influence whether politicians become advocates of the consumer cause and, by logical extension, whether they are amenable to forming political alliances with private consumer advocates. These alliances can increase the likelihood that advocates will choose assimilative strategies over extrainstitutional ones when trying to influence policy decisions.

Informal norms, which are much more difficult to identify because of their cultural overtones, include styles of decision making and methods of informal contact among various groups or individuals in the consumer policy process. Norms differ from formal rules in that they are not subject to formal enforcement procedures, although they can be informally enforced through peer pressure. I should also add that in Japan, where much of the wheeling and dealing of politics takes place outside mainstream channels of interest articulation and where informal institutions are often used to compensate for the perceived inadequacies of formal ones (Curtis 1999:4), attention to informal institutions can help us understand why consumer advocates do what they do in the policy process. For example, norms governing bureaucratic advisory council (*shingikai*) deliberations that stifle consumer demands help explain why advocates put so much emphasis on activating or manipulating public opinion when these councils are in session.

In accordance with the historical institutional perspective, I pay close attention to policy and institutional change, both of which can explain sudden shifts in the strategic behavior of consumer advocacy organizations. I am therefore careful to point out "critical junctures" or "formative moments" in a movement's development, which I define as periods in which advocates discover new opportunities for political activism resulting from policy and/or institutional shifts, gain or lose access to key resources, and reassess their strategic behavior. The Occupation period (1945–1952) and the years immediately following the enactment of the Consumer Protection Basic Law are two examples of critical junctures that had positive long-term effects on the Japanese movement.

Although I put great store in the potential of institutions to shape the strategic behavior of consumer advocacy organizations, I do not assume that institutions explain everything. As we noted earlier, institutions *condition* the menu of strategic options available to advocates, but they do not necessarily determine them. Nor do institutions always tell us how advocates will choose from among their strategic options. To fully explain the options and choices of consumer advocates, therefore, we must also consider socioeconomic developments, the nature of consumer issues, the preferences of individual consumer leaders, and cultural factors.

Finally, I argue that even though movement strategies are conditioned over the long run by a range of institutional and other variables, the impact of those strategies on policymaking is ultimately determined by one of the most important informal institutions of consumer politics: alliances between government and business actors at specific points in the policy process. The effects of elite alignments on movement leverage vary according to whether those alignments are characterized by consensus or conflict. Specifically, consumer organizations that are well equipped with human and financial resources and that operate within "open" institutional structures will have virtually no power over the policy process if business and government actors are closely allied in opposition to movement demands. Consumer organizations that are less fortunate politically and financially and that have little or no formal access into the policy process, however, may find themselves exercising leverage over that process when business and government representatives are poorly organized and/or at odds with each other.

Analyzing the behavior and influence of consumer organizations within the public policy process is admittedly a complicated task. As the reader has no doubt inferred from the preceding pages, my theoretical aim in this book is *not* to derive simple explanations of causation from the complex and often contradictory details of consumer politics in Japan or other advanced industrial democracies. Rather, I hope to use the theoretical insights outlined in this chapter to identify major patterns in the relationship between Japanese consumer movement activism and the broader political system while simultaneously highlighting the political and social meaning of those patterns. By injecting an element of cross-national comparison into the analysis, I also intend to show that Japanese consumer organizations are logical and even influential reflections of their historical and political circumstances.

2   Consumer Advocacy in the United States and Britain

The phenomenon of consumerism has given rise to a rich and varied literature on the political development of consumer advocacy organizations in the United States.[1] Few of those works, however, systematically address the impact of political institutions and policies on the historical trajectories and political fortunes of those organizations; fewer still compare their American subject matter with organized consumer movements abroad.[2] This chapter aims to partially rectify this gap in the literature by comparing how governmental policies and the institutional configurations of consumer protection policymaking in the United States and Britain have influenced the strategies and political impact of their respective consumer advocacy organizations. In the process, I outline two contending institutional models of consumer policymaking—the United States's pluralist, decentralized system and Britain's centralized, semicorporatist system—to serve as points of comparison for my more in-depth analysis of the Japanese consumer movement.

My decision to bring the U.S. and British cases into an analysis of the Japanese consumer movement is based on the following considerations. First, all three countries have enjoyed comparable levels of economic development since the late 1960s and have faced broadly similar consumer problems, yet the strategies and impact of their respective consumer organizations are quite different. These differences, which are summarized in chapter 9, can be explained using the analytical framework described in chapter 1.

Second, although the U.S. movement differs quite markedly from the British and Japanese cases in regard to both the political and institutional context of movement activism and the movement's strategic behavior and impact on policy, it should be included in any comparative analysis of consumer advocacy if for no other reason than it has served as a model for consumer activism around the world. This is particularly true for Japanese advocates, many of whom have looked to Ralph Nader and his network of organizations for standards against which to measure their own performance. More important, singling out the contextual differences between the American and Japanese movements helps us understand the boundaries of consumer advocacy in Japan.

While the U.S. movement tends to be the outlier of the three cases, the British movement closely resembles the Japanese case in terms of its structural institutional context of movement activism. The fact that British consumer advocates tend to have more direct influence over policy than Japanese organizations do, therefore, gives us more clues to the sources of idiosyncrasies in the Japanese case. Many of those clues, I argue in later chapters, are rooted in the informal institutional practices of Japanese policymaking in particular and in political trends more generally.

The United States: A Century of Consumerism

For most Americans, the phrase *consumer movement* conjures up images of Ralph Nader and his impassioned and highly effective crusade against the excesses of business and government. Few, however, realize that the wave of consumer power that swept the political world during the 1960s and 1970s under Nader's watch was a phenomenon without precedent in American consumer history. And it is a long history, beginning at the turn of the twentieth century and punctuated by a series of political fits and starts.

The First Wave: The Turn of the Twentieth Century

Consumer advocates first appeared on the American political scene during the 1890s in the midst of rapid urbanization and a population explosion, the rise of mass production and the branding of products, the development of national markets in the wake of expanding rail links, mass advertising, and large cost-of-living increases (Herrmann and Mayer 1997:585). These socioeconomic developments contributed to mounting concerns among urban dwellers about the safety and quality of consumer goods and, in turn, defined many of the issues that gave early consumer representatives their initial raison d'être.

Consumer advocates were, in many ways, products of the Progressive Movement, with its reformist and humanitarian outlook (Mayer 1989:10, 18) and tendency to look to government as the primary instigator of social and economic reform (Herrmann and Mayer 1997:585). Accordingly, many of the organs that engaged in consumer politics during this period were not consumer organizations in the strict sense of the term but, rather, organizations that embraced a broad range of social and economic issues in addition to consumer-related concerns. Many of those organizations were led by women and were particularly active at the state and local levels (Brobeck 1997:531). The more overtly "consumer" organs, meanwhile, mixed broad social reform with consumer issues in their agendas. For example, the Consumers League of New York, the country's first consumer organ, made its mark by publicizing a "white list" of shops that provided not only quality consumer goods but also good working conditions for their staff members (Herrmann and Mayer 1997:585).

As a result of the institutional context of consumer activism, the United States's early consumer organizations had almost no direct influence over the direction of national policymaking. In theory, the potential for congressional support for consumer issues certainly existed. The lack of a strong tradition of party discipline in both houses of Congress, for example, meant that legislators could champion consumer and other public-interest issues with relative political impunity. In practice, however, the likelihood that long-term advocates of the consumer interest would emerge in the legislative branch of government was weakened by the predominance of business-related interests in the polity.

The legislative record shows how preoccupied lawmakers were with the affairs of industry. Since the vast majority of regulatory measures introduced at this time were designed to promote efficient commerce rather than consumer protection, benefits bestowed on consumers as a result of those measures were either incidental or of secondary concern to legislators (Mayer 1989:11). The expansion of consumer choice as a result of antitrust policies designed to regulate industry is the best example of this tendency.

The informal alliance between government and business was reinforced by a deep-seated distrust of expanding governmental regulation in anybody's interest, let alone the consumer's. The business lobby and its allies among southern Democrats were particularly vocal in this regard (Herrmann and Mayer 1997:586). Not surprisingly, these sentiments often translated into vehement opposition to consumer protection proposals that threatened to restrict industry's economic freedom.

For consumer advocates, the upshot of these informal political alignments and the basic policy orientations of Congress was not only a paucity of close consumer allies in the policymaking system—a key resource for citizen groups seeking to influence policy—but also a distinct unlikelihood that consumer lobbying would have a direct impact on legislative developments. It is largely for these reasons that consumer organizations resorted to boycotts and nonviolent forms of protest to express their political views while looking outside the mainstream political system for support.

Among the more important allies of the organized movement were the muckraking journalists who were themselves both cause and reflection of the Progressive Movement. Many of these journalists featured consumer reform as part of their crusade against governmental corruption and shady business practices. The *Ladies Home Journal* and *Colliers*, for example, were zealous proponents of food and drug safety (Nadel 1971:13). Media attention to consumer issues lent an air of legitimacy to two of the early organized movement's most prominent objectives: the introduction of governmental regulation to enhance the safety of basic consumer products and the development of a "consumer consciousness" in the public at large.

Although consumer organizations achieved few of their regulatory objectives before World War I, they did manage to raise the awareness of ordinary citizens about their identities as consumers—so much so, in fact, that Walter Lippmann felt compelled to remark that the consumer consciousness had begun to outpace the class consciousness of labor (Herrmann and Mayer 1997:586). The development of a nascent consumer identity did not, however, translate into mass support for consumer organizations; nor, for that matter, was it matched by a commensurate level of legislative support for regulation in the consumer interest.

How, then, do we explain the consumer protection measures introduced at this time?

The passage of the Meat Inspection Act and the Pure Food and Drug Act in 1906 offers some clues. Starting in 1892, consumer organizations diligently lobbied both Congress and the White House for passage of a pure food act but were continually defeated by a loose legislative coalition led by southern Democrats and supported by business groups (Herrmann and

Mayer 1997:586). Then the tide quickly turned in favor of the bill's supporters following the publication in 1906 of Upton Sinclair's best-selling book *The Jungle*. A shocking account of the unsanitary conditions of Chicago's meatpacking industry, the book caused an immediate public sensation and prompted President Theodore Roosevelt to throw his support behind a meat inspection bill (Nadel 1971:11). The Pure Food and Drug Act was passed shortly thereafter by an overwhelming majority of both houses.

Put simply, consumer protection legislation was the product of eleventh-hour presidential backing in response to scandal and public outrage (Herrmann 1974:12). Presidents have every incentive to respond to such outbursts because they are elected at large; to ignore public opinion in such circumstances, in other words, is to invite a loss of support at the polls. Consumer organizations and their media allies played a supporting role in the immediate denouement of legislative events by publicly endorsing these last-minute presidential initiatives and the legislators who eventually transformed them into law. Perhaps more significantly, consumer advocates had a longer-term and more indirect impact on the policy process by influencing public opinion. In the case of the Meat Inspection Act and the Pure Food and Drug Act, advocates helped shape the very public sentiments that ultimately persuaded the president to take action in 1906.

As witness to the country's first consumer organizations and the development of a nascent consumer consciousness, the period spanning the final years of the nineteenth century and the first two decades of the twentieth was without a doubt a formative moment in the development of the American consumer movement. That said, the United States at this time was by no means a consumer-oriented polity. As a result of the pro-business policies and political alignments of key policymaking actors, the few governmental consumer protection measures that were introduced during this period were the result not so much of routine policymaking in the so-called consumer interest than of legislative accident or, more rarely, of last-minute presidential responses to public backlashes against the egregious abuses of the health and safety of consumers.

The Second Wave: The 1930s

Consumer activism experienced a lengthy lull as a result of World War I, the decline of the Progressive Movement, and the "business dominated spirit of the 1920s" (Nadel 1971:16). By the 1930s, however, prevailing socio-economic conditions made the movement appear ripe for a revival. In addition to the myriad socioeconomic crises normally associated with the Great Depression, American citizens faced a proliferation of consumer problems resulting from the expansion of mass production and mass advertising. The country was also in the midst of adapting to electricity and the diffusion of electrical appliances (Mayer 1989:19), products that were prime targets for proponents of enhanced consumer safety.

Some consumer activists responded to these economic developments by publishing a spate of new antibusiness exposés that strengthened the country's burgeoning consumer consciousness. Among those exposés was *100,000,000 Guinea Pigs: Dangers in Everyday Foods, Drugs, and Cosmetics*, a best-selling book by Arthur Kallet and F. J. Schlink that described the subjection of unwitting consumers to untested and potentially dangerous products and pointed out the weaknesses of the Pure Food and Drug Act.[3] Schlink later helped establish a consumer organization that in 1936 evolved into Consumers Union (cu). CU, which publishes *Consumer Reports*, is today regarded as the country's leading product-testing organization and one of its most influential consumer advocacy organs.

While a deepening consumer consciousness and the establishment of Consumers Union are reasons enough to designate the 1930s as a second formative moment in the movement's history, the lack of meaningful access to the policy process prevented consumer representatives from exercising the kind of policy influence that one might expect during periods of economic distress. The fate of the Consumer Advisory Board of the National Recovery Administration (NRA) is a case in point. While consumer organizations hailed the board as the first formal access point for consumer representatives into the federal bureaucracy, movement efforts to have the consumer interest embodied in NRA policy were often rebuffed as board members focused on reinvigorating business (Mayer 1989:23) in response to the policy priorities of the Roosevelt administration. Consumers, in other words, had representation at the national level but, as a result of the policy priorities and informal institutional practices of the 1930s, virtually no voice.

The inability of consumer organizations to gain meaningful inroads into the corridors of policy formulation and implementation was reinforced by a growing distrust in governmental circles of radical political tendencies in the general population. By the end of the decade, many consumer advocates had been put on the political defensive following investigations of Consumers Union by the House Committee on Un-American Activities for alleged communist activities. Although the charges proved groundless, the incident led to a decline in CU membership (Herrmann and Mayer 1997:588) that was not reversed until well after World War II.

In keeping with both historical precedent and consumer representatives' limited inroads into the policy process, pro-consumer laws introduced during the 1930s were once again the product of scandal and last-minute executive sponsorship, as opposed to congressional initiatives supported by consumer lobbying. The long-anticipated overhaul of the 1906 Pure Food and Drug Act in 1938, for example, was the handiwork of Rexford G. Tugwell, the assistant secretary of agriculture (Nadel 1971:16), and occurred only after the tragic deaths in 1937 of more than 100 consumers of a tainted medicinal drink (Herrmann 1974:18). Clearly, the era of New Deal politics did not include a new deal for the organized consumer movement. Now, as before, consumer advocates operated from the sidelines of interest articulation.

The Third Wave: The 1960s and Early 1970s

After a long period of dormancy triggered by World War II, the political fortunes of the organized consumer movement changed dramatically during the 1960s (Nadel 1971:3). In accordance with historical precedent, the third wave reflected problems inherent in the act of consumption, this time caused by rapid economic growth and the proliferation of new product lines, the expanded use of credit, and the globalization of production (Mayer 1989:13). Moreover, as Americans became more affluent, they grew less tolerant not only of the problems plaguing them as the consumers of goods and services but also of governmental graft and the widening power imbalance between themselves and the country's flourishing business community. To some scholars, the frustrated expectations of American consumers were the source of the movement's coming of age during the 1960s (Finch 1985:25). If the history of the American movement is any indication, however, we can safely assume that socioeconomic grievances will not result in politically powerful consumer organizations if policy and institutional opportunities for consumer activism are not in place. What made the 1960s and early 1970s significant for the American movement was the appearance of precisely those kinds of opportunities.

It all started in 1962 when President John F. Kennedy delivered the country's first consumer message to Congress. In that statement, Kennedy identified the need for greater government involvement in consumer protection and outlined four basic consumer rights that were to define the parameters of that involvement: the rights to safe products, to consumer-related information, to a range of product choice at competitive prices, and to be heard by both industry and government. By the late 1960s, the list was expanded to include the right to redress for damages caused by defective products and unfair business practices.

Kennedy's commitment to consumer protection made good political sense because it required little budgetary outlay and yet appealed to the electorate at large at a time of rising "public expectations about the capacity of government to improve the quality of life in American society" (D. Vogel 1989:40). Recognizing the political benefits of toeing the consumer line, Kennedy's successors—including Richard Nixon—followed his lead by delivering their own consumer messages to Congress and sponsoring consumer-related legislation.

In a classic example of the impact of policy change on institutional configurations, the elevation of consumer protection on the presidential agenda was quickly followed by the introduction or expansion of executive institutions that were responsible for formulating and executing consumer policy. Kennedy, for example, established the Consumer Advisory Council as an adjunct of the prestigious Council of Economic Advisors. The advisory council served as an intrabureaucratic representative of consumer issues and an adviser to the president (Nadel 1971:51). Similar offices were maintained by subsequent presidents throughout the 1960s and 1970s, although their influence was curtailed during the Republican administrations of Nixon and Ford. Institutional developments elsewhere in the bureaucracy included the establishment in 1973 of the Consumer Product Safety Commission (CPSC), an independent regulatory agency responsible for implementing a wide range of consumer protection statutes (Fise 1997:164), and the expansion of the regulatory powers of the Federal Trade Commission (FTC) and the Food and Drug Administration (FDA).

The policy and institutional changes of the 1960s are particularly remarkable when measured against past trends. As we noted earlier, business and southern Democrats at the turn of the century were loath to sanction the growth of governmental regulatory controls in both areas pertaining to consumer affairs and in the economy more generally. By the 1930s, President Franklin Roosevelt's New Deal policies had enlarged the regulatory role of governmental officials in the economic realm, but that role did not encompass consumer protection to a significant degree. The policies of the Kennedy administration, by contrast, marked the beginning of a new wave of governmental expansion—of a paradigmatic shift, in other words, toward a more public-interest approach to consumer protection that legitimized direct governmental interference in the affairs of business on behalf of consumers.

Members of Congress also jumped on the consumer bandwagon during the 1960s in response to both the reorientation of governmental consumer policy and institutional changes in Congress that were taking place independently of executive initiatives. In the Senate, for example, the decentralization of decision making, the enhanced powers of junior members, increases in the size and influence of committees and subcommittees, and the Democratic landslide of 1964 injected a heavy dose of youth and liberalism into the chamber (D. Vogel 1989:40) and increased the propensity of entrepreneurial politicians (Wilson 1980a:370)[4] to support new public-interest issues. For many politicians—particularly Democrats—consumer protection was quickly identified as one such issue (see Mayer 1988:89, 1989:32; Nadel 1971:111–12).

The story of Senator Warren Magnuson's (D-Wash.) conversion to the consumer fold is a telling illustration of this trend. During the 1940s, Magnuson had made a mark for himself as a political spokesman of Boeing Aircraft, one of the largest employers in his home state. After almost losing the 1962 election, Magnuson swung his support behind a number of consumer protection bills and assumed the chairmanship of the Senate Subcommittee on the Consumer in an effort to broaden his political support base. The senator was rewarded for his actions by a landslide victory in 1968.

Warren Magnuson's congressional career attests to the impact of broad policy shifts and institutional change in the United States on the willingness of individual politicians to develop consumer-friendly platforms. These contextual developments in turn had a profound effect on the resource configurations of private consumer advocates. For the first time in the movement's history, advocates now had a number of powerful sympathizers and allies in the corridors of national power who were both willing and able to trumpet the consumer cause. The United States is unusual in this regard, for as we observed in chapter 1, organized consumer movements normally have trouble forging alliances with policymakers. It is important to remember, however, that the movement's advances were attributable not so much to the power and savvy of movement advocates as to policy trends and the institutional configurations of the broader political system.

By the mid-1960s, presidential policy initiatives, the expansion of the consumer-related functions of bureaucratic organs, and the decentralization of power and concomitant rise of consumer movement allies in Congress had led to the enactment of a number of laws that marked the birth of a comprehensive consumer protection policy regime.[5] Like social movement organizations more generally, American consumer advocates did not instigate these institutional changes, nor did they play a defining role during the initial upsurge in legislative activity. These institutional and legislative developments did, however, encourage consumer organizations to expand their lobbying networks in support of further reform. After years of focusing almost exclusively on product testing, for example, Consumers Union ventured into advocacy politics during the 1960s by establishing offices in Washington, D.C. The era also witnessed the formation of the Consumer Federation of America (CFA), an umbrella group of 200 national and state organizations (Mayer 1989:43) responsible for coordinating consumer lobbying activities and organizing the annual national consumer conference known as the Consumer Assembly.

The most widely recognized organizational development in the American consumer movement at this time was, of course, the appearance of Ralph Nader and his network of advocacy groups. Nader's first foray into the public's consciousness came in 1965 as the author of *Unsafe at Any Speed*, an exposé of General Motors' shoddy manufacturing standards. The following year, as Nader was testifying before Congress for highway and automobile safety legislation, the *New York Times* revealed that Nader's private life had been the target of an investigation by GM. Almost overnight, *Unsafe at Any Speed* became a best-seller and Nader a household word. The publicity surrounding the scandal not only led to a strengthening of the original provisions of what in 1966 became the National Traffic and Motor Vehicle Safety Act, but it also raised the public's awareness of consumer issues and of efforts by the organized movement to pressure the government to do more for consumers (Nadel 1971:141). Nader cashed in on his newfound fame and the expansion of institutional opportunities for political action by establishing his network of organizations and, in the process, paving the way for a flood of highly skilled public-interest lawyers—one of the U.S. movement's most valuable resources—to play a leading role among consumer advocates. In a year or two, Nader and his band of Raiders had transformed the mission of consumer protection in America into a veritable crusade.

Despite the numerous institutional inroads into the policy process that were opening to the organized consumer movement, the consumer crusade was not an easy one for private advocates. Like consumer organizations everywhere, Nader's consumer network and other key consumer organs never had as many of the resources required for effective lobbying campaigns as did their wealthy opponents in the business community. To compensate for this weakness, many organizations allied with activists in the labor movement. Ties between labor—including the AFL-CIO—and the consumer movement are consequently quite close; unions, for example, participate actively in the Consumer Federation of America and offer many consumer organizations financial support and manpower (Herrmann and Mayer 1997:599).

Consumer advocates also used the courts to enhance their leverage in the policy process. In many cases, judges proved amenable to the consumer cause as a result of several policy-related changes that had been taking place in the court system during the 1960s: the expansion of the doctrine of standing, the strengthening of the courts' willingness to overturn regulatory agency decisions, and the recognition of the right of private citizens to participate in the decisions of administrative agencies (D. Vogel 1989:108). Throughout the late 1960s and 1970s, highly publicized consumer lawsuits—particularly class action suits and those filed under administrative procedure rules—helped shape consumer protection policy by convincing both the general public and bureaucratic officials of the need for reform (Berry 1977:289) while simultaneously making firms more sensitive to consumers' needs (Schweig 1980:200).

When all is said and done, consumer advocates would have made few if any advances in the policy process during the 1960s and early 1970s had it not been for the lack of concerted opposition from the business community. Business had been caught unawares by the sudden and unprecedented upsurge in pro-consumer legislation, and, as a result, was slow to respond (D. Vogel 1989). At the root of the problem was the fact that the business community was poorly organized at this time and bereft of the strong, institutionalized ties with policymakers needed to fend off the consumer attack. Indeed, one could make the case that there was no pressing need for business to be otherwise; this was, after all, an era of economic expansion from which all interests could benefit. It was not until after the 1973 oil shock, when the country entered a period of prolonged economic recession, that business representatives and their political allies were able to organize an effective counterattack against consumerism and its costly economic side effects. Until then, advocates had both the institutional and ideological space in which to press for the fulfillment of their public-interest goals.

Consumer Strategies and Policymaking Roles

When compared with business organizations, the AFL-CIO, or even the National Rifle Association, American consumer organizations have had a relatively weak impact on policy. As we noted in chapter 1, this should come as no surprise given the difficulties confronted by consumer advocates when mobilizing both resources and a highly diffuse consumer constituency. But when we compare the record of American consumer organizations during the 1960s and early 1970s with that of their counterparts abroad, their ability to influence the agenda-setting and policy-formulation processes and to blow the whistle on governmental incompetence looks quite impressive. The key to those successes has been the institutional structure of the American policy-making system.

The impact of consumer advocates on agenda setting and policy formulation was made possible by unprecedented presidential initiatives in the consumer realm and the establishment of informal relationships with pro-consumer congressional entrepreneurs who appeared after the decentralization of Congress. These developments facilitated Nader's efforts to raise the issue of automobile and highway safety in Congress, for example, and to influence the content of corresponding legislation. Access to the courts and to sympathetic officials in the bureaucracy, moreover, enabled advocates to expose graft, administrative errors, and undemocratic procedures in the public sphere.

That consumer advocates managed to achieve a fair number of policy objectives during the 1960s and 1970s is testament to the effectiveness of a finely tuned strategy of persuasion[6] that included the dissemination of product-testing results, the publication of carefully researched books and articles, and effective lobbying and litigation techniques. Together, these tactics influenced policymakers both directly and indirectly through the formation or activation of public opinion. On many occasions, for example, consumer publications and lawsuits helped turn vague consumer problems into contentious political issues (Mayer 1988:87), which in turn raised public expectations for commensurate solutions at the policymaking level.

As resource mobilization theorists argue, the overall effectiveness of consumer movement strategies in the policymaking process is contingent on access to capital, strategically placed allies, media attention, policy-related information, and intramovement expertise. During the heyday of consumer activism, advocates may not have been as well endowed as wealthy business lobbyists, but they were much better off than their counterparts in many other advanced industrial democracies. Governmental tax exemptions for donors to nonprofit organizations, proceeds from the sales of publications like *Consumer Reports*,[7] and, less frequently, foundation and government grants[8] generated enough money for the country's main consumer organizations to sustain their research programs and lobbying campaigns. As for strategically placed allies, consumer organizations, as we have already noted, had a fair number of supporters in Congress, the White House, and the regulatory agencies, many of whom also served as important sources of insider information about the policy process. Consumer representatives also enjoyed an enduring and productive relationship with the media that continues to this day, a relationship that is undoubtedly one of the most important prerequisites for getting the consumer message to the public (interview, James, May 1999). Finally, the movement's access to expertise was, and continues to be, more than adequate. Although most consumer organizations continually struggle with the problem of personnel shortages, many are staffed by individuals who are highly trained in the law, economics, and even the natural sciences. The remarkably high level of expertise in the organized movement is itself a reflection of the relative openness of both national and state governmental institutions to pressure from citizen advocates. Had such institutional opportunities not existed, talented professionals would have had few incentives to devote their careers to advancing the consumer cause.

In sum, consumer advocacy organizations during the 1960s and 1970s had sufficient inroads into the policy process and access to key resources to adapt to that process in an assimilative manner, pursuing tactics based on rational persuasion, rather than street demonstrations, emotive appeals to the public, and other forms of traditional protest. In this way, consumer organizations behaved much like mainstream interest groups rather than mass-based social movement organizations. This is not to suggest, however, that advocates routinely cooperated with the "enemy"; to the contrary, they took pains to preserve their political independence and to avoid co-optation by either business groups or the state. They sought, in other words, to be "in" the system, not "of" it.

Recent Trends

By the mid-1970s, consumer advocates could claim victory on a number of fronts: products were now safer than ever before; consumer fraud was on the decline; and both industry and government were much more attentive to the voices of consumers. But the political fortunes of consumer organizations had begun to change by this time in response to a confluence of developments: the economic slowdown of the post–oil shock period, the reorganization of business interests at the national level, the dissemination of new ideas about consumer protection in the policymaking realm, and the devolution of powers from the federal government to the states.

As economic growth slowed after the mid-1970s, an increasing number of scholars, policymakers, and business representatives called for the state's retreat from the affairs of private business as a way to jump-start growth rates. Although consumer protection was far from the forefront of this neoliberal rethink, proponents justified regulatory reform to consumers on the grounds that it would lead to lower prices, more technological innovation in the marketplace, and, consequently, a greater range of product choice. This free-market approach to consumption was reminiscent of the first two waves of consumer movement history when the consumer interest was addressed via the beneficial but nevertheless incidental side effects of pro-business, market-oriented policies. By the Reagan administration—a "cruel time," in Nader's words (New York Times, May 10, 1989)—the approach had once again placed consumer representatives on the political defensive.

The consumer retreat was fueled not only by shifting governmental policies and ideas about consumer protection but also by the mobilization of firms in response to the regulatory gains of the public-interest movement (New York Times, May 10, 1989). A few of those firms established rival "public-interest" organizations of their own to disseminate the new neoliberal creed and to discredit the accomplishments and reputations of Nader and other consumer advocates (New York Times, April 22, 1982).[9] Others simply intensified their lobbying efforts for deregulation. In response to these policy and political realignments, the budgets and consumer-related responsibilities of regulatory agencies like the Federal Trade Commission shrank (New York Times, May 26, 1981); the role of the president's consumer adviser was scaled back; and the balance of power in Congress shifted toward the proponents of regulatory reform. For consumer representatives, the net effect of these developments was a decline in the number of institutional opportunities to disseminate their ideas and influence the policy process.

As the number of institutional opportunities for consumer activism at the national level decreased, so, too, did the political and economic resources at the disposal of representative organizations: the number of potential allies in Congress dwindled; the flow of public-interest lawyers into consumer organizations slowed; and access to government grants narrowed (interview, James, May 1999). Not surprisingly, the ability of consumer organizations to achieve their policy-related goals decreased accordingly. From the late 1970s, when long-term movement efforts to establish a national consumer agency were roundly defeated in Congress,[10] through the 1980s, the rate of introduction of new consumer protection legislation fell dramatically.

Consumer organizations may have suffered an overall decline in their capacity to influence the content of national public policy following the resurgence of business and the narrowing of access points into the policy process, but they certainly did not disappear. In fact, some consumer organizations continued to exert limited influence over both public opinion and the national agenda-setting and policy implementation processes—a feat that speaks volumes about the success of the organized movement's past policy gains, its organizational flexibility, and its ability to expand the conceptual boundaries of consumer activism.

On the issue of regulatory reform, for instance, Nader's well-publicized "populist critique" (Derthick and Quirk 1985:41) of national regulatory agencies (D. Vogel 1980/81:609) encouraged governmental actors to reform the system. As early as the Nixon administration, for instance, a well-publicized Nader exposé led to the wholesale overhaul of the Federal Trade Commission. Selective movement support for the government's deregulatory proposals also had an influential impact on public opinion. Advocates worked hard, for example, to strengthen public support for airline, telephone, and banking deregulation, although many later criticized some of the specifics of deregulation on the grounds that they led to higher prices for low-income consumers (Brobeck 1991). Finally, although Nader's network, in alliance with labor unions, ultimately failed to prevent the passage of the North American Free Trade Agreement,[11] it was instrumental in raising public awareness of the social and environmental costs of economic globalization and in placing the domestic and international ramifications of free-trade agreements on the national political agenda (D. Vogel 1980/81:1; interview, James, May 1999).

The continuing impact of consumer organizations on public opinion has been facilitated by the expansion of opportunities for consumer activism at the subnational level. Both state and local governments have been involved in consumer protection since the late nineteenth century, but it was not until the 1960s and 1970s that their consumer-oriented roles expanded with the establishment of state consumer affairs offices (Gregg 1997:527) and, by the end of the 1970s, the rapid expansion of the consumer-related responsibilities of state attorneys general (Blanke 1997:538; *New York Times*, February 8, 1988). These trends continued into the 1990s as numerous states established independent councils or agencies to represent the legal and economic interests of consumers before bureaucratic commissions overseeing utilities, insurance, health care, and other consumer-oriented programs (Gregg 1997:531). In these and other cases, institutional innovations at the state level were facilitated by interstate cooperation through such organizations as the National Association of Consumer Agency Administrators and the National Association of Attorneys General (Gregg 1997:531).

Institutional developments at the subnational level led to some interesting changes in the organized movement as it sought new inroads into the policy process and closer contacts with the citizenry during the era of regulatory reform. Consumers Union, for example, established regional chapters in Texas and California during the late 1970s. Together with other organizations at the state level, these chapters have indirectly influenced national policy on such issues as insurance and health care by helping set consumer precedents at the state and local levels via the courts and legislative assemblies (interview, James, May 1999). Ralph Nader, meanwhile, poured his energies into the expansion of his state and local consumer networks.[12] Although the diffuseness of the consumer constituency and the relative weakness of consumer grievances will undoubtedly prevent the American consumer movement from becoming a truly mass movement, the aim of Nader and other advocates has been to inject a stronger grassroots element into the overall movement (*New York Times*, April 27, 1982) now that the level of direct consumer access into the national policy process has diminished. The strategies of these organizations, meanwhile, appear to have remained more or less the same. What is distinctive about consumerism after the late 1970s is the fact that the number of governmental targets of movement strategies has expanded.

As consumer organizations responded to institutional shifts in the national policymaking system, many of their policy priorities changed as well. Now that consumer organizations are more firmly entrenched in the nation's cities, for example, they are more in tune with the problems of elderly and low-income consumers (interview, James, May 1999), whereas in the past they were mainly spokespersons for the middle class. Furthermore, as consumer organizations try to extend their appeal to a broader cross section of the population, more and more are addressing such issues as good governance, environmentalism, health care, taxation, and other issues that thirty years ago were only minor points on the consumer agenda (see Kroll and Stampfl 1981). Clearly, the concept of "consumer" has been taking on more and more attributes of "citizenship" as the movement adjusts to the changing institutional opportunities of consumer activism at the turn of the new century.

British Consumerism

The politics of postwar consumerism in Britain raise some intriguing questions for students of comparative consumer movements. Between 1875, when the country's first food and drug act was enacted, and the early 1990s, Britain introduced more consumer protection laws than did the United States (M. J. Smith 1993b:201). At the same time, however, Britain's network of consumer advocacy organizations has not been nearly so politicized as the American consumer movement; nor does it enjoy comparable levels of influence over the national policy process. Where, then, do these laws come from? Are governmental policymakers simply more pro-consumer than their American counterparts, thereby negating the need for a more active consumer movement?

Institutional factors hold the answers to these questions. While American consumer organizations have been characterized by a high degree of organizational independence in relatively pluralist and adversarial interest-group and policymaking settings, Britain's leading advocacy organizations have cooperated with governmental and business actors in a semicorporatist institutional setting based in the national bureaucracy. The ramifications of these institutional arrangements for the politics of consumer protection policymaking in Britain are at least twofold. First, since leading consumer advocates are not only "in" the system but also "of" it, they have fewer incentives to build a more politicized network of private consumer organizations, or, for that matter, to adopt aggressive lobbying tactics. Second, while British policymakers are not necessarily any more enlightened than their American counterparts, they do have strong institutional incentives to encourage compromise between consumer and business actors and to formulate policies that accommodate the interests of both. The result is a body of consumer protection law that, while extensive, is far softer on business than are comparable American statutes.

The following is a brief overview of these institutional arrangements and their impact on the historical development, political strategies, and policy-related influence of British consumer advocacy organizations.

The Institutional Backdrop

Although the British consumer movement can trace its roots to the early nineteenth century, when the consumer cooperative movement was first launched,[13] routinized consumer participation in national policymaking processes is widely regarded as a postwar phenomenon (see Hornsby-Smith 1986; J. Mitchell 1997). As in the United States, the politics of consumer participation in these processes are conditioned by formal and informal institutional opportunities for the representation of the public interest by various actors in the political system. Unlike the United States, however, those opportunities are relatively narrow in scope. Although party competition has encouraged virtually all parties to incorporate consumer issues into their political platforms, for example, the potential for the British Parliament to give rise to political entrepreneurs who distinguish themselves by their commitment to consumer policy is curbed by such informal institutional features as party discipline and centralized decision making, particularly in the powerful House of Commons. Furthermore, the prime minister, who is chosen from among members of Parliament rather than elected directly by the public at large, like the American president, has fewer incentives to espouse broad consumer interests as part of his or her political platform. Finally, the courts have not developed into a powerful alternative avenue for the articulation of the public interest. For years, lawsuits were harder to launch and much more costly than in the United States, and onerous procedural barriers discouraged plaintiffs from bringing cases to completion (Smith and Swann 1979:150–51). By the mid-1970s, however, this began to change as measures were introduced to simplify and reduce the costs of small-claims cases at the county court level (Wraith 1976:51–52). Consumer access to the courts expanded further during the 1980s and 1990s as more and more British lawyers accepted cases on a contingency basis (O'Connor 1998:67–68). These changes notwithstanding, the British courts are still much more costly and complex than their American counterparts and hence harder for consumers to access.

With regard to the processes of policy implementation, moreover, consumer representatives or private citizens have fewer opportunities to alter or reverse bureaucratic decisions. This is particularly true for regulatory policy. In the United States, agency procedures hold regulators publicly accountable for their actions, while a decentralized judicial system enables private citizens to contest individual regulatory decisions. The same cannot be said of Britain, however, where decision making is more centralized and discretionary and private citizens still face considerable legal barriers in the court system when seeking retribution for damages caused by, say, antitrust enforcement (Swann 1989:7). British consumers do have access to administrative redress via the Parliamentary Commissioner for Administration, a kind of ombudsman established in 1967 for citizens whose interests have been harmed by executive actions, but its effectiveness as spokesperson for consumers is weakened by the fact that it must deal with a wide range of nonconsumer issues as well.

In keeping with trends in many other policymaking fora (see Jordan and Richardson 1982:81), consumer protection policymaking throughout much of the postwar era has been carried out in an informal institutional context of "bureaucratic accommodation" and consensus building. Centered in the bureaucracy, the process involves consultation and negotiation with concerned groups linked to the government in subunits resembling policy communities (Jordan and Richardson 1982). Consumer organizations have assumed a fairly well-defined place in these subunits, performing in them the twin functions of setting agendas and providing decision makers with specialized information about consumer-related issues.

The Advocates: Public and Private . . .

The most influential consumer advocacy organs in this policymaking configuration have been the National Consumer Council (NCC) and the Consumers' Association (CA). Formed by the Labour government in 1975, the NCC is a publicly funded,[14] nonstatutory body (Hornsby-Smith 1986:292) with a wide-ranging mandate to conduct research on consumer-related issues and to represent the interests of consumers in the bureaucracy, Parliament, and, in the past, nationalized industries (G. Smith 1982:272). While the NCC resembles consumer agencies at the state level, there is nothing like this organ at the national level in the United States aside from the presidential consumer adviser, who performs far more limited functions and is backed by a much smaller staff.

The NCC's position as official spokesperson for the consumer interest has often been criticized because the council is not a mass-membership organization (Cullum 1997; J. Mitchell 1997:577). One might also argue that it runs the risk of being captured by governmental actors, industry, or the political parties, given its close association with government. In practice, however, there is no compelling evidence that the NCC is controlled by any of these actors (J. Mitchell 1997:577; M. Smith 1991:125); to the contrary, some analysts regard the council as a "genuine public-interest organization" and applaud its political neutrality (M. Smith 1991:125). That said, the NCC's close and institutionalized ties with the government do encourage cooperative relations with other interests—even business groups. For example, the NCC forms alliances with the major parties and business groups to support specific policy proposals. Although American organizations have allied with other interests like labor unions and environmental groups on certain issues—particularly during the past two decades in response to their relative political decline—alliances with business groups have been rare.

The NCC has never approximated the policy-related influence of American consumer organizations during the 1960s and early 1970s. In accordance with the informal institutional custom of bureaucratic accommodation, this is largely attributable to the comparatively close ties between business groups and the government and the resulting influence of business interests over policy. Consequently, NCC policy proposals are often defeated or watered down in response to business demands, and consumer policy in general tends to be much more solicitous of business interests than is comparable policy in the United States.

By the same token, since the mid-1970s the NCC has helped secure important protections for British consumers because of the quality of the information it provides, information that is well regarded by both civil servants and politicians (M. Smith 1991:124). In this respect, the NCC's ability to persuade other policymakers of the need for stronger consumer protection measures resembles that of many American consumer organizations. What distinguishes the NCC from American organizations is the fact that persuasion is carried out from a highly institutionalized position *within* the centralized policy process.

As noted earlier, the institutionalized relationship between the NCC and the government has had ramifications for consumerism as a politicized movement, for by establishing an effective body within the purview of the policymaking system that is mandated to speak out on consumers' behalf, the government has in effect weakened incentives for the further mobilization of private advocacy groups (M. J. Smith 1993b:204). It has also weakened the inclination of other consumer organizations to adopt the aggressive political tactics of many American organizations. This is not to suggest that there are no Nader-like organizations in Britain; indeed, a few of them do exist, particularly for specific issue areas (G. Smith 1982:291). They are, however, an exception to the norm.

If any one private organization epitomizes the "British norm" of consumer activism, it is the Consumers' Association. Since 1957, when it was established with the financial help of the Consumers Union in the United States, the CA has addressed the problems of middle-class consumers (Hornsby-Smith 1986:304) by adopting the model of consumerism perfected by its American mentor. For example, it launched *Which?* the British equivalent of *Consumer Reports*, a magazine that provides members[15] with product-related information generated by its in-house product-testing facilities. In the first week of its existence, *Which?* attracted more than 10,000 members to the CA (J. Mitchell 1997:595),[16] a telling illustration of the public's need for up-to-date information in the new consumer culture. By the 1960s, the CA had replaced consumer cooperatives as the leading nongovernmental spokesperson for the consumer interest.

Like Consumers Union, the CA focuses on product testing and the provision of information to its members and employs full-time advocates who lobby government for specific consumer protection policies. Proceeds from *Which?* and affiliated publications, moreover, have given the organization a healthy resource base that in 1994 totaled roughly $60 million (*The Economist*, June 18, 1994:62).[17] It is here that the similarities end. Whereas Consumers Union has maintained a careful organizational distance among itself, the federal government, and business interests, the CA tends to take assimilative politics to new heights by linking arms with the NCC in cooperative relationships with such actors. The CA has even supplied personnel to both the NCC and the Office of Fair Trading (Hornsby-Smith 1986:304), Britain's equivalent of the Federal Trade Commission and one of the few bureaucratic organs with a consumer affairs division. By the 1980s, the CA had become such a fixture in the political establishment that it was no longer seen as a serious threat by business. In the words of one analyst, "The CA is now as much a part of the conformist British scene as the House of Lords, tea, and the test match" (G. Smith 1982:290).

Finally, a note about consumer-related activities at the local level. Although local governments are not as involved in consumer protection as the American states are—a reflection of Britain's unitary system of government, which grants the localities little more than the power to execute national policies—consumer activity at the local level did increase during the 1960s and 1970s, when the number of local consumer groups reached a postwar high of about fifty (J. Mitchell 1997:578).[18] It was during this time that local governments introduced some interesting consumer-related institutions, the most important of which were the nonstatutory Consumer Advice Councils, which offered local consumers advice and, in some cases, conciliation and arbitration services (G. Smith 1982:280). Operated by staff members trained by the CA, the Consumer Advice Councils served as pivots for close working relations among the CA, local consumer groups, and local governments (G. Smith 1982:280).

. . . And Their Roles in the Policymaking System

Like American organizations, the impact of British organizations on policy depends on their ability to persuade policymakers that stricter consumer protection measures are in everyone's best interest. Unlike American organizations, however, their "strategies of persuasion" put far more emphasis on the routine dissemination of information in government circles than on the publication of scathing exposés, litigation, and aggressive lobbying, a strategy that reflects their limited but entrenched position in the policymaking system.

The institutional space occupied by consumer advocacy organizations and the resulting emphasis on strategies of rational persuasion enable those organizations to perform the following functions in the policymaking system. First, because of the NCC's mandate to represent the consumer interest in both Parliament and throughout the bureaucracy, both the NCC and, to a lesser extent, the CA, perform important consultation services for other actors in the policy process. The quality of such services in turn positions the two organizations to influence the processes of agenda setting and policy formulation, although these functions should not be overestimated, given the power of countervailing business interests in the decision-making process. Both functions are carried out in a centralized and consensus-oriented political system that encourages consumer organizations to balance the consumer interest against other contending interests in society. As we noted earlier, the result is consumer policy that fulfills many consumer protection objectives but that is often much softer on business than is corresponding policy in the United States.

What, then, is the role of public opinion in the British consumer policy process? Like consumer organizations in the United States and elsewhere, British organizations try to enhance their policymaking influence by conditioning public opinion about consumer issues. The NCC and the CA do this by publishing high-quality reports, books, and consumer magazines and by cooperating closely with the media on an issue-by-issue basis.[19] Although the activation or manipulation of public opinion can be a significant—albeit indirect—determinant of the willingness of policymakers to strengthen national consumer protection policies, it is not as important a political strategy as it is in the United States, since key consumer advocates are already so firmly entrenched in governmental circles.

Over the years, the NCC and the CA have been recognized as influential forces behind the introduction of a number of consumer statutes. During the 1960s and early 1970s, for example, these organizations helped with the implementation of incomes and pricing policies[20] by taking part in efficiency audits of specific industries and submitting suggestions for investigations to the National Board for Prices and Incomes (G. Smith 1982:15–17). They also contributed to the introduction of toy and electrical safety regulations, the enactment of the Unsolicited Goods and Services Act of 1971, and the Unfair Contract Terms Act of 1977 (G. Smith 1982:288; J. Mitchell 1997:576), the partial lifting of controls on retail shopping hours, and the introduction of regulations governing car safety and food hygiene (J. Mitchell 1997). Last but not least, the NCC was instrumental in the passage of the Credit Unions Act of 1979 and the Consumer Safety Act of 1986 (J. Mitchell 1997:579).

Consumerism During the Thatcher Era

As in the United States, British consumer organizations lost some of their political influence during the 1980s as the government grappled with such pressing economic problems as industrial decline and the loss of international competitiveness, inflation, high taxes and low income levels, and low-quality social services. As the official opposition during the late 1970s, the Conservative Party interpreted these problems as caused by excessive governmental involvement in the affairs of business (Fleming and Button 1989:85–86). Following her ascension to power in 1979, Margaret Thatcher consequently embarked on a long-term program of neoliberal political and economic reform that focused on the privatization of industry, deregulation, and a strict monetary policy.

Since the Thatcher reforms were driven primarily by politicians, they represented a departure from traditional modes of bureaucracy-centered policymaking. Thatcher's efforts to override tradition did not, however, go completely unchecked; before long, she was forced to abandon some of the more radical aspects of her proposals as a concession to her opponents. Her government did manage, though, to shift the focus of consumer policy from an interventionist governmental stance in the economy to one that left far more to market forces.

In keeping with these new policy pronouncements, the size of the government's consumer administrative apparatus was scaled down. For example, the Department of Prices and Consumer Protection, which had been an important ally of consumer organizations during the Labour governments of the 1970s, was abolished and its functions subsumed under the junior-ranking minister for consumer affairs and small firms in the Department of Trade and Industry. Although the NCC was retained, financial support for that organ dropped precipitously.

Public and private consumer organs at the local level also felt the pinch. Most of the Consumer Advice Councils that had been established during the 1960s and 1970s, for example, disappeared after the Thatcher government ended its financial support in 1979 (G. Smith 1982:281). Not surprisingly, the loss of a local governmental ally had a deleterious effect on private consumer groups at the grassroots level, the number of which dropped to a postwar low of just sixteen by the mid-1990s (J. Mitchell 1997:577).

Although opportunities for consumer organizations to influence the policy process were reduced as a result of the policies and institutional changes of the Thatcher era, consumer protection policy did not take as much of a beating as it did in the United States during the Reagan administration. In fact, the government actually *strengthened* legal and regulatory protections for consumers by introducing the Consumer Safety Act and a number of other statutes and by shielding the country's social regulatory regime from deregulation. This suggests that despite Thatcher's free-market and anti-bureaucracy persuasions, the long-standing policymaking customs of bureaucratic accommodation and compromise among contending interests still prevailed. It also attests to the entrenched position of consumer advocates in the policy process, a position that was not easily usurped by a change in governmental personnel. By the early 1990s, the consumer's enhanced position in the economy was officially recognized in the so-called Citizens' Charter, a governmental statement of what consumers should reasonably expect from their public institutions: high standards, information, openness, choice, nondiscrimination, accessibility, and redress (Cullum 1997:174).

Consumer organizations contributed selectively to the reform process by conveying valuable information to both politicians and bureaucrats. With

regard to airline deregulation, for instance, the country's leading organizations extensively researched the economic and safety ramifications of comparable reforms in the United States and concluded that deregulation was
in the consumer's best interest (Swann 1989:17). Consumer advocates also
supported the deregulation of the professions and efforts by the General
Agreement on Tariffs and Trade (GATT) to lower international trade barriers
(G. Smith 1982:13), and opposed the inflationary Common Agricultural
Policy of the European Union. In each instance, advocates were determined
to lower consumer prices and increase the range of product choice in the
marketplace.

The fact that privatization policies occupied such an important position
in the neoliberal agenda of the Thatcher government had interesting—and
unique—results for both regulation and the role of consumer organizations
in the policymaking sphere. In many cases, the privatization process resulted
in the "re-regulation" of a number of sectors in order to control competition
where monopolies had once existed.[21] In keeping with their traditionally
consultative functions, consumer advocates went on to perform watchdog
functions in agencies like the Office of Telecommunications (OFTEL) that
were established to oversee these new regulatory controls (M. Smith
1993a:154). Consumer organizations may have played only a minor role in
the movements to privatize and deregulate industry in Britain, but the end
result of those policies was the establishment of new governmental agencies
that in some ways enhanced the representation of the consumer interest in
the political system.

Although contemporary British consumers are in many ways better off
politically than their American counterparts, consumer advocates have not
done as much as American organizations to expand their constituencies and
adjust their principles and policy goals to the socioeconomic and institutional changes now confronting the movement. The CA and the NCC, for
example, have done little to coordinate their advocacy activities with the
wishes of smaller advocacy organizations and local consumer groups, many
of which have vociferously opposed governmental efforts to deregulate the
economy and privatize public corporations. Neither organization, moreover,
has done much to embrace environmentalism, which is of increasing concern to consumers (Middleton 1998:213–27). Nor, with the partial exception
of the NCC, has the organized movement shed its middle-class orientation
by appealing more to underprivileged consumers (*The Economist*, June 18,
1994:62). The Consumers' Association, for example, continues to champion
the kinds of consumer issues that were popular two or three decades ago

while failing to address many of the problems affecting "consumers-as-citizens" at the turn of the century. Had consumer advocacy organizations enjoyed broader membership bases or been faced with more narrow or less secure inroads into the policy process, they, like their American counterparts, might have proved more flexible in their organizational and conceptual approaches to consumerism. For now, however, they appear stuck in an increasingly outdated "middle-class groove" (*The Economist*, June 18, 1994:62).

Conclusion

The American and British consumer advocacy movements share a number of characteristics. Both experienced their most formative moments during the postwar period, when mass production and mass consumption had created a plethora of consumer-related problems and rising expectations of the quality of consumer life had reached new heights. Both movements, moreover, were largely guided from above by consumer advocates rather than fueled from below by grassroots citizen activism. Finally, consumer organizations in both countries looked primarily to their governments as the most capable guarantors of the consumer interest and suffered institutional setbacks when those guarantors retreated from the affairs of business.

American and British consumer organizations differ, however, in how they have articulated the consumer interest in the policy process and in their impact on policy outcomes. These differences, as the previous analysis has shown, can be largely explained with reference to the institutional contexts of the two movements. The relatively pluralist, decentralized, and fluid consumer policymaking process of the United States, for instance, has given American consumer organizations the kinds of political access and resources that have enabled them to maintain their organizational independence and to adopt aggressive but assimilative—as opposed to protest-oriented—strategies in the policy process. When the alliance between business and government is relatively weak and diffuse, those organizations perform agenda-setting, policy formulation, and bureaucratic whistle-blowing functions that have contributed to one of the most progressive consumer policy regimes in the world.

In Britain, by contrast, a more rigid, centralized, and semicorporatist consumer policy process combined with a closer and more enduring government-business relationship has compelled consumer organizations to cooperate much more closely over the long term with other actors in the political system. As a result, advocates perform broad consultative functions in the policy process, as well as agenda-setting, policy formulation, and watchdog functions, and are more likely to seek compromise with business interests than their American counterparts are. At the same time, British consumer advocates throughout most of the postwar period have played a highly routinized role in the institutions of consumer policymaking while American advocates must constantly adapt to the vicissitudes of the United States's more fluid, decentralized political system. British consumer organizations, in other words, are more secure in their respective institutional context but have been largely incapable of bringing about the kind of progressive consumer protection policies that marked the heyday of American consumer movement activism.

In Japan, the institutional context of consumer politics resembles that of Britain in that policymaking is centered in the national bureaucracy and based in many ways on consensus building among different interests. But whereas British consumer organizations participate regularly and meaningfully in national consumer protection policymaking, Japanese consumer representatives have little more than symbolic representation in that process. On the surface, at least, the Japanese consumer policy process can be likened to a system of "corporatism without consumers."[22] The reasons for the virtual exclusion of consumer representatives from national policymaking circles are rooted in the institutions of Japanese politics, especially those that appeared in the context of one-party dominance. How this particular state of affairs arose, as well as the efforts by evolving consumer organizations to permeate the system from below, are the subjects of the next three chapters.

3 The Politics of an Emerging Consumer Movement: The Occupation Period

> Our pioneering leaders exclaimed: "Capitalism is a double-edged sword! We are exploited both as workers and consumers!" The battle to abolish the exploitation of workers has progressed; the trickery of exploiting consumers, however, has been taken to the extremes of ingenuity and it threatens the livelihood of the masses. . . . The social responsibilities of consumers, particularly of women, are extremely great. . . . Let us raise our voices and assert the consumer position.
>
> —Consumer declaration, February 1957

So proclaimed Oku Mumeo, the founder of Shufuren (Japan Federation of Housewives' Associations), before an assembly of 700 consumer advocates from around the country at the first annual National Consumer Rally (Zen nihon shōhisha taikai) in Tōkyō. Resonating with the incendiary rhetoric of the times, Oku's words expressed a deep-seated frustration among consumer representatives with the pro-business policies of the early postwar conservative establishment, the failure of both business and government to respect consumer interests, and the lack of consumer representation in the decision-making processes of both business and government. At the turn of the twenty-first century, this sense of moral outrage still lingers as the postwar movement celebrates more than fifty years of economic and political activism.

My purpose in this and the next chapter is to survey the early postwar history of one of Japan's most enduring social movements before the institutionalization of the post-1968 consumer protection policymaking system. In this chapter, I explore the structural and strategic evolution of consumer organizations from war's end to 1955, when the Liberal Democratic Party (LDP) first came to power. This was an important period for our purposes, not only because it witnessed the formation of several of Japan's flagship consumer advocacy organizations, but also because it spawned many of the characteristics of Japanese consumerism that still are present today. As a period of rapid political transformation, moreover, the decade exemplifies the effects of policy change, institutional developments, and broad political alignments on the evolution of social movements. Of particular significance, as we shall see, was the so-called Reverse Course,[1] a reorientation of Occupation priorities toward conservative, pro-business goals that in some cases changed the opportunities for consumer activism.

From Bamboo Shoots to Blooming Flowers: The Socioeconomic and Political Context of Early Postwar Consumerism

Whereas the contemporary American and British consumer movements were largely the products of firmly entrenched democratic systems and the economic affluence of the 1960s, the most formative years of the Japanese consumer movement were those of the immediate postwar period, an era of economic chaos, political and institutional instability, and unprecedented opportunities for citizen activism.

From Japan's defeat in World War II until 1950, when the advent of the Korean War finally put the country on the road to economic recovery, Japanese citizens faced triple-digit inflation and severe food and product shortages, problems caused in many instances by a draconian rationing system and a burgeoning black market. To stem the ravages of malnutrition, many Japanese were reduced to trading their possessions for food on the black market and foraging for provisions in the countryside. In the words of those who lived through the period, it was a "bamboo shoot lifestyle" (*takenoko seikatsu*), a metaphor for life below the subsistence line.[2]

In a manner similar to that of the environmental citizens' movement two decades later, Japanese consumers mobilized quickly and spontaneously at the local level against this economic backdrop in pursuit of a life-and-death objective: the restoration of the supply of basic necessities to the marketplace at affordable prices. It was, quite simply, a time of mass participation in pursuit of consumer goals—a rare occurrence when compared with the postwar histories of the U.S. and British movements.

In contrast to both environmental groups, with their relatively affluent middle-class members (see McKean 1981), and to their American, male-dominated counterparts, Japan's early postwar consumer organs were composed primarily of impoverished women from diverse social backgrounds.

They compensated for their lack of resources with a newly found sense of political efficacy that emerged from a common political wellspring: the democratic policies and institutions introduced by the Allied Occupation of Japan.

Shortly after arriving in Japan, the Supreme Commander of the Allied Powers (SCAP) lifted the authoritarian controls of the prewar and wartime eras and granted citizens a number of basic democratic rights and freedoms that paved the way for a veritable explosion of interest-group and citizen-group activity (Tsujinaka 1988:73). Among those who took full advantage of these developments were the country's newly enfranchised women, many of whom lost no time jumping into the political fray. Indeed, some women got involved in democratic politics even before the Occupation forces set foot on Japanese soil. Ichikawa Fusae, for example, one of Japan's best-known feminist activists, formed the first of many postwar women's groups only ten days after the surrender.[3] Legend has it that she was inspired by flyers hinting at the democratic changes to come that had been dropped by American airmen onto the fields surrounding her home (KSS 1997:5). During the final months of 1945 and throughout the next year, women around the country swelled the ranks of the unions and the political parties (Garon 1997:181), organized for welfare rights for mothers and children and the elevation of the status of women, and campaigned for lower prices, an end to black marketeering, a more efficient rationing system, and other consumer-related issues. Although many of these groups were short lived, the degree of activism among Japanese women during this period was unprecedented. It was, as Oku Mumeo's daughter Nakamura Kii recounted a half century later, "a time when women jumped into action like flowers blooming all at once" (K. Nakamura 1996:10).

It was also a time when economic and political circumstances contributed to a qualitative and structural overlap of the consumer and women's movements. In this context of economic scarcity, many of the problems that plagued women-as-consumers were closely intertwined with their roles as mothers and housewives. One of the most important tasks performed by housewives during the early Occupation years was to line up each day— sometimes for hours at a time—to collect their families' daily rations (Garon 1997:181; K. Kobayashi, April 1994:41). When the rationing system did not work properly (which was often the case during the Occupation), the housewives had trouble meeting their families' nutritional needs. Thus it was no accident that many of the organizations that we now associate with the women's movement, like Ichikawa's League of Women Voters (Fujin yūken-sha dōmei), became involved in consumer-related campaigns during the Occupation. This practice continues to this day, although to a lesser degree. Meanwhile, organizations like Shufuren, which made their mark after World War II mainly as consumer advocates, have simultaneously pursued objectives designed to eliminate prostitution, promote the status and protection of women, and so on. In contrast to the U.S. and British movements during the early postwar period, virtually no organs focused exclusively on consumer issues.

While the newly institutionalized democratic rights and freedoms of the Occupation period were instrumental in spurring Japan's nascent consumer organs into action, those rights and freedoms were not accompanied by routinized participation in the mainstream decision-making processes of government. This was particularly true from 1947/48, when a reorientation of Occupation policy led to the introduction of pro-growth policies that both enhanced the influence of business spokespersons in the policy process and weakened the legitimacy of nonbusiness interests like labor and consumers. Accordingly, consumer activists, along with most other citizen groups at the time, pursued the tactics of the politically dispossessed: noisy street demonstrations, the petitioning of bureaucratic officials, boycotts, direct confrontation with local businessmen, and other forms of overt political protest. In keeping with their lack of financial resources and political and economic expertise, many activists also resorted to publicly berating those in authority for abusing the public trust.[4]

Although consumer protest may not have yielded the policy results that more established interest groups might expect to obtain in the mainstream political process, it was important as a form of citizen participation in politics for at least two reasons. First, the noisy, iconoclastic nature of consumer activism helped educate otherwise passive citizens about their identities as consumers, the extent of consumer abuses in the postwar marketplace, and, finally, the legitimacy of standing up to the vaunted producer on behalf of consumer protection. It was, in many ways, an early postwar example of what Susan Pharr termed "status-based conflict" (Pharr 1990:5)—of efforts by consumers to assert their identities and to challenge the authority of political and economic leaders who had suppressed them in the past. Second, consumer activists in many instances successfully used protest tactics to shame the perpetrators of egregious consumer abuses into changing their business practices. Their successes, in turn, encouraged many activists to establish formal organizations, some of which went on to become part of the nucleus of the contemporary consumer advocacy movement.

Japan's Flagship Consumer Organizations

Kansai shufuren

One such group was the forerunner of one of the most influential consumer organizations in western Japan: the Kansai shufuren (or Kansai shufurengōkai, Kansai Federation of Housewives' Associations). In October 1945, Higa Masako, a Christian activist and educator, led a group of fifteen women from a suburb of Ōsaka to the offices of the local rationing authorities to protest the persistent and lengthy delays in the supply of rice rations (K. Kobayashi, April 1994:38–41). Armed with empty *furoshiki*,[5] the women arrived at the rationing station just as the attending officials were sitting down to a midday meal complete with ample portions of freshly cooked rice — enough, in fact, for a "week's supply of rice gruel" (K. Kobayashi, April 1994:41). The women immediately took the officials to task for pilfering the public rice supply and clamored for the timely resumption of rations to the neighborhood. Miraculously, supplies were restored later that very same day. The incident was one of the first examples of what was later dubbed the "Give us back our rice *furoshiki* movement" (Kome yokose furoshiki undō),[6] a campaign that attracted consumers from all over Japan.[7]

Spurred on by her unexpected victory, Higa and her cash-strapped followers decided to form a small women's group that eventually expanded into the Ōsaka shufu no kai (Ōsaka Housewives' Association), a small organization that survived on the meager donations of its members. In 1949, the association merged with twenty-nine other local women's groups to form the Kansai shufuren. A nonpartisan organization consisting of both individual members and independent women's groups, the Kansai shufuren promoted international peace, an end to black marketeering and inflation, the reform of the rationing system, and a number of other issues that symbolized the association's origins in the wake of wartime destruction.

Among the organization's most successful programs was the "housewives' shop" (*shufu no mise*) designation for exemplary local retailers. Comparable to the "white list" issued by the Consumers League of New York at the end of the nineteenth century,[8] the designation was awarded through democratic balloting procedures to retailers who avoided black market practices, sold their products at reasonable prices, and treated their customers with courtesy and respect (KSS 1997:17). Over time, retail practices improved markedly in a number of Ōsaka neighborhoods as shopkeepers began competing for the designation as a way to attract customers. The women who chose the designations, meanwhile, acquired an unprecedented sense of power over a distribution system that had long been viewed as immune to consumer control (K. Kobayashi, November 1994:50). The "housewives' shop" campaign quickly spread to other parts of the country and was widely regarded as one the movement's most effective market-oriented tactics for changing the behavior of business.

Nihon shufurengōkai

Consumer protest against the rationing system also included efforts to restore to the marketplace the supply of potatoes, sugar, vegetables, kerosene, and a number of other staples (Nomura 1990:3). These campaigns, together with protests against inflationary price hikes, were fittingly referred to as the Movement to Defend Livelihoods (seikatsu bōei no undō). Although the tactics often varied according to locality, the most common were direct confrontation with those deemed responsible for the shortages—the tactic of choice for the politically weak and financially destitute who eschewed the use of violence.

Among the better-known campaigns in the movement to protect and improve livelihoods was a rally organized by Tōkyō housewives to demand the removal of defective matches from the marketplace (Furyō matchi tsuihō taikai). The brainchild of Oku Mumeo, who had been inspired by the protests of the Ōsaka shufu no kai (K. Nakamura 1996:8), the rally is widely touted as one of the most symbolic events in the postwar history of the organized movement.

During the early postwar period, when electricity was in short supply, matches were an indispensable household commodity controlled by the rationing system. Since rations often fell short of their specified allotments, however, consumers were frequently reduced to purchasing them at highly inflated prices on the black market (Takada 1979:60). Matches were not only expensive and hard to come by, but many of them would not even light when struck.[9] After failing to extract a promise from manufacturers and local authorities to rectify the problem (Shufurengōkai 1973:12), Oku and a small group of supporters arranged for consumers to exchange their defective matches for good ones at a rally scheduled for September 3, 1948, in the Shibuya ward of Tōkyō (NHSK 1980:22).

The event, which was widely covered by the media, was an enormous success (Oku 1988:177). The organizers collected an entire truckload of defective matches (*Shufuren dayori*, December 1948:2), obtained a public apology from the manufacturers in attendance, and extracted an agreement from officials representing the Daily Necessities Department (Nichiyōhinka) of the Ministry of Commerce (Shōkōshō) and the Economic Stabilization Board (Keizai anteihonbu) to regulate the quality of matches in the future (Takada 1979). Heartened by the effectiveness of the campaign, Oku and her expanding circle of supporters organized Shufuren (Nihon shufuren-gōkai, Japan Federation of Housewives' Associations) in October 1948, arguably Japan's leading consumer organization. By 1949, Shufuren was estimating a membership of more than 500,000 in the Tōkyō metropolitan area alone (*Shufuren dayori*, May 1949). By the early 1990s, it consisted of about 500 individual members and roughly 400 local organizations from around the country (Keizaikikakuchō 1991c:26).

Oku Mumeo's political philosophy has heavily influenced Shufuren in its efforts to protect the rights of both women and consumers.[10] A feminist and labor activist who had associated in the past with such prominent figures as Ichikawa Fusae and the socialist leader Osugi Sakae, Oku believed strongly in the advancement of consumer and women's rights through both education and political activism, and she was a major figure in the establishment of prewar women's and cooperative organizations. Oku was also one of a small handful of postwar consumer activists to obtain public office. In 1947, she was elected to the Upper House for the first of three consecutive terms as a member of the People's Cooperative Party. Throughout her tenure, she used her platform to articulate the problems specific to both women and consumers and to press (unsuccessfully) for the establishment of a consumer agency at the national level. Oku also served as a member of several governmental *shingikai* (government advisory councils) during these early years and publicized some of the contents of the proceedings—which were officially closed to the public—in the organization's monthly newsletter, *Shufuren dayori*. Although she had very little power compared with that of her male counterparts in the conservative parties, Oku was, in effect, the movement's most prominent voice in the mainstream political system.

When she finally relinquished her seat, Shufuren experienced a drop in direct political influence (interview, Shimizu, July 1999) that it was never able to recover.

With the rice paddle (*oshamoji*) as its symbol,[11] Shufuren engaged in a number of activities during the late 1940s and early 1950s to advance the status of consumers, including product testing, consumer advising and education; the designation of "housewives' shops" (*shufu no mise*) in the Tōkyō area (*Shufuren dayori*, April 1949); rallies; and signature drives. Like its Kansai counterpart, the organization viewed itself as nonpartisan and politically independent. Oku's association with prewar feminist and labor organizations and her pursuit of progressive policies as a member of the Upper House, however, gave the organization a slightly left-of-center political hue.

The fujinkai *and Chifuren*

Another important player in the contemporary consumer movement that formed during the early postwar period was the National Federation of Regional Women's Organizations (Zen nihon chiiki fujinkai rengōkai), or Chifuren, an association of regional women's organizations and their constituent local women's groups (*fujinkai*).

The *fujinkai* had a controversial prewar history—a product, in large part, of the nature of their relationships with national and local authorities. Although many groups formed spontaneously and independently from the late nineteenth century through mid-1945 (Zenchifuren 1973:13), others were mobilized from above or became the target of local governmental interference in support of state-sponsored goals. During the 1930s and the early 1940s, for example, *fujinkai* were established to participate in national defense training, campaigns to promote savings, and other programs designed to facilitate the execution of national wartime policies (NHSK 1980:25; see also Garon 1997). In some instances, groups were organized into national federations; the Women's Patriotic Association (Aikoku fujinkai), which was supervised by the Home Ministry, and the Women's Association for the Defense of Japan (Dai nihon kokubō fujinkai), organized by the War Ministry, were two of the best-known examples (K. Kobayashi, July 1995:48).

The *fujinkai* were disbanded by the Occupation forces in 1945 as inherently undemocratic, only to reappear in semialtered form shortly thereafter. The extension of the franchise to women in late 1945, combined with official Occupation policies designed to promote the free and democratic association of Japanese citizens at the local level, helped spark a mushrooming of these groups around the country. In many instances, however, there was nothing voluntary about the mobilization process at all; in fact, existing evidence suggests that many women were still steeped in the social mores of prewar Japan and joined the *fujinkai* only out of a sense of obligation to their communities (K. Kobayashi, November 1995:45).

As Garon notes, although SCAP prohibited governmental interference in the formation and maintenance of these groups, many *fujinkai* received funding from local authorities who were eager to use the groups as "subcontractors" for local governmental projects (Garon 1997:189). In blatant disregard for the spirit of democracy, moreover, some localities offered guidance to the *fujinkai* on how to organize and conduct themselves "democratically" (NHSK 1980:26). Not surprisingly, many of the postwar *fujinkai* looked strikingly like their prewar predecessors in regard to both the gap between their leaders and rank-and-file members and their close relations with governmental organs—a testament, so to speak, to the resilience of prewar and wartime organizational customs even in the midst of expanding opportunities for democratic change (Garon 1997:188; K. Kobayashi, November 1995:188).

The *fujinkai* were interested in a much wider range of social and political issues than were the women's groups that participated in the Kansai shufuren and Shufuren. The 1948 schedule of activities of the Federation of Women's Associations of Shizuoka Prefecture illustrates this point. Throughout much of the year, the organization focused on reforming marriage customs, relieving earthquake victims, and commemorating the anniversary of a visit to Japan by Helen Keller (K. Kobayashi, November 1995:46). By contrast, lowering prices and attacking black market practices encompassed a relatively small portion of the group's energies.

By 1951, the *fujinkai* had formed regional federations in more than 70 percent of the prefectures (K. Kobayashi, November 1995:47). SCAP forbade them, however, from establishing a national federation for fear that it would interfere with the democratic participation of women at the local level (KSS 1997:69). With the end of the Occupation in 1952, these restrictions were lifted and the National Federation of Regional Women's Associations— Chifuren—was duly established under the leadership of Yamataka Shigeri, a leading activist in the prewar *fujinkai* and a suffragist associated with Ichikawa Fusae. Today, Chifuren has about 6 million members (Keizaikikakuchō 1993a:62).

Chifuren differs from Shufuren in several ways. First, whereas Shufuren often focuses on political activism at the national level, Chifuren has a more regional outlook. Second, although Shufuren is involved in a number of issues relating to politics and women, the organization is known primarily as a consumer organization that engages in both education and advocacy. Chifuren, on the other hand, has embraced a much wider range of political and social issues, including the promotion of clean elections, the prevention of juvenile delinquency, a ban on prostitution, the promotion of welfare programs and gender equality,[12] and opposition to nuclear weapons (NHSK 1980:45).[13] Over the past three decades or so, however, Chifuren has been increasingly recognized as one of the country's leading consumer advocacy organizations.[14] Third, Chifuren is much more closely aligned with conservative, pro-business forces in Japanese politics than Shufuren is. Although it is not formally allied with any political party, Chifuren is politically conservative and often referred to derogatorily as the *fujinkai* of the Liberal Democratic Party, an image that is partly attributable to the fact that many *fujinkai* members are wives of locally prominent, upper-middle-class personages. As a result of its conservative political leanings, Chifuren often conflicts with other consumer organizations over the choice of appropriate tactics and slogans during political campaigns (interview, consumer activist, April 1994).

The Consumer Cooperatives

Like Chifuren, the history of the Japanese consumer cooperative[15] movement extends back to the Meiji era, although it was not until the Taishō period (1912–1925) that the movement came into its own (Katsube 1979:54). Small in size and often very short lived, many of the early co-ops were organized by the workers of large corporations and had strong ties to the Communist Party. Others, particularly in the Kansai area, were heavily influenced by the Christian Socialist thinking of such well-known evangelists as Kagawa Toyohiko. No matter what their political orientation, all were formed as a consumer-controlled counterbalance to the increasing power of big business interests during a period of rapid industrialization.

Unlike their postwar counterparts, the prewar cooperatives consisted primarily of men. Many of the leaders of these groups were very progressive in their views of women, however, and actively supported female suffrage (Uchida 1983). The co-op movement consequently attracted the participation of such leading female activists and educators as Hiratsuka Raichō, the founder of the Taishō feminist journal *Bluestocking* (*Seito*); Oku Mumeo; Nomura Katsuko, a prominent postwar consumer activist; and Hani Motoko, a Christian socialist educator and the founder of the Jiyū gakuen school in Tōkyō. Many of these women embraced the socialist cooperative principles established in 1844 by England's Rochdale Society of Equitable Pioneers: open membership, democratic control, education, and cooperation among cooperatives (Iwadare 1991:430–31), features that social scientists now associate with new social movements.

These early feminist and consumer pioneers looked to the cooperatives as democratic fora in which women-as-consumers could interact with men on an equal basis in the hopes of building a more just and equitable society (K. Kobayashi, September 1993:40–44). But as a result of their leftist orientations and the introduction of a rationing system and other state-led controls over the economy that negated their economic usefulness, the co-ops were suppressed by the state following the outbreak of hostilities with China (Nomura 1973:3).

The consumer cooperatives quickly reappeared during the Occupation period with the blessing of SCAP. From SCAP's point of view, these organizations performed useful functions in the local distribution of scarce goods and services and served as vehicles, together with the agricultural cooperatives, for the democratization of Japanese society (Nomura 1973:3). The co-ops also helped educate consumers in coping with economic scarcity. By 1947, the roughly 6,500 small co-ops around the country boasted a combined membership of about 3 million people (KSS 1997:48). The late 1940s also witnessed the formation of what later became Seikyōren (Nihon seikatsu kyōdō kumiai rengōkai, Japan Consumer Cooperatives Union, or JCCU), a nonpartisan national umbrella organization and the foremost political representative of the cooperative movement at the national level (Iwadare 1991:429).[16]

The Japanese consumer cooperative movement, now one of the largest in the world with roughly 44 million members (Keizaikikakuchō 1997:3), is as varied as the organized consumer movement is as a whole. While many of the larger prefectural cooperatives provide myriad services for their members in settings that rival those of sophisticated Japanese department stores, others consist primarily of *han*: small groups of residents who gather regularly to place orders and receive deliveries from a local cooperative distribution center. The political preferences of the cooperatives also run the gamut of the political spectrum, from the highly politicized and progressive Seikatsu Club[17] of the Kantō area to the small and largely apolitical joint buying clubs that deal directly with local farmers. All of them, however, are imbued to varying degrees with qualities often associated with new social movements, including democratic participation in decision making, environmentalism, and equality of the sexes. The fact that the co-ops have adopted these organizational principles and the *fujinkai* have not is due primarily to their democratic prewar history and emulation of British cooperative norms.

Although the consumer cooperative movement eventually managed to become one of the largest and most economically resilient wings of the postwar consumer movement, its future was very uncertain during the early postwar years. Following the upsurge of cooperative mobilization during the democratization phase of the Occupation, the movement fell on hard times with the introduction of economic austerity measures during the politically conservative Reverse Course years (1947/48–1952). For example, many co-ops succumbed to bankruptcy as the government took steps to increase the level of competition in the market. By October 1950, only 130 or so of the roughly 6,000 co-ops that had been active in June 1947 were still in existence (KSS 1997:49).

The economic problems of the early postwar co-ops were further compounded by the stipulations of the 1948 Consumers' Lifestyle Cooperative Law (Shōhi seikatsu kyōdō kumiai hō), or Co-op Law. Before the war, consumer cooperatives—or "buyers' cooperatives" (*kōbai kumiai*), as they were often referred to at the time—were subject to heavy governmental regulation under the 1900 Industrial Association Law (Sangyō kumiai hō), a law that was intended to protect the interests of farmers and small and medium enterprises (KSS 1997:50). In 1947, SCAP and Japan's first socialist government began drafting a law designed exclusively for the consumer co-ops. With SCAP's backing, co-op representatives were directly involved in the drafting process, an unprecedented opportunity in the history of the co-op movement that attests to the relatively open political atmosphere of the first few years of the Occupation. Activists took advantage of this opportunity to press for legislation that would prevent the kind of arbitrary governmental interference that had culminated in the suppression of the co-ops during the 1930s and to lay the groundwork for the movement's long-term growth.

As luck would have it, shifts in the political alliances that governed the formal legislative process eventually shunted the co-op representatives to the sidelines of that process. It all began around late 1947 when many of the movement's New Deal allies in SCAP headquarters returned to the United States and the pro-growth stage of the Occupation gathered steam (KSS 1997:52). These personnel and policy developments not only reduced the number of political opportunities for co-op participation in policymaking, but they also led to the co-optation of the legislative process by a tightly knit coalition of conservative politicians and small business representatives who felt economically threatened by the co-ops (NHSK 1980:31–32).

The Co-op Law met most of the demands of small businessmen and their political sponsors. The law forbade, for example, the amalgamation of pre-fectural cooperatives,[18] thereby preventing the formation of powerful, na-tionwide chains. It also restricted co-op sales to members only, a stipulation that led to the direct monitoring of cooperative business practices by the Ministry of Health and Welfare (interview, Hiwasa, February 1994), the min-istry in charge of implementing the law. Finally, the law failed to meet many of the co-ops' specific demands, including access to special tax exemptions and the right to deal in credit and insurance transactions. All in all, the law was designed to promote free competition between the cooperatives and mainstream businesses on the basis of equality between the two (KSS 1997:53), much to the chagrin of co-op activists who had pressed for the legal recognition of consumer cooperatives as nonprofit organizations. For cooperatives that were struggling to stay afloat, the new law sounded a death knell. Today, restrictions on the size and activities of the co-ops explain in part why they account for only 2.5 percent of the Japanese retail market.[19]

Ironically, even though the Co-op Law was originally designed to contain the growth of the consumer cooperative movement, it presented the co-ops with a good excuse to get involved in consumer advocacy politics.[20] No sooner was the law enacted than co-op leaders mobilized both themselves and their members to pressure the government for amendments.[21] The law was also an incentive for the co-ops to cooperate with other consumer or-ganizations in support of strong consumer protection measures and an end to collusive business practices in both the small and big business commu-nities, practices that were weakening even further the co-ops' vulnerable economic position.

Despite their financial problems during the Occupation, the consumer cooperatives distinguished themselves in subsequent years as the most fi-nancially secure of consumer-related organizations. Their financial security in turn strengthened the political independence of the co-ops, a few of which—including the Seikatsu Club (see Gelb and Estevez-Abe 1998;

LeBlanc 1999)—have fielded candidates in local and prefectural elections. Most co-ops tend not to become involved in electoral affairs, however, particularly those, like Seikyōren, that have played a leading role in national legislative and regulatory campaigns. But regardless of the extent of their involvement in legislative activities, the cooperatives have the potential to mobilize virtually millions of consumers behind consumer-related goals— even though only a tiny portion of cooperative members join for political purposes[22]—and are therefore key components of the contemporary consumer advocacy movement.

The Early Postwar Strategic Repertoire

Indoctrinated for generations to rely passively on governmental authorities to take the initiative in setting the nation's political agenda and solving its problems, Japanese citizens during the early years of the Occupation were suddenly confronted with a whole new array of opportunities for democratic participation in politics. Now, the name of the game was liberal democracy, and for the first time in their history the Japanese were openly encouraged by higher-ups to exercise their new rights at the local PTA and as members of unions and citizens' groups. As might be expected in a country that had had little exposure to democratic practices in the past, many Japanese citizens reverted to their old political behavior by functioning as passive players in hierarchically structured groups, much to the frustration of the Occupation authorities (see, e.g., van Staaveren 1994). Others, however, took full advantage of these new political opportunities and pursued more democratic styles of internal decision making.

The forces of continuity and change were evident not only in the structure and internal behavior of consumer organizations but also in the strategic behavior of those organizations vis-à-vis their governmental and business adversaries. From the repertoire of the impoverished and politically weak, consumer organizations for the first decade of their postwar existence relied heavily on protest strategies designed to shame recalcitrant businesses into fulfilling their responsibilities to consumers. The adaptation of prewar strategies to postwar contingencies was hardly a matter of choice for consumer organizations, given their almost complete exclusion from mainstream political processes. Consumer organizations simply did not have the resources or the formal and informal links to bureaucrats and politicians that would have enabled them to work through formal institutionalized channels to bring industrywide pressure on business.

In a few short years, however, some consumer organizations managed to partially transcend their peripheral position in Japanese politics by developing new ways of getting their points across to both the public and those in positions of authority. The "housewives' shops" movement was certainly one example of this. So, too, were the market-displacing transactions carried out by the consumer cooperatives. A third example of consumer innovation that we have yet to examine was product testing.

In 1950, Shufuren established the Basic Commodities Research Department (Nichiyōhin shinsabu), the first of its kind in Japan. Under the leadership of Takada Yuri, a certified pharmacist and leading figure in the organization, the department armed Shufuren with scientifically derived information that helped legitimize the organization's political demands and discredit the arguments of its opponents. Product testing marked an important step forward in Shufuren's efforts to strengthen its power of persuasion, a power, as we have seen in the case of the American and British movements, that enhances the effectiveness of public-interest groups in both the marketplace and the policy process.[23]

Some of the early findings of Shufuren's testing facilities had a major impact on public opinion. In 1951, for instance, Shufuren publicized the use of a potentially carcinogenic yellow food dye in *takuan*, a popular pickled radish. Following a public backlash, the Ministry of Health and Welfare launched its own investigation and in 1953 banned further use of the dye. Comparable results were achieved following the subsequent discovery of dangerous substances in plastic food containers (see, e.g., Takada 1996:82–83). In other cases, Shufuren had a more direct impact on business practices. The publicity surrounding its discoveries that manufacturers were falsely representing the contents of products like margarine, beef, soy sauce, soap, and milk, for instance, was all it took to prod those manufacturers into changing their labeling practices. These early victories led to subsequent expansions of Shufuren's testing facilities and helped stem the flood of defective products into the marketplace. The *takuan* incident, moreover, proved to be a flagship case in the campaign to promote food safety (NHSK 1980:37–38), the consumer movement's top political priority throughout the postwar era.

That the market-oriented strategies of consumer organizations occasionally succeeded in changing the behavior of industry and prompting regulatory responses from officials is in part a reflection of the issues in question. In most cases, consumer organizations were tackling problems that were easy to understand and widely regarded as blatant abuses of the safety and economic well-being of consumers. As we shall see in later chapters, direct confrontation with business adversaries and the dissemination of data produced by product-testing facilities proved far less effective once consumer issues became mired in legal jargon and the complexities of contemporary politics.

Relations with Government Authorities

The forces of change and continuity also permeated the relationships between consumer organs and governmental authorities. Sometimes those relationships were highly cooperative and reminiscent of prewar norms, but at other times, conflict was the norm. One notable example of close cooperation was the formation of a "consumer federation" to oppose black market practices, particularly those that raised consumer prices. Led on the government side by regional branches of the Price Agency (Bukkachō) and the Economic Stabilization Board (Keizai antei honbu), the federation included the Ōsaka shufu no kai (predecessor of the Kansai shufuren), Sōdōmei (All-Japan General Federation of Trade Unions), and Sanbetsu kaigi (Congress of Industrial Organizations)—a rather unlikely quintet of players given the potential for conflict among them. Higa Masako, the head of the Ōsaka shufu no kai, balked at first at the idea of linking up with these groups for fear of the corrupting influence that such an association might have on her organization (K. Kobayashi, May 1994:40). But she eventually changed her mind on the grounds that refusing to cooperate would have appeared chauvinistic and "petty" (chachi) (KSS 1997:18). She was also impressed by the manner in which bureaucrats had humbly asked for her assistance in these matters, a sign, she believed, of the changing times (K. Kobayashi, May 1994:40). Finally, Higa was aware that SCAP had encouraged governmental initiatives to combat inflation and the black market with the cooperation of citizens' groups (KSS 1997:18–19).

Cooperation among consumers, governmental authorities, labor, and business representatives included boycotts of goods sold on the black market, the dissemination of consumer information in partnership with the media, joint supervision of local business practices, and the like (K. Kobayashi, May

1994:40). In addition, Ōsaka shufu no kai and its successor, Kansai shufuren, embarked on a number of independent campaigns aimed at destroying black-market practices and lowering consumer prices that met with either tacit or overt governmental approval—the "housewives' shop" campaign being the most significant case in point. We should note that the federation did not last long; after only a few months, it disbanded following a conflict between Ōsaka shufu no kai and the labor organizations over leadership tactics (KSS 1997:17).

One of the most controversial examples of cooperation between consumer organizations and governmental authorities was the New Life movement (Shin seikatsu undō). The movement, which had historical precedents in the prewar Daily Life Improvement and wartime Renovation of Daily Life campaigns (Garon 2000:75), was begun in part by newly formed citizen groups in rural areas and then spread to other parts of the country with the explicit endorsement of Katayama Tetsu's socialist government. Although the movement's specific themes varied from region to region, the ultimate aim as eventually envisioned by government authorities was the democratization of daily life and the promotion of modernization through the free association of citizens at the local level, an end to the hold of tradition on the lives of individuals in the household and local community, and the encouragement of a strong work ethic (NHSK 1980:45). The movement, in short, covered a dizzying array of social and economic issues and was supported by a wide range of groups, including the fujinkai, Chifuren, Shufuren, and, to a lesser extent, the consumer cooperatives.

The government-sponsored movement was a boon to the long-standing efforts of the housewives' organizations to educate citizens about "rationalizing lifestyles" (seikatsu no gōrika) (Shufuren dayori, January 1955). Accordingly, these organizations were most conspicuous in programs designed to improve access to quality food, clothing, and housing, to teach household accounting and child-rearing methods, to promote household savings,[24] and the like. There were even campaigns to curb the incidence of disease by reducing the production of household garbage and eliminating flies and mosquitoes in local communities (Shufuren dayori, August 1955). These and other programs often entailed cooperation among the housewives' organizations and served as platforms for activists to promote other pet projects not directly related to the New Life movement, such as the promotion of female politicians (Shufuren dayori, June 1955).

The state's involvement in the movement escalated under Prime Minister Hatoyama Ichirō, who in 1954 established the Special New Life Movement

Committee (Shin seikatsu undō tokubetsu iinkai) to provide advice and financial aid to affiliated groups. The committee was immediately branded by the media as a front for governmental control over grassroots groups, an accusation that was categorically denied by many of the *fujinkai*, some of which had apparently gone to great lengths to resist governmental interference in their affairs (KSS 1997:82). To ward off further criticisms, in 1955 the government established an independent organization called the New Life Movement Association (Zaidan hōjin shin seikatsu undō kyōkai), with regional branches at the prefectural level, which was ostensibly designed to help affiliated organizations help themselves. As might be expected, there was nothing independent about the associations at all, given their near total dependence on government for both funding and personnel (KSS 1997:82).

Although it lingered well into the 1970s and 1980s, the New Life movement entered a period of decline by the end of the 1960s. As urbanization and economic affluence accomplished much of what the movement was originally supposed to achieve, namely, the modernization of lifestyles at the local level, many of the *fujinkai*, youth groups, and other affiliated organizations disintegrated. Between 1962 and 1965, the New Life movement associations tried to reinvigorate the movement by promoting regional economic development, but their efforts were largely unsuccessful (NHSK 1980:47). Meanwhile, many of the movement's issues were taken up by local lifestyle schools (*seikatsu gakko*) as governmental involvement in the movement decreased.[25]

For every instance of cooperation between consumer activists and governmental authorities, one can find an equally compelling example of confrontation. In August 1948, for instance, the Ōsaka shufu no kai—the Price Agency's partner in the Movement to Promote Price Stability—took action against high beef prices in the area and the Price Agency's refusal to take appropriate countermeasures. Activists organized an extensive boycott of the product, bombarded the agency with petitions, and even sent Higa Masako to appeal personally to agency higher-ups at their headquarters in Tōkyō. The boycott was the first of its kind in postwar Japan and received nationwide coverage from the media. It did not, however, result in victory for the consumer side. Although activists managed to extract a promise from the Price Agency to consult more regularly with consumers, the boycott failed to bring down prices (KSS 1997:22–26).

Another example of confrontation was the Movement to Oppose Increases in Public Bath Fees (Furodai neage hantai undō), organized in Tōkyō by Shufuren with the participation of the consumer co-ops (Oku

1988:189). In August 1948, the adult admission to public bathhouses in Tōkyō rose from six to ten yen—a huge increase for poverty-stricken Japanese families who had no bathing facilities of their own. A few months later, the bathhouses applied to the Price Agency for permission to raise their fees to twenty yen in order to accommodate "rising energy costs." Shufuren promptly lodged a protest with the agency, a move that provoked the bath owners into lowering their request by five yen (K. Kobayashi, September 1994:44). After failing to persuade the agency to block the increase altogether, Shufuren proceeded to discredit the bath owners by conducting a few "scientific" surveys of its own. Over the space of a few days, the organization dispatched teams of women disguised as ordinary bathers to facilities around the city and, on the basis of their observations, made rough calculations of the overhead costs incurred by the average bath owner. At an open meeting with Tōkyō governmental officials and bathhouse representatives, they announced their findings: the bathhouses were already faring quite well economically compared with other small businesses, and the proposed fee hike was actually greater than projected increases in the price of coal (NHSK 1980:33). The Price Agency responded by banning any further fee increases for ten months (K. Kobayashi, September 1994:45).

In an interesting and in some ways typical turn of events, Shufuren then joined forces with the bath owners in pursuit of a common goal. During their public meeting with the Price Agency and the bathhouse owners, the women displayed samples of murky brown water that they had surreptitiously taken from the baths during their inspection tours and rebuked the owners for their low hygienic standards. The bath owners retorted that no matter how much fresh water they added to the baths, they could not keep them clean when their customers refused to soap up before entering the tubs. In a show of sympathy with the owners' predicament, Shufuren mounted posters on the walls of the bathhouses to alert patrons to proper bathing conduct: "Soap up and rinse off before you enter the baths!" "Don't put your towel into the water!" "Treat the water as if it were in your own home!" (K. Kobayashi, September 1994:45). The so-called Bathing Etiquette campaign (Nyūyoku echiketto undō) eventually achieved its desired results and, in the process, restored a modicum of civility to the relationship between Shufuren and Tōkyō's public bathhouses.

These four cases highlight several important features of early postwar consumer organizations and their relationship to governmental authorities and business, not the least of which was the persistence of maternalistic tendencies to shape and supervise consumer behavior on even the most intimate level. It was a classic case of moral suasion (*kyōka*).[26] Second, the cases illustrate the fact that cooperation was carried out on an ad hoc basis and, as in the case of Ōsaka shufu no kai's association with the Price Agency, was often preceded by intense discussions about the terms of cooperation. Such preliminaries were not surprising given the absence at that time of regular channels of cooperation between the two sides.

Third, the cases underscore a relationship among consumer activists and business and governmental actors that was cooperative on some issues but combative on others. The criterion for cooperation was a commonality of interests. When those interests coincided, as they did during the Movement to Promote Price Stability, the New Life movement, and the Bathing Etiquette campaign, many—but by no means all—consumer activists communicated frequently with governmental authorities (or, in the case of the bathing campaign, with business) and sometimes received official financial aid. But when those interests conflicted, Japan's large consumer organizations were quick to disassociate themselves from the government.

Fourth, the cases highlight the lack of unity in both the consumer and governmental camps. Some consumer organs, for example, cooperated frequently with government, but others did not. Among those that did cooperate, many, like Shufuren, did so very selectively and often criticized the authorities when their interests conflicted. Nor did the government speak with a unified voice when working with consumer organizations. The Price Agency, for instance, cooperated with consumer representatives for very pragmatic reasons and with SCAP's overt encouragement. Prime Minister Hatoyama, on the other hand, seemed as interested in controlling the activities of grassroots groups as he was in achieving social and economic goals, and he frequently clashed with officials in the Finance Ministry who opposed such interference (NHSK 1980).

These observations defy the often stereotypical views of many Western and Japanese commentators that the organized consumer movement was beholden to either government authorities or business interests. In reality, the relationship between consumer advocates and these other interests was marked by both cooperation and conflict. The relationship was, in short, as varied as the consumer movement itself.

The question that then arises is, why would consumer activists cooperate with the government at all, particularly if they were so concerned about preserving their organizational integrity? The severe economic crisis of the immediate postwar period was certainly one reason the two sides came together. As Higa Masako's experiences show, cooperating with the government on some issues was viewed by many activists as a logical and efficient way to solve problems pertaining to both consumption and public health that these activists would have tackled anyway on their own. Once the consensus between consumer representatives and the government began to break down, however, as it did by the mid-1950s, instances of cooperation were much less frequent.

Second, since consumer activism was a new phenomenon in early postwar Japan, cooperating with the government on issues espoused by both sides served to legitimize consumer organs in the eyes of a population still influenced by conservative traditions. Third, cooperation with government authorities often provided consumer activists with scarce financial resources. It is no accident that the organs that have cooperated the most with governmental authorities since World War II were those with the fewest resources. Shufuren, for example, has constantly struggled to stay afloat financially and consequently has depended on occasional governmental assistance in the form of subsidies for product testing, consumer-related surveys, and the like (interview, Takada, April 1994).[27] The consumer cooperatives, by contrast, with their independent financial base, have worked far less frequently with officials. Although it would be a gross overstatement to assert that Japan's consumer movement was manufactured by the government, it is fair to say that were it not for occasional governmental support for the activities of Shufuren and other cash-strapped organizations, the organized movement would never have advanced as far as it did (K. Kobayashi, November 1994:48).

Finally, and perhaps most important, consumer organizations recognized that in order to make a difference in consumer protection, they needed inroads into the political system. Despite the introduction of democratic principles and institutions during the early stages of the Occupation, consumer representatives lacked routinized representation in those institutions, particularly at the national level. Accordingly, consumer activists sometimes regarded ad hoc and informal cooperation with the government as their only avenue into the decision-making process, an avenue that was all the more attractive when it resulted in access to sorely needed financial resources.

An Emerging Consumer Identity

If there is one overriding image that emerges from the first decade of the consumer movement's postwar history, it is an image of diversity. Consumer organizations differed markedly in their internal structure, goals, access to financial resources, and relations with both business and government.

These differences made it difficult for many consumer organizations to cooperate with one another. Despite the professed commitment of many of them to joint action, examples of intramovement cooperation were actually quite rare. In fact, the early history of these organizations is peppered with stories of interorganizational strife, personal animosities between rival leaders,[28] and even conflicts within organizations.

These differences notwithstanding, citizens' organs in their consumer capacity were motivated by a common socioeconomic goal during the first decade of the postwar period: the elevation of the economic status of Japanese citizens in the wake of wartime destruction. While pursuing this objective, consumer organizations fashioned a loose consensus on what it meant to be a consumer (*shōhisha*), a consensus that reflected the organizations' economic and political experiences and that had an impact on their goals and relations with other groups in society in later years. This process of defining the interests of consumers in a changing socioeconomic context resembled what social movement theorists refer to as "framing": the fashioning by social movement activists of "shared understandings of the world and of themselves that legitimate and motivate collective action" (McAdam et al. 1996b:6). Framing is particularly important to our purposes because it highlights some of the political and cultural forces that influenced the strategic choices of individual activists.

At the root of Japan's emerging consumer identity during the early postwar period were negative attitudes toward the purely economic conceptualizations of "consumer" and "consumption" (*shōhi*).[29] These attitudes were certainly not without historical precedent. During the 1920s, for instance, consumer cooperativists were struck by the adverse reactions of ordinary consumers to phrases like "buyers' cooperative" (*kōbai kumiai*) and "consumer cooperative" (*shōhisha kumiai*). Many citizens seemed to dislike the term *consumption* because of its passive and allegedly antiproducer overtones that were in no small part conveyed by the very linguistic makeup of the term: *shō*, after all, means "to extinguish," and *hi* means "waste." In a similar vein, many people distrusted the seemingly innocuous expression "buyers' cooperative" on the grounds that it implied not-for-profit economic activities that were of benefit to self-seeking consumers rather than to the economy as a whole (Yamamoto 1982:674).

During the mid- to late 1940s, the use of the term *consumer* as a category of individuals in their consuming and, by logical extension, nonproductive capacities struck many activists as particularly inappropriate in the context of sweeping economic destruction. Recognizing that Japanese citizens had been stricken by economic adversity not only as consumers but also as farmers, laborers, and small businessmen, many of these activists stood up for all these groups against the harmful activities of big business and governmental negligence.

In response to the economic contingencies of the times, the concept of consumer was, in effect, stretched by many in the movement to reflect the overlap between the consumer and other competing identities and in a way that took advantage of the new political opportunities of the early postwar period. Thus, consumers were not just users of the fruits of production, they were also human beings struggling to survive in a context of economic scarcity, as the Movement to Defend Livelihoods succinctly illustrated. In many cases, consumers were also producers or laborers or the spouses and dependents of such individuals. This aspect of the emerging consumer gestalt, if we can refer to it as such, was significant, since most so-called consumer activists were women married to workers or small businessmen. Finally, and as Oku Mumeo often pointed out on the floor of the Diet, consumers were citizens not only of a particular country (*kokumin*) but also of civil society (*shimin*).

A multifaceted approach to the consumer's place in the polity and the economy was in and of itself a tacit recognition of the mutually reinforcing features of these various identities. One had to consume, for example, in order to survive and produce (or obtain sustenance from someone who did) in order to consume. One's identity as a citizen (*shimin*), in turn, entitled one to the basic rights and freedoms stipulated by the 1946 constitution, not least of which was the right to life or survival. Needless to say, conflict is also inherent in this conceptual approach to consumption. The protection of one's position as a producer, for instance, could prove detrimental to one's consumer identity, and vice versa. In more recent years, and as American trade officials are eager to point out, one's identity as a citizen of Japan (*kokumin*), which often entails support for economic protectionism, can run counter to one's interests as a price-conscious consumer. When all is said and done, this emerging consumer gestalt stressed the need for a workable balance among these different identities.

This informal juxtaposition of producer, citizen, and consumer identities under a single conceptual banner bears a striking resemblance to more contemporary definitions of the term *seikatsusha* (lit. "lifestyle person"). A vague concept that defies precise translation, a *seikatsusha* connotes for some users and theorists a consumer-as-citizen, while for others it incorporates the worker identity as well.[30] Although the term has prewar origins and was circulating during the early postwar period in various guises, there is little evidence that it was widely used by consumer activists outside the consumer cooperative movement.[31] Nevertheless, given the broad similarities between the early postwar consumer gestalt as fashioned by consumer activists and more contemporary usages of the term *seikatsusha*, for the sake of simplicity, I will henceforth refer to the former as "the early *seikatsusha* identity."

The early *seikatsusha* identity symbolizes an important difference between the Japanese and many Western consumer movements insofar as it collapses elements of the consumer, producer, and citizen identities into a single concept. During the heyday of the U.S. movement, the consumer and producer identities were manufactured as almost polar opposites by consumer advocates intent on distinguishing themselves from producers and forging a sense of solidarity in the consumer camp. As we saw in the last chapter, however, American activists have stretched the concept in recent years to more fully embrace the notion of citizenship, particularly as the movement's political fortunes decline and the issues confronting consumers spill outside the confines of mere consumption. The experiences of both the American and Japanese movements suggest that definitions of consumer and other related terms reflect much more than just the idiosyncrasies of the authors of those definitions. They also are symbolic of the socioeconomic and political contexts in which they are used.

This early *seikatsusha* identity was politically correct in many circles as well as conceptually appealing. Take, for example, housewives. As mentioned earlier, those who took the brunt of inflation, the black market, and an inefficient rationing system during the Occupation were housewives responsible for shopping, raising children, and managing family finances. In the context of economic scarcity, consumption evolved into much more than just the passive act of purchasing and consuming goods and services; it also became an important prerequisite for the survival of the family and, therefore, for the ability of women to perform their various functions as housewives. Shufuren and Chifuren members consequently took to the political stage as women, mothers, and the wives of producers or laborers as well as consumers—as newly enfranchised female citizens, in other words, who felt compelled by unprecedented economic circumstances to take an integrative and mutually compatible approach to consumption and production.[32]

Seikatsusha and its root noun *seikatsu* ("lifestyle" or "livelihood") also provided the consumer cooperatives with an avenue out of the historical controversies inherent in the terms *consumer* and *consumption*. As the co-ops regrouped in the wake of defeat, many adopted names like "livelihood cooperative society" (*seikatsu kyōdō kumiai*, or *seikyō*)—names that implied consumption not for its own sake but, rather, for the purpose of improv-ing one's livelihood or lifestyle (Oku 1988:167). In this way, the rather in-nocuous expression enabled the emerging co-op movement to appeal to consumers without overtly offending small retailers while simultaneously recognizing the producer and consumer functions inherent in co-op mem-bership. It was, in short, an ideal response to the challenges of building up a movement for consumers in a context of economic stagnation, not to mention an ingenious way to attract members from the labor unions and agricultural and fisheries cooperatives.

The emerging *seikatsusha* identity can be viewed as both a source and a reflection of some of the priorities—or lack thereof—and strategic choices of early consumer advocates. It gives added meaning, for instance, to the movement's willingness during the Occupation to ally with labor, small busi-ness, and government to work toward common objectives. It also makes sense of the movement's seemingly irrational support for agricultural pro-tectionism over the years and of its willingness to ally with rice farmers toward that goal. As noted earlier, protectionism has been an integral com-ponent of the citizenship (*kokumin*) dimension of the early *seikatsusha* iden-tity, as well as a reflection of the movement's determination to promote self-sufficiency in food production. The *seikatsusha* identity also helps explain aspects of movement behavior at the end of the twentieth century: opposition to the imposition of a 3 percent consumption tax during the late 1980s, which brought advocates into alliance with small business; and cooperation with local merchants' associations against the loosening of the Large-Scale Retail Store Law, a development that ostensibly threatened the culture of local shopping districts and the livelihoods of small retailers.

Although the Japanese consumer movement has clearly taken a more holistic approach to consumption and production than has its Anglo-American counterparts,[33] this should by no means suggest that consumer activists have been reluctant to criticize producers when the specific interests of consumers are abused. To the contrary, and as the long-standing attack by consumer organizations and the co-ops on collusive behavior in the small business community attests, most consumer activists are all too willing to go on the offensive when that balance between the consumer and contending identities is upset. Thus, many of the more combative advocates in the con-temporary movement have avoided the term *seikatsusha* altogether in their efforts to clarify the nature of their ongoing conflict with business interests (interview, Hara, July 1999).

Conclusion: Consumer Organizations in Comparative Perspective

As the organizational expressions of an emerging social movement, consumer organs during the early postwar period resembled the environmental citizens' movements (*shimin undō*) of the 1960s and 1970s in regard to their nonideological political orientation and attention to issues that affected the livelihoods of average citizens (see, e.g., Krauss and Simcock 1980:190; McKean 1981:8). Unlike the citizens' groups of later years, however, the issues espoused by consumer organs were not the "quality-of-life" concerns of an affluent population but, rather, those of a society living well below the poverty line.

The early organized consumer movement also differed from the environmental citizens' groups of the 1960s and 1970s in that it quickly manifested itself at the prefectural and national levels. This discrepancy can be partly explained by the nature of the issues and objectives adopted by the two movements. While environmentalists tended to focus on eradicating pollution on a local case-by-case basis (Broadbent 1998:183), many consumer activists concentrated on reforming consumer-producer relations at a much broader, more systemic level. A more persuasive explanation, however, has to do with the institutional and political contexts of the two movements' formative years. Many of Japan's flagship consumer organizations were established in a relatively fluid institutional context and progressive policy environment, at least for the first few years of the Occupation period. As a result, consumer leaders encountered comparatively few obstacles as they flexed their democratic muscles and set up shop at the prefectural and national levels. Environmental groups, on the other hand, appeared on the scene when an unsympathetic government-business alliance was firmly in command of the political system. As Jeffrey Broadbent observed, these "political institutions . . . encouraged local [environmental] protest movements to stay local, rather than joining hands and maturing into a powerful national interest group presence" (Broadbent 1998:184).

This is not to say that the consumer presence at the national and prefectural governmental levels was a particularly powerful one during the early postwar period. Although the movement did manage to organize and score a few victories in the marketplace, it failed to gain a meaningful foothold in a policy process that was increasingly dominated by pro-business interests, as the cooperative movement's attempts to influence the content of the 1948 Co-op Law so clearly illustrates. As a result of the movement's position on the periphery of decision-making power, advocates were left with a menu of strategic choices that consisted of protest, the dissemination of information, and cooperation with erstwhile adversaries—the strategies of the politically disenfranchised. As the next chapter shows, the strategic choices of consumer organizations were to remain more or less unchanged between 1955 and the late 1960s, with the advent of conservative party dominance and the institutionalization of a strong government-business alliance.

4 Consumer Politics Under Early One-Party Dominance: 1955 to the Late 1960s

In 1956, after GDP growth rates had finally matched prewar highs, the Japanese government officially announced the end of the period of postwar reconstruction and the beginning of an era of economic expansion (Bronfenbrenner and Yasuba 1987:95). For consumers, the ensuing years were ones of increasing consumption and unprecedented economic affluence, dual phenomena that were both sources and side effects of Japan's economic catch-up with the West. As often happens in countries that grow rapidly, this veritable revolution in consumption patterns both transformed Japanese living standards and led to a profusion of consumer problems that lent a new sense of urgency to the organized movement.

If any one feature of consumer politics stands out between the mid-1950s and the end of the following decade, it is the reluctance of the pro-business conservative regime to respond in more than a haphazard fashion to the movement's demands for a comprehensive policymaking and administrative system geared toward consumers. Since 1955, when the Liberal Democratic Party first took control of government, through the late 1960s, when its grip on power began to loosen, national policymaking in the political-economy realm was oriented to promoting producer interests. In a manner reminiscent of the United States before World War II, the particular problems of consumers were addressed only as a secondary concern.

In this chapter, I analyze consumer activism during the first fifteen years or so of the era of one-party dominance, paying particular attention to the limits of the movement's protest- and market-oriented strategies vis-à-vis the policy process. I also explore the opening of new opportunities for consumer activism at the prefectural level, opportunities that enabled advocates to begin exploring alternative avenues of interest articulation. Those avenues, as we shall see in later chapters, facilitated the movement's subsequent expansion and policy-related successes at the national level.

The Crisis of Consumer Affluence

Japan's "consumer revolution" (*shōhisha kakumei*) was officially acknowledged in the government's 1959 *White Paper on Citizen Affluence* (Maki 1979:45). At its most mundane, the phenomenon marked the advent of rampant materialism as consumers scrambled to acquire the latest in consumer technology, with the so-called three sacred treasures (*sanshu no jingi*)—television sets, refrigerators, and washing machines—topping the list of coveted items. Pejorative terms like "electrification madame" (*denka madamu*) and "automated lady" (*ōtome fujin*) (NHSK 1980:60) crept into the popular discourse as housewives struggled to outpurchase one another, reflecting not only the mounting affluence of a population long held captive by state-enforced frugality but also the erosion of simpler and more traditional lifestyles.[1]

At a more systemic level, the consumer revolution entailed deep-seated changes in the relationship between producers and consumers. As industrial innovation contributed to the twin phenomena of mass production and mass consumption, consumers became increasingly separated from producers by layers and layers of middlemen. Gone were the days when shoppers could purchase most of their goods and services from small producers on the basis of direct, personal relationships. Although such vendors have remained fixtures in the market for basic foodstuffs, for larger and more technologically sophisticated items, consumers found themselves at the tail end of increasingly complicated networks of manufacturers, wholesalers, distributors, and retailers.

As consumption grew more complex, the problems confronting consumers mushroomed in both number and scope. Among the more conspicuous were the high prices caused by cartels and the expanding distribution system, and the indiscriminate use of synthetic additives in processed foods. Consumers also grappled with consumer fraud, the inevitable by-product of fierce and often unregulated competition among producers and retailers. In many cases, the race by manufacturers and retailers for ever bigger market shares was accompanied by outrageous marketing strategies to promote consumer acceptance of artificially inflated prices, the development of a "throwaway culture" (*tsukaisute bunka*), and an end to that old wartime mind-set that "extravagance is the enemy" (*zeitaku wa teki da*) (NHSK 1980:60–61).[2]

To the surprise of many who associate contemporary Japanese products with superior quality, the most pressing consumer issue of the late 1950s and 1960s was the flood of defective products into the marketplace. In some instances, the consumption of those products resulted in catastrophic consequences for their users. Some of the better-known examples of this are the 1955 incident involving arsenic poisoning in a powdered milk formula produced by the Morinaga Corporation that sickened more than 12,000 infants; the thalidomide incident of 1962 that affected about 700 babies; the 1968 Kanemi cooking oil disaster (*Kanemi yushō jiken*) involving PCB poisoning in cooking oil and approximately 1,600 casualties; and the SMON incident of 1970 in which more than 11,000 consumers were disfigured by a tainted antidiarrhea medicine.[3]

As students of the Japanese environmental movement have shown (see, e.g., Broadbent 1998; McKean 1981), the negative side effects of rapid economic growth were symptomatic of a corporate culture that clung blindly to the objective of "growth at all costs" as the nation strove to catch up economically with the West. Buttressed by such practices as lifetime employment and corporate loyalty and by a deepening relationship between producers and conservative politicians, that culture often proved impermeable to the complaints of ordinary citizens who bore the brunt of manufacturing excesses (Kimoto 1986:55).

As the sheer number and severity of those excesses grew, however, governmental authorities began to respond to consumer movement pressures for the establishment of a consumer *kakekomidera* at the governmental level—of a bureaucratic entity (or entities), in other words, that would listen to the concerns of consumers, assume responsibility for the formulation and implementation of consumer protection policy, and, in the process, function as a consumer-oriented, institutional counterbalance to the numerous inroads into the policy process enjoyed by business interests. The degree to which these demands were fulfilled, however, varied markedly according to the level of government.

Early Consumer *kakekomidera* at the National and Local Levels

Prefectural and local governments took the lead in establishing consumer-oriented bureaucratic facilities. The localities had several incentives to embrace the consumer cause: (1) a presidential-style electoral system for many heads of government which encouraged governors and mayors to embrace consumer, environmental, and other public-interest issues; (2) a unitary system of government which prompted many localities to look for innovative ways to distinguish themselves administratively from the powerful central government; (3) the 1947 Local Autonomy Law which, at SCAP's behest, singled out the localities as the country's primary laboratory for democratization; (4) a centuries-old popular tradition of looking to the localities to solve problems confronting local residents; and (5) as the 1960s wore on, the proliferation of progressive local governments eager to establish more responsive lines of communication with local citizens.

It all began in Tōkyō, where the national consumer organizations were based and consumer consciousness was relatively strong (Suzuki 1979:260). In 1961, the Tōkyō metropolitan government responded to a campaign organized by a local assemblywoman from Chifuren and to the recommendations of the Tōkyō Consumer Price Policy Advisory Council (Tōkyōto shōhiseikatsu bukka taisaku shingikai) by setting up the nation's first Consumer Economics Section (Shōhikeizaika) in its Economics Department (Keizaikyoku). Elevated to the status of a division (*bu*) in 1964, the organ was in charge of developing product safety, pricing, and consumer education policies in the Tōkyō area. From the start, the division was plagued by low morale and inertia among officials, many of whom viewed their new consumer-related assignments as demotions (Sahara 1979:216). Such problems aside, similar sections and divisions were set up by other prefectures and large cities around the country in a process of intergovernmental communication and policy diffusion.[4] By 1966, a total of twenty-one prefectural and twenty-five city organs had been established (NHSK 1980:73).

Tōkyō was also the first locality to incorporate consumer participation into local decision-making processes in what was clearly a reflection of progressive governmental efforts to establish "pipelines to the people" (Steiner et al. 1980a:19). In 1961, the Tōkyō government established the predecessor of what is now known as the Consumer Lifestyle Policy Advisory Council (Shōhi seikatsu taisaku shingikai), a commission that makes consumer-related policy recommendations to the governor and includes representatives from consumer organizations. The following year, it set up the Consumer Lifestyles Monitor, a government-run network that solicits opinions about consumer issues from 1,000 residents from all walks of life. This was followed up two years later with the establishment of a governmental consumer con-sultation facility that became the nucleus of a consumer center later in the decade. Finally, in 1967, the government began publishing *The Wise Con-sumer* (Kashikoi shōhisha), a monthly periodical on local consumer-related problems, as well as *Documents on the Consumer Movement* (Shōhisha undō shiryō), a long-running series that chronicles the activities of consumer or-ganizations in the metropolitan area (Suzuki 1979:260).

Tōkyō was certainly not the only locality to institute novel consumer-related facilities. Similar developments were also occurring in the Kansai area. In 1965, the Hyōgo prefectural government set up a semigovernmental facility known as the Citizens' Lifestyle Science Center (Kokumin seikatsu kagaku sentaa) that developed consumer education programs and carried out consultation services for aggrieved consumers in the prefecture. By de-cade's end, the center had become a model for consumer centers throughout the country (Sahara 1979:216).

When all is said and done, consumer-related institutional developments at the local level were ad hoc, sporadic, and insufficient responses to the myriad problems that plagued consumers during the 1960s. But they were far more progressive than comparable developments at the national level, where an unspoken policy of "growth at all costs" held sway as a result of a strong relationship among the ruling LDP, economic bureaucrats, and lead-ing members of the business community. In 1963—two years after the Tōkyō metropolitan government established its Consumer Economics Section— the Ministry of Agriculture, Forestry, and Fisheries became the first national ministry to establish an in-house consumer division, followed by the Ministry of International Trade and Industry (MITI) the next year. Although welcomed by consumer advocates as administrative steps in the right direction, these sections proved to be far less interested in "consumer protection" than in promoting higher levels of "consumption" in the consuming population. Unlike their local counterparts, moreover, they did very little to incorporate consumer participation into ministerial decision-making processes (NHSK 1980:92).

The Economic Planning Agency, which lacked ministerial status and was looking for ways to expand its jurisdiction, did the most at the national level to address the concerns of consumers. In 1965, it established the Citizen's

Lifestyle Bureau (Kokumin seikatsu kyoku), a bureaucratic space that became the coordinating bureau for consumer policy throughout the national bureaucracy. Limited participation by consumer representatives in consumer-related agency decision making was introduced with the establishment of the Social Policy Council (Kokumin seikatsu shingikai) in 1965, an advisory organ falling under the jurisdiction of the Prime Minister's Office that is administered by the agency and deliberates on a wide variety of social issues. These administrative and advisory organs eventually made a number of recommendations to the government in favor of stronger consumer protection laws and a larger national consumer administrative system (Miyasaka et al. 1990b:56). Unfortunately for consumers, however, many of those recommendations were all but ignored until the end of the decade.

Although a comprehensive and more uniform system of consumer protection policymaking and administration spanning both levels of government did not materialize until after the 1968 enactment of the Consumer Protection Basic Law, several features that characterized consumer bureaucratic affairs throughout the latter part of the twentieth century became apparent during this time. The first was the bureaucratic subordination of consumer issues to the goal of economic growth, a phenomenon common to the United States and other advanced industrial democracies that spread consumer-related functions throughout their bureaucracies rather than concentrating them in one central ministry/department or agency.

Weak representation of consumer interests in the national bureaucracy was (and still is) further aggravated by *tatewari gyōsei* (vertical administration): the vertical organization of ministries along functional lines. *Tatewari gyōsei* reinforces the subordination of consumer functions to the particular economic or social focus of each ministry and is characterized by a lack of horizontal coordination of those functions *across* ministerial lines (Kimoto 1986:14). This is in marked contrast to Britain, where consumer-related administrative functions tend to be concentrated in a small handful of ministries.[5] The Japanese system complicates the task of articulating the consumer interest by dispersing opportunities for consumer participation in bureaucratic policymaking over a very wide range of administrative access points. Combined with the ministries' already strong disposition toward the interests of producers during the high-growth era, vertical administration weakened the efficiency of consumer lobbying efforts and strained the resource base of movement advocates as they struggled to establish long-term informal relations with a diverse array of government officials.

Tatewari gyōsei was not the only institutional feature of the national bureaucracy that weakened the effectiveness of consumer lobbying efforts. Advocates were also hindered by the fact that bureaucrats were regularly rotated
from position to position in their particular ministries and agencies and, in
some cases, between ministries and agencies. This made it very difficult for
advocates to establish lasting allies in the bureaucracy. Last but not least,
the fact that most regulatory functions are carried out by the economic
ministries, as opposed to independent regulatory agencies and commissions,
made it all the more difficult for advocates to find sympathetic ears in the
bureaucracy. Japan differs in this respect from the United States, where
independent regulatory commissions have produced some of the organized
movement's most influential and enduring allies.

In sum, while the national bureaucracy appeared to be perforated with
multiple access points for consumer advocates, the effectiveness of those
potential inroads into the policy process was weakened by the structure of
bureaucratic institutions and by many of the rules and customs governing
those institutions. This is not to suggest that consumer advocates lacked any
connection whatsoever with officialdom. The housewives' organizations, for
example, were occasionally commissioned by the ministries to carry out consumer surveys and product testing. Leaders from both Chifuren and Shufuren
also served as members of governmental *shingikai* (governmental advisory
councils) that deliberated on social and economic policy issues, positions that
accorded them access to classified information that was often quietly distributed to other activists. But advocates did not have the kind of close relationships with government officials that business representatives enjoyed. To the
contrary, their requests for private meetings with individual bureaucrats were
often denied and their opinions in *shingikai* proceedings all but ignored. For
all intents and purposes, consumer advocates played second fiddle to their
business adversaries in a policymaking process that accorded them little more
than symbolic representation. It was a relationship, as we shall see in later
chapters, that persisted even after the post-1968 institutionalization of a more
comprehensive consumer bureaucratic system.

As consumer organizations were "turned away at the gate" (*monzenbarai*)
of the national policy process during much of the 1960s, relations between
consumer organizations and prefectural and local governments took something of a different turn. As noted earlier, institutional innovations at the
local level—particularly in localities of a progressive political persuasion—
represented governmental efforts to address consumer problems in local ju-

risdictions and to incorporate consumer participation into policymaking processes. Relations between local governments and consumer organs were not always consistently productive or "democratic" across localities. In Saitama Prefecture, for instance, many consumer groups were co-opted by the prefectural government as they clamored for government subsidies (Kimoto 1986:245). Other prefectures and cities, meanwhile, ignored the concerns of consumers altogether, while those that did the most for consumers were often criticized by advocates for not doing enough. When all is said and done, however, the institutional innovations at the local level proved to be much more progressive and beneficial for consumer advocates than those at the national level, a trend that continued after 1968.

The Diversification of the Organized Consumer Movement

The period of early one-party dominance also witnessed an expansion of the organized consumer movement at an average rate of sixty-nine new organs per year (Tsujinaka 1988:73). This rate marks a drop from the democratization phase of the Occupation period, when 648 new groups or organizations were formed in 1945 alone (Keizaikikakuchō 1997:9),[6] and the mid-1970s, when the rate of movement expansion reached its post-Occupation zenith. The vast majority of organs that were established during the late 1950s and 1960s were local or prefectural,[7] a trend that can be at least partly explained by the localities' forward-looking bureaucratic innovations. That said, several new organizations were also established at the national level, many of which went on to play important roles in the movement. The following is a brief survey of some of those groups and organizations.

The Lifestyle Schools

Most of the groups that appeared during the late 1950s and 1960s were either *fujinkai*, the local women's groups often affiliated with Chifuren, or small groups consisting primarily of housewives that arose in response to specific grassroots problems. Although little is known about the structure, goals, and longevity of many of these small groups, it appears that some organized spontaneously and in response to pressing consumer concerns and worked hard to maintain their political independence, whereas others were either organized under the guidance of local bureaucrats or went on to form clientelistic relationships (Tsujinaka 1988:57) with local authorities. As might be expected, the presence of captured local organs has tarnished the organized movement's overall reputation as an independent political entity.

Perhaps the most conspicuous examples of captured local consumer groups are those that participated in the post-1964 Lifestyle Schools movement (Seikatsu gakkō undō). Like the national housewives' organizations, the small lifestyle schools[8] promote the education of local consumers on such basic issues as household accounting and comparison-shopping techniques (NHSK 1980:83). Unlike the national associations, however, the lifestyle schools tend to avoid overt political protest and other forms of political advocacy, although occasional confrontation with local industry and officials is certainly not out of the question when warranted by concerns for the health and safety of local consumers.

The apolitical tendencies of the lifestyle schools stem in part from their links with government organizations. During the first few years of their existence, many championed the cause of the New Life movement and relied on both the national and prefectural New Life movement associations for start-up grants and other forms of funding. Then, as the movement began to lose steam, the schools turned to the localities as their main source of financial aid. Their close financial links to local government eventually contributed to their undoing as the media and other consumer organizations branded them as mere appendages of the localities. Politicians, meanwhile, criticized the more politicized schools for using taxpayers' money to oppose state policies (NHSK 1980:85). The fact that the schools often duplicated many of the educational functions performed by the larger housewives' associations and the *fujinkai* merely added to their struggle to survive. Despite efforts to establish an independent financial base and diversify its activities, the Lifestyle Schools movement declined rapidly from the 1970s and today occupies only a small proportion of the organized consumer movement.[9]

The Japan Consumers Association

Another important product of the rapid-growth period that focused on the dissemination of consumer-related information rather than political advocacy was the Japan Consumers Association (Nihon shōhisha kyōkai), a controversial semigovernmental organ whose history is representative of national governmental efforts to defang private consumer organizations by co-opting some of their functions and encouraging movement cooperation with industry.

The Japan Consumers Association began as a small committee in the Japan Productivity Center (Nihon seisansei honbu), a MITI-affiliated organization established in 1955 with the support of business, labor, and the U.S. government (KSS 1997:43–44) to foster rapid economic growth and the introduction of foreign (i.e., modern) technology and management techniques to Japan. In 1958, on the premise that productivity could not be enhanced without advancing the interests of the consumers of Japanese products, the center set up an internal Consumer Education Committee (Shōhisha kyōiku iinkai) consisting, among others, of government officials and representatives from private consumer organizations.[10] Both the committee and its immediate successor, the Consumer Education Room (Shōhisha kyōiku shitsu), promoted cooperative linkages between individual consumers and private firms and sponsored public lectures on various product lines (K. Kobayashi, December 1996:37). The center also established comparable programs at the regional level,[11] published an educational magazine called *Smart Shopping* (Kaimono jōzu), and sponsored inspection trips (*shisatsu-dan ryokō*) abroad (KSS 1997:45) for cash-strapped consumer advocates like Oku Mumeo to investigate foreign consumer programs.

The center's consumer activities were instrumental not only in raising consumer awareness of the nature of consumption but also in introducing several consumer-related expressions to Japan, including "the consumer is king" (*shōhisha wa ōsama da*) and "virtuous consumption" (*shōhi wa bitoku*), as well as the more basic term "consumer education" (*shōhisha kyōiku*) (NHSK 1980:66–69). These and other slogans highlighted the center's determination to promote the development of a home market for Japanese products. The center's activities were also an example of effective cooperation between government officials and private consumer activists toward a common goal: the education of Japanese citizens about consumption in the context of rapid economic growth. Relations between the two sides, however, were not always harmonious. Consumer advocates, for example, criticized the Japan Productivity Center for paying far more attention to encouraging consumer demand than to promoting consumer protection, a tendency symbolized by the center's promotion of "virtuous consumption" as its consumer-related catchphrase of the day. The center eventually took heed of these criticisms in 1961, when the organ responsible for consumer education broke off from its parent organization to form the Japan Consumers Association (Zaidan hōjin shōhisha kyōkai).

The Japan Consumers Association is a MITI-affiliated organization with regional chapters that provides educational materials to consumer organs, schools, and businesses; carries out consumer research and product testing; provides consultation services to aggrieved consumers; and publishes *The Monthly Consumer* (*Gekkan shōhisha*), a well-respected journal consisting of product assessments and other consumer-related articles. The association is also responsible for training and certifying consumer lifestyle consultants (*shōhiseikatsu konsarutanto*) who are employed by local governments and private businesses as both advisers on consumer-related issues and liaisons between their employers and the consuming public.

Although individual members of the Japan Consumers Association have been known to participate in consumer protest and legislative campaigns over the years, the association itself tends to avoid involvement in consumer movement campaigns.[12] As a result of its dependence on subsidies from both MITI and industry (Maki 1979:45), the association's role as an independent spokesperson for the consumer interest warrants suspicion (Sahara 1979: 215). The well-funded association has also weakened the raison d'être of some of the less well-off private consumer organizations. For example, its sophisticated research and testing facilities were partly responsible for the eventual termination of Shufuren's own product-testing program. These criticisms notwithstanding, the association was an important part of Japan's network of consumer organizations during the rapid-growth period and is highly regarded for its contributions to the development of consumer informational services and of a consumer identity in the public at large.

The Consumption Science Center and the Consumption Science Federation (Shōkaren)

Another organization that appeared during this period was the Consumption Science Center, a privately funded consumer entity led, until her death in the early 1990s, by Mitsumaki Akiko. Mitsumaki was at one time a vice-president of Shufuren who caused something of a media stir in 1964 by breaking away from that organization following a leadership dispute (KSS 1997:102). At the heart of Mitsumaki's decision to leave Shufuren was her desire to establish comprehensive programs to teach Japanese citizens about consumer rights and practical consumer-related issues, an objective that Mitsumaki believed could not be fully met by the politically active Shufuren.

Shortly after leaving Shufuren, Mitsumaki founded the Consumption Science Center (Shōhikagaku sentaa), one of the few juridical organizations (*zaidan hōjin*) in the organized movement.[13] The center's principal function has been to run the Consumer University (Shōhisha daigaku), a Tōkyō-based lecture and seminar program covering a wide range of consumer issues (Shōhi kagaku sentaa 1989:6–7). Women's groups affiliated with the federation carry out similar programs in areas around the country. A month after establishing the center, which can be viewed as an educational consumer organ, Mitsumaki set up Shōkaren (Shōhi kagaku rengōkai), the center's "movement organization" that participates frequently in political advocacy campaigns.

Mitsumaki's organizations also administered a small consumer cooperative that grew out of a movement to provide consumers with low-priced milk during the mid-1950s. Launched while the leaders of Shōkaren were still Shufuren members, the project involved the "spot selling" (*sokubai*) of milk for ten yen a bottle in the busy Shibuya ward of Tōkyō. The leaders of the project obtained the milk directly from dairy farmers and eventually arranged to have it delivered to the homes of interested consumers. In conjunction with the eventual proliferation of refrigerators, a formal cooperative was established to cover a much wider range of products.

Shōkaren's spot-selling efforts were part of publicity activities (*gaitō senden katsudō*) designed to alert consumers to the effects and pervasiveness of price increases. As such, they were also a vehicle for mobilizing consumers into protest and legislative campaigns, some of which distinguished Shōkaren as a maverick organization in the consumer movement. For example, in stark contrast to Shufuren and despite the organization's links with local farmers, Shōkaren supported at least a partial liberalization of the domestic rice market and the reform of the government's food staple control system in order to both lower the price of rice and provide consumers with a wider range of product choice (KSS 1997:9–10).[14] This unusual stance, which debunks the stereotypical view advanced by the media that consumer organizations are uniformly opposed to the liberalization of rice, was the product of Mitsumaki's personal philosophy and her many years of experience as the only consumer representative on the central government's Rice Price Advisory Council (Beika shingikai). It may also result from the fact that Shōkaren is not nearly as well organized locally as, say, Shufuren and Chifuren, both of which adopted far more conservative positions on the issue of rice liberalization in response to the preferences of their rural and semirural members (interview, Shōda, December 1993).

Japan Consumers Union

The personal preferences of movement leaders also help explain the distinctive objectives and strategies of Japan Consumers Union (Nihon shō-hisha renmei), a consumer organization that combines both educational and advocacy functions. The organization was established in 1969 by Takeuchi Naokazu, a former bureaucrat from the Ministry of Agriculture, Fisheries, and Forestry (MAFF) who left his post to protest what he argued was bureaucratic support for a cartel to raise milk prices (KSS 197:115). Takeuchi, like many other consumer advocates, has been a vocal supporter of agricultural protectionism but is not, as van Wolferen and other critics assert, a handmaiden of the MAFF (see, e.g., van Wolferen 1990:53). To the contrary, Takeuchi is a radical and outspoken critic of governmental policy (see, e.g., Takeuchi 1990).

Financed almost exclusively by proceeds from its publication, *Shōhisha report* (Consumer report) (interview, Tomiyama, March 1994), Consumers Union is one of only a handful of national organizations that has a significant male membership.[15] In order to protect its politically nonpartisan stance, the organization forbids other consumer organs to become members, allowing only individuals to join (KSS 1997:115). It is also one of the smallest national consumer organizations, with only 4,000 or so members (Keizaikikakuchō 1993a:78). In marked contrast to Shufuren, which relies heavily on proceeds from corporate advertising in *Shufuren dayori*, its in-house newspaper, Consumers Union stays clear of such links with the business community. It is, in short, the most independent of all the major consumer organizations.

It is also the most radical and controversial. Taking its cue from Ralph Nader's style of political activism (K. Kobayashi, November 1996:42), Consumers Union has become well known for confronting firms in an unusually aggressive and "accusatory" manner (*kokuhatsugata*) that some might argue is tantamount to harassment. Its methods consist of bombarding the alleged perpetrators of consumer abuses with pointed questionnaires known as *ya-*

bumi (lit. "a letter tied to an arrow") (KSS 1997:117). If the business in question refuses to answer the questionnaires or, over time, to change its behavior, Consumers Union will publicize the names of the company and its products in *Shōhisha report* and, if possible, the mainstream media. The organization has also taken—or threatened to take—its opponents to court. Since its chances of winning lawsuits have been very slim, however, the tactic can be viewed as a device for attracting broad attention to a particular issue and alerting citizens to their rights as consumers.

The union's confrontational style, die-hard support for agricultural protectionism, and fight for additive-free food products have invited the disdain of the bureaucracy and precluded any possibility of individual members serving on ministerial advisory councils. Its radical overtones have also led to conflicts with other, more politically moderate consumer organizations, particularly over questions of strategy. Whereas the housewives' organizations and the cooperatives have been willing to cooperate with business and government and to pursue assimilative political strategies, Consumers Union has generally avoided any association with its ideological adversaries, preferring instead to rely on market-oriented tactics and political protest. With its go-it-alone approach to political activism, Consumers Union is the most unusual and least representative organization in the movement.

Shōdanren

An inevitable side effect of the proliferation of consumer organs was the organizational fragmentation of the consumer movement as a whole. To help overcome this problem, which threatened to weaken the movement's political and economic effectiveness, the consumer cooperatives and Shufuren spearheaded the establishment of a horizontal umbrella group known as the National Liaison Committee of Consumer Organizations, or Shōdanren (Nihon shōhisha dantai renrakukai), in December 1956 (interview, Ono, March 1994). In later years, comparable liaison committees were established at the prefectural level as well. Although Shōdanren occasionally performs educational functions for the consuming public, its raison d'être is consumer advocacy.

The immediate impetus behind Shōdanren's establishment was the enactment of the Special Measures Law for the Adjustment of Retail Trade (Kouri shōgyō chōsei tokubetsu sotchi hō) (Ono 1996:41), a law that permitted cartel-like agreements among specified groups of small retailers. Arguing that it gave small businessmen an unfair competitive advantage over consumer cooperatives, Shōdanren strongly protested the legislation.

Shōdanren originally consisted of representatives from eleven organizations, including Shufuren, Seikyōren, several smaller women's groups, Sōhyō, and one other labor federation. Over time, the organization quadrupled in size, and membership by labor unions all but disappeared as the labor movement declined.

In addition to its role as a leading proponent of consumer rights in Japan, Shōdanren made its mark as a vocal critic of all forms of collusive business practices during the rapid-growth era and was a key supporter of a stronger Antimonopoly Law—issues that, not coincidentally, affected the economic well-being of the co-ops. Shōdanren has been instrumental in orchestrating interorganizational cooperation on specific issues and continues to organize and sponsor an annual consumer rally (shōhisha taikai) of consumer representatives from around the country. Comparable functions are performed at the local level by regional Shōdanren chapters.

The history of Shōdanren has been a rocky one. During the late 1950s and 1960s, the organization was very dependent on financial contributions from Sōhyō (interview, Ono, March 1994), Japan's foremost labor organization at the time and one of Shōdanren's most politically powerful and financially secure members. To appease Sōhyō, Shōdanren occasionally softened its otherwise aggressive stance toward consumer problems that had a bearing on labor-management relations, such as the reform of the Antimonopoly Law (interview, Ono, March 1994). Since the decline of organized labor, however, Shōdanren has distanced itself politically from the unions (interview, Hiwasa, February 1994) and diversified its funding sources. Shōdanren's efforts to orchestrate joint activism during these early years, however, were impeded by the fact that many of its constituent organizations had little in common and had not yet mastered the technique of working together. Even today, Shōdanren is handicapped by the absence of Chifuren, although the housewives' federation does cooperate with the umbrella organization on an issue-by-issue basis.

Financial problems, an overdependence on labor support, and poor management techniques prevented Shōdanren from effectively fulfilling its self-declared mandate during the 1960s (interviews, Ono, March 1994, and Hiwasa, February 1994). It did little, for example, to confront problems involving false labeling and advertising and industrial pollution—problems that were occupying the attention of other social movement organizations at the time (interview, Hiwasa, February 1994). In subsequent years, however, the organization honed its skills as an interorganizational coordinator and political lobbyist and, from the 1970s, played a leading role in most consumer protection legislative campaigns (Shōdanren 1987b:17). As such, it can be credited for bringing some semblance of organizational unity to an otherwise highly fragmented movement.

The Emergence of a "Dual Structure" in the Japanese Consumer Movement

By the eve of the enactment of the 1968 Consumer Protection Basic Law, the organized consumer movement showed signs of becoming two movements in one: one local and the other national in scope. The local movement, as we have seen, encompassed a wide assortment of groups. Some of those groups were *fujinkai* affiliated with Chifuren or groups established under the auspices of Shufuren, while others were founded as part of the New Life movement. Still others were independent grassroots groups that arose in response to purely local issues. Although there are no nationwide statistics to prove this point, it appears that many in the latter group were eventually captured by the local bureaucracies with which they cooperated (interview, Andō, February 1993), a trend that continued throughout the 1970s and 1980s. Others, by contrast, worked hard to preserve their political independence and exhibited many of the traits that scholars normally associate with environmental citizens' movements and other new social movements, such as the spontaneous organization of middle-class citizens at the grassroots level, democratic participation in group-decision making, and attention to quality-of-life issues. Based on my own personal observations and interviews with national consumer activists, it appears that most of these small, grassroots groups were preoccupied with local environmental and food safety issues and only rarely got involved in large-scale political advocacy campaigns.

Private organizations at the national level, by contrast, looked in many ways like the advocacy organs of the United States during the 1960s. Many of them, for example, pursued quality-of-life, public-interest goals on behalf of very broad constituencies and, with the notable exceptions of Chifuren and, to a lesser extant, Shufuren, had no more than minimal contact with grassroots consumers or consumer groups as they went about their day-to-day business. As might be expected, this organizational feature of the movement made it difficult for national advocates to mobilize public opinion behind movement goals (interview, Shōda, December 1993).

Whereas local groups focused on solving consumer-related problems by directly confronting industry on a case-by-case basis, many of the national and prefectural organizations addressed consumer problems more systemically by pursuing three broad objectives. The first—pressuring government into institutionalizing a more comprehensive consumer protection policy-making and administrative system—we have already examined. The other two were reflections of the government's reluctance to do more to protect consumers from the hazards of rapid growth: the development of consumer education programs designed to increase citizens' awareness of consumption and their rights as consumers, and the introduction of stricter consumer protection laws and regulations by the national and prefectural governments.

Consumer Education and the Notion of Consumer Rights

Whether public or private, financially secure or dependent on government largesse, many consumer organizations during the 1960s launched programs to educate the public about consumption and consumer rights. To some scholars, education was the most important responsibility shouldered by consumer activists, for one important reason: the absence in the general public of a strong civic consciousness and awareness of individual rights (Kimoto 1986:35; Shōda 1989; interview, Shōda, December 1993). In the U.S., British, and German cases, consumer movements were grafted onto individuals' preexisting awareness of their civic rights and responsibilities. In Japan, by contrast, the birth of the postwar consumer movement *preceded* the entrenchment of such an awareness (Shōda 1989:118).[16] In order to overcome this barrier to consumer consciousness-raising, many consumer advocates became much more than mere representatives of the "consumer interest," however defined; they also functioned as vehicles for the dissemination and articulation of "citizenship"—of that element of the early *seikatsusha* identity that had been introduced from above during the Occupation and that was slow to take root in Japanese soil. Although many consumer organs in the United States and Britain combine educational and advocacy functions in their day-to-day affairs, the overlap between the two was taken to unprecedented heights in Japan in response to these political and historical considerations.

Generally, consumer education programs were designed to cultivate either "wise consumers" (*kashikoi shōhisha*) or "active consumers" (*kōdōsuru shōhisha*). The first objective, pursued by virtually all consumer organs and local governmental consumer offices, included the dissemination of information about such basic consumer skills as recognizing bargains, comparing prices, and avoiding defective products. As such, consumer education was a politically innocuous affair that served to rationalize consumption without upsetting the political and economic institutions and practices that shaped the processes of production.

As the 1960s wore on and the problems confronting consumers proliferated, some consumer organs became more and more interested in cultivating active consumers (Kimoto 1986:45), that is, consumers who were willing to stand up for their interests and to exercise their rights as both consumers and citizens. This was, of course, a politically loaded undertaking, since it meant confronting industry and, in some cases, tacitly rejecting many of the government's pro-business policies.[17] It also involved a great deal of "learning by doing"—of raising consumer and civic consciousness by means of product boycotts, street demonstrations, petition drives, and the like. As might be expected, the Japan Consumers Association and local groups that had formed clientelistic relations with the localities steered clear of such overtly political activities, while Shōdanren, Shufuren, Consumers Union, and other private consumer advocacy organizations took the lead.

The promotion of consumer rights in a country that had not yet digested the more general notion of civil rights proved challenging for consumer advocates. As in many other advanced industrial democracies, consumer rights are not entrenched in civil law (Kimoto 1986:63). For guidance on how to legitimize those rights in the eyes of the public, therefore, advocates could only refer to articles 13 and 25 of the constitution dealing with the right to health and happiness and the right to life, respectively. They also took their cue from President John F. Kennedy's 1962 speech to Congress that outlined the consumer's rights to safety, choice, information, and representation. These rights, together with the right to redress, have since become indelible principles of the Japanese movement.

Even with this arsenal of ideas at their disposal, activists by the mid-1960s found the task of instilling a consumer consciousness and an appreciation of consumer rights in the general public to be particularly onerous. The challenge stemmed in part from the nature of consumer problems in advanced industrial countries. As noted in chapter 1, a consumer consciousness tends to develop slowly in a society because the burden of consumer "injustices" like defective products and high prices is often shared, to varying degrees, by all socioeconomic groups. Consumers have few incentives, in other words, to distinguish themselves from other groups in society on the basis of those injustices. Without that kind of "us versus them" mentality, however, few citizens are motivated to think carefully about their rights as consumers.[18]

During the late 1950s and 1960s, Japanese citizens had even fewer incentives to dwell on their consumer identities; this was, after all, an era of "growth at all costs"—of pro-producer policies generated by a conservative political system that was firmly behind the national goal of economic "catch-up" with the West. To go against the grain of this national creed by championing the interests of consumers was to appear unpatriotic. Against this backdrop, many consumers were disinclined to speak up for their interests, preferring instead to delegate the resolution of consumer problems to those in governmental authority (*okami ni makaseru*) or to passively "cry themselves to sleep" (*nakineiri suru*) as mere victims of producer-instigated abuse. These habits proved hard to break for those who had been educated under the crushing yoke of authoritarianism.

The flip side of this victim mentality and dependence on authority was the government's distinctive conceptualization of its role vis-à-vis the consumer. In the United States and Britain, the government has assumed the role of *guarantor* or *caretaker* of consumer rights that are vested in the individual and that entitle individual consumers to legal redress upon demand. In Japan, by contrast, the task of protecting consumers from the negative externalities of production during the rapid-growth era was approached—if at all—as an *obligation* of a paternalistic government.[19] Although the government was certainly beholden to fulfill its obligations in those few consumer-related areas that were defined by law, the absence of legally entrenched consumer rights gave it the upper hand when dealing with consumer issues that had yet to be formally defined. Not surprisingly, when faced with unforeseen problems, the government, in its preoccupation with economic growth, tended to uphold the interests of producers over those of consumers.

For these reasons, many consumer activists in Japan view consumer "protection" as a mixed blessing. Consumer protection normally entails the introduction of laws and regulations by governments to shield consumers who cannot protect themselves from the harmful side effects of business activities. In the United States, consumer protection also implies the guarantee of basic consumer rights. But in a country like Japan where the notions of individual and consumer rights are not so deeply entrenched in the political culture, consumer protection runs the risk of preserving the status quo by reinforcing consumer passivity, governmental paternalism, and the power of business interests.

Clamoring for Government Protection: Consumer Movement Campaigns

Despite the disadvantages of relying too heavily on government for consumer protection, consumer advocates realized they had little choice but to do precisely that, given the weakness of the courts as guarantors of individual rights—a point that will be explored in later chapters—and the sheer power of the business community. Advocates, in other words, needed the government on their side in their bid to narrow the yawning political and economic gap between producers and consumers. The late 1950s and 1960s, therefore, were peppered with campaigns to pressure government into assuming an expanded consumer protection role. As in the United States before World War II, however, consumer protection policies were normally the product of scandal or converging interests between consumers and producers, rather than consumer participation in established channels of interest articulation. The following is an overview of three representative consumer campaigns, two of which ended in success, the other in failure.

The Nise Canned Beef Incident and the Product-Labeling Movement

As businesses scrambled for market share during the rapid-growth era, consumers were increasingly exposed to incidents of consumer fraud (NHSK 1980:61). One of the most glaring examples of this was the so-called Nise Canned Beef incident (Nise gyūkan jiken), a scandal that revealed the paucity of national regulatory measures to protect the consumer.

It all started in September 1960 when a lone consumer contacted the Public Health Department (Eiseikyoku) of the Tōkyō metropolitan government to complain about a fly she had discovered in a can of beef produced by the Nise Corporation. The department immediately launched an investigation into what seemed to be a straightforward violation of public-health regulations. It quickly became apparent, however, that false labeling was also at issue, for the cans of "beef" had been packed with whale meat.

The incident caused a minor media sensation and drew attention to the inadequacy of Japan's weak labeling regulations. Since whale meat in no way posed a threat to the health of consumers, both the Public Health Department and the Ministry of Health and Welfare were powerless to change the labeling practices of the Nise Corporation. For Shufuren, whose product-testing department had long been aware of fraudulent labeling by manufacturers, the Nise case presented a long-awaited opportunity to mobilize for stricter labeling regulations (KSS 1997:90–91).

In 1962, the national government responded to the findings of the Tōkyō government and the burgeoning consumer backlash by enacting the Law to Prevent Unjustifiable Premiums and Misleading Representations (Futōkeih-inryū oyobi futōhyōji bōshi hō), the first piece of legislation since the Anti-monopoly Law to cite consumer protection as one of its primary objectives (Sahara 1979:214–15). The process surrounding the enactment of the law was unusual, however, in that the bill met with virtually no resistance from firms. In fact, many manufacturers welcomed the measures because they promised to stem the proliferation of unfair trade practices—if the provision of premiums to consumers can be regarded as such—which advantage some firms over others.[20] The law was, in short, widely viewed in the business community as a regulatory safeguard against that age-old bugaboo of "competitive chaos" (katō kyōsō).

The Nise case was significant not only because it was one of the only legislative campaigns in which the interests of business and consumers coincided but also because it marked the beginning of a long-term and very successful consumer movement to improve product-labeling practices. It also highlighted both the sympathy of local officials for the interests of consumers and the impact of local government initiatives on the introduction of national regulatory measures. Indeed, the case was one of the earliest examples of a loose partnership between consumer activists and local authorities to enact stronger consumer protection measures. It was a partnership that was to expand considerably as the years passed.

The Newspaper Boycott

Throughout the 1960s, consumer advocates pressured bureaucrats and politicians to quell the swelling "price typhoon" (bukka taifū) that was hitting consumers squarely in the pocketbook (Shōdanren 1987b:24). Realizing that inflation was bad for business as well as consumers, the Ikeda government responded by introducing an ambitious assortment of anti-inflationary policies.[21] Unfortunately, however, those policies were not completely successful, in part because of the government's reluctance to simultaneously tackle collusive business practices and other structural causes of inflation. This was at no time more apparent than during Shōdanren's newspaper boycott.

In 1959, Japan's major national and regional newspapers announced within several days of one another a whopping 18 percent increase in their subscription rates. Convinced of intraindustry collusion, Shōdanren filed a formal request for an investigation (*shinsa seikyūsho*) with the Japan Fair Trade Commission (JFTC) under article 45 of the Antimonopoly Law. The commission proceeded to collect evidence of collusion from the national Newspaper Association (Shimbun kyōkai) and from comparable organizations at the regional level. Shōdanren, meanwhile, persuaded more than 1 million newspaper subscribers (Shōdanren 1987b:20) to refuse to pay the difference between the old and new subscription rates. Swayed by arguments that the increases had been warranted by rising paper costs and in effect ignoring the evidence of collusion, the JFTC finally ruled in August that it would not press charges against the newspaper companies (Misono 1987). Incensed by the decision, consumer organizations filed appeals with the Tōkyō District Court and, later, the Tōkyō High Court, both of which upheld the commission's decision.

The boycott, which was closely covered by the nation's smaller newspapers, proved to be the biggest show of consumer protest since the Occupation. Although the major dailies promised to consult with consumer representatives before implementing future price hikes (interview, K. Nakamura, April 1994), Shōdanren nonetheless viewed the campaign as a major failure for the consumer movement (interview, Ono, March 1994). Activists were particularly disappointed by the JFTC's unwillingness to carry out the spirit of the Antimonopoly Law by responding to the demands of ordinary citizens and combating the problem of collusive business practices (Ono 1996). Unfortunately, the inability of consumer organizations to counter collusive business practices was revealed again and again during the 1960s as Shōdanren and unaffiliated consumer organizations fought against collusive price hikes by the utilities sector, public bath owners, and barber and beauty shop proprietors (Shōdanren 1987b:24). Together, these were classic examples of *monzenbarai*— of being turned away at the gate of ostensibly pro-consumer national bureaucratic organs that had been captured by producer interests.

The Color TV Boycott

The high point of consumer activism during the rapid-growth period was reached in 1970/71, when five consumer organizations working together with the leaders of Shōdanren organized a nationwide boycott of television sets that had been grossly overpriced as a result of intraindustry price fixing.

In 1970, Chifuren was commissioned by the JFTC to investigate the prices of color television sets. Both Chifuren and, in subsequent inquiries, the JFTC, discovered that manufacturers were displaying artificially high list prices (*genkin seika*) on their products (Kirkpatrick 1975:243), thereby enabling designated sellers to charge inflated "discount" prices. The ploy proved misleading—not to mention costly—to consumers who were not savvy enough to negotiate discounts. This was, consumer advocates concluded, a glaring example of unfair trade practices (*futō torihiki hōhō*), a violation of the 1961 Law to Prevent Unjustifiable Premiums and Misleading Representations, and an infringement of the consumer rights to information and product choice at fair prices. To rectify the problem, they insisted, among other things, on the public disclosure of the actual list prices, a demand that the industry categorically ignored.

The United States, meanwhile, was pressuring the Japanese government to do something about the enormous price discrepancy between sets sold in Japan and the United States. According to a study conducted jointly by JETRO (Japan External Trade Organization) and MITI, nineteen-inch models produced by Japanese color television manufacturers were selling in America for roughly one-third less than the price of comparable models in Japan (NHSK 1980:137). These dumping charges, together with Chifuren's findings on the industry's pricing practices at home, attracted widespread media coverage and outraged the Japanese public.

In early 1971, when it became clear that the industry was not about to comply with the JFTC's recommendations to liberalize prices (Zenchifuren 1973:158) and that MITI did not intend to rectify the problem, Chifuren launched a consumer boycott against color TV sets with the support of four other consumer organizations, including Shufuren. Seikyōren, the national consumer cooperative umbrella organization, helped raise public awareness of the color TV problem by producing its own model and selling it in affiliated co-op stores for almost half the price of mainstream brands.

The timing of the boycott could not have been more fortuitous. First, it was carried out when millions of Japanese consumers were on the threshold of replacing their old black-and-white sets with the color models that had just hit the market. Consumer organizations took advantage of this buying trend by skillfully convincing consumers to "refrain from buying" (*kaibikae*) their new TVs until the sets were priced more fairly. Second, since it was launched at the height of the New Year's buying season when shoppers were armed with their year-end bonuses, the campaign contributed to a sharp decrease in sales at a time when they should have been at their highest. Finally, consumer leaders were able to activate the boycott quickly and effectively when circumstances were at their most favorable because of extensive media coverage, much of which had been fueled by the controversy's international dimensions (interview, K. Nakamura, April 1994).[22] Consumer activists, in other words, had at their disposal a recipe for a successful boycott: good timing, media coverage, public support, and a powerful and indignant (foreign) ally.

As the boycott progressed and American anger intensified, advocates welcomed two more allies into their fold: MITI and the JFTC, both of which caved in to domestic and international pressures by urging the industry to lower their prices and cut back on exports. In February 1971, as profits dropped precipitously and inventories swelled, manufacturers finally agreed to meet these demands. The boycott drew to a close.

The color television boycott was a milestone in the history of the postwar consumer movement in that it marked the first time that a disparate group of consumer organs had joined to successfully combat the collusive business practices of a powerful industry. Over the next two decades, Shōdanren and the "five organizations" (*go dantai*: Shufuren, Chifuren, Japan League of Women Voters, Seikyōren, and Consumers Association of the (Tōkyō) Bunkyō Ward) that formed the campaign's organizational nucleus cooperated frequently on several consumer-related issues. Intracoalition relations were not always smooth, however, and disagreements over tactics resulted in a number of hard-won compromises. In the color TV boycott, for example, the organizations battled over what kind of terminology to use in their attempts to attract the participation of consumers. Chifuren opposed the actual use of the word *boycott* (*fubai* or *boikotto*), insisting instead on more modest expressions like *kaibikae* ("refrain from buying") in the hopes of winning over consumers who hesitated to participate in a highly publicized social movement. Some of the other organizations disagreed with Chifuren but ultimately conceded in order to keep the federation—with its huge membership—involved in the campaign (interview, K. Nakamura, April 1994).

The success of the color television boycott prompted both Japanese and foreign observers to sit up and take notice of what appeared to be a new consumer phenomenon. Maki Shōhei, a frequent commentator on Japanese consumer issues, viewed the affair as much more than a transient occurrence and marveled at the ability of activists to mobilize literally millions of citizens (Maki 1979:46–47). In a similar vein, Maurine Kirkpatrick observed that the boycott and other successful consumer campaigns represented

> an attempt to broaden the bases of interest articulation and represen-
> tation, and . . . had the effect of serving as a vehicle for popular dis-
> satisfaction as well as providing feelings of individual efficacy. . . . In
> the context of this new political environment, . . . the consumer move-
> ment . . . acquired a meaning extending beyond mere interest in fair
> treatment for consumers. The consumer movement [became], like
> citizens' movement activism, another channel of expression for citi-
> zens' demands and dissatisfactions.
>
> (Kirkpatrick 1975:235)

Although analysts were certainly correct to point out the broad significance of consumer movement activism for Japanese politics, they erred on two points. First, many were approaching their subject matter as if consumer activism were a recent phenomenon, when in fact the boycotts and other market-oriented campaigns that had captured so much media attention to-ward the end of the rapid-growth era had been fixtures of consumer politics for almost a quarter century.

Second, many analysts overestimated the power of the boycott as a move-ment strategy. As we noted in chapter 1, boycotts are extremely difficult to organize given the diffuseness of the consumer constituency and are doomed to failure if the media neglect to cover them or the government decides to support the targeted manufacturers. Their success, moreover, depends heavily on good timing and luck—two ingredients that were present in the TV boycott case but have been hard to duplicate in other instances. It should come as no surprise, then, that the color TV boycott was not only the first large-scale boycott to truly succeed in postwar Japanese history; it was also the last.

Conclusion

The period stretching from the advent of the 1955 system to the late 1960s or so was one of both institutional constraints and opportunities for

Japanese consumer activists. First and foremost under the category of constraints was the government's failure to effectively incorporate the consumer interest into national decision-making processes by establishing a more comprehensive system of consumer protection policymaking and administration. For all intents and purposes, consumers were still excluded from the corridors of power by a political establishment consisting of conservative politicians, bureaucrats in the economic ministries, and representatives from the business community. The predominance of pro-business interests was particularly apparent in the JFTC's unwillingness to acknowledge the legitimacy of consumer movement appeals for stricter antitrust enforcement, a topic explored in greater detail in chapter 6.

Against the backdrop of pro-business political alignments and bureaucratic institutions that excluded consumer activists from meaningful participation in national policymaking, consumer advocates found sympathetic allies at the local level. As illustrated by the Nise Canned Beef incident, local administrations were much more open to the demands of consumers than was their national counterpart; in some instances, moreover, local initiatives on the consumer front helped spark policy innovation at the national level. This emerging relationship between the localities and the national government in the sphere of national consumer protection policymaking was only to intensify in subsequent years.

The first decade and a half of the 1955 system also underscored the limits of market-oriented strategies to wrest concessions from business interests. As the short case studies explored in this chapter show, activists were able to achieve their goals only in those rare instances when business had been hit squarely in the pocketbook or when their interests in a particular piece of "consumer" regulation or legislation coincided with those of consumer advocates. In cases of pure confrontation between consumers and business, without effective inroads into the national policy process, consumers were doomed to failure. As we shall see in the next chapter, however, consumer access to national decision-making processes promised to expand with the 1968 enactment of the Consumer Protection Basic Law and the subsequent introduction of a comprehensive system of consumer protection policymaking and administration.

5 The Post-1968 Consumer Protection Policymaking System and the Consumer Movement's Response

Nineteen sixty-eight was a year of symbolic anniversaries and new beginnings for the Japanese consumer movement. First, it marked the twentieth anniversary of the founding of Shufuren and the enactment of the Co-op Law, two events that have come to represent the early postwar upsurge of consumer activism and the laws and political institutions that have simultaneously constrained and provoked that activism.

Nineteen sixty-eight was also the 100th anniversary of the Meiji Restoration and Japan's entry into the "modern" world. In the parlance of the organized consumer movement, it had been a century of public support for economic growth, producer supremacy in the political economy, and, in many cases, economic progress achieved at the expense of consumers. It was, many activists believed, a century that needed to end.

Even more important to those activists, 1968 witnessed the enactment of the Consumer Protection Basic Law (Shōhisha hogō kihon hō), an event that marked the culmination of more than two decades of market-oriented activism and the beginning of a new phase of consumer advocacy based on consumer participation in policymaking processes. As such, the Basic Law came to represent both change and continuity for the organized movement: change, insofar as it represented an important governmental concession to pressures from below and laid the groundwork for an institutionalized system of consumer protection policymaking and administration, and continuity, in that it left more or less intact many of the basic political alliances that had governed national consumer policymaking in the past. It was, in short, another potent symbol of both the challenges and opportunities of postwar Japanese consumer politics.

This chapter examines the politics leading up to the enactment of the Basic Law, the law's impact on the institutions of consumer protection policymaking and administration, and the resulting opportunities—or lack thereof—for consumer advocacy both nationally and locally. The analysis is based on the theoretical observation made in chapter 1 that new laws or policies can create new institutional configurations that in turn can either empower or restrain societal interests. I conclude the chapter with an overview of the menu of strategic choices available to consumer advocates since 1968. In chapters 6 through 8, I look at how advocates have used those strategies to influence the direction of consumer protection policymaking.

The 1968 Consumer Protection Basic Law

The Political Backdrop

The Consumer Protection Basic Law was enacted in part because it made good political sense. The law was, after all, a long-overdue policy response to the myriad distortions of rapid economic growth that had been plaguing consumers for well over a decade (Kimoto 1993:10). More specifically, it was a much-needed antidote to a consumer bureaucratic system that was far too informal and fragmented to keep up with contemporary consumer problems (Sunada 1968:6), as well as a concession to consumers who had grown weary of the government's unspoken policy of "growth at all costs."

The ruling Liberal Democratic Party (LDP) had some compelling reasons of its own to support the law. By the mid- to late 1960s, a confluence of problems had created a political situation in which the pro-business party could no longer afford to ignore the issue of consumer protection: the product-related disasters of the late 1950s and 1960s; mounting citizen activism at the grassroots level directed at both environmental and consumer issues; and the threat to conservative party rule posed by the rise of progressive local governments, many of which were taking innovative steps in the consumer policy realm. Not coincidentally, the party had just seen the Basic Law on Environmental Pollution through the Diet. A similar statute dealing with consumer protection, many in the party now believed, could be just what the LDP needed to appease Japan's increasingly disgruntled voters before they took their frustrations to the polls. For all intents and purposes, the LDP was acting in anticipation of a political "crisis" in the consuming electorate in a manner comparable to the "crisis and compensation" dynamic explored by Calder (1988).

The politics behind the enactment of the Basic Law were a rare example of conservative party initiatives in consumer policy formulation, initiatives that heretofore had been taken by the bureaucracy or, less frequently, by the opposition parties. Originally, the bill was to be drafted by the Economic Planning Agency[1] with the cooperation of the pertinent ministries and then introduced to the Diet with the backing of the cabinet (Sunada 1968:17). Two developments, however, catapulted the policy process outside regular decision-making channels. The first was the specter of endless interministerial squabbling among the eighteen ministries and agencies that were to have a hand in the bill's drafting. The second was the tabling of alternative bills by a number of progressive opposition parties at a time when the LDP's position at the polls was very uncertain (KSS 1997:108). The LDP's answer to these challenges was to seek multiparty sponsorship of a private member's bill.

Accordingly, a bill was drafted in the LDP's Policy Affairs Research Council (PARC) and then submitted to a subcommittee in the Lower House's Special Committee on Price Problems. During the ensuing interparty negotiations, Sunada Jūmin,[2] a second-generation LDP Diet member from Hyōgo Prefecture and the head of the subcommittee, played a key role in allaying fears in the LDP rank-and-file that a comprehensive consumer statute would be detrimental to business progress (Shōdanren 1987b:109) and in gathering support from the opposition parties, most of which had criticized the LDP bill for not doing *enough* for consumers. Thanks largely to Sunada's efforts, an interparty alliance was eventually forged among the LDP, the Japan Socialist Party, the Kōmeitō, and the Democratic Socialist Party, an alliance that looked very much like the ones identified by Calder during the formulation of welfare, environmental, and small-business legislation (Calder 1988:444).

The bill passed unanimously on May 24, 1968, and went into effect six days later (Oikawa 1993:6). Consumer organizations, which had been completely excluded from the decision-making process, had no say over the law's contents. The legislative process was significant, however, for at least three reasons. First, and most important to our purposes, the law ushered in a new phase of consumer politics characterized by enhanced opportunities for routinized consumer participation in policymaking. However disappointing those opportunities may have been, they marked the end of a long period of consumer advocacy based primarily on market-oriented protest. Second, and as noted earlier, it was a rare example of LDP initiative in the consumer sphere, not to mention a concession to citizen demands after years of prioritizing producer interests. Finally, it was one of few private member's bills ever enacted into law in the history of the Diet, as well as an extraordinary example of interparty cooperation. As such, the Consumer Protection Basic Law can be viewed as an early manifestation of the willingness of a politically besieged LDP to cooperate more closely with the opposition parties in the Diet.[3]

The Consumer "Constitution"

The price paid for bipartisan support was a piece of legislation that many critics summarily dismissed as a mere "propaganda law" (*senden rippō*) (Oikawa 1993:7). Indeed, on the surface of things at least, the law resembles most other basic laws[4] in both its tacit declaration that "there ought to be more laws!" and its omission of measures that might give concrete meaning to that declaration. That said, the Basic Law does have value insofar as it lays out the principles, objectives, and institutions of consumer protection policymaking and administration in Japan. As such, the law fulfills its reputation as the country's "consumer constitution."

The purpose of the Consumer Protection Basic Law is to "secure the stability and improvement of consumer lifestyles" by defining the responsibilities of the state, localities, business enterprises, and consumers themselves toward the interests of consumers (Keizaikikakuchō 1999:154). What is significant about this phrase is the implicit recognition that consumers have unique problems of their own. As Japanese legal scholars have often noted, the Civil Code and supporting statutes, which had guided consumer-related transactions in the past, overlooked the fact that consumers were weak relative to big business in terms of economic power and access to product-related information (Japan Consumer Information Center 1989:2; Miyasaka et al. 1990b:31). The Basic Law helps level the playing field by acknowledging the inherent inequality of the consumer-producer relationship and by providing in principle for the kinds of legal measures that would protect consumers from abuse. The law also addresses the problems of consumers head-on (Sunada 1968:15–16), unlike most other consumer-related laws which, like comparable American statutes before the 1960s, did so only indirectly.

The law consists of four sections. The first outlines the responsibilities of the state and the localities toward the interests of consumers. It also calls on firms to cooperate with both entities in executing consumer-related policies and ensuring the provision of safe and reliable products and product-related information to their customers. The section ends with an appeal to individual consumers to take the initiative in acquiring consumption-related information and to behave "self-reliantly and rationally."

Section 2 authorizes the state to set national standards for product safety, correct weights and measures, proper labeling, and free and fair competition;[5] states the roles of all levels of government in soliciting and reflecting the views of consumers in policy formulation and implementation; and calls on the state to establish product-testing facilities and to provide citizens with consumer-related information and educational opportunities. It also authorizes the state, localities, and private companies to establish institutions to deal with consumer complaints.

Section 3 provides for the establishment of state and local institutions to facilitate the execution of consumer policies and stipulates the role of the state in taking "necessary [steps] for the encouragement of sound and self-reliant organizational activities in which the consumer may endeavor to stabilize and improve his consumer life." The final section establishes the Consumer Protection Council (Shōhisha hogo kaigi) under the Prime Minister's Office. Headed by the prime minister, the council consists of eighteen ministers and agency directors (Keizaikikakuchō 1993a:16) and is responsible for annually formulating broad consumer protection policies.

The Institutional Configurations of Consumer Protection Policymaking and Administration

"New policies," proclaimed E. E. Schattschneider during the 1930s, "create new politics" (Schattschneider 1935:288). And so it was in Japan following the enactment of the Consumer Protection Basic Law. Within seven years of its promulgation, seventeen preexisting consumer-related laws were strengthened, and fourteen new ones—most of which carried out the stipulations of the Basic Law—were enacted (NHSK 1980:116). It was a historically unprecedented flurry of legislative activity in the consumer realm. And although many of the statutes were subsequently attacked by consumer representatives and legal scholars for being "deboned" (*honenuki*), or soft on business, even the most stalwart critics had to admit that they improved the lot of consumers by strengthening product safety standards, increasing access to information and redress mechanisms, and enhancing consumer representation in governmental decision-making processes. As such, they were a victory for consumer organizations, many of which had campaigned long and hard for such measures.

The Basic Law also had a major impact on the consumer-related institutions of the national and local bureaucracies. By outlining governmental responsibilities toward the consumer and sanctioning and promoting the expansion of a consumer-oriented bureaucratic space, for example, the statute increased the odds that ideas pertaining to consumer protection would mature into concrete laws and policies. For bureaucrats entrusted with protecting consumers, the law had an immediate impact on morale, particularly at the local level where consumer protection, together with environmental administration, was becoming a respected local governmental function. These developments in turn help explain the upsurge in consumer protection legislative activity both nationally and locally during the late 1960s and early 1970s (Sahara 1979:216).

The law also legitimized the preexisting role played by the localities in consumer protection by broadly stipulating their responsibilities in executing state policies and formulating local policies, functions that were formally incorporated into the 1947 Local Autonomy Law by an amendment introduced in 1969. The immediate effect of these provisions was the acceleration of earlier efforts by local governments to take a leading role in the day-to-day implementation of consumer protection policy, the formulation of a number of new policies oriented toward local consumer problems, and the development of consumer-related services and education programs. Accordingly, during the late 1960s and 1970s, prefectural, city, and town governments expanded their facilities to deal with consumer issues and frequently took the initiative in directing the public's attention to problems affecting consumers.

Last but not least, by highlighting the need for consumer legislative action in the future, the Basic Law led to both the introduction of new policy-making and administrative organs and the expansion of old ones. Together, these institutions quickly evolved into a comprehensive system of consumer protection policymaking and administration spanning both levels of government. The main political and institutional features of that process before the downfall of Liberal Democratic Party rule in 1993 were as follows.

The Consumer Protection Policymaking and Administrative System

As the highest-ranking decision-making body in the consumer protection policy process, the Consumer Protection Council functioned as a horizontal bureaucratic forum for identifying consumer issues, setting policy targets, and coordinating consumer policy in the national bureaucracy. In practice, however, the council was weakened as a policymaking organ by the fact that it met only once a year. Moreover, given the large number of bureaucratic voices that had to be coordinated by the council, its recommendations often reflected little more than the lowest common denominator of official thinking on consumer issues.

The Consumer Protection Council was further hampered by the fact that it was run by top-ranking politicians who had little experience — or interest — in consumer affairs. On that note, one of the curious features of consumer politics that set Japan apart from the United States was the failure of the political parties — both conservative and progressive — to elevate consumer issues as priority items in their policy platforms (Kitazawa 1979:261–63). As we noted in the case of Britain, this can be partly explained by the tendency of parliamentary systems to weaken incentives for prime ministers to champion broad public-interest issues and for individual backbenchers to become "political entrepreneurs" in the consumer realm. Also to blame was the former "single nontransferable vote multimember district system" that encouraged politicians to cultivate votes by promising the distribution of particularistic favors to their potential constituents rather than promoting broad quality-of-life issues.

Although the opposition parties occasionally helped shape the terms of the debate on some of the more politicized consumer issues by fielding private members' bills and stoking public opinion, consumer advocates who allied with the opposition parties behind consumer policy initiatives often expressed disappointment that those parties did not do more to advance the consumer cause. The parliamentary and electoral constraints faced by all political parties notwithstanding, opposition inertia on the consumer front is certainly intriguing, particularly given the potential for consumer issues to set those parties apart from the LDP in the minds of the voters. The reliance of both the Socialist and Democratic Socialist Parties on labor union support may be one reason for this, if we can assume that emphasis on the affairs of workers deflected party attention away from the broader concerns of consumers. The opposition's status as the Diet's "permanent opposition" before 1993 and the policy-related inertia that consequently set in is certainly another.

Given the Diet's relative weakness as a forum for the articulation of consumer-related concerns, the business of consumer protection formulation fell primarily to the ministries in a manner comparable to that of Britain. This is not to say that LDP politicians played no role in this process; to the contrary, they could and would jump in when interministerial conflict or intense business opposition was involved. Even when consumer policymaking was routine and uneventful, ruling politicians influenced the process indirectly through their veto power. Since the cabinet did not normally adopt policies that were unpalatable to the party in power, in other words, bureaucrats constantly tried to determine—or at least anticipate—the prerequisites for cabinet approval. Finally, the LDP became more directly involved in consumer policymaking on those few occasions when consumer issues threatened to affect the party at the polls. Consider, for example, the LDP's active involvement in the enactment of the Consumer Protection Basic Law and, two decades later, in the introduction of the controversial consumption tax.

While the ministries were responsible for drafting and implementing consumer-related laws pertaining to their respective jurisdictions, the Economic Planning Agency served as the coordinator of interministerial consumer policymaking. The agency was in charge, for example, of a monthly meeting of section chiefs (*katchō*) from the eighteen ministries and agencies that deliberated on overall consumer policymaking and administration, and a smaller meeting of pertinent officials from the agency, the Ministries of Health and Welfare and Agriculture, Forestry and Fisheries, and the Fair Trade Commission to discuss food-related policies (Keizaikikakuchō 1993a: 17). As horizontal mechanisms for interministerial cooperation, however, these meetings were often the venue of decision-making inertia and turf battles caused by the institutional phenomenon of "vertical administration" (*tatewari gyōsei*).[6] Moreover, the role of the Economic Planning Agency as chief conductor of the consumer policymaking process was weakened by the agency's lack of ministerial status in the cabinet. In keeping with pre-1968 bureaucratic trends, the post-1968 consumer protection policy and administrative processes remained fragmented and laden with conflict.

According to the Basic Law and several supporting statutes, business and labor representatives, consumer advocates, academics, and other nongovernmental interests could participate in ministerial consumer policymaking in one of two ways. The first was membership on *shingikai*: bureaucratic "consultative bodies" (*shimon kikan*) that function as advisory organs to ministerial and agency heads during the early stages of policymaking (Schwartz 1998:52). Most of the *shingikai* that had played a role in consumer policymaking in the past had mandates that extended far beyond the consumer realm — MITI's Industrial Structure Council (Sangyō kōzō shingikai) being one of the better-known cases in point. For policies that touched on the jurisdictions of several ministries, the Social Policy Council (Kokumin seikatsu shingikai) usually stepped in. Since the final reports released by *shingikai* often formed the basis of a ministry's official position on a particular issue, the councils performed an important legitimizing function for the ministry concerned. Like other deliberative councils, however, consumer-related *shingikai* often functioned as mere rubber stamps for bureaucratic policies or fronts for behind-the-scenes bureaucratic networking (see Schwartz 1993:217–41).

The second, more indirect avenue for the articulation of citizen interests was the Japan Consumer Information Center (Kokumin seikatsu sentaa,[7] or JCIC) and its affiliated network of local consumer centers.[8] The JCIC is a public organization established under the jurisdiction of the Economic Planning Agency by the 1970 Japan Consumer Information Center Law (Kokumin seikatsu sentaa hō). It carries out product testing, consumer-related research and public opinion surveys, public education on consumer issues, advice for aggrieved consumers, and mediation (*assen*) and conciliation (*chōtei*) in disputes between businesses and consumers. Comparable functions are performed at the local level by "consumer centers" (*shōhisha sentaa*, also known as *shōhi seikatsu sentaa*, or "consumer lifestyle centers"). These are semigovernmental organizations established by local ordinances and affiliated with the JCIC. Between the early 1970s and 1993, the centers and the JCIC together functioned as an institutional network for the public dissemination of consumer-related information and as an administrative feedback mechanism in which the results of local consumer administration were funneled into the national bureaucracy through the Economic Planning Agency.

The role of the localities in these policymaking and administrative processes was an important one. On one level, the localities served as financially subsidized executors of national policies and of consumer-related programs centered in the ministries. The localities were also authorized by the Basic Law to enact consumer protection ordinances to address problems specific to the jurisdictions of the localities in question, a feature that was lacking in the Basic Law on Environmental Pollution before the 1970 amendments (McKean 1981:243). Finally, and as we shall see shortly, the localities occasionally functioned as receptacles of local public opinion which, in some circumstances, could have a significant impact on policymaking at the center.

Consumer Organs and the Post-1968 Policymaking System

After 1968, consumer representatives were presented with new inroads into the national consumer protection policymaking and administrative processes. But just how effective were those inroads? The Basic Law may have expanded the scope and significance of the consumer protection policymaking system, but can the same be said for the influence of consumer organizations within that system?

If the underlying principles of the Basic Law are any indication, the answer to the second question is a resounding no. Consider, for example, article 2, the Basic Law's own version of the "harmony clause" of the 1967 Basic Law on Environmental Pollution: "The state has the responsibility of establishing and executing overall policy concerning consumer protection *in accordance with the development of economic society* (emphasis added)." In one short sentence, consumer protection is ranked second to economic growth and producer interests as a domestic policy goal. Although the Basic Law on Environmental Pollution was eventually freed of this provision (Broadbent 1998: 120–22), the consumer version remains intact.

Another feature of the law that weakened consumers as political players before 1993 is the omission of any mention of individual consumer rights. Although the concepts of product safety, information, choice, consumer representation, and redress are addressed to varying degrees by the statute, they are approached not as rights vested in the individual but as privileges bestowed on the people by business and government with an eye to the "development of economic society." This feature, which conforms closely with long-standing Japanese approaches to state-consumer relations, has been roundly criticized by consumer organizations, academics, and legal specialists for elevating the interests of producers over those of consumers and for encouraging consumers to depend heavily on those in political and economic authority for solutions to consumer-related problems (see, e.g., Kimoto 1986:86–88; Oikawa 1993:6–7).

A third feature of the Basic Law that warrants attention here is the stipulation in article 17 that "the state and local governments shall take necessary measures for the encouragement of sound and self-reliant organizational activities with which the consumer may endeavor to stabilize and improve his consumer life." This is not a validation of consumer protest or a green light for the organizational expansion of the consumer movement. To the contrary, when viewed in tandem with the rest of the law and the absence of any discussion of consumer rights, the article suggests governmental support for apolitical consumer organs that support "rational" consumption, that provide for the education of "wise" (*kashikoi*) consumers—as opposed to "active" (*kōdōsuru*) ones—and that cooperate with state and local authorities in the "development of economic society." The law, in other words, seeks to depoliticize the organized consumer movement while protecting the supremacy of producer and bureaucratic interests in the policy process. In this way, the law mimics the underlying intentions of the Basic Law on Environmental Pollution (see Upham 1987:58).

Clause for clause, the Consumer Protection Basic Law gives us little reason to expect an expansion of consumer leverage over the policy process. How, then, were the principles of that law actually carried out? In the environmental realm, as Upham has shown, the objectives of the Basic Law on Environmental Pollution and its supporting legislation were duplicated on the ground by local dispute resolution mechanisms that effectively prevented the politicization of environmental conflicts (Upham 1987:56–58). The spirit of the Consumer Protection Basic Law, on the other hand, was implemented almost to the letter at the national level, but not in the localities. The results of this discrepancy have been far-reaching not only for local consumer policymaking, but also for decision making at the center.

Consumer Representation at the National Level

By all accounts, opportunities for direct access to the national policy process were extremely disappointing for consumer advocates before 1993. The opinions of consumer leaders who served on consumer-related *shingikai*, for example, were frequently overpowered by business representatives who benefited directly from the rules and informal customs governing committee deliberations. Advocates often spoke bitterly of their experiences as *shingikai* members, complaining about the exclusion of consumer representatives whose opinions did not mesh with those of the ministries (interview, Shimizu, February 1993), bureaucratic control over agenda setting and the report compilation process, the haphazard distribution of pertinent documents to council members just hours before meetings were to convene (interview, Y. Itō, April 1994), the fact that many documents were written in English or other foreign languages, and the lack of public access to *shingikai* meetings. In disputes between consumer and business representatives, moreover, they claimed that business often won out, whereas the dissenting opinions of consumer leaders went unrecorded in the final *shingikai* reports.[9] These consumer-related *shingikai* resembled *shingikai* more generally insofar as they functioned "in ways downright inimical to their intentions" (Schwartz 1998:52).

Consumer representatives also lacked informal access to bureaucrats in the policy process. In most ministries dealing with consumer issues, requests by consumer representatives for meetings with pertinent officials were often turned down or granted by low-ranking bureaucrats with little more than ten minutes or so to spare. Advocates fared somewhat better in the more sympathetic Economic Planning Agency, the center for consumer policy coordination in the bureaucracy, but their ties to individual bureaucrats in the agency were relatively weak and at times even inconsequential, given the agency's lack of clout in the bureaucracy as a whole.

Symbolic representation in the consumer policy process by consumer organizations was mirrored by close, institutionalized relationships between business interests and officials. Since most consumer-related policies involve the regulation of business practices, business was heavily represented in the national decision-making process to ensure the smooth implementation of policy. Business input into that process was both formal and informal. The opinions of industry leaders who served as members on ministerial *shingikai* that deliberated on consumer issues, for example, were given careful consideration when reports were compiled. Business leaders also cultivated long-term, private relationships with key bureaucrats that were frequently tapped as informal channels of interest articulation and mutual consultation throughout the policy process. Consumer organizations, meanwhile, lacked such avenues into the ranks of officialdom.

Consumer Representation at the Local Level

The Consumer Protection Basic Law produced a set of corporatist institutions that, for all intents and purposes, excluded representatives of the consumer interest from the post-1968 consumer protection policymaking system. "Turned away at the gate"(*monzenbarai*) of the national corridors of power, consumer advocates looked to the localities as alternative channels of interest articulation. Their efforts proved to be surprisingly successful.

For starters, advocates managed to form useful ties with politicians at both the city and prefectural levels, where, as we noted in an earlier chapter, electoral incentives and historical precedent encouraged politicians to embrace public-interest issues. Advocates also had direct and effective access to bureaucratic decision-making processes. Consumer leaders were regularly consulted on the composition of local *shingikai* memberships (interview, Andō, February 1994), and their representatives on the councils were closely involved in the compilation of council reports, which reflected more or less accurately the various opinions both for and against particular policy proposals. *Shingikai* meetings were also open to the public, thereby giving non-council members from consumer organizations an opportunity—which they did not have at the national level—to keep abreast of consumer-related debates in local governments. Consumer movement advocates who served on local *shingikai* generally expressed moderate to high degrees of efficacy and were considerably more satisfied with local deliberative organs than with those at the national level (interview, Andō, February 1994; NHK 1993).

The local consumer centers constituted another avenue for consumer organizations into the local policy process. While the dispute resolution mechanisms of these centers sometimes worked against the interests of consumer representatives by preventing individual consumer disputes from becoming politicized—just as local dispute resolution procedures do in the environmental realm[10]—the centers served the political interests of consumer movement advocates in several ways. For example, consumer representatives often worked with center officials to carry out consumer education programs and product testing, projects that brought them into close contact with local policymakers. In addition, many of these centers had at least one staff member on hand who was responsible for implementing local governmental policies pertaining to these groups and serving as liaisons between the center and consumer representatives (interview, Kudō, December 1997).

Although the individuals who occupied these positions were rotated every three years or so in accordance with Japanese bureaucratic custom, some of them developed close and informal relationships with consumer representatives that were coveted by the latter as both sources of information and opportunities for the articulation of movement preferences. In this sense, the centers developed into the kinds of *kakekomidera* ("temple for seeking refuge") that advocates longed for at the national level.

The extent of consumer input into local policymaking procedures was particularly apparent during the formulation and implementation of consumer ordinances. The drafting of Tōkyō's highly regarded Consumer Ordinance (Shōhisha jōrei, 1975),[11] for example, was the responsibility of a prominent local *shingikai* in which consumer representatives played a major role (Suzuki 1979:261). Consumer leaders had additional opportunities to influence the policy process by participating in the Residents' Council to Protect Livelihoods (Seikatsu wo mamoru tōmin kaigi), a citizen's forum established by the Tōkyō metropolitan government during the 1960s that has since played a leading role in monitoring the implementation of consumer and other ordinances (Suzuki 1979:263).

The significance of consumer-related ordinances should not be underestimated. For one thing, those ordinances have tended to be far more proconsumer than comparable statutes are at the national level. In a striking divergence from the Consumer Protection Basic Law, for example, the Tōkyō Consumer Ordinance posits a number of basic consumer rights. As a measure of the government's sincerity in recognizing the existence of those rights, moreover, the ordinance empowers consumers to directly request their executive heads of government to investigate consumer problems (Suzuki 1979:261–63). In some instances, local ordinances have even improved the lot of consumers nationwide by setting new standards for consumer policy at the center—a trend that has been particularly noticeable in product labeling (Kitazawa 1979:42). This feedback relationship among consumer advocates, local government, and the national policymaking system resembles that of the United States following the national anticonsumer movement backlash of the 1980s.

The Basic Law was the initial impetus behind the expansion of local responsibilities regarding the consumer, but the extent to which the localities carried out those responsibilities went well beyond the spirit of the law. This was largely due to the legacy of progressive local governments that came to power in the 1960s and early 1970s and actively fostered direct contact between local decision makers and residents in accordance with the demo-cratic principles embodied in the Local Autonomy Law.[12] Local govern-mental activism in the consumer realm was further encouraged by heightened citizen demands for more comprehensive local consumer poli-cies, particularly after the 1973 oil shock. Over time, Japan's local consumer *kakekomidera* became even more active and influential than those of a com-parable unitary state: Britain.

The expansion of institutional opportunities for movement participation in local policymaking and policy implementation was not without drawbacks for the organized consumer movement. As we noted in earlier chapters, close cooperation between local governments and consumer advocates during the early postwar period was often purchased at the price of the latter's indepen-dence. The post-1968 period was certainly no exception, for as the number of local consumer organs grew during the early and mid-1970s, so, too, did the number of groups that had been "captured" by government. Even for organs that managed to preserve their political independence, the expansion of local governmental facilities led to the co-optation of important movement functions. The fact that local governments now played a major role in the education of "wise" (*kashikoi*) consumers and the provision of consultation services to aggrieved consumers, for example, rendered more or less redun-dant comparable functions in less well endowed consumer organizations. These developments not only weakened organs that were struggling to re-define their organizational raison d'être, but they also increased the incen-tives for consumer advocates to depend heavily on local administrations for resources, advice, and information. At the same time, however, and as the next section illustrates, relations between movement organs and the localities often developed into political alliances that had a significant impact on consumer policy both locally and nationally.

Post-1968 Consumer Movement Strategies

Throughout their early postwar history, consumer organizations had re-lied on a mixture of protest, boycotts, and other market-oriented strategies as they worked to improve the economic and political lot of consumers. Oku Mumeo's position as an Upper House Diet member, occasional mem-bership by consumer representatives on national *shingikai*, and examples of government-movement cooperation on specific consumer issues notwithstanding, the politics of consumer protection were fought mainly from the periphery of the Japanese political system.

As a result of the post-1968 institutionalization of a comprehensive system of consumer protection policymaking and administration, "the periphery" took on new meaning for consumer representatives. Now, as before, consumers were often excluded from the national policymaking processes that were controlled by bureaucrats, conservative politicians, and business interests. Unlike those earlier years of consumer activism, however, advocates enjoyed access to local channels of interest articulation that at times proved invaluable to movement campaigns. Local government—or the "periphery," if we can refer to it as such—had become an integral part of Japanese consumer protection politics.

The importance of the localities during consumer campaigns is rooted in the kinds of resources that were channeled into the organized movement. In accordance with the Basic Law's provisions for governmental support of consumer organizational activities promoting the "stabilization" and "improvement" of consumer livelihoods in harmony with economic development, for example, the localities supplied consumer groups with start-up fees and project grants, resources that in turn spurred the rapid growth of the grassroots movement after 1973. National consumer organizations also benefited from local largesse. Local consumer-related bureaus and consumer centers supplied consumer organizations like Shufuren and Shōdanren with product-testing equipment, space for consumer-related exhibitions, sponsorship for consumer lectures and symposia, and spacious and well-equipped rooms for interorganizational meetings of movement leaders. The main branch of the Tōkyō Consumer Center, for instance, often provided meeting places for advocates and advertising support for issue-specific study groups that were held during Shōdanren's annual National Consumer Rally (Zen nihon shōhisha taikai). In addition, as the next three chapters reveal, the center supplied both national and local advocates with rooms for leadership meetings and organizational support for lectures by prominent lawyers and academics during national political campaigns. Last but not least, advocates occasionally found important allies in their benefactors, a few of whom supported movement goals as private citizens.

Over time, consumer advocates learned through trial and error how to use these local resources to influence policymaking at the national level. By 1993, when the era of one-party dominance drew to a close, those advocates had developed a repertoire that combined traditional social movement strategies like lobbying, litigation, and, to a lesser extent, protest, with more innovative ones reflecting the particular institutional opportunities of the local level. Those strategies can be summarized as follows.

Issue Definition

"Issue definition" (*mondai teigi*), as advocates themselves refer to it, marked the start of consumer advocacy on a particular issue. The strategy, which involved nothing more than identifying consumer problems from the point of view of consumer rights, was implemented by consumer representatives with two policy-related goals in mind: (1) defining the terms of the debate in the policymaking sphere and (2) activating public opinion.

It is important to note that issue definition had only a minimal impact on the agenda-setting stage of the policy process. In keeping with the corporatist features of national consumer policymaking, the government would elevate a consumer issue onto the agenda not so much in response to public pressure as to the appearance of a "focusing event" (Kingdon 1984:104): a crisis, symbol, or related issue that highlighted the political importance of a particular consumer problem to powerful economic and political actors. As the antitrust, anti-deregulation, and product liability case studies attest, focusing events in the consumer realm included foreign legislative trends, foreign trade pressure, the introduction of nonconsumer policies requiring commensurate adjustments in the consumer realm, or, more rarely, the specter of political crisis.

It was only once the agenda had been set and the early policy formulation stage begun that advocates mobilized scarce resources for issue definition and other strategies designed to influence the policy process. Issues were defined in part through the distribution of movement pamphlets, organ newspapers, flyers, and even full-length books to rank-and-file members and other concerned citizens. Normally, this literature consisted of simple descriptions of the problem at hand, definitions of basic terminology, explanations of the connection between the problem and consumer rights, and the alleged role of business and/or government in both contributing to and solving the problem. In some cases, these messages were conveyed through simple cartoon dialogues between disgruntled consumers (many of them portrayed with their fists clenched in anger or with tears running down their faces) and their business and government adversaries.

Consumer advocates were also quite adept at organizing public lectures and study groups on important issues, many of which were held at consumer centers. Organizers used those occasions to promote movement positions, distribute literature, and, in some cases, solicit signatures for petitions. Depending on the issue, those events often attracted audiences of a hundred or more. Needless to say, media cooperation in publicizing such events and covering the consumer message could have a profound effect on issue definition's ultimate impact on public opinion.

Although they did not refer to it as such, American and British consumer organizations also engaged in "issue definition" whenever they publicly defined a consumer-related problem and demanded a solution from business and/or government. Japanese advocates differed from their foreign counterparts in both the length and the intensity of this activity. Whereas U.S. and British advocates tended to pursue this strategy mainly during the early stages of movement campaigns, the Japanese engaged in issue definition with surprising alacrity throughout the policy process and, as I discovered after attending numerous movement meetings, at the expense of public discussions on how to take political action on a particular issue.[13] This was because issue definition doubled as an important consciousness-raising and movement-building device in a country where public awareness of consumer rights was still quite weak.

Although one might expect issue definition to be fairly straightforward, it was a daunting task for many Japanese advocates. As we noted in earlier chapters, consumer organizations are staffed not by politically savvy public-interest lawyers or, as in the case of the NCC in Britain, governmental insiders, but by housewives—many of whom joined the organized movement during the early postwar period and never acquired the legal, economic, and political training that would have enabled them to tackle single-handedly the complex issues that affect modern consumers. In the words of one academic observer, the movement lacked its own "fountain of wisdom" (*chiebukuro*) (interview, Shōda, December 1993). Furthermore, forced by personnel shortages to embrace several issues simultaneously, advocates were often left with little time to devote to one particular issue area and to cover that area well. Thus, they came to rely not only on local government for infrastructural and PR support but also on members of the academic and legal communities to help them define pertinent consumer issues. Issue definition was by necessity a team effort.

The Dissemination of Information

The generation of scientifically derived information to both consumers and policymakers in support of consumer movement positions was an important prerequisite for issue definition in particular and for the activation or manipulation of public opinion more generally. Unfortunately for many consumer organizations, the successful implementation of this strategy was hampered by both the aforementioned resource deficiencies and local governmental co-optation of consumer movement functions since the early 1970s. Unlike the United States's Consumers Union or Britain's Consumers' Association, contemporary consumer organizations simply did not have the money, expertise, or research facilities to carry out extensive scientific research and large-scale public opinion surveys on their own.

Accordingly, many consumer organizations came to rely heavily on the research of lawyers, scholars, foreign sources, the JCIC, local consumer centers, and, to a lesser extent, the Economic Planning Agency and the Fair Trade Commission. Unlike many American and British consumers organizations that have been known to generate their own information, the contribution of Japanese organizations to the public discourse on consumer issues lay in the dissemination of information generated by other organizations to sectors of society that might not otherwise have access to it: housewives who participated in consumer organizations, members of the consumer cooperatives, and citizens with connections to local governments and consumer centers.

Litigation

Since the early 1970s, a number of consumer organizations, including Shufuren, the consumer cooperatives, and Consumers Union, occasionally sued business and government in their efforts to extract concessions for consumers.[14] Although few movement litigants and their supporters expected to win those suits, their courtroom battles often took on the dimensions of a crusade. At the crux of the consumer mission was a determination to instill a sense of injustice, knowledge of consumer issues, and an awareness of consumer rights in the public at large.[15] Litigation, in other words, was largely fought for purposes that lay outside the courtroom.

Consumer advocates were able to accomplish their nonlegal objectives in many instances because consumer lawsuits were closely watched by the media and hence the general public. Media attention can be attributed to the fact that before the early 1990s, lawsuits were an infrequent phenomenon, and for good reason: lawsuits were very difficult to launch and sustain in Japan, as they have been in Britain and many other European countries. Japanese consumer organizations, with their narrow financial base and lack of legal expertise, were barred from easy access to the courts by high filing fees, complicated and time-consuming legal procedures, overloaded court schedules, weak discovery provisions, a shortage of lawyers willing to volunteer their time to consumer movement causes, and, in many cases, a narrow standing to sue.[16] Clearly, the institutional features of the Japanese court system were much less "consumer friendly" than those of the United States, where Ralph Nader and other consumer advocates have frequently used the courts as an alternative—and often highly effective—channel of interest articulation.

During the 1970s, Tōkyō and several other prefectural governments began compensating consumers for the absence of a small-claims court system by subsidizing citizens involved in consumer lawsuits. In Tōkyō, these subsidies have been granted in suits involving small claims and large numbers of plaintiffs (Tōkyōtō seikatsu bunkakyoku 1994:15)—suits in which the value of court-related fees by far exceeds that of damages claimed.[17] In at least one instance, consumer advocacy organizations were also the recipients of this kind of local government largesse.[18] Even with these subsidies, however, litigation was a very costly and time-consuming strategy used only in exceptional circumstances.

Lobbying

Although consumer advocates lobbied policymakers at key points in the policy process, resource constraints, political institutional features, and attitudes in the movement itself weakened the overall effectiveness of this strategy. Unlike business organizations, with their full-time staffs of lobbyists and researchers, consumer organizations lacked the personnel and political shrewdness to carry out sustained onslaughts on conservative politicians and bureaucrats. When given the choice between contacting Diet members or bureaucrats, moreover, consumer leaders normally focused on bureaucrats (interview, Shimizu, July 1999), given their close, day-to-day involvement in the consumer policy process and their access to pertinent information. As a result of staff shortages, by contrast, individual Diet members often failed to follow up on the demands of consumer lobbyists.

Consumer advocates were also deterred by a weak sense of political efficacy under LDP rule. Because they usually associated the party with business interests, why should they waste precious resources on lobbying politicians who would only turn a deaf ear to their demands—assuming, of course, that they would even agree to meet with advocates in the first place? In some instances, advocates felt so powerless over LDP politicians that they failed to take advantage of good lobbying opportunities when they did arise. The LDP's Machimura Nobutaka, for example, noted that four months after taking over as chair of the Policy Affairs Research Council's subcommittee on product liability, he still had not heard from a single consumer representative, even though the organized movement was by that point campaigning full throttle for the law. Antiproduct liability lobbyists from the business community, on the other hand, had showed up on his doorstep within a matter of days (interview, Machimura, June 1993).

Depending on the issue, consumer advocates usually put most of their lobbying eggs into one or more of the following institutional baskets: the Economic Planning Agency, the Fair Trade Commission, and the opposition parties. Once a particular policy process was in full swing and it was deemed strategically feasible to do so, advocates would selectively lobby the economic ministries and the LDP as well.

Since private hearings with powerful bureaucrats and politicians were relatively hard to come by, consumer advocates would often take full advantage of those opportunities by visiting those policymakers in groups, armed with petitions or other indicators of public opinion. Meetings tended to be short and, in some instances, very spur-of-the-moment. During the final stages of the movement to enact a product liability law, for instance, a group of four movement leaders accosted Prime Minister Hosokawa Morihiro in the halls of a governmental office after weeks of frustrated attempts to obtain a formally scheduled meeting with him, thrust a list of policy-related demands into his hands, and asked for his support. After the prime minister acknowledged the advocates with a brief nod and a promise to read over the materials, the meeting ended. Although the encounter had lasted only a few moments, the advocates considered themselves fortunate (interviews, consumer advocates, March and April 1994).

Local Mobilization Activities

Since meetings with high-ranking policymakers were often futile, consumer organizations found innovative ways to pressure those individuals from afar by mobilizing public opinion at the local level—where opportunities for political activism were most abundant—and then channeling the indicators of that opinion to the center. For major campaigns, advocates first set up *renrakukai* (liaison committees) linking advocates at the national level to regional organizations and regional organizations to local groups. Frequently organized under the auspices of both the national and regional chapters of Shōdanren, these committees served as both channels of communication between various levels of the organized movement and mechanisms through which to coordinate the mobilization of grassroots public opinion. Some of those *renrakukai*, moreover, were important conduits of information between members of national *shingikai* and others in the organized movement. As we shall see in the case of product liability reform, advocates used the *renrakukai* to disseminate *shingikai* information to other advocates and, in some cases, to channel local public demands to the *shingikai*. Much of the organizational business of these *renrakukai* was conducted in consumer center facilities.

Local public opinion was targeted in a number of ways through these liaison committees. Advocates, for example, occasionally organized postcard campaigns among local groups affiliated with the co-ops and housewives' organizations, small consumer groups connected to the localities, and individual consumers. The campaigns involved postcard-size *ikensho*, or "opinion statements," written demands for specific policy-related initiatives signed by individuals or consumer groups that were mailed directly to both local and national policymakers.

Petitions were another popular method for channeling local opinion to the center and, like the opinion statements, could include detailed policy recommendations in addition to demands for a policy response to a particular issue. Some of those petitions were sent directly to national policymakers, others to local assemblies for formal resolutions either for or against a particular policy position. Organizers then tallied up the number of local resolutions passed across the country and bombarded national policymakers with the resulting figures. In some cases, as we shall see, these resolutions served as powerful indicators of local public opinion, not to mention an innovative way for the localities, in partnership with citizen activists, to influence national policymaking.

Lectures, seminars, and symposia—many of which were held at the Japan Consumer Information Center and local consumer centers—were another way for *renrakukai* to get the word out to the general public. The audiences at these events, however, normally consisted of individuals who were members of either the co-ops or consumer advocacy organizations. From what I could tell, few of these events attracted unaffiliated consumers. Nevertheless, since many of these movement members then took what they had learned to their local group, *han* or co-op store, or neighborhood, lectures and seminars played an important indirect role in the mobilization of public opinion.

Most of the strategies designed to mobilize local public opinion were extremely labor intensive and not always effective. According to some of my contacts in the organized movement, for instance, opinion statements, petition campaigns, and public lectures were somewhat less successful in rural areas, where consumers tended to be more conservative and less politicized. These challenges notwithstanding, the strategies of mobilizing public opinion through local institutions helped compensate the organized movement for its lack of direct influence in the national policymaking process and of the mass followings that gave many other types of social movement organizations their political clout.

Protest

Although consumer organizations increasingly pursued "assimilative" strategies after 1968—strategies that worked with and through political institutions rather than against and outside them—many advocates still resorted to traditional protest activities at key points in the policymaking process in order to underscore their policy positions and their opposition to governmental practices. Once a consumer-related issue reached the governmental agenda, for example, consumer advocates occasionally demonstrated in the streets of Nagatachō, chanting slogans and, in the case of Shufuren, brandishing placards in the shape of a rice paddle (*oshamoji*). Advocates also made impassioned speeches on crowded street corners, decrying business and governmental recalcitrance on particular policy issues in a manner reminiscent of the confrontational strategies of the early postwar period. Speakers used those occasions to urge passers-by to convey their consumer-related preferences to their elected representatives, sign petitions, read up on movement literature, and the like.

Unfortunately for those who participated in these events, consumer protest did not attract much attention. Although opposition politicians were occasionally on hand to greet and encourage street demonstrations, for example, the media were often conspicuous in their absence. Few Japanese, moreover, stopped to listen as advocates trumpeted their cause through microphones on busy sidewalks. That protest strategies were ignored by most Japanese was symptomatic of the fact that they had become common occurrences in Japanese politics—indeed, it was a rare day that Nagatachō did not bear witness to protest in one form or another.

That said, protest strategies with long historical precedents helped foster a sense of purpose, consumer solidarity, and historical continuity among advocates as they pursued more mainstream (and mundane) forms of pressure politics.[19] Like any other ritual, protest strategies had a greater impact on those who carried them out than on the witnesses to those activities. For these reasons, protest remains even today a small but significant part of the organized movement's strategic arsenal.[20]

This fact was underscored for me in November 1993, when I participated as an "observer" in a Nagatachō demonstration for product liability legislation. More than 2,000 activists, decked out in colorful cotton *happi* jackets adorned with the names of their co-ops or consumer organizations, marched from Hibiya Park to the Diet waving placards and shouting pro-product liability slogans. As we approached the Diet, I asked one of the organizers why there were no journalists from the mainstream press in attendance.

"They never come anymore," he responded, "but that's OK. We don't expect them to show up."

It was a demonstration, in other words, for the demonstrators.

Forming Alliances

The resource deficiencies of consumer organizations made the formation of alliances with other actors in the polity a crucial task, one that supplemented each of the strategies just listed. As sources of information, local scholars and lawyers were particularly important to consumer advocates. But advocates did not always get along with their legal and academic partners, nor were the three camps always capable of maintaining a united front in the political sphere. The relationship between advocates and scholars, for example, tended to be cohesive during the agenda-setting stage of the policy process and in regard to the more straightforward question of whether or not a particular policy should be adopted. But once the process progressed to deliberations on policy-related details, legal scholars, with their far more nuanced view of consumer policy and jurisprudence, would sometimes part company from their consumer allies.

Lawyers, by contrast, would stick with consumer advocates until the bitter end. Increasingly since 1968, the National Bar Association of Japan (Nichibenren), which has a special division devoted exclusively to consumer law, joined forces with consumers on issues that advanced the interests of both parties. All of the twenty or so lawyers who worked with the organized consumer movement on an issue-by-issue basis did so for free. Most, moreover, were exemplary individuals with a passion for advancing the public interest. All in all, lawyers were key allies for the organized movement, so much so, in fact, that many consumer organizations were criticized by both members and outsiders for relying too heavily on their legal allies.

As resource mobilization theorists have pointed out, the presence of allies in the mainstream political system is an important ingredient for social movement success in the policy realm. As the case studies in the second half of this book illustrate, consumer organizations occasionally had fairly influential allies in the Fair Trade Commission, the Economic Planning Agency, and in the persons of Sunada Jūmin and Prime Ministers Miki Takeo and Hosokawa Morihiro, to mention a few. Since links between consumer organizations and these agencies and individuals were not nearly as strong as those between, say, business representatives and MITI, governmental allies might be more accurately referred to as movement "sympathizers." No matter what their title, however, the mere presence of actors in the mainstream policymaking system who were willing to speak out occasionally on behalf of consumer interests lent an air of credibility to the consumer movement stance. When those actors were lacking, as we shall see, exercising leverage over the national policy process became all the more difficult.

Consumer organizations also forged alliances on an issue-by-issue basis with members of the opposition parties. Since the opposition parties did not play a large role in the bureaucracy-centered consumer policymaking process, they were not as valuable to consumer advocates as the Economic Planning Agency, the Fair Trade Commission, or even the odd maverick politician in the LDP, let alone legal scholars and lawyers. Although consumer advocates would cooperate with key individuals in the opposition parties during movement campaigns, it was not until after a bill had been submitted to the Diet for passage that the parties become truly important allies for those advocates.

There was far more cooperation between consumer advocates and local and prefectural politicians. Although subnational legislative assemblies certainly did not have the authority to enact sweeping consumer protection laws, they were able to put pressure on the center by passing resolutions favoring particular policy options. Many of these resolutions, as we noted earlier, were issued in response to petitions assembled by advocates at the local level. Advocates also cooperated with both prefectural and local bureaucrats and assembly members as they deliberated on local consumer-related regulations and ordinances in the fora introduced earlier in this chapter. As illustrated by the movement to enact an information disclosure law,[21] local initiatives could have an impact on policymaking at the center in a manner similar to that of the United States in recent years.

Although labor unions were important allies for consumer advocates in the past, this was no longer the case after the early to mid-1980s. During the late 1940s and 1950s, when the labor movement was reaching its postwar peak in terms of militancy and political influence, consumer advocates and labor unions often worked together to oppose the black market, inflation, and the development of monopoly capitalism. Sōhyō, as we saw in chapter 4, was a founding member of Shōdanren and an important financial donor to that organization until shortly before the labor federation's demise. But as the rise of enterprise unionism encouraged workers to equate their own welfare with that of their companies and the political impact of labor decreased, the alliance between workers and consumers declined commensurately. By the early 1990s, the unions did not often see eye to eye with consumer advocates on consumer goals, many of which threatened to raise corporate costs, nor did they participate in Shōdanren or serve as sources of financial support for consumer organizations.

Consumer advocates also allied with farmers, particularly in regard to food-related issues. In keeping with their common experiences during the immediate postwar period and the nature of the early *seikatsusha* identity, both consumer advocates and members of the farming cooperatives linked arms in defense of food safety and national self-sufficiency in food production. This long-standing alliance had a conservative influence on the positions of many consumer organizations, particularly those like Chifuren whose members are drawn disproportionately from rural and semirural areas (interview, Shōda, December 1993).

Last but not least, one of the most important allies of the organized movement was, of course, the media. In contrast to the United States, where the working relationship between many consumer advocates and journalists has often been very close and mutually beneficial, the relationship was much less fruitful in Japan, particularly toward the last years of the twentieth century. During the heady days of early postwar democratization, consumer campaigns, like most forms of political protest, were eagerly covered by newspapers that had just emerged from the fetters of authoritarian censorship. During the major consumer legislative campaigns of the 1980s and 1990s, however, the media often picked up on consumer issues only after they had reached key positions on the government agenda, ignoring, in the process, earlier movement efforts to draw attention to those issues. There are several reasons for this. First, as we observed earlier, many of the strategies employed by consumer organizations to publicize consumer issues were no longer considered newsworthy. Second, consumer organizations, like other social movement organizations, suffered from a relatively poor reputation in Japan. As a result of the violent student uprisings of the late 1960s and early 1970s, the arguments, data, and activities of social movement organizations were often viewed with suspicion by reporters and editors alike (interview, *Asahi shimbun* reporter, March 1994). Consumer organizations fared somewhat better than many other social movement organizations, primarily because of the conservative image of their most prominent leaders and their reliance on relatively reliable sources of information. Third, few consumer issues were as headline grabbing as, say, environmental pollution, a topic covered much more extensively by the media (Groth 1996:220).

Finally, the media's internal structure contributed to a relatively weak relationship between their members and consumer advocates. The organization of top newspaper journalists into "reporters' clubs" (*kisha kurabu*)[22] connected to individual ministries and parties, for instance, gave newspapers an incentive to rely on official sources, rather than consumer advocates, for information about consumer protection. Those who did cover consumer issues, moreover, normally worked for the less prestigious lifestyle sections of their newspapers and were rotated out of those positions every few years (interview, Hosokawa, July 1999). As a result, there were virtually no journalists in Japan who carved long-term career niches for themselves out of the consumer beat, as many have done in the United States. Consumer organizations in the past thus faced the time-consuming task of cultivating relationships with the media on an issue-by-issue basis.

The Impact of Consumer Organizations
on National Policymaking

With the exception of lobbying, the common denominator of all these strategies was the importance of public opinion as a consumer movement resource. As we noted in chapter 2, public opinion has been a significant resource for the U.S. and British movements as well. As a result of their lack of meaningful access to the formal policymaking process, however, the activation or manipulation of public opinion as a movement weapon against the prevailing powers that be has proved to be far more important in the Japanese case.

The question that then arises is, to what extent did national policymakers in Japan actually pay attention to the demands of public opinion? An anecdote from my fieldwork may offer some insight into this question. A few months before the enactment of the Product Liability Law, I met with a mid-level bureaucrat from the Ministry of Health and Welfare who was involved in the "PL" policy process. When I asked whether his division had received any opinion statements (*ikensho*) from consumers on this issue, he pointed to two fairly large cardboard boxes in a distant corner of his noisy, crowded office, both of which were filled to the brim with postcards. Surprised, I asked if anyone in his office had read them all.

"Well, no," he replied, "We glance at most of them to get a rough idea about what the public wants, but we certainly don't read them for details" (interview, Ministry of Health and Welfare official, February 1994).

His answer, as I later discovered during my interviews with movement advocates, was just what those advocates would expect from a bureaucrat in a major economic ministry. Opinion statements and petitions were valued by bureaucrats and conservative politicians as measures of the public's support for, say, tighter regulatory control over the use of synthetic additives, product liability reform, or stricter antitrust policy. In most cases, however, the actual details of those policy initiatives were decided by bureaucratic experts in cooperation with the ruling party and members of the business community and with virtually no input from consumer representatives.

This is not to suggest that bureaucrats and politicians always paid attention to the wishes of consumers. Indeed, sometimes even the largest public opinion campaigns yielded nothing in the way of policy change. Only when there was dissension in the alliance of bureaucrats, politicians, and business interests did public opinion affect the direction of policymaking. In instances like these, public opinion functioned like a swing vote in the decision-making process, propelling policy debate toward a conclusion when it might otherwise have ended in stalemate. But when the alliance between business and government was close and based on consensus, public opinion had little effect on the policy process. In short, and as the next three chapters show, the impact of consumer advocacy on post-1968 consumer protection policy was ultimately determined by a single variable: the level of cohesiveness among the pro-business interests that controlled the policy process.

Part 2

Case Studies: The Impact of Japanese
Consumer Advocacy on Policymaking

6 The Right to Choose: The Movement to Amend the Antimonopoly Law

> People of the same trade seldom meet together, even for
> merriment and diversion, but the conversation ends in a conspiracy against the
> public, or in some contrivance to raise prices.
> —Adam Smith, *The Wealth of Nations*

There is a commonly held perception on both sides of the Pacific that Japanese consumer advocates care little about high price levels or the economic forces that contribute to them.[1] This is not true. Consumer advocates may be willing to tolerate high prices for the sake of protecting domestic markets and ensuring high-quality products, but they have been quick to oppose price increases that do not fulfill those objectives. There is plenty of evidence to support this observation. Recall that many of the movement's most prominent consumer organizations were established during the Occupation in order to combat inflation, the black market, and price fixing. In 1970, advocates organized a highly successful boycott against the color television industry for the glaring price discrepancy between sets sold at home and those sold abroad. Consumer advocates took the oil industry to court for unfairly jacking up kerosene prices after the 1973 oil shock and put unrelenting pressure on local governments during the 1970s and 1980s to lower utility rates. Finally, the organized movement has been a zealous supporter of stricter antitrust enforcement; in fact, Shōdanren was established in 1956 with that very objective in mind.

Of all the issues that occupied the attention of Japanese consumer organizations during the second half of the twentieth century, reform of the Antimonopoly Law was among the most important. For decades, advocates upheld stronger antitrust enforcement as central to fulfilling the consumer's basic right to a range of product choice at fair prices. Efforts to achieve that goal, however, were often defeated by well-organized businesses and their governmental allies, many of whom looked to cartels and other forms of collusive business practices as inevitable side effects of free-market mechanisms, as well as effective solutions to market inefficiencies.

Antitrust, in short, was an issue that pitted Japanese consumers and producers against each other in a conflict that was inherently biased toward the latter. By 1974, however, a fortuitous confluence of economic and political events sparked the first large-scale legislative campaign in the history of the postwar consumer movement, a campaign that culminated in a modest but nevertheless unprecedented series of antitrust reforms in May 1977.

Why do consumer advocates consider the Antimonopoly Law (AML) to be such an important component of consumer protection in Japan? What have advocates done in the past in order to strengthen the law's provisions? Finally, to what extent did the organized movement influence the 1977 reform process, and how can we explain that influence? Some Japanese scholars have argued that the failure of consumer advocates to organize a large mass movement for AML reform was responsible for the narrowness of the amendments that were ultimately introduced (see, e.g., Kimoto 1981:4). Arguments such as these, I believe, err on two counts. First, by assuming a linear relationship between the consumer movement's input into the policy process and the content of specific policies, they overestimate the potential power of diffuse societal interests over public policy and neglect the institutional and political variables that mediate between movement activism and policy outputs. By the same token, these arguments underestimate the significance of the movement's contribution to the reform process via the mobilization of public opinion. The impact of consumer activism on antitrust policy may have been unavoidably narrow, in other words, but the *nature* of that impact highlights the circumstances in which diffuse societal interests can extract concessions — however modest — from Japan's pro-business political establishment.

The Early Postwar History of Antitrust in Japan

The Antimonopoly Law was enacted in 1947 as an integral part of the Allied Occupation's policy of economic democratization. Designed in part to maintain a competitive economic structure following the planned breakup of the collusive *zaibatsu* and modeled closely on American antitrust statutes, the law rested on the premise that the prevention of monopolies and collusive business practices should be pursued as ends in themselves.

In keeping with this "per se illegal" principle,[2] the law prohibited cartels and interlocking directorates; provided for the breakup of companies (*kigyō bunkatsu*) with market shares exceeding certain specified levels; and imposed strict regulatory controls over company mergers, the admissible shareholding levels of individual companies, and the involvement by Japanese corporations in cross-national business agreements. The quasi-judicial Japan Fair Trade Commission (JFTC) was created to implement the law's provisions (Caves and Uekusa 1975:483), and laws and regulations contradicting the spirit of the AML were amended or abolished (*Nihon keizai shimbun*, May 23, 1974). The result of all this legislative activity was an antitrust statute that was at least as strict as its American prototype.

Taking the Punch out of Antitrust

No sooner had the ink dried on the new law than it was subjected to a round of revisions that underscored the ideas and principles that shaped the outlook of both big business and government toward the statute. As the main thrust of the Occupation's economic policy shifted from democratization to economic reconstruction in response to the onset of the cold war, American authorities feared that the AML's strict provisions would slow the process of economic recovery by obstructing the flow of foreign investment into Japan and the development of trade relations with other countries. Harboring similar concerns, the business community carried the debate one step further by calling into question the law's "per se illegal" premise, arguing instead that it was the *effects* of collusive business practices, rather than the practices themselves, that should be regulated (Misono 1987:47).

Thus, in 1949, the AML was amended under the guidance of the Occupation (Haley 1991b:409) in order to loosen restrictions on interlocking directorates, intercorporate shareholding, and mergers and to relax governmental controls over international business agreements. In 1953, less than a year after the Occupation ended, the conservative government enacted yet another round of amendments. Ostensibly designed to help businesses weather the economic downturn that had followed on the heels of the Korean War, this second set of amendments constituted a clear attack on the "per se illegal" principle that was causing so much consternation in the business community. The revisions included a further loosening of restrictions on intercorporate shareholding, mergers, and interlocking directorates;

the abolition of measures requiring the divestiture of very large companies; the authorization of recession and rationalization cartels; and the exemption of certain resale price maintenance systems from the purview of the law (*Nihon keizai shimbun*, May 23, 1974). To reinforce these changes, a number of other statutory and regulatory measures were initiated during the 1950s, including a reduction of the JFTC's powers (1952), the enactment of several industry-specific laws that authorized the formation of cartels, and the abolition of the Trade Association Law (Jigyōsha dantai hō) which had been enacted during the Occupation to curb the formation of large business organizations. Taken together, these changes were a major victory for the business community.

In sum, the government's increasingly pro-cartel policy constituted, along with protectionist measures, an attempt to shield businesses from the vicissitudes of competitive market forces and to facilitate economic growth as the country struggled to catch up with the West. Despite talk about the need to regulate the effects of oligopolistic industries and collusive business practices in accordance with the "public interest," there was little evidence that the interests of *consumers* had been considered during these early years. For all intents and purposes, the "public interest" had been equated with that of producers.

The Consumer Response

Because the 1949 amendments were introduced before many of Japan's leading consumer organizations had been established, there was no official consumer response to the weakening of the country's antitrust policy until 1953. Even then, the movement's activities were limited to an occasional petition, intramovement research on the issue, and the odd public statement calling for an end to monopolies, cartels, and other collusive business practices restricting consumer access to competitively priced goods in the marketplace (interview, Ono, March 1994). Although these sporadic grumblings were, in the final analysis, politically inconsequential, they did mark the official start of several decades of consumer activism on the antitrust issue.

Despite their severe resource deficiencies and virtual exclusion from the corridors of political power, consumer organizations launched a number of campaigns after 1953 designed to shore up the nation's battered antitrust regime. Shufuren and Seikyōren, for example, organized a long-term movement to revoke the resale price maintenance provisions of the revised AML.

As the decade wore on, consumer protest was widened to include the so-called bypass laws (tekiyōjogaihō) that exempted specific businesses from antitrust enforcement—laws administered primarily by MITI to maintain ministerial control over the stimulation and rationalization of industries and sectors deemed essential to long-term economic growth.[3] Finally, both the housewives' associations and the consumer cooperatives were vocal opponents of the 1957 amendments to the Environmental Sanitation Law (Kankyō eiseihō) and the enactment of the Small and Medium Business Organization Law (Chūshō kigyō dantai soshikihō). Pushed through the Diet by the LDP as concessions to small businesses that felt threatened by the heightened concentration of big business, both laws authorized the formation of price cartels among designated small and medium enterprises.

Although none of these campaigns resulted in victories for the consumer side during the 1950s and 1960s, they were important for several reasons. First, they brought consumer organizations into frequent contact with the relatively sympathetic JFTC, contact that became one of their most important resources during the AML reform movement two decades later. They also highlighted the leading role played by the consumer cooperatives in the reform movement. Although the cooperatives are exempted from the AML, their size and activities are constrained by the Co-op Law. The notion of looser AML enforcement, therefore, raised the specter of unfair competition from large and powerful businesses in the economy (Shōda and Sanekata 1976:260–61). Clearly, the consumer cooperatives were concerned about not only the effects of lax antitrust enforcement on the "consumer interest" but also the threat to their own economic survival posed by collusive business practices. Finally, these early campaigns served as incentives for consumer advocates to fine-tune their definitions of antitrust in relation to consumer protection in a way that appealed to their consumer constituency and distinguished them from their business adversaries. Given the prevailing climate of opinion on antitrust during the 1950s and 1960s, this task must have struck many advocates as a thankless one.

Issue Definition: Antitrust and the Consumer Interest

Interpreting the relationship between the "consumer interest" and antitrust policy in Japan is difficult given the ambiguities of the law itself. Consider, for example, article 1, which outlines the objectives of the statute:

This act, by prohibiting private monopolization, unreasonable restraint of trade and unfair trade practices, by preventing excessive concentration of economic power and by eliminating unreasonable restraint of production, sale, price, technology, and the like, and all other
unjust restriction of business activities through combinations, agreements . . . aims to promote free and fair competition, to stimulate the
creative initiative of entrepreneurs, to encourage business activities of
enterprises, to heighten the level of employment and people's real
income, and thereby to promote the democratic and wholesome development of the national economy as well as to assure the interests
of consumers in general.[4]

This unwieldy preamble raises a number of interpretive problems. What,
for example, is the ultimate aim of the statute, the advancement of free and
fair competition, the promotion of the "national economy" (*kokumin keizai*),
or the advancement of the consumer interest? What, moreover, is the relationship among business interests, consumer interests, and the national
economy? Needless to say, these questions can be answered in a number of
ways. The promotion of free and fair competition, for instance, can be interpreted as a way of protecting consumers. Alternatively, consumer protection can be viewed simply as a positive side effect of the overriding goal of
promoting free and fair competition in the economy. Finally, if we are to
equate the welfare of the national economy with the interests of both producers and consumers, the ultimate aim of the statute could be interpreted
as striking a balance between consumer and business interests.

As might be expected, the ambiguities of the AML sparked a lively debate
in both the academic and policymaking communities over how the law
could and should be interpreted.[5] Consumer organizations, predictably, argued throughout the "issue definition" (*mondai teigi*) stages of antitrust-
related campaigns that the ultimate purpose of the law was consumer protection, and they pressured the JFTC to implement the law in a manner
commensurate with that view. Consumer advocates also became quite adept
at wrapping proposals for AML reform in the language of consumer rights.
Consumers, they contended, had a fundamental right to a range of product
choice at competitive prices, and even though the Antimonopoly Law did
not mention consumer rights per se (indeed, it did not even define what
was meant by the term *consumer*), it was the most important guarantee of
that right.

The business community and its allies in MITI and the LDP approached the statute much differently. As evidenced by the preceding overview of the AML's early history, this camp viewed the law as an unwelcome constraint on business activities. Since abolishing the law altogether was never a viable option for Japan, the pro-business camp settled for an interpretation of the law that equated the "national economy" with business interests and in turn justified the lax implementation of the law's provisions. The JFTC, by contrast, embraced a more flexible interpretation over the years, sometimes bending to the winds emanating from MITI and other times carving an independent niche for itself in the overall scheme of competition policy by stressing the law's consumer-oriented dimensions. The JFTC's shifting stance on antitrust policy, as we shall see, had a major impact on efforts by the organized consumer movement to amend the law.

The 1958 Reform Movement

These conflicting interpretations of the Antimonopoly Law were particularly evident during the government's 1958 efforts to amend the law yet again. Toward the end of the decade, MITI became an increasingly vocal proponent of looser antitrust legislation in response to the growing internationalization of business. Concerned that Japanese companies would not be able to compete internationally as the ministry's controls over capital flows and exchange rates were reduced, MITI sought to minimize restrictions on market concentration in the belief that larger companies would be more competitive in world markets. In response, the Kishi cabinet established the Antimonopoly Law Advisory Council to deliberate on reform and packed it with representatives from the business community.[6] During the deliberations, the council solicited the views of numerous sectors of society and the economy. Of the industries surveyed, the vast majority supported the loosening of AML restrictions on business activities (Misono 1987:104–5). Among the opponents of the proposed changes were consumer organizations, labor unions, agricultural cooperatives, and small and medium enterprises, all of which voiced their support for stricter controls over cartels and for an expansion in the size and investigative powers of the JFTC (Misono 1987:106).

The reform bill that was eventually submitted to the Diet incorporated the demands of MITI and the business community to ease the standards governing the formation of recession and rationalization cartels and further reduce the JFTC's powers (Haley 1991b:414). A number of political developments, however, prevented the bill from getting past the committee stage of the Lower House's deliberations. First, the Japan Socialist Party, which now was much more vocal on the antitrust issue than it had been in 1953, took steps to stall the proceedings. Second, many LDP Diet members from agricultural constituencies attacked the bill in response to intense pressure from farmers, many of whom opposed the formation of cartels in agriculture-related industries for fear that they would result in higher prices for fertilizers, feed, and farming equipment. Third, impatience in the Diet toward the conservatives' alleged high-handedness was running high following the defeat of the government's unpopular attempts to weaken the Performance of Police Functions Act (Keisatsukan shokumu shikkō hō) in 1958. These developments, combined with extensive media coverage of the proposed AML revisions, sparked a public backlash against the government's apparent disregard for the welfare of nonbusiness interests.

Clearly, the governmental and business interpretations of antitrust policy that had underpinned the first two waves of AML revisions had hit a wall, thanks in part to the unrelenting opposition of consumer organizations. In just five years, the organized movement had acquired a higher level of intellectual sophistication on antitrust policy and, with the establishment of Shōdanren in 1956, a somewhat more unified organizational structure. The influence of consumer organizations on policymaking should not be exaggerated, however, since they still lacked governmental allies and direct access to decision-making processes at this time. To make themselves heard, therefore, Shōdanren resorted to pressuring the opposition parties and other interest groups in the polity—to playing, in other words, a role that supported the better-connected opponents of reform. For example, it stayed in close contact with the Japan Socialist Party in 1958, making numerous representations to the party as it conducted research on the antitrust issue (interview, Ono, March 1994). Shōdanren also went to great lengths to convince contacts in Zenchū that a loosening of restrictions on cartels would be contrary to the farmers' interests. Zenchū, which had access to antitrust policymaking through its close ties with rural LDP Diet members, eventually became one of the most vocal and influential opponents of the reforms. Indeed, as the then general secretary of Shōdanren noted, had it not been for consumer pressure, Zenchū might never have become such an influential player in the reform debate (interview, Ono, March 1994).

The government may have failed to defang the AML in 1958, but it did manage to put the JFTC on the defensive. Over the next decade, the JFTC's investigations of alleged violations of the law dropped dramatically as the number of mergers and cartels—many of them encouraged by MITI—multiplied (*Nihon keizai shimbun*, May 26, 1974). The commission also proved incapable of curbing collusive and unfair business practices, as exemplified by its failure in 1959 to reverse a concerted increase in the subscription rates of Japan's major national and regional newspapers, an incident that ignited the largest AML-related consumer campaign to date.

The failure of the newspaper boycott, as we noted in chapter 4, ushered in a period of decline for Shōdanren, which was also struggling with financial and management problems and the declining participation of Sōhyō in consumer movement affairs. Indeed, Shōdanren was having trouble orchestrating consumer activism on *any* issue, let alone those pertaining to antitrust. As a result, the movement in favor of stricter antitrust enforcement lost much of its organizational unity during the early 1960s and was reduced to piecemeal activism by individual organizations on an issue-by-issue basis.

Single-Issue Consumer Campaigns

Surprisingly, it was the JFTC that put the spark back into the consumer antitrust movement. As its power over collusive business practices and the structure of industry dwindled in response to pressure from MITI and the LDP, the commission tried to assert its organizational independence during the 1960s by expanding into consumer administration (Misono 1987:115). The move had the tacit approval of public opinion, which was, at the time, favoring a shift toward a more consumer-oriented society in the context of rising economic affluence. Japanese citizens were particularly affected by the escalation of such unfair trade practices (*futō torihiki hōhō*) as false advertising and product labeling, the attachment of premiums to the sale of consumer products,[7] and various forms of misinformation resulting from rebate practices, commission sales, and canvassing activities.

The JFTC's activism gathered steam after the Nise Canned Beef incident and its subsequent backing of the 1961 Law to Prevent Unjustifiable Premiums and Misleading Representations (Shōda and Sanekata 1976:37). Although the law served the interests of producers as much as it did consumers by putting a brake on excess competition—a move that equated the welfare

of the "national economy" with the interests of both parties—it was nevertheless regarded as an integral part of Japanese consumer protection policy
(Matsushita 1978:71). Heartened by this landmark statute and, by the end
of the decade, the enactment of the Consumer Protection Basic Law, consumer advocates around the country stepped up their activities against high
prices and for stricter antitrust enforcement. By the early to mid-1970s, consumer organizations had become much more adept at cooperating with one
another when working toward common goals (KSS 1997:144–47) and were
actively fostering a climate of public opinion that later became an essential
resource in the movement to amend the Antimonopoly Law.

Public opinion favoring a stricter antimonopoly law was first activated
through mini-campaigns that targeted specific issues relating to the country's
overall antitrust regime. The details of the first campaign—the color TV
boycott—we examined in chapter 4. The success of the boycott was crucial
to the overall AML movement because it boosted intramovement morale and
solidarity, helped strengthen a nascent alliance between the JFTC and consumer organizations, and presented advocates with an unprecedented opportunity to educate consumers about antitrust policy and its relationship to
basic consumer rights. The boycott also laid the organizational groundwork
for subsequent efforts to draw attention to the country's lax antitrust regime,
including opposition to the resale price maintenance system and the juice
and kerosene trials (Shōdanren 1987b:40).

Reform of the Resale Price Maintenance System

The five organizations that had been active during the TV boycott formed
the nucleus of a concurrent movement to attack retail price maintenance
(*saihanbai kakaku iji*) systems. Resale price maintenance (RPM) is a form of
price fixing in which the manufacturer of a particular product sets the prices
charged by both wholesalers and retailers and forces both parties to abide
by those prices. Since the practice tends to stifle competition among sellers
of the same brands of products, the system—which can be likened to a kind
of "vertical cartel"—is considered an unfair trade practice and, therefore, a
violation of the Antimonopoly Law (Matsushita 1978:71). As noted earlier,
however, a limited number of product lines had been exempted from the
AML ban on RPM as a result of the amendments of 1953.

Throughout the 1960s, the number of RPM arrangements expanded as
business struggled to overcome the uncertainties of competitive pricing in

the context of an expanding economy. Some of those arrangements had been approved by the JFTC under the AML's 1953 amendments; others, like the one in place in the color television industry, were implemented illegally.[8] Legal or otherwise, the practice was criticized by scholars, Shufuren, and other consumer organizations for contributing to inflation and violating the consumer's right to product choice at competitive prices (KSS 1997:137). In response to these and other pressures, the Economic Planning Agency launched an investigation into the practice in 1966, and the JFTC soon followed suit. The end result of these inquiries was a reduction in the number of officially designated product lines from nine to five, a total that involved about 120 manufacturers and approximately 3 percent of small retail sales (*Nihon keizai shimbun*, May 10, 1974).

Consumer organs refused to accept what they condemned as a partial solution to the problem and continued to clamor for a total ban on the practice. Accordingly, advocates launched a grassroots campaign urging consumers to avoid shops where RPM systems were in place and to shop in stores that offered discounts (Shōdanren 1987b:41). In late 1973, in the context of mounting inflation, the sharp curtailment of official price fixing in West Germany and Britain, and the JFTC's increasingly activist stance under the new leadership of Takahashi Toshihide, consumer efforts finally bore fruit as the list of officially designated product lines was reduced to three: medicines, books, and cosmetics priced at under 1,000 yen (*Nihon keizai shimbun*, May 10, 1974).

Consumer representatives were faced with a number of very difficult challenges during their campaign to abolish the RPM system. The first involved the issue's low level of popular appeal: "resale price maintenance" is a relatively complicated economic concept that few consumers understood, and it took advocates a great deal of effort to educate themselves on this issue, let alone the public (interview, K. Nakamura, April 1994). Second, given the wide range of products targeted by RPM, it was all but impossible for advocates to organize national boycotts of those products. Boycotts might have been partially successful had the media paid more attention to the issue, but unlike the color TV boycott, RPM was not a headline grabber. Finally, in the case of cosmetics, consumer advocates faced an industry that was closely tied to the center of political power. Shiseidō, for instance, had several influential allies in the LDP who opposed governmental efforts to reform the system. As Shufuren leader Nakamura Kii once commented, with powerful opponents like these, efforts to completely abolish RPM practices were bound to fail (interview, K. Nakamura, April 1994).

In addition to the partial victories of the anti-RPM crusade, consumer activism on this issue contributed to heightened public knowledge on matters pertaining to antitrust. Chifuren, for example, helped raise public awareness of the problems associated with RPM by manufacturing and marketing Chifure, its own line of cosmetics that sold for less than one-tenth the price of comparable products produced by Shiseidō and other mainstream cosmetics companies (Tanaka 1996:130). Second, the RPM issue inspired consumer representatives to expand from five to eight the number of organizations that had formed the nucleus of the color television boycott, a development that was facilitated by the fact that RPM was the focus of virtually no interorganizational disagreement (interview, K. Nakamura, April 1994).

The Juice Trial

Although the Law to Prevent Unjustifiable Premiums and Misleading Representations was extolled by consumer organizations and legal scholars during the 1960s and early 1970s as a pillar of consumer protection, instances of lax enforcement were by no means uncommon. This problem became a headline news item during the early 1970s in response to Shufuren's campaign against the labeling practices of domestic juice manufacturers.

In 1968, Shufuren's product-testing division launched an investigation into canned and bottled juice products on the suspicion that artificial fruit juices were being falsely designated as "100 percent pure." Completed in the autumn of the following year, the tests revealed that of 100 samples marked "100 percent juice," only 3 percent had been accurately labeled. About a fifth of the samples consisted entirely of artificial juices, and the remainder were between 10 and 30 percent pure juice (NHSK 1980:168). To rectify what was clearly a case of deceptive labeling and a violation of the consumer's rights to choose and to know, Shufuren appealed to the JFTC under the Law to Prevent Unjustifiable Premiums and Misleading Representations to have more stringent labeling standards applied to the juice industry.

In March 1971, the JFTC announced that it had concluded a "fair competition agreement" (Kōsei kyōsō kiyaku) with juice manufacturers to clarify the industry's labeling standards, an agreement that failed to satisfy Shufuren's demands. The new standards did nothing to prevent application of the label "100 percent juice" to products consisting primarily of artificial ingredients, while the labels for products containing no real juices merely had to note the presence of artificial flavors and/or colors.

Arguing that the new labeling requirements still deceived consumers, Shufuren, for the first time in its history (Shufurengōkai 1978:4), filed a formal "statement of dissatisfaction" (fuman mōshitate) with the JFTC under the Law to Prevent Unjustifiable Premiums and Misleading Representations that included demands for stricter and more accurate labeling standards. Two years later, the JFTC ruled that Shufuren was not qualified to make such an appeal.[9] In a sudden about-face, the commission then announced that the juice manufacturers would have to comply with stricter labeling standards after all, standards that reflected Shufuren's demands almost to the letter.

Although Shufuren was pleased that five years of activism had finally led to the introduction of proper labeling standards in the juice industry, the blatant disregard with which the commission had handled its formal appeal infuriated the organization. Since ignoring the problem was tantamount to a tacit approval of the JFTC's ruling, the organization appealed the decision to the Tōkyō High Court. Known interchangeably as the Consumer Rights trial (Shōhisha no kenri no saiban) and the Juice trial (Jyūsu saiban), the suit was a test case of the consumer's right to be heard—of the right of average consumers and consumer organizations to appeal administrative decisions pertaining to consumer protection. It was also the largest and most widely publicized example of movement litigation to date.

After several months in court and with the financial and moral support of other consumer organizations and scores of legal scholars and lawyers who served as volunteer counsel, Shufuren lost the case. In its July 1974 ruling upholding the JFTC's decision, the Tōkyō High Court argued that consumer protection was an important aim of the Law to Prevent Unjustifiable Premiums and Misleading Representations and that consumers did indeed have the right to contest administrative decisions that violated the interests of consumers. They did not, however, have the legal standing to demand a repeal of the "fair competition agreement" that had set the juice industry's labeling standards, because the "agreement"—which was not legally binding—had no direct bearing on the interests of consumers (Shufuren dayori, August 15, 1974). Viewing this as yet another example of being "turned away at the gate" (monzenbarai) of "democratic" institutions, Shufuren appealed to the Supreme

Court with the backing of forty influential legal scholars. In 1978, the Supreme Court ruled in favor of the Tōkyō High Court, arguing that neither consumers nor consumer organizations were qualified to lodge formal complaints against administrative measures that aimed to protect the "public interest" (*kōeki*) (Yamane, Seryō, and Mori 1998:70).

As with many issues related to Japanese competition policy, conflicting interpretations of the public interest were at issue in the Juice Trial. While consumer organizations and their legal allies were equating "public" with "consumers" and propounding a "per se illegal" approach to unfair trade practices, juice manufacturers were arguing that since consumers benefited from what was in the best interests of business, trade practices should be deemed "fair" or "unfair" on the basis of their overall effects on the economy. After initially siding with business on this point, the JFTC acknowledged the blatant injustices inherent in the 1971 labeling agreement and ordered the industry to alter its standards in ways that satisfied consumer demands for truth in labeling. Ultimately, then, the controversy was resolved in a way that equated the public interest with the consumer interest.

Legally, however, the case marked a profound defeat for consumer organizations. By arguing that the labeling agreement had nothing to do with consumer interests and that consumers lacked the legal standing to contest the definition of the public interest as implied in the Law to Prevent Unjustifiable Premiums and Misleading Representations, the JFTC and the courts were protecting their authority to have the final say in what constituted the public interest and denying the consumer's alleged right to contest administrative decisions. The case was, in short, an illustration of narrow consumer access to the legal system as an alternative channel of interest articulation—even when access had been provided for by law.

The JFTC's capriciousness in the Juice trial was not entirely unwarranted. The commission has, after all, a mandate under the AML to promote competitive business practices in the economy *and* to protect consumers. These mandates are bound to conflict, particularly given the AML's ambiguous treatment of the relationship between the two. The JFTC's waffling suggests, moreover, that the commission had been caught between its desire to uphold the consumer interest and pressure from the bureaucracy and the business community for lax antitrust enforcement.

Although Shufuren's defeat in the Juice Trial marked a low point for consumer organizations, it did add fuel to the fire for AML and JFTC reform. By symbolizing the JFTC's lack of accountability to consumers like no other incident since the 1959 newspaper subscription rate increase, the issue helped raise the public's consciousness of their rights as consumers and the commission's frequent inability—if not unwillingness—to uphold them. The timing of the Tōkyō High Court's ruling, moreover, proved propitious for the movement to strengthen the Antimonopoly Law. Handed down just as the JFTC was fielding its own proposals for reform, the ruling attracted extensive media coverage and galvanized both consumer organizations and public opinion behind the burgeoning legislative movement.

The Kerosene Trials

Another landmark consumer campaign that overlapped with and fed into the movement to strengthen the Antimonopoly Law involved three lawsuits against Japan's powerful oil cartel. Like the Juice trial, these cases illuminated the difficulties confronted by consumer organizations in the court system and ultimately ended in defeat. More important, the cases had a major impact on public opinion regarding antitrust, at least during the early stages of the reform movement.

The story of the kerosene trials began in 1971, when President Richard Nixon's suspension of the gold standard led to a long wave of yen appreciation. Consumer advocates had hoped that the increasing value of the yen would lead to lower prices for consumers, but this was not to be. In fact, in some instances, the prices of imports actually increased. Meanwhile, MITI, despite a barrage of complaints from consumer organizations, did virtually nothing to correct the problem (Yamane et al. 1998:75).

Consumer organizations were particularly incensed after the 1973 oil shock, when sharp increases in the price of oil contributed to exponential price hikes and a concomitant drop in the supply of such basic consumer necessities as paper, soap, sugar, and toilet paper (Zenchifuren 1986:127). By year's end, newspapers were filled with stories of panicked consumers buying up supplies of "scarce" commodities faster than retailers could keep them on the shelves. Many of those incidents were the result of rumors about pending shortages that had been fanned by the media (NHSK 1980:177–78); others were legitimate responses to retailer hoarding and collusive business practices designed to jack up prices.

Of particular concern to consumer advocates and the JFTC was evidence of a powerful cartel in the oil industry. Taking their cue from the commission's 1973 decision to launch a formal investigation into this matter, a number of national consumer organizations took steps of their own. Their target was kerosene, an increasingly popular and relatively clean energy source used for space heaters. In 1974, Consumers Union (Shōhisha renmei) took the first step by organizing 343 of its members into the "Consumer Association for Getting Back What Was Taken Away" (Torareta mono wo torikaesu shōhisha no kai), a group of plaintiffs that filed suit against the kerosene manufacturers with the Tōkyō District Court in September 1974. Over the next few months, ninety-six members of Shufuren and the Kawasaki Consumer Cooperative filed a similar suit in Tōkyō, followed by 1,654 co-op members in Tsuruoka, Yamagata Prefecture. The plaintiffs in the two Tōkyō cases filed under article 25 of the Antimonopoly Law, and the Tsuruoka plaintiffs, under article 709 of the Civil Code (KSS 1997:153). In each case, the consumer side requested damages amounting to less than 2,400 yen per person (Yamane et al. 1998:75). In all three instances, hundreds of potential plaintiffs were disqualified on the grounds that they no longer possessed the proofs of purchase necessary to prove damages. Those who requested duplicates of their receipts, meanwhile, were often turned down by kerosene retailers who feared retaliation from their suppliers (NHSK 1980:182), a development that simply underscored the extent of the cartel's control over the distribution system.

As often happens in Japan, the trials dragged on for years. In 1981, Consumers Union's case was settled out of court, and by 1989, the other two lawsuits, after a series of appeals that ultimately reached the Supreme Court, had been defeated.[10] In the Tsuruoka case, the Supreme Court argued that the plaintiffs had failed to prove that consumers had suffered damages at the hands of the cartel (KSS 1997:153).

Like the Juice trial, the kerosene trials revealed how difficult it was in Japan to obtain compensation for alleged violations of consumer rights and interests through the court system. In civil cases, the courts often side with large groups of plaintiffs who have suffered severe bodily harm at the hands of business. But when consumers file suit on matters of political principle, the system is far less sympathetic. This discrepancy may be partly attributable to the legal ambiguities and requirements of the statutes under which the suits are filed. Article 25 of the Antimonopoly Law, for example, is unclear about the circumstances under which consumers can sue for damages, nor for that matter, does it specify the meaning of "damages." As a result, relatively few suits have been filed under these provisions.[11] As we shall see in the chapter on product liability, article 709 of the Civil Code involves a heavy burden of proof for the victims of business negligence. In suits involving large numbers of consumers who have suffered clear bodily injury, public pressure and basic morality often take over, and the burden of proof is suspended.[12] In suits pertaining to political principle, by contrast, this virtually never happens.

The myriad barriers confronting consumers-as-plaintiffs notwithstanding, lawsuits were an effective way of educating citizens about their rights as consumers and attracting both media and public attention to consumer-related issues.[13] As one consumer advocate commented, consumer organizations filed suits that were destined to fail simply because there was no better forum for publicizing the status of consumer rights in Japan (interview, Nishikawa, March 1994). Since the mid-1970s, using the courts for these purposes has been further legitimized by local governments, many of which passed ordinances permitting local government subsidies for consumer lawsuits. In the kerosene case filed by Shufuren and the Kawasaki cooperatives, for example, Shufuren received a total of 1.8 million yen from the Tōkyō metropolitan government to help cover some of its legal expenses (Shufur-engōkai 1998:55).

The Movement to Reform the "Cartel Archipelago"

By the mid-1970s, consumer movement opposition to high-priced color television sets, the resale price maintenance system, misleading information in the marketplace, and the oil cartels had contributed to the creation of a growing public constituency in favor of AML reform. Negative fallout from the oil shock also proved propitious for the advocates of reform as mounting evidence of collusion in numerous sectors of the economy exposed the many weaknesses of the existing antitrust regime. Finally, international trends in the context of a rapidly changing world economic environment added fuel to the reform fire. In 1973, both West Germany and Britain strengthened their antitrust laws and regulations, and the United States was in the midst of considering similar reforms. Although the impact of foreign developments should not be overestimated, they served, along with the oil shock, as useful "focusing events" for Japanese reform advocates and lent credence to the argument that strict antitrust enforcement was a trend of the times.

The trigger behind the first official reform bill came in the person of Takahashi Toshihide, a former Ministry of Finance official who became the JFTC commissioner in 1972. Under Takahashi's tutelage, the JFTC took a more activist stance toward the eradication of collusive business behavior and unfair trade practices than at any time since the mid- to late 1950s. Well known for such comments as "our country is a cartel archipelago" (*waga kuni ga karuteru rettō da*) (*Asahi shimbun*, February 6, 1976), Takahashi was almost single-handedly responsible for increasing the number of official JFTC investigations into alleged violations of the AML. In fiscal 1973, for example, the JFTC investigated 194 such cases and took disciplinary action in sixty-six, or 36 percent. Figures for the previous fiscal year were thirty indictments out of 166 investigations, a rate of only 18 percent (Misono 1987:225; see also Sanekata 1986:385). Takahashi was also instrumental in reforming the resale price maintenance system and indicting the oil cartels after the oil shock. As such, he was a key consumer movement sympathizer in the campaign for AML reform.

The fact that oil and consumer prices did not drop after the JFTC's actions against the oil cartels was interpreted by the JFTC as evidence that the AML was in pressing need of reform (*Mainichi shimbun*, July 17, 1974). And so, in December 1973, Takahashi established the Antimonopoly Law Study Group (Dokusenkinshihō kenkyūkai) in the commission to debate reform options. Composed of thirteen members, most of whom were university professors specializing in law or economics,[14] the group released a report in September 1974 that formed the basis of the commission's subsequent proposals.

Since the JFTC lacked the authority to submit bills to the Diet, its recommendations were released in the form of a "tentative proposal" or "draft" (*shian*) that later served as an influential reference point for public and governmental deliberations on reform (Shōda 1982:247). The draft was by no means revolutionary, however. The question of limiting the scope of legal cartels, for instance, was conspicuously absent, as were other points that the JFTC deemed politically unfeasible (Yamamura 1982a:90).

The key recommendations of the JFTC draft were as follows:

1. Company divestiture (*kigyō bunkatsu*): authorization of the JFTC to order the divestiture of companies approaching monopoly or oligopoly proportions, regardless of whether or not those companies were violating the AML.
2. Restrictions on stockholding (*kabushikihoyū seigen*): restrictions of large companies from holding shares valued at more than one-half the total stock value of the issuing company. Corresponding ceilings for financial institutions to be set at 5 percent of the value of the issuing company's stock value.

3. Public disclosure of cost prices (*genka kōhyō*): authorization of the JFTC to require the disclosure of the cost price of products produced by companies engaged in collusive pricing practices.
4. Orders to return to previous price levels (*kakaku no genjō kaifuku meirei*): authorization of the JFTC to order members of cartels to lower their prices to precartel levels.
5. Surcharges (*kachōkin*): authorization of the JFTC to levy surcharges against members of price cartels.
6. Punitive provisions: raise to 5 million yen the maximum value of fines levied against individuals who knowingly violate the AML.

The Ruling Triad Responds

The JFTC's proposal evoked strong opposition from the big-business community. In May 1974, a few months before the draft was formally released, Keidanren, under the leadership of Dokō Toshio, publicly expressed misgivings about the reform process (*Sankei shimbun*, May 30, 1974) and quickly established itself as the center of AML-related debate in the business community. Keidanren subsequently established its own in-house study group to further clarify its position, dispatched teams of researchers to Europe to study foreign antitrust systems, and solicited the opinions of industry representatives. About a month after the JFTC's draft was released to the public, the organization publicized its opposition to all but the recommendation for higher surcharge ceilings. It then went on to attack the JFTC by proposing that the commission be placed directly under the jurisdiction of an economic ministry and called for the formation of a cabinet-level committee to coordinate future deliberations on reform (*Yomiuri shimbun*, October 16, 1974). The latter request was ultimately granted.

Business leaders found a powerful ally in MITI under Nakasone Yasuhiro and, after December 1974, Komoto Toshio. Both the ministry and Keidanren opposed the JFTC draft on the grounds that greater JFTC interference in business affairs—particularly pricing decisions—would constitute a violation of free-market principles (*Mainichi shimbun*, September 28, 1974), prevent firms from responding effectively to changes in the global economy, and detract from the ministry's ability to implement industrial policy (*Nihon keizai shimbun*, July 5, 1974).

Predictably, consumer organizations took issue with these arguments by accusing MITI and Keidanren of denying the link between collusive business practices and high prices (*Nihon keizai shimbun*, July 28, 1974) and ignoring the growing public constituency in favor of AML reform. As revealed by well-publicized surveys conducted by both consumer organizations and the press, their arguments were backed by public opinion (Misono 1987:232).

In response to these public opinion indicators, Keidanren softened the tone of its rhetoric. On July 24, 1974, Dokō announced at a press conference that the organization's earlier statements opposing the JFTC draft did not reflect Keidanren's formal position. Subsequent commentary on AML reform was accordingly much more discreet and cautious, with only passing mention of specific recommendations or positions (Misono 1987:232). Keidanren was clearly concerned about a public backlash against the business community and was trying to strike a more conciliatory posture toward the advocates of reform. But its softer public stance did not signal the end of its opposition to AML reform. Rather, it signified its withdrawal from the public arena and an increased reliance on behind-the scenes efforts to block the passage of the proposed amendments.

The LDP was also sensitive to public opinion, but its initial attempts to appease it were tempered by conservative elements in the party which sided with MITI and big business in their opposition to stronger antimonopoly legislation. The party began deliberating on the issue just as the JFTC was preparing to announce its tentative draft. Headed by Kuranari Tadashi, a member of the (anti-reform) Nakasone faction and himself an opponent of reform, the intraparty meetings on AML uncovered strong opposition to the JFTC proposals (*Sankei shimbun*, September 19, 1974). At the same time, however, some party leaders were viewing the public's growing intolerance of cartels and inflation as a future electoral threat (*Mainichi shimbun*, November 29, 1974), while others were swayed by calls from the small-business community, as represented by the Tōkyō Chamber of Commerce and Industry, for stronger antitrust regulations (*Nihon keizai shimbun*, July 28, 1974). The LDP eventually conceded to public demands for action by setting up the Special Investigative Committee on AML Reform (Dokkinhō kaisei tokubetsu chōsakai) under the leadership of Yamanaka Sadanori and giving it the task of drafting a reform bill (*Mainichi shimbun*, November 29, 1974). It was a classic case of the positive impact of public opinion on a divided elite. As luck would have it, however, the party was *too* deeply divided to come to a consensus on the reform issue. This meant that for the time being, at least, the terms of the debate would be set by the forward-looking JFTC.

Miki Takeo's ascension to the prime ministership in December 1974 helped strengthen pro-reform elements in the ruling party. Throughout his tenure as prime minister, Tanaka Kakuei had assumed a rather passive stance on the issue of amending the AML (*Sankei shimbun*, September 19, 1974), refusing to declare himself either for or against reform. Miki, however, responded to the public's growing antibusiness sentiments and disillusionment with his predecessor's scandal-ridden government by making reform a focal point of his economic policy. Miki's clear declaration of support for a stronger Antimonopoly Law partially discredited the opposition of conservative LDP politicians and marked the start of more effective intraparty negotiations (*Asahi shimbun*, December 6, 1974). By the end of December, a roundtable (Dokkinhō kaisei mondai kondankai) had been set up in the Prime Minister's Office to research the issue and make recommendations for a cabinet-sponsored bill. What was still unclear, however, was the extent to which business interests would agree to compromise on the details of reform.

Consumers React

The announcement of the JFTC's proposals provided consumer organizations with a window of opportunity to mobilize further for change. Since advocates lacked direct access to the policy process through institutionalized links with the LDP and the bureaucracy, they were reduced to nonmainstream channels of interest articulation. As with all consumer campaigns, this involved the mobilization of public opinion through local petition drives, lecture series, the distribution of books and pamphlets, and an occasional street demonstration. Unlike subsequent large-scale movements, however, consumer organizations were still learning how to carry out these tactics within the institutional infrastructure of the localities. This was 1974—only six years after the enactment of the Consumer Protection Basic Law—and the formal and informal mechanisms linking consumer organizations to the localities were still being established. Consequently, there were fewer instances of working through local bureaucratic facilities to reach the citizenry or pressuring local assemblies into issuing resolutions in favor of reform. During the mid-1970s, consumer activism was focused on mobilizing public opinion at the grassroots level, but the tactics designed to achieve that objective were implemented as much on the street and in the confines of consumer organizations themselves as through local government institutions.

Fortunately for consumer advocates, public opinion was already favorably disposed in 1974 toward the idea of reform as a result of the single-issue campaigns pursued by consumer organizations in the past and in response to the economic effects of the oil shock. Indeed, the oil shock may have been the best thing that could have happened to the pro-reform movement. By hitting individual consumers in the pocketbook, the event enhanced public awareness of both cartels and unfair business practices and helped create a climate of public opinion that was susceptible to manipulation by consumer advocates.

In large consumer federations like Shufuren and Chifuren and in the consumer cooperatives, the organizational apparatuses for tapping into and aggregating the opinions of individual consumers had long been in place and were quickly activated at both the local and national levels. As the president of the Tōkyō chapter of Chifuren observed, housewives were banding together with little prompting from the organization's central leadership to discuss the impact of cartels on prices and how strengthening the AML would improve the lot of consumers (*Yomiuri shimbun*, September 20, 1974). Political and economic circumstances, in other words, had transformed an otherwise obscure issue into one of immediate concern to average housewives, thereby sparking the growth of a movement that was as much the product of grassroots (*kusa no ne*) activism as skillful leadership from the center (*chūō shidō*). This kind of spontaneous activism declined sharply in subsequent years as consumer issues became more and more complex and divorced from the daily lives of average consumers.

Although public opinion was stoked with relative ease, articulating that opinion to central policymakers proved challenging. Fortunately, since the oil shock had transformed the issue of reform into a headline issue, the media provided ample coverage of the activities of consumer advocates and portrayed the organized movement as a whole as the most prominent and active advocate of reform next to the JFTC (*Tōkyō shimbun*, June 25, 1975). At the same time, consumer advocates felt a need to lobby policymakers directly, a tactic that was carried out with mixed results.

Contacts with the JFTC proved to be the most valuable inroad into the policy process, particularly during the early stages of the debate. Shortly after assuming his post as commissioner, Takahashi set out to enhance the power of the JFTC and to establish a popular constituency in support of his efforts. His ongoing dialogue with top consumer leaders was an important part of this strategy. Consumer leaders spoke highly of the commissioner and his willingness to meet with them regularly and at length (interview, K. Nakamura, April 1994), and they took advantage of those meetings to lodge petitions with the JFTC (*Nihon keizai shimbun*, September 25, 1974).

Given the strength of the opposition to AML reform, consumer organizations felt that their best strategic option was to rally behind the JFTC in a unified show of support (interview, Ono, March 1994; *Nihon keizai shimbun*, September 19, 1974), even though they had hoped the commission would do far more to meet the demands of the organized movement. Consumer advocates had lobbied the commission to include the following stipulations in its tentative draft: (1) the complete abolition of resale price maintenance systems, (2) a total ban on recession and rationalization cartels, (3) the introduction of mechanisms to enhance citizen participation in JFTC investigations,[15] and (4) access to quick and adequate consumer compensation for damages incurred as a result of AML violations.[16] Since the politically astute commission was intent on drafting a moderate proposal that would not completely alienate powerful forces in the government and business community, these pro-consumer stipulations were shelved for the time being.

In sharp contrast to the JFTC, MITI was often impermeable to consumer lobbying efforts. Even though the relationship between MITI officials and consumer representatives had never been a close one, it was at a particularly low ebb when Nakasone headed the ministry. Nakasone never distinguished himself as a champion of the consumer interest, and his reluctance to meet with advocates was a source of anger and frustration among consumer advocates.[17] Predictably, meetings between the two sides were few and far between.

Consumer ties to the LDP were also weak and ineffective, which was hardly surprising given the party's strong links to the business community. Consumer advocates did, however, manage to cultivate some useful contacts with opposition politicians who looked to AML reform as an opportunity to check the power of big business and score points against the LDP. With the exception of the Japan Communist Party, all the opposition parties conducted intraparty discussions on AML reform, many of which were attended by consumer representatives. Several of the parties also submitted reform bills of their own to the Diet during the early months of the debate (*Sankei shimbun*, September 27, 1974). These bills—like most private members' bills fielded by the opposition—had little chance of passing, but they did help advance the consumer cause by raising the public's awareness of the issue.

Finally, consumer organizations had an enthusiastic advocate in Prime Minister Miki. Of all the postwar prime ministers, Miki Takeo was one of the most accessible to consumer representatives. His support for the development of a more consumer-oriented society, moreover, struck a responsive chord in a public that was extremely disillusioned with the scandal-ridden

Tanaka administration. Immediately after assuming his post, Miki announced his support for a stronger Antimonopoly Law and pressed for the inclusion of divestiture procedures, price disclosure requirements, and restrictions on stockholdings and mergers (*Mainichi shimbun*, October 15, 1974). More important to consumers interested in fulfilling their right to be heard, he also recommended the incorporation of measures to strengthen the JFTC's accountability to private citizens and to facilitate access to compensation in the event of consumer damages caused by violations of the AML. Miki was without a doubt the organized movement's most influential governmental ally; unfortunately, however, he lacked the power to push forward his vision of reform.

Defeat of the Five-Party Reform Bill

Prime Minister Miki campaigned long and hard to draw up a cabinet bill that would incorporate these pro-consumer elements but, in the end, was left with a bill that did not even meet the standards of the more modest JFTC proposal. The processes leading up to the bill's adoption and its aftermath were telling illustrations of the extent of business, bureaucratic, and LDP opposition to AML reform (*Nihon keizai shimbun*, March 8, 1975), not to mention the internal dynamics of *shingikai* politics.

At the center of the deliberative process was an eighteen-member roundtable committee established by Miki in the Prime Minister's Office in December 1974. Two veteran consumer representatives sat on the committee: Tanaka Satoko, president of the Tōkyō chapter of Chifuren, and Nakamura Kii, vice-president of Shufuren. Initially, the two women called for a reform bill that would incorporate not only the JFTC draft provisions but also measures to strengthen consumer redress procedures and to abolish cartels and the resale price mechanism system. After carefully weighing the balance of political forces in the committee, however, they and about seven other members, several of whom represented organized labor, threw their support behind the JFTC proposal. Business representatives, meanwhile, comprising roughly a third of the membership, opposed the JFTC proposal and pressed for a weakening of the commission's authority to interfere in the economy (*Mainichi shimbun*, September 25, 1975). The remaining third, consisting mostly of legal and economic scholars, supported reform in principle but opposed any amendments that would give the JFTC the authority to interfere in the pricing mechanisms of private firms. Even though a majority of the committee supported some sort of reform, the lack of consensus resulted in a stalemate that enabled pro-business elements to seize the initiative in other deliberative venues in the LDP and the economic ministries. It was, from the vantage point of consumer politics, a typical turn of events.

Of particular importance were the results of MITI's intraministerial deliberations on reform. In its own draft bill, the ministry spelled out the limits of its willingness to compromise with the pro-reform camp (*Nihon keizai shimbun*, March 2, 1975). The cabinet bill that was officially adopted in April 1975 met MITI's demands almost to the letter, thereby marking a significant departure from the provisions of the JFTC draft: price disclosure and reversion stipulations were removed; restrictions on stockholding were loosened (Misono 1987:246); and the amounts that could be charged in criminal fines were lowered. The authority of the JFTC to order the divestiture of large businesses, moreover, was emasculated by the requirement that the commission confer at least twice with an economic ministry before taking such steps (*Mainichi shimbun*, April 15, 1975).

Consumer organizations and much of the scholarly community condemned the cabinet bill as a complete sellout to MITI and business interests. Tanaka and Nakamura complained that the interests of consumers had been completely overlooked (*Nihon keizei shimbun*, March 5, 1975) and the alternative opinions expressed by the prime minister's committee all but ignored (*Asahi shimbun*, May 17, 1975). The two advocates organized a press conference to express their disgust with the results of the bureaucratic deliberations, held a private meeting with Prime Minister Miki, and then boycotted a party held at the prime minister's residence to celebrate the drafting of the bill (*Shufuren dayori*, May 15, 1975; interview, K. Nakamura, April 1994).

Diet deliberations, which began in May 1975, were immediately mired in stalemate. As expected, the opposition parties denounced the bill as "deboned" (*honenuki*) and demanded revisions. Prime Minister Miki refused to comply on the grounds that amending the bill would unravel the governmental constituency that backed it (*Mainichi shimbun*, May 9, 1975). A number of prominent conservative LDP politicians, meanwhile, attacked the bill as too tough on business (*Asahi shimbun*, May 15, 1975). Unfortunately for the pro-reform camp, the bill was shelved in late June in response to more pressing legislative priorities (*Asahi shimbun*, June 20, 1975).[18]

The move brought an immediate outpouring of grassroots consumer protest in the form of street demonstrations, signature drives, and *ikensho* campaigns. The uproar had the effect that consumer representatives had hoped for: in a sudden about-face, LDP politicians in the Lower House Commerce Committee picked up the issue once again and cobbled together a compromise agreement with members of the opposition parties. The so-called Five-Party Reform Bill that was passed unanimously by the Lower House and submitted to the House of Councilors on June 24 incorporated several of the opposition parties' demands, including an increase in the surcharge ceiling and an end to the requirement that the JFTC inform a pertinent economic ministry before launching an investigation into illegal business behavior. (The JFTC was still obligated to confer with an economic ministry before implementing divestiture measures.) In addition to the bill, the Commerce Committee passed a resolution calling for future investigations into measures that would facilitate consumer access to the courts when filing civil suits under the AML (*Mainichi shimbun*, June 25, 1974).

Consumer organizations rallied behind the Five-Party Reform Bill as an acceptable compromise. Fearing that the bill would not make it through the Upper House, where LDP opposition to antitrust reform was more deeply entrenched, Shōdanren orchestrated an intensive lobbying campaign of individual politicians. Their efforts, however, were in vain. When the chamber turned to other pressing items of legislative business, the bill died in committee.

The Five-Party Reform Bill may have failed, but its legislative history speaks volumes about the extent of consumer movement influence over the public policy process. The principal contribution of consumer advocates to the reform movement was to keep the stalemate-ridden deliberative process moving despite strong pressures from the pro-business camp to abandon it altogether. Advocates accomplished this task by stimulating a climate of public opinion that was already favorably disposed toward reform; putting pressure on policymakers at key points in the policy process; allying with individuals like Miki and Takahashi who, despite their political weaknesses, were vocal proponents of reform; and standing firmly behind the JFTC's proposal, even though that proposal fell far short of the movement's expectations. These tactics proved effective in the context of conflict between small and big business interests and among LDP politicians over the desirability of reform. The outpouring of consumer protest in cooperation with the opposition parties also appeared to influence the content of the Five-Party Reform Bill, which came closer to meeting consumer demands than previous government drafts had. Consumer influence should not be exaggerated, however, for as subsequent stages of the legislative process revealed, pro-business representatives were willing to go only so far in their efforts to compromise with organized consumer interests.

Strike 2

With the failure of the Five-Party Reform Bill, the movement to amend the Antimonopoly Law slipped into political dormancy. Prime Minister Miki, however, refused to give up on what was tantamount to a personal mission and announced in January 1976 that he would push to have a similar bill enacted before the year was out. Consumer organizations and their allies in the opposition parties and the academic community hardly reacted to the news. Now that the public—which was increasingly preoccupied with the effects of the recession—no longer harbored the strong antibusiness sentiments of the previous year (*Asahi shimbun*, January 24, 1975), the time was simply not ripe for another full-scale consumer campaign.

If anything, the LDP's opposition to AML reform had intensified during the winter of 1975/76. Fearing a loss of political funding from big business in the wake of stricter political finance regulations, the party was more sensitive than ever to JFTC interference in private business practices and was contemplating further proposals to weaken the commission's powers (*Asahi shimbun*, January 24, 1975). But after Miki caved in to conservative elements of his party and agreed to tone down his position on reform, the LDP's Special Investigative Committee on AML Reform agreed to take up the issue once again. The committee's recommendations formed the basis of a cabinet bill that was much softer on business than the Five-Party Reform Bill, in that it provided for a decrease in the JFTC's investigatory powers and eliminated all divestiture provisions (*Asahi shimbun*, May 26, 1976).

Submitted to the Lower House in late April 1976, the bill was doomed from the start. The product of LDP politicians who opposed reform and yet recognized the need to go through the public motions of settling an issue that was of extreme importance to the prime minister, the bill was condemned by opposition politicians, many of whom refused even to consider it during committee deliberations (*Asahi shimbun*, April 16, 1976). The opposition parties retaliated by jointly resubmitting the Five-Party Reform Bill shortly after the cabinet version was introduced to the Diet (*Asahi shimbun*, October 22, 1976). In the meantime, consumer organizations and their academic allies issued joint declarations to the press, the JFTC, and the prime minister opposing the government bill and called for the enactment of the Five-Party Reform Bill (*Asahi shimbun*, April 28, 1976).

The ability of the more conservative elements in the LDP to dictate the terms of the debate at this stage was the result not only of the effects of the recession but also of the sudden resignation of Takahashi Toshihide as chairman of the JFTC in February 1976 for reasons of declining health. Takahashi had been the standard bearer of AML reform in the government and one of only a handful of top governmental officials who had spoken out on behalf of the consumer interest. His departure, therefore, marked the loss of a very important ally for both consumer organizations and Prime Minister Miki. Takahashi's successor, Sawada Yasushi, was more accommodating to the wishes of the business community and sided with the conservative elements of the LDP in early 1976 by supporting a watered-down version of the Five-Party Reform Bill (*Nihon keizai shimbun*, December 9, 1976). Even though the resulting cabinet bill would have introduced only minor changes to the country's antitrust policy, it was too unpopular to gain passage. In November 1976, after weeks of stalling by the LDP, the bill was shelved.

"Doing It Honestly the Third Time Around"

Unlike most consumer protection issues, the issue of antitrust reform was so politicized by the mid-1970s that it became an electoral issue.[19] Publicizing the death of the government's second reform bill as a sign of LDP indifference to the welfare of consumers, all the opposition parties included reform in their campaign platforms during the December 1976 Lower House election. Although it is unlikely that the issue affected actual voting behavior, the results of the ballot were nevertheless auspicious for the future of reform insofar as they strengthened political parity in the Diet between the LDP and the opposition parties and forced the conservatives to cooperate with the opposition more than before. Recognizing both the public's demand for change and the limitations inherent in the new political alignments, Prime Minister Fukuda Takeo voiced his strong support for the speedy enactment of a reform bill shortly after taking office (*Nikkan kōgyō shimbun*, January 17, 1977; Sanekata 1986:395). AML reform had become a test case of the government's professed commitment to political change and the welfare of consumers.

The strengthened position of the opposition parties was also responsible for the LDP's willingness to adopt a bill that was tougher on business than the one that had been submitted to the Diet in 1976. Many observers were surprised by this development because in the context of the lingering recession, enthusiasm for AML reform was at a low ebb in the LDP (*Nihon keizai shimbun*, January 9, 1977). The big-business community, hoping that the Fukuda government would adopt a much more pro-business stance than its predecessor, was particularly taken aback by the new prime minister's activism on the issue (*Nikkan kōgyō shimbun*, January 17, 1977). Analysts suspected that Fukuda and his followers were trying to shore up their public image in anticipation of the Upper House elections scheduled for the following summer (*Nihon keizai shimbun*, January 9, 1977).

To highlight the new government's determination to make AML reform a reality, the motto "doing it honestly the third time around" (*sandome no shōjiki*) was attached to the deliberative process and was quickly disseminated by the press (*Nihon keizai shimbun*, January 9, 1977). In the spring of 1977, after extensive behind-the-scenes negotiations with the opposition parties and attempts to win over the big-business community (*Asahi shimbun*, March 13, 1977), the Fukuda government came up with a series of proposals that, given the inclusion of limited divestiture measures and restrictions on company stockholding, were accepted by the proponents of reform as a major improvement over the second Miki cabinet bill (*Nihon keizai shimbun*, April 1, 1977). The proposals did not, however, meet with the approval of MITI officials, who demanded the insertion of stipulations requiring that the JFTC consult with the economic ministries before implementing such measures. A heated turf battle consequently ensued between MITI, which was trying to assert its ultimate control over the structure of the economy, and Fukuda, who feared that conceding to MITI's demands by weakening the JFTC would provoke a major confrontation with the opposition parties and hurt his already dwindling popularity (*Nihon keizai shimbun*, April 12, 1977). MITI's opposition had the effect of delaying the deliberative process, even though the other ministries supported Fukuda's proposals (*Nihon keizai shimbun*, April 6, 1977).

As a concession to MITI—whose support was of fundamental importance to the smooth implementation of reform legislation—Fukuda and the other ministries agreed to insert measures demanding close consultation between the JFTC and MITI before divestiture procedures were carried out. The cabinet then formally adopted a bill that was submitted to the Lower House in

April. Although the opposition parties considered the legislation a retreat from the Five-Party Reform Bill, the bill was nevertheless passed by a unanimous vote on May 13, together with a resolution calling for close cooperation between MITI and the JFTC in the implementation of antitrust policy in order to placate the "crisis mentality" of the big-business community (*Nihon keizai shimbun*, May 13, 1977). In the Upper House, where the resistance of LDP politicians to reform was still much more deeply entrenched than in the Lower House, a number of provisions were added to the bill that effectively weakened the JFTC's divestiture powers and called for the coordination of antitrust policy and industrial policy. Both stipulations were concessions to big-business demands for the flexible implementation of the law (*Asahi shimbun*, May 27, 1977). On May 27, the bill was passed almost unanimously (Sanekata 1986).

Consumer organizations had little impact on the actual details of this round of legislative decision making, but they were instrumental in keeping the process alive. The organizations were certainly conspicuous in their activities, sending petitions to the Diet and making statement after statement to the media demanding the enactment of a reform bill. The aim of all this activity was to get something—indeed, anything—passed. As the president of Shōdanren remarked to the press at the time, "If something, somehow, is not passed at this time," the opportunity for antitrust reform would be lost forever (*Mainichi shimbun*, February 24, 1977).

The amendments to the AML that were introduced in 1977 included (1) surcharges on unfair profiteering by cartels, (2) limited divestiture provisions, (3) the authorization of JFTC investigations into parallel price increases by oligopolies, (4) increased fines for AML violations, and (5) stockholding restrictions (Caves and Uekusa 1975:479). In hindsight, observers disagree as to the effectiveness of these provisions. Some analysts view them as an "epoch-making" development in the history of the law (Matsushita 1993:84) and point to the decline of cartels in the economy since 1977 as proof that the amendments made a difference (Matsushita 1993:482). The increase in the number of reports of illegal activities by the public to the JFTC (Matsushita 1993:482), moreover, suggests that the JFTC's accountability to consumers had been enhanced and that public awareness of AML-related problems had risen as a result of the reform movement. In other respects, however, the revisions met with public criticism. Stipulations requiring close consultation between the JFTC and MITI, for example, were blamed for the weak enforcement of many AML provisions. Finally, consumer advocates were dissatisfied because the public still lacked the power to obtain quick and effective redress for AML violations. In response to these problems, a number of consumer advocates continued to pay close attention to the implementation of Japanese antitrust policy and to press for further revisions in the Antimonopoly Law (interview, K. Nakamura, April 1994).

Conclusion

The reform of the Antimonopoly Law during the 1970s was a unique case in the history of Japanese consumer politics. Most consumer-related legislation and regulation is hammered out primarily in the bureaucracy with only *pro forma* input by societal interests. The highly politicized AML reform battle, however, involved a wide cross section of the polity and was carried out in a diverse array of institutional settings, both formal and informal.

As such, the story of AML reform highlights the conditions under which diffuse societal interests can wrest concessions from the political powers that be. To reiterate one of the themes of this study, the key to success lies not in the size or wealth of those societal interests but in the nature of informal alliances among policymakers in decision-making processes. This observation is borne out by the three stages of the AML amendment process summarized earlier. As we saw, consumer advocates during Prime Minister Miki's reign campaigned vigorously for AML reform yet achieved little as a result of big business's hold over Miki and other reform elements in the LDP. Under Prime Minister Fukuda, on the other hand, advocates achieved far more in terms of policy outputs, even though levels of consumer mobilization had remained more or less the same. What made a difference during this later stage of the reform process was a decrease in popular support for the LDP during the 1976 Lower House election. This loss forced LDP leaders to abandon some of their more stalwart big business allies and to compromise with pro-consumer elements in the Diet and the polity. A breakdown in the cohesiveness of the government-business alliance, in other words, had increased the political leverage of the organized movement.

Postscript

Antitrust policy, as Robert A. Katzmann points out with reference to the United States, can serve one or more of the following interrelated purposes: (1) the attainment of heightened levels of business performance in the economy, (2) limitations on the power of big business, (3) the guarantee of fair standards of business conduct, and (4) the nurturing of competitive market processes as an end in itself (Katzmann 1980:156). This framework serves as an illuminating road map for understanding not only the shifting priorities of Japanese antitrust policy in response to specific political and economic circumstances but also the unique features of Japanese attitudes toward this important component of capitalist economies.

During the early Occupation period, as part of an overall policy of economic democratization, the primary objectives of antitrust policy were limiting firm size and promoting competitive market forces. From the late 1940s through the 1950s, as the nation prioritized economic growth, the emphasis shifted to the achievement of higher levels of economic performance. In the 1960s, when the side effects of economic growth became politically intolerable, the guarantee of fair business standards became a major concern.

Consumer representatives have long recognized the impact on consumer protection of restricting company size and guaranteeing fair business standards. By preventing the growth of monopolies and oligopolies in the marketplace and prohibiting unfair business practices, consumers stand a better chance of gaining access to a wider range of competitively priced goods and services and to the information needed to make wise consumer choices. Consumer advocates have consequently lobbied long and hard for stricter antitrust enforcement in both these areas, as well as for greater accountability by the JFTC to consumers and more effective redress mechanisms for the victims of AML violations.

In contrast to their counterparts in the United States or Britain, however, Japanese consumer organizations have never been enthusiastic supporters of antitrust policy as a guarantee of competitive market forces (Shōda 1982:243). Instead, Japanese advocates, like their business adversaries, have harbored deep-seated misgivings toward unfettered competition and have downplayed the role of antitrust policy in this area. This inherent distrust of free-market forces is certainly not limited to the antitrust realm. As the next chapter shows, similar sentiments conditioned the organized movement's stance toward deregulation in particular and the consumer-government relationship more generally.

7 The Right to Safety: The Movement to Oppose the Deregulation of Food Additives

Hiwasa Nobuko is in many ways a typical Japanese consumer leader. Like thousands of other housewives, she joined a consumer cooperative during the mid-1970s out of concern for the nutritional well-being of her children. Troubled by what she termed the "distortions" (*yugami*) of rapid economic growth and the dearth of information about the food she and her family consumed, Mrs. Hiwasa was attracted to the co-ops by their commitment to foods that were free of agricultural chemicals and synthetic additives (interview, Hiwasa, February 1994). Drawn to political activism by interest in these and other consumer issues, she was soon playing a major role in movement campaigns to ban the use of synthetic food additives. Today, Mrs. Hiwasa is secretary-general of Shōdanren, the national umbrella organization that coordinates many of the country's consumer campaigns.

Mrs. Hiwasa's ascension to the pinnacle of consumer movement power symbolizes the leading role of food safety in Japanese definitions of the consumer interest. Throughout the postwar period, consumer organizations campaigned tirelessly for comprehensive food-labeling standards, strict regulatory controls over the use of synthetic additives in foods, limits on the usage of agricultural pesticides, and a ban on imported foods treated with postharvest chemicals. Some advocates have even tolerated high food prices for the sake of maximum safety,[1] a stance that many Americans, with their penchant for convenience and low prices, find difficult to understand. The importance of food purity to the organized movement was further highlighted by the profound crisis of confidence that it suffered during the early

1980s following its failure to reverse the deregulation of eleven controversial synthetic additives and to strengthen the nation's bureaucratic system for guaranteeing food safety. Occurring against a backdrop of LDP resurgence in Japanese politics, this setback marked the advent of a long "winter period" (*fuyu no jidai*)[2] in the movement's history that lasted until the early 1990s.

The movement to oppose the deregulation of food additives is the focus of this chapter. As one of the largest single-issue campaigns in Japanese consumer history[3] and an example of movement failure, it serves as a prime case study for several of the issues and questions introduced at the beginning of this volume: the relationship between a movement's level of organization and its impact on policymaking, the political determinants of movement influence, and the role of institutions in determining the extent to which the voices of diffuse societal interests are incorporated into central governmental decision making. The case also touches on a number of additional themes that underscore the distinctive features of the Japanese consumer movement, namely, the relationship between consumers and governmental authorities in the regulatory sphere, the impact of culture on consumer movement priorities, and the role of foreign pressure, or *gaiatsu*, in Japanese consumer protection policymaking.

The Regulatory, Cultural, and Historical Backdrop

Consumer Protection and Governmental Regulation

Organized consumer movements have traditionally adhered to the "public-interest" theory of regulation.[4] Based on the twin convictions that free-market mechanisms have the potential to harm consumers and that public policymaking is dominated by narrow economic interests, this theory looks to government as the only entity strong enough to act in the best interests of the general public. The primary mechanism for protecting the public interest is regulation: the governmental "imposition of controls and restraints and the application of rules" over firms' economic decisions (Swann 1989:3).

Regulation can be roughly divided into three broad categories, each of which has a bearing on consumer protection. Economic regulation, which gives governments the authority to control major decisions pertaining to price, output, rates of return, and entry and exit in specific industries (Gerston, Fraleigh, and Schwab 1988:27), can benefit consumers by stabilizing the prices and supplies of goods and services in the marketplace. Antitrust regulation, which enables governments to interfere in business activities in order to prevent collusive business behavior, protects consumers from both high prices and unfair business practices.

Consumer protection is achieved as a by-product of economic and anti-trust regulation, whereas social regulation targets the consumer directly. Based on the recognition that consumers are frequently incapable of evaluating complicated information that will allow them to make sound judgments about the goods and services they purchase, social regulation sets standards for the kinds of qualitative results that industries must achieve in the productive process (Gerston et al. 1988:30). Examples include automobile emission standards, approval procedures for drugs and cosmetics, and, more important to our purposes, product-labeling requirements and controls over the use of food additives and agricultural pesticides. As might be expected, social regulation has been a major focus of consumer movement activism throughout the industrialized world.

As I explain in more detail later on, American consumer advocates over the years have been selectively supportive of public proposals to disengage from the affairs of private firms, particularly when governmental regulatory mandates have been abused or unfulfilled. This, I believe, is partly a function of their capacity to curb the excesses of business behavior through an activist court system. British organizations have also supported a number of deregulatory programs in part because of their ability to perform officially sanctioned watchdog functions over deregulated industries. Both movements, moreover, tend to embrace liberal economic principles, preferring free-market mechanisms to governmental controls as means to advance consumer interests.

Japanese consumer representatives, by contrast, have clung with almost religious tenacity to a public-interest approach to consumer protection, even when that approach was losing political legitimacy. There are several reasons for this. First, the country's legacy of state-led economic development legitimized an activist governmental role not only in the affairs of business but also in the consumer realm. This has been borne out, as we have seen in previous chapters, by the establishment of semigovernmental consumer organizations that compete with private organizations for control over various consumer-related functions and that play a leading role in consumer education. Second, with the weakening of private consumer organizations relative to governmental organs, consumers were given strong incentives to lean heavily on government for consumer protection services. This tendency was further reinforced by weak conceptualizations of individual and consumer rights and the absence of an activist court to champion those rights.

Consumer advocates in Japan did not like having to submit to the often arbitrary protections of a paternalistic state, but as long as the courts remained weak and civil law (as opposed to regulatory) protections of consumers few in number, they were loath to support deregulatory measures that would expose consumers to the negative side effects of business activities. They were not necessarily opposing deregulation per se, as some critics of the movement would have us believe; they were simply opposed to deregulation *without* accompanying legal protections.

Culture Matters

Another reason that Japanese consumer organizations have projected an "anti-deregulation" image is that in 1983, in one of its first forays into the deregulatory realm, the government targeted social regulations governing the use of synthetic food additives, a move that elicited a torrent of protest from consumer advocates. In the United States and Britain, social regulation was largely untouched by the reform movements of the 1980s. Had the reverse been true, one can be certain that American and British consumer advocates would have been equally vociferous in their reactions.

Consumer concerns about food safety are common to virtually all advanced industrial societies and for a variety of reasons that are by no means specific to any one country. Scholars have found, for example, that like other quality-of-life issues, heightened food safety concerns tend to reflect higher income levels (see, e.g., Swinbank 1993). On the basis of a survey of consumer attitudes in Seattle and Kobe, Japan, moreover, Jussaume and Judson contend that declining confidence in the safety of the food supply generally increases with age and in households with children under eighteen (Jussaume and Judson 1992:243). They also observe that the level of concern is much higher in Japan than in the United States, and for reasons that appear to pertain to culture (Jussaume and Judson 1992:247). They do not, however, pursue this observation in detail.

According to Douglas and Wildavsky, popular attitudes toward risk are conditioned by a society's shared values (Douglas and Wildavsky 1982:8). If this is indeed the case, what are the cultural sources of the Japanese un-willingness to take food-related risks? The Shintō and Buddhist premium placed on cleanliness and purity is certainly one source. The etiological view of disease, explored by Ohnuki-Tierney, may be another.

According to Ohnuki-Tierney, traditional beliefs about the origins of dis-ease involve demarcations between the safe and controlled surroundings of one's home or personal space and the possible dangers emanating from "without." The common cold, for instance, is widely believed to be the product of germs contracted from the "outside"; hence the importance of removing one's shoes before entering a home, washing one's hands after being outdoors, and soaping up and rinsing off before entering the com-munal bath. Ohnuki-Tierney argues that the linkage between impurities contracted from outside and one's physical health is so strong in the minds of many Japanese that to neglect these ritual acts and ablutions is tantamount to a transgression of common morality (Ohnuki-Tierney 1984:21–50).

A concern for purity permeates basic consumption patterns as well. Con-sider, for example, the unwillingness of many Japanese consumers to eat while strolling down the street. If Ohnuki-Tierney's theory is correct, this is attributable not to a dislike for foods that lend themselves to ambulatory consumption but, rather, to a fear of eating in uncontrolled environments that have been subjected to a host of contaminants.[5] And what first-time visitor to Japan has not marveled at the Japanese penchant for peeling the skin off fruits — even grapes — before consuming them? Again using Ohnuki-Tierney's theory, those skins are the locus of germs and chemicals that may pose a risk to the health of consumers, even after washing. The skin of a fruit, in other words, is the bearer of impurities that were contracted from "outside" and that separate the consumer from the purity of the fruit "inside." As a foreigner living in Japan, I could certainly understand the hygienic rationale of this custom but failed to comprehend its moral value, as I dem-onstrated all too often by popping unpeeled grapes into my mouth in front of my disapproving Japanese friends.

If the mere thought of eating a piece of fruit with the skin still intact is anathema to most Japanese, imagine their reaction to foods containing chemical additives. In many advanced industrial countries, the use of such additives escalated after World War II, when mass production, the establish-ment of sophisticated distribution systems, and the proliferation of super-markets made it possible to produce processed foods for national markets. In this context, the use of synthetic additives enabled food processors to produce foods with a shelf life of weeks and even months. In response to these trends, the number of synthetic additives permitted for use in Japan increased from a mere sixty in 1957 to 356 by 1969 (*Kobe shimbun*, April 23, 1983).[6] For Japanese consumers long used to purchasing unprocessed foods from small neighborhood shops, the proliferation of additives was an affront to their notions of purity, what with their unnatural origins and possible side effects and the unknown consequences of consuming large mixtures of additives over a lifetime. It also contributed, I would argue, to an already deep-seated distrust of free-market principles and to the determination of many consumers to look to a paternalistic government for regulatory protection.

The History of Food Safety Issues in Postwar Japan

That culture may be a more important determinant of food safety awareness in Japan than economic affluence is apparent in the fact that consumer awareness of the potentially harmful effects of chemical additives first arose during the latter years of the Occupation, when consumers were still struggling economically. In 1951, in one of its first forays into product testing, Shufuren uncovered the use of an allegedly carcinogenic food dye in *takuan* (pickled radishes), a discovery that eventually prompted the Ministry of Health and Welfare to ban the substance. Consumer activism regarding food safety issues was also flourishing at the local level, where housewives were becoming increasingly conscious of the effects of postwar food shortages on the nutritional health of their children. Tani Mitsuei's experiences serve as a good example. A prominent consumer advocate in Niigata Prefecture, Mrs. Tani got her start in consumer politics during the early 1950s by organizing a study group on food-related issues. In a few years, the prefectural government responded to pressure from the group by establishing one of the country's first food-testing facilities at the prefectural level. By decade's end, Mrs. Tani had helped establish a regional *renrakukai* (liaison committee) of consumers to promote the use of natural food additives. One of the distinguishing features of the *renrakukai* was its close working relationship with the prefectural government. The committee not only relied heavily on the findings of the prefecture's testing facilities, but it also cooperated with the government on a number of fronts to promote food safety and nutritional awareness in the prefecture (Tani 1996:117–20). It was an early but nevertheless representative case of local governmental initiative and cooperation with consumer advocates.

The consumer cooperative movement also benefited from consumer concerns about food safety. By the end of the 1950s, the co-ops were struggling to attract members and to stay afloat financially. During the 1960s and 1970s, however, membership was booming in what organizers called "the golden age" of the cooperative movement (interview, Kurimoto, November 1992). The movement continued to flourish through the 1980s and into the 1990s and, by 1992, boasted a membership of roughly 15 million households, one-quarter of all households in Japan (interview, Kurimoto, November 1992). According to a 1988 survey of co-op members conducted by the Japan Consumer Cooperative Unions (Seikyōren), 76.5 percent of co-op households joined the movement in order to gain access to safe, higher-quality foods (Iwadare 1991:433). Paralleling and complementing this trend was the establishment of local joint-buying clubs based on direct purchasing relationships between groups of local consumers and organic farmers. The clubs gave consumers access to guaranteed sources of healthy produce and enabled farmers and consumers alike to circumvent the often byzantine—and costly—distribution system.

According to co-op officials, the consumer cooperatives were the first to provide consumers with organically grown produce and food products free of synthetic additives. These products were popular among consumers who had seen their food supply quickly transformed by rapid economic growth and were increasingly distressed by news of mass injuries caused by tainted milk products,[7] cooking oil laced with PCBs,[8] and other food-related disasters. The growing popularity of the co-ops eventually prompted mainstream food retailers to follow suit. Today, organic and additive-free products are readily available to consumers in a wide range of stores, a development that by the early 1990s resulted in a leveling off of cooperative membership (interview, Hiwasa, February 1994). It is a trend that simply underscores the long-term success of the consumer cooperative movement as a whole.

Throughout the postwar period, consumer advocates have taken a number of steps to ensure the safety of the nation's food supply and to heighten consumer awareness of this issue. One way of achieving these goals has been to campaign for stricter product-labeling (hyōji) standards. Many organizations, for example, pressured the Ministry of Health and Welfare to require detailed descriptions of synthetic additives used in processed foods, an objective they failed to achieve until *after* the anti-deregulatory movement of 1983/84. The delay, it appears, was caused by pressure from food manufacturers who balked at the inconvenience of conforming to new labeling standards (*Mainichi shimbun*, July 30, 1983). Many also feared that the inclusion of more information pertaining to potentially controversial additives would hurt business by scaring consumers away.[9]

Consumer advocates have also grouped together on a number of occasions to ban the presence of potentially dangerous food products in the marketplace and to pressure the Ministry of Health and Welfare into introducing stricter regulations governing the food supply. As the following two examples show, their efforts met with mixed results.

In late October 1969, the Ministry of Health and Welfare announced a recall of all food products containing cyclamates in response to evidence uncovered by American scientists that the substances were carcinogenic.[10] Although Japanese food processors had a vested interest in the continued authorization of cyclamates, which comprised more than 80 percent of the artificial sweeteners in use at the time, a few companies responded to public concerns by voluntarily pulling their products from store shelves well before the recall was to go into effect. Then, in a last-minute about-face, the ministry postponed the recall in early January 1970, following a similar move by the American government and mounting opposition from the majority of Japanese food processors.

Shortly after the recall was postponed, five consumer organizations, led by Chifuren, launched a nationwide movement to boycott products containing cyclamates. The boycott, which attracted the participation of several million consumers, was testament to the organizational skills of consumer advocates,[11] but it failed to convince the Ministry of Health and Welfare to revoke the postponement. The use of cyclamates is still permitted in Japan today, although many companies have stopped using them in anticipation of further consumer boycotts.

Consumer activism was much more effective in the movement to ban the use of AF2, a germicide used in tofu, ham, sausages, and Japanese fish paste. AF2 had been officially authorized by the Ministry of Health and Welfare in 1965, but independent research conducted during the early 1970s on laboratory animals revealed carcinogenic properties in the substance. Although AF2 was not a focus of international pressure, the Ministry of Health and Welfare sided with food processors and refused to ban the substance in response to organized consumer demands.

Consumer organizations responded by taking their cause to the grassroots level. The campaign began in 1972 in the Tōkyō area, where local consumer groups organized boycotts of neighborhood shops that sold products containing AF2 (Inaba et al. 1979:11; see also Suginamiku shōhisha no kai 1982:63–64), and soon spread to other cities around the country. After several weeks of this, the Ministry of Health and Welfare caved in to the movement's demands by authorizing its Food Sanitation Deliberation Council (Shokuhin eisei chōsakai) to look into the problem. Before the council publicized its opinion that AF2 may indeed be carcinogenic, however, countless large food-processing companies and retail outlets voluntarily stopped using or selling the substance, turning instead to alternative—usually natural—additives that performed similar functions. In August 1974, the ministry formally removed AF2 from its list of approved additives.

In his study of Japanese food safety regulations and their impact on trade, David Vogel suggests that consumer representatives and Japanese business have seen more or less eye to eye on the question of strict standards governing synthetic food additives (D. Vogel 1992:146). The cyclamate and AF2 campaigns, however, indicate that consumer-business relations on this issue are much more conflicted than Vogel suggests: consumer representatives *will* take businesses to task for violating consumer safety expectations.

The cases are also typical examples of the politics governing the regulation of potentially harmful additives. The Ministry of Health and Welfare usually will respond to consumer activism and ban the use of an additive *if* it can be easily replaced by other additives and there is no foreign pressure for its continued use. But even when consumer organizations fail to evoke a ministerial response, they still can curb the usage of controversial additives by boycotting them. As we have observed in other chapters, the effectiveness of this time-consuming tactic should not be overestimated—particularly when two or more product lines have been targeted.

The Regulatory Process and the Consumer Movement's Response

All advanced industrial democracies regulate the use of food additives to some degree. In some countries, food processors are free to use any additive so long as it has not been specifically banned by the government; in others, including Japan, the United States, and Britain, manufacturers can use only those additives that have been expressly approved by government authorities (D. Vogel 1992:120). In some ways, the Japanese regime is more lax than those of its Anglo-Saxon counterparts; it does not, for example, regulate natural food additives. But in regard to synthetic additives, Japanese regulations are stricter than those of the United States[12] and Britain, although this has not always been the case. Before the European Union moved to harmonize the regulation of additives among its member states during the early 1990s, Britain had authorized the use of roughly 300 additives (D. Vogel 1995:51–52), many fewer than the 336 approved by the Japanese government on the eve of deregulation in 1983.[13]

In the past, the Japanese government went to great lengths to assure the population of its commitment to food safety. In 1972, as consumer activism on this issue was reaching its postwar peak and the AF2 movement at the grassroots level was gathering steam, the Diet passed a resolution alongside an amendment to strengthen the 1948 Food Sanitation Law (Shokuhin ei-seihō)[14] which pledged to restrict the number of additives approved in the future. In keeping with that resolution, the Ministry of Health and Welfare authorized only seven additives between 1972 and 1983 (Nihon keizai shimbun, May 18, 1983). In 1975, in response to mounting domestic fears concerning the possible presence of dangerous additives and pesticides in imported foods, the Miki cabinet resolved that additives should be authorized only on the basis of studies conducted by Japanese governmental organs, universities, or other domestic research organizations in a position of authority (Mainichi shimbun, July 14, 1983),[15] the implication being that foreign data would not be accepted as an alternative. These moves met with a mixture of resounding approval from consumer representatives and criticism from abroad that the Japanese government was erecting nontariff barriers to trade in food products.

Even though the Japanese regulatory regime governing synthetic food additives acquired a reputation abroad for being one of the strictest in the world, consumer organizations complained that it was not strict enough. In accordance with the cultural premium placed on cleanliness and purity, consumer organizations have in principle opposed the use of synthetic additives on the grounds that safer, natural substances[16] can be used to perform the same functions.[17] Some organizations like the Consumers Union (Shōhisha renmei), moreover, have even gone so far as to insist on a blanket ban on all synthetic additives. Most consumer advocates refuse to accept the scientific argument that some controversial additives are harmless to human beings when consumed in minute quantities, pointing out that science has yet to disprove the possibility of toxic side effects resulting from the prolonged consumption of many different kinds of additives. Consumer organizations have, in other words, equated "safety" with "zero risk." The Ministry of Health and Welfare, meanwhile, like many of its foreign counterparts, equates safety with the "absence of significant risk" (D. Vogel 1992:120).

Consumer organizations have also contested the manner in which synthetic additives have been approved for use in Japan. The Food Sanitation Law stipulates that before it can be approved by the Minister of Health and Welfare, an additive must first be assessed by the Food Sanitation Deliberation Council (Shokuhin eisei chōsakai), an advisory council that answers to the minister. The 1972 Diet resolution on food safety requires that council membership mainly reflect the opinions of consumers. In practice, however, scientists and business interests are much more heavily represented than consumer interests, with only one representative from consumer organizations permitted on the council at any given time. Much to the chagrin of the organized movement, moreover, consumer representatives are not designated as such. For example, Takada Yuri, a prominent vice-president of Shufuren and the first consumer representative to sit on the commission, was required to serve in her capacity as a pharmacist, a title that she felt undermined the significance of her proclamations made on behalf of consumers. Her successors—both of them well-known consumer representatives—served on the council as "individuals of learning and experience" (gakushiki keikensha). In keeping with consumer misgivings about governmental shingikai in general, all three consumer advocates have complained vehemently about the paucity of consumer representation on the council and its tendency either to override or ignore their opinions (interviews: Y. Itō, April 1994; Kanamori, April 1993; Takada, April 1994; KSS 1983:126).

According to the rules and regulations governing council procedures, additives can be approved only when (1) there is actual proof (jisshō) or confirmation (kakunin) of the safety of those additives and (2) the additives are deemed both indispensable to a food product and beneficial to consumers (Mainichi shimbun, July 12, 1983).[18] Again, the consumer representatives who have served on the council tell a different story. Council members have often been known to devote only a few hours of discussion to safety issues, and the documentation on which such deliberations are based has often been provided by food-processing companies rather than independent research organizations or the Ministry of Health and Welfare. In addition, members are often given only a few days to read hundreds of pages of documents, many of which are written in complicated academic styles that are often incomprehensible to laypersons. To complicate matters further, many of the documents are written in English and other foreign languages, with no translations provided (interview, Y. Itō, April 1994). Finally, until recently members were forbidden to discuss the contents of the documents with noncouncil members, a requirement that obstructed attempts by consumer representatives to obtain outside assistance or, for that matter, to disseminate information about the policy process to other advocates. Together, these informal norms and customs governing the regulatory policy process effectively excluded the systematic incorporation of consumer voices in that process.

By the early 1980s, consumer advocates were complaining that the policy process surrounding the regulation of synthetic additives was a slipshod, undemocratic affair sorely in need of reform. The government disagreed. To consumer representatives, Ministry of Health and Welfare officials justified the closed-door sessions as necessary to ensure free and open discussions by council members, the majority of whom have been scientists (*Shō-hisha Report*, July 27, 1983). They also argued that decisions reached in the council were based on international standards of safety and that consumer advocates had underestimated the ability of modern technology to determine the exact levels at which various kinds of additives could be safely consumed by humans.

Toward the Comprehensive Deregulation of Synthetic Additives

Neoliberalism and the Movement Toward Deregulation

By 1980, regulation as a mechanism for protecting consumers was falling into disfavor in the United States, Britain, and, to a lesser extent, Japan. At the root of this trend was a widespread rejection of the premise expounded by many scholars and policymakers that economic regulation was serving the "public interest." During the 1960s and 1970s, academics of the Chicago school developed the so-called capture theory of regulation, which stated that regulatory agencies were serving the interests of the regulated rather than those of the public at large. George Stigler, for example, viewed the regulatory process not as a forum for the advancement of the consumer interest but, rather, as a kind of political marketplace in which politicians offered industry protective regulation in return for votes and financial backing (Stigler 1971). Milton Friedman, whose writings became a major cornerstone of the neoliberal economic "rethink" in Britain as well as the United States, argued that government efforts to protect the consumer through regulation had failed because they excluded many products from the marketplace and reduced the overall range of consumer choice (Jordan 1993:23).[19]

Although the capture theory of regulation has since been partially refuted by a number of American scholars (see, e.g., Wilson 1980b), it nevertheless found a receptive audience among business representatives and conservative policymakers during the late 1970s and 1980s in all three countries following the economic slowdowns and mounting budget deficits of the post–oil shock period. Academic proposals for governmental disengagement from the economy, meanwhile, had become viable solutions to contemporary problems relating to economic performance. This did not mean that consumer protection was no longer a consideration for policymakers; rather, it meant that there was a growing belief that consumer protection was best achieved through freer market mechanisms. Consequently, terms like *self-regulation* and *self-responsibility* assumed the dimensions of deregulatory slogans in the United States, Britain, and Japan, underscoring a basic trust the market's ability to provide industries with the incentives to establish their own rules governing entry and exit and product safety standards, and for consumers to take care of themselves.

In many ways, the notions of self-regulation and self-responsibility conflict with the traditional beliefs of organized consumer movements. Consumer advocates do not view consumption as a strictly economic act but, rather, as a multifaceted activity that affects such quality-of-life concerns as one's life, health, and standard of living. In the past, consumer advocates in Japan and elsewhere put very little trust in the ability of unfettered markets to guarantee the rights and interests of consumers. Instead, they pressed for governmental economic regulation to control prices and supply and for social regulation to guarantee product quality and safety.

One therefore might have expected consumer advocates during the 1980s to oppose the neoliberal movement toward deregulation. In both the United States and Britain, however, this was not always the case. Although consumer organizations expressed misgivings about certain aspects of deregulation, many eventually supported proposals for airline and other forms of deregulation in the expectation that consumers would be better off in the long run. In Japan, consumer organizations were vociferous in their opposition to deregulation, a development partly attributable, as we noted earlier, to the *kind* of deregulation being proposed. In the United States and Britain, reform focused on *economic* regulation which, when loosened, stood to benefit consumers by lowering prices and expanding product choice. *Social* regulation, meanwhile, emerged from the reform process more or less unscathed. In Japan during the early 1980s, the neoliberal spotlight focused not only on economic regulation but also on product safety standards, governmental controls over the use of synthetic additives, and other forms of social regulation. Consumer organizations responded by opposing deregulation across the board.

Enter gaiatsu

The Japanese government's interest in social deregulation reflected both international developments in food processing and, more important, outright pressure from the United States for the liberalization of Japanese agricultural markets. Foreign trends and *gaiatsu* (foreign pressure) had had an impact on rules governing the use of food additives well before the neoliberal reform movement of the early 1980s. During the mid-1970s, for example, Japanese government authorities were monitoring worldwide reassessments of food safety standards that were contributing to the expanded use of synthetic additives in countries around the world.[20] Second, and in response to the mounting trade imbalance between Japan and the United States, Washington had begun to criticize Japan's strict controls over the use of additives as nontariff barriers to trade (see D. Vogel 1992). The Japanese government responded to these pressures during the mid- to late 1970s by authorizing the use of a handful of additives, including, in 1977, a highly controversial fungicide known as OPP found on imported citrus fruits.[21]

Whereas governmental efforts during the 1970s to appease the Americans were largely ad hoc, the response of the Nakasone government (1982–1987) to American trade pressure was far more systematic. Shortly after taking office, Nakasone authorized a comprehensive reassessment of economic and social regulatory controls that were allegedly functioning as barriers to imports. In 1982, the OTO (Overseas Trade Ombudsman, Shijō kaihō mondai kujō shōri suishin honbu) was established under the jurisdiction of the Economic Planning Agency to monitor feedback from Japan's trade partners about Japanese trade practices. As might be expected, complaints concerning Japan's stringent food and product safety standards—most of them lodged by American businesses—topped the list. With regard to food additives, Americans were particularly concerned that Japan had failed to authorize the use of 128 synthetic additives that were on the United Nations' Food and Agriculture Organization / World Health Organization (FAO/WHO)'s A1 list and that were widely used by American food-processing companies. It is in this context that the Nakasone government decided in 1983 to increase the number of synthetic additives permitted for use in Japan.

The Consumer Backlash

Among the eleven additives targeted for authorization in 1983 were the controversial artificial sweetener aspartame, fungicides used in breads and other baked foods, colorants found in chocolates and candies, and an additive used in beer to speed up the fermentation process. Along with those additives, the government also deliberated on BHA, an antioxidant widely used both in Japan[22] and abroad that had long been opposed by consumer advocates. Research conducted in the 1970s and early 1980s by the Ministry of Health and Welfare and a team of scientists at Nagoya University had shown that BHA caused cancer in rats. The ministry responded to these findings in the summer of 1982 by informing the GATT of a decision to ban the substance (*Nihon keizai shimbun*, February 1, 1983). Following an outpouring of complaints from the American, British, and Canadian governments that the ban constituted a nontariff barrier to trade, Prime Minister Nakasone and Mori Yoshirō, the minister of health and welfare, conferred in January 1983 and agreed to suspend the ban until international scientists had ruled conclusively that BHA was unsafe for human consumption (*Mainichi shimbun*, February 1, 1983; *Yomiuri shimbun* February 1, 1983). Consumer organizations were outraged by the move and argued that the ban should have stayed in place, given the substance's potentially carcinogenic properties. Although BHA was not one of the eleven additives formally authorized by the Ministry of Health and Welfare in August 1983, the ministry did decide at that time to extend the suspension of the ban. Despite the continued opposition of consumer representatives, BHA is still used today.

From the government's point of view, loosening governmental restrictions on the use of synthetic additives was, comparatively speaking, a politically painless but fruitful affair. For one thing, the deregulatory process could be carried out relatively simply and effectively in the Ministry of Health and Welfare and without any formal input from the Diet. Deregulation also had the support of domestic food processors that opposed governmental controls and all the tedious paperwork and other forms of governmental interference that accompanied them. Finally, authorizing several additives all at once could be seen as a signal to Japan's trading partners that the country was "serious" about deregulation and committed to opening its agricultural markets.

The authorization of the eleven additives resulted in a major consumer backlash. Several issues were at stake for consumer advocates, not the least of which was the culturally based concern for the safety of the nation's food supply. Although all the targeted additives were listed on the FAO / WHO's A1 list, advocates opposed authorization on the same grounds that they had opposed the use of synthetic additives in the past: the lack of evidence that the prolonged consumption of such substances would not result in damaging side effects.

Ongoing problems in the nation's product-labeling standards were also of concern to consumer advocates. Before 1983, only one-fifth of the 336 authorized synthetic additives had to be listed on the labels of food products. Manufacturers were not required to state those additives by name so long as their functions were clearly indicated (*Sankei shimbun*, August 10, 1983). Much more lenient than those of the United States and most Western European countries, Japanese food-labeling standards gave manufacturers the freedom to withhold information from consumers regarding controversial additives. These standards undermined the validity of the pro-deregulatory slogan of "self-responsibility," since consumers could not be expected to make informed choices about the foods they purchased if they were not given information on which to base those choices.

The role played by *gaiatsu* in the unraveling of governmental controls over synthetic additives was grist for the consumer movement's mill. Although advocates have been known to welcome foreign interference in domestic political affairs as a boost to the consumer cause,[23] such has not been the case for food safety. Condemning American demands for the liberalization of food additives during the late 1970s and 1980s as a threat to the health of Japanese consumers, advocates, like their counterparts in many European countries, argued that the international harmonization of regulations affecting trade flows should not impinge on national safety standards reflecting the culinary habits and cultural traditions of a particular society (*Shōhisha undō nenpan* 1987:17). Advocates also worried that foreign pressure on the additives issue would jeopardize the future of Japanese agriculture by destroying barriers to food imports. Heavily influenced by the famines of the early postwar period, by their long-standing political partnership with the farming community, and by Japanese conceptualizations of what it means to be a consumer in society, the majority of older advocates have consistently supported agricultural protectionism as a prerequisite for self-sufficiency in the nation's food supply, even if it leads to higher prices for consumers. According to Takeuchi Naokazu of Consumers Union, these cultural, safety, and nationalist considerations warrant the placement of food products *outside* the mainstream commodity economy (Miyachi 1984). The failure to do so, he argued, would allow Americans to "occupy the stomachs" of the Japanese (Takeuchi 1990:104).

Finally, consumer advocates viewed the whole affair as evidence that the Japanese government could not be trusted to respect the wishes of consumers. More specifically, they condemned the Nakasone government's decision to authorize the eleven additives as a violation of past policies to protect the health of consumers, particularly the 1972 Diet resolution and the Miki cabinet's 1975 proclamation (*Asahi shimbun*, June 11, 1983).

The Deregulatory Process

Consumer advocates also criticized the Food Sanitation Deliberation Council for issuing its recommendation after only a few short weeks of deliberations, for ignoring evidence generated by Japanese scientists that several of the additives caused cancer in rats,[24] and, as the council chairman himself later admitted during a press conference, for failing to build a viable consensus among the membership in favor of deregulation (*Mainichi shimbun*, July 13, 1983).

The harried pace of deliberations meant that many of the members had little chance to absorb the reams of documents provided by the Ministry of Health and Welfare. This matter was later the target of a heated exchange in the Diet's Social Labor Committee (Shakai rōdō iinkai) between a Shaminren Diet member and the head of the Ministry of Health and Welfare bureau that serves as the secretariat to the Food Sanitation Deliberation Council:

SHAMINREN: When were the documents delivered to the members of the [council]? Also, how many were delivered?

MINISTRY OF HEALTH AND WELFARE: I think about a week before-hand.

SHAMINREN: I heard that documents [for the April 11 meeting] were delivered once on April 3 and once on April 6. Is that correct?

MINISTRY OF HEALTH AND WELFARE: That's correct.

SHAMINREN: I heard that the documents were enough to fill two cardboard boxes and that they amounted to 6,000 pages—many of which were written in English. Minister [of Health and Welfare] Mori says it is enough to feed a horse. Is this true?

MINISTRY OF HEALTH AND WELFARE: I think that's about right.

SHAMINREN: So the members had one full week to read the first set and only three to five days to read the second set. And with that, they're to carry out careful deliberations?

MINISTRY OF HEALTH AND WELFARE: I think they were able to deliberate sufficiently, since each member was to read only those documents pertaining to his field of specialty.

(Mainichi shimbun, July 13, 1983)

Although accounts differ as to the precise timing of the distribution of documents (*Mainichi shimbun*, July 13, 1983), the fact remains that the members were unable to make informed decisions based on a thorough evaluation of the data at their disposal.

The haphazard deliberations of a council whose membership was skewed toward business interests suggests that the decision to deregulate had been made *before* the issue reached the council and that the council itself was little more than a *kakuremino* (lit., an "invisibility-granting fairy cloak"; Schwartz 1993:230), a forum for legitimizing behind-the-scenes political maneuvering by key policymakers. This was in turn facilitated by the fact that the main actors behind the decision to authorize the additives were few in number: Prime Minister Nakasone, the minister of health and welfare, several high-level bureaucrats in the Ministry of Health and Welfare,[25] and business representatives.[26] This pro-deregulation coalition was able to control the decision-making agenda for two reasons, both of which pertain to the institutional configurations of the decision-making process. First, since only the Ministry of Health and Welfare had bureaucratic jurisdiction over additives in Japan, it did not have to coordinate its position with that of other ministries, a process that can lead to long-winded turf battles and policy-making stalemates. Second, the centralization of decision making in the bureaucracy enabled Nakasone and his supporters to sidestep the protests of the opposition parties during the early stages of the policy process and to prevent the further politicization of this highly controversial issue. The discrete nature of the policy process in turn allowed key decision makers to act quickly and decisively before their bureaucratic or political opponents had a chance to mobilize—a feature that distinguishes the additives case from the antitrust and product liability cases, both of which were mired from the start in jurisdictional battles and political conflict.

Superimposed on this decision-making process was a sense of urgency precipitated by American trade pressure. This should not suggest, however, that the additives case was one of simple Japanese capitulation to American demands. As Schoppa argues in his analysis of the Structural Impediments Initiative (SII) talks, *gaiatsu* is successful when it resonates with the demands of a domestic political constituency (Schoppa 1997). Without such a commonality of interests, Schoppa contends, *gaiatsu* works only when it is accompanied by a serious diplomatic threat (Schoppa 1997:7). In the additives case, it is clear that the demands of American trade negotiators had found a receptive audience among the likes of Prime Minister Nakasone, one of the leading proponents of deregulation; the Ministry of Health and Welfare, which was much more liberal in its approach to regulating additives than Japanese consumers were; and Japanese food manufacturers and retailers, many of whom looked to the expanded use of synthetic additives as a ticket to higher sales. It is also clear that threat was *not* a major component of American trade pressure in this instance. Although Americans were certainly complaining about the role of Japanese product safety standards as nontariff barriers to trade, the threats of retaliation that accompanied those complaints did not carry nearly as much punch as they did after 1988, when the Super 301 provision of the Omnibus Trade and Competition Act enhanced the capacity of Congress and the U.S. trade representative to change the behavior of America's "recalcitrant" trade partners. Indeed, when all is said and done, American pressure in the additives case did not preempt the role of pro-business actors in consumer politics; rather, it complemented and legitimized that role.

The Anti-Deregulation Campaign

After the government presented the public with a fait accompli—sanctioned by a council that purported to speak for the public interest—the media zoomed in on the issue. A flood of critical newspaper articles spoke of a government that had caved in to foreign pressure and resorted to underhanded tactics in forcing what amounted to a highly unpopular decision. Consumer organizations, for their own part, cashed in on the mounting sense of public outrage to build a nationwide anti-deregulation movement.

The movement grew rapidly during the summer and autumn of 1983 as both local groups and national organizations campaigned aggressively at the local level to bring about a reversal of the government's decision (*Asahi shimbun*, June 11, 1983). As part of the *mondai teigi* (issue definition) stage of their campaign, advocates educated consumers on the alleged dangers of chemical additives by sponsoring public lectures and symposia using the facilities and public relations assistance of local consumer centers and by distributing tens of thousands of leaflets and booklets to concerned citizens. In addition, rallies and demonstrations were held around the country. One such rally of more than 10,000 people was staged in Tōkyō on the heels of an official state visit by President Ronald Reagan (Nihon seikyōren 1984:20). The largest consumer rally to date, it was surpassed only by those of the anticonsumption tax movement later in the decade. Advocates also pressured thirty-three prefectural and 392 city, town, and village assemblies into passing resolutions calling for a reversal in the government's policy (Nihon seikyōren 1984:20) and persuaded a number of localities to enact ordinances banning several of the controversial additives (*Kobe shimbun*, July 5, 1983). Finally, appeals signed by hundreds of prominent personalities from a range of professions were published in the newspapers, and more than 8 million signatures were collected for petitions that were sent to both the Diet and local assemblies (Zenchifuren 1986:136), a number that far exceeded those of the antitrust and product liability movements. Most of these tactics were carried out under the guidance of the Central Executive Committee for Opposing the Deregulation of Food Additives (Shokuhin tenkabutsu no kisei kanwa hantai chuō jikkō iinkai), a liaison committee established in October 1983 by ninety-six national, regional, and local consumer organs and with the selective support of labor activists, lawyers, and the agricultural cooperatives (Zenchifuren 1986:136).

Judging from the sheer number of the petitions and the attendance levels at rallies and demonstrations, efforts to elicit a response from the public at large had been very successful. The response was not all that surprising, however, given the population's cultural predisposition to take an interest in food safety issues. The results of public opinion surveys underscore this point. In a survey of about 500 housewives conducted in December 1983 by a Tōkyō consumer-related study group, 68.2 percent of the respondents said that they were very worried about the deregulation of additives. Only 2.2 percent stated that they were unaware of the issue (*Mainichi shimbun*, December 20, 1983).

Consumer organizations also tried to lobby LDP politicians, but their requests for meetings were often refused. One tactic that was carried out quite successfully vis-à-vis the political parties, however, was the submission of questionnaires to various party headquarters. Although the questions asked were often rhetorical and yielded information that was largely irrelevant to the policy process, they did uncover some interesting insights into the politics of deregulation and provided consumer advocates with verbal ammunition against the government. In the spring of 1983, for example, a coalition of consumer organizations distributed a questionnaire to the parties that consisted of the following politically loaded questions:[27] (1) Do you approve of deregulating additives in response to trade friction and without proof that the substances are safe? (2) Do you support the 1972 Diet resolution proclaiming that the use of additives should be restricted "to the utmost" (*kyokuryoku seigen suru*)? and (3) Do you feel that the deregulation of additives without conclusive proof of their long-term safety will alarm the general public?

The LDP responded to the first question by stating that the deregulation of additives was necessitated by (1) Japan's international obligation to open its markets by harmonizing product standards and licensing procedures according to international norms and (2) the diversification of domestic culinary habits and the diffusion of processed foods. This position was seconded by the New Liberal Club. The JSP, Kōmeitō, and the JCP, by contrast, all responded that they opposed deregulation on the grounds that the safety of the targeted additives had not been conclusively determined. The Democratic Socialist Party (DSP) took the middle ground by supporting the need to liberalize domestic markets while criticizing the government's refusal to respect the public's wishes.

As for whether or not Japan should still abide by the 1972 Diet resolution, the LDP evaded the question by arguing that the safety of the additives was "internationally recognized" (*kokusaiteki ni kakunin sarete*) and that the additives were necessary given the nation's changing culinary habits. The New Liberal Club toed a similar line. The other opposition parties (with the exception of the DSP, which did not respond to the second and third questions) replied that the resolution should indeed be respected through strict control of the total number of additives authorized for use in Japan.

The LDP avoided the third question by asserting once again that the additives were safe and posed no dangers to public health. The New Liberal Club was much less evasive in its response, arguing that given the lack of conclusive information on the effects of prolonged consumption of many different kinds of additives, steps should be taken to allay the fears of the populace. The other opposition parties were more stringent in their demands that the long-term effects of additives be more thoroughly investigated. The Socialist and Communist Parties also called on the government to respond to public pressure by assigning more consumer representatives to the Food Sanitation Deliberation Council and opening deliberations to the public.

These responses clearly indicate that the LDP, which used *gaiatsu* as an excuse for implementing unpopular political measures, was unwilling to publicly acknowledge consumer concerns regarding the safety of synthetic additives. Most of the opposition parties took a "safety first" stance, acknowledged the need to keep the public informed and to address their demands, and generally portrayed themselves as allies of consumers. The LDP cited the existence of scientific information to justify its claims, whereas the opposition parties pointed to the lack thereof to support theirs. It was classic party politics.

Consumer organizations responded to the LDP's position as elucidated in these and other statements by taking the moral high ground. In both movement publications and through the national media, advocates tried to depict the ruling party as completely oblivious to the welfare of its citizens. In July 1983, for example, the *Mainichi shimbun* reported on a heated exchange over the safety of the prolonged use of synthetic additives between consumer representatives and Mori Yoshirō, the minister of health and welfare. Once it became painfully clear that his answers had failed to satisfy his opponents, an irritated Mori demanded: "Has anyone ever fallen ill because of additives?" (*Mainichi shimbun*, July 12, 1983).

The press, for its own part, had a field day with the issue. Food safety is one of the few contemporary consumer issues that is relatively easy for the average consumer to understand.[28] Moreover, given the penchant for Japanese citizens to judge a food product "unsafe until proven absolutely safe," the issue can be conveyed with few ambiguities. Articles reporting the estimates of a Dōshisha University professor that the average Japanese adult was consuming as much as 4 kilograms of synthetic additives a year (*Hokkaidō shimbun*, May 19, 1983), therefore, were bound to provoke the consternation of consumers. In short, the controversy surrounding the eleven additives made good copy as headline news in the home economics sections of the national and local newspapers.

In addition to the safety issue, the deregulatory process itself was a topic of media attention, even for the pro-business *Nihon keizai shimbun*. On the day the council delivered its final decision, the newspaper criticized the fact that the council had stated not that it would endorse the authorization of the additives but, rather, that it "would not stand in the way" (*sashitsukaenai*) of such a move (*Nihon keizai shimbun*, May 18, 1983). Other newspapers also raised some thought-provoking questions about the way in which the council deliberations had been carried out. In a highly informative and well-researched series of articles published in July, for example, the *Mainichi shimbun*[29] quoted inside sources who revealed that the actual issue of safety had been the focus of only three to four hours of deliberations and that many of the documents used for those deliberations were biased. One council member alleged that the documentation used to prove the safety of the artificial sweetener aspartame, for example, had been provided exclusively by the American firm that manufactured the substance (*Mainichi shimbun*, July 14, 1983). These and other articles were written in a style that would easily outrage readers who were concerned about their rights to be heard and to product safety. They were, in short, a boon to the anti-deregulation movement.

The opposition parties also took up the consumer banner by pitting themselves against a seemingly indifferent government as champions of the consumer interest. Although opposition politicians did not work closely with consumer advocates and were criticized by the movement for not acting quickly enough on the issue,[30] they did articulate the consumer position in the policymaking sphere on several occasions. As illustrated earlier, questions concerning the content of deliberations in the Food Sanitation Deliberation Council were frequently raised in both chambers of the Diet, and a number of politicians—including the future socialist prime minister Murayama Tomiichi—took the LDP and the Ministry of Health and Welfare to task for handling the deregulatory process in an undemocratic and haphazard fashion (*Shufuren dayori*, May 15, 1983). On one occasion, JSP politicians organized a debate with Ministry of Health and Welfare officials and invited consumer representatives to observe. When asked why the council deliberations had been closed to the public, the officials responded that it was to preserve the academic freedom of the members, most of whom were scientists. They also stated that even though the meetings were closed, the public could later view the minutes upon request. This came as a surprise to many of the consumer representatives in the group, who had found it next to impossible to gain access to that documentation (*Shōhisha Report*, July 27, 1983).

More than any other consumer campaign either before or after, consumer organizations, their allies, and the general public spoke with a single voice in their opposition to the deregulation of the eleven additives. This upsurge of public protest from the grass roots of society did not, however, lead to success in the policy realm. The Ministry of Health and Welfare's decision to deregulate the eleven additives went ahead as planned, largely because of the strength of Nakasone's coalition, which operated in a discrete and highly controlled institutional environment. It was a crushing disappointment for the organized movement.

Postscript

In addition to loosening the regulations governing food additives, Nakasone and his allies simplified the government's food inspection system. In mid-1983, sixteen laws governing safety checks on imported foods were amended as part of the governmental policy of administrative reform and in response to pressure from the United States (Nihon seikyōren 1984:4). Also in 1983, the Food Sanitation Supervisory Office (Shokuhin eisei kanshi jimusho), the governmental body in charge of supervising the nation's inspection procedures of food imports, was abolished and its duties transferred to the Quarantine Office. As a result of these administrative changes, the number of inspections of imported foods declined sharply. Consumer organizations, their allies in the legal community, and opposition party politicians opposed these cutbacks in the country's food inspection administrative apparatus and continued to demand tighter regulatory controls over inspection procedures well into the 1980s.

From the point of view of consumers, the deregulatory movement of the early 1980s did have one positive side effect: following the authorization of the eleven additives and the postponement of the ban on BHA, the Ministry of Health and Welfare announced that it would strengthen the nation's food-labeling standards in order to provide consumers with the information to make more informed choices about the foods they purchased. Seventy-eight additives, including the eleven slated for authorization in 1983, now had to be identified by name on product labels. All but five of that total, moreover, had to be identified according to function as well (D. Vogel 1992:128). Although the changes were in keeping with the deregulatory slogan of consumer self-responsibility, they were received rather grudgingly by food-processing companies, many of which criticized the new standards as just another form of regulation that would require investment in new labeling designs. To accommodate businesses and much to the annoyance of consumer organizations, the Ministry of Health and Welfare ruled that the new standards would not go into effect for another two years. While welcoming the changes as a protection of the rights to know and to choose, consumer advocates criticized the government's decision as an attempt to defuse conflict over what was, in the final analysis, an unresolved public safety issue (*Shufuren dayori*, July 15, 1983). True to their long-standing faith in the merits of the public-interest theory of regulation, moreover, many advocates paternalistically questioned the ability of consumers to properly evaluate the information at their disposal concerning the foods they consumed.

Finally, it should be noted that a few consumer organizations softened their opposition to deregulation by the late 1980s as the government abandoned its efforts to carry out social regulatory reform. Today, organizations like Shufuren, Chifuren, and the consumer cooperatives support reforms that enhance consumer access to a wider range of products at lower prices. At the same time, however, advocates maintain their vigilance over both the processes and long-term ramifications of regulatory reform. With regard to the deregulation of medicinal products, for example, concerned advocates remain wary of proposals to introduce sweeping changes that would make more over-the-counter medicines available to consumers. Advocates like Itō Yasue, a Shōkaren executive and former member of the Food Sanitation Deliberation Council, contend that such products should be deregulated on a case-by-case basis and only after extensive investigations into their safety have been completed (interview, Y. Itō, December 1998). Japanese consumer organizations, in short, accept deregulation as a political inevitability, but they are determined to prevent the kinds of deregulatory excesses that might prove harmful to consumers.

Conclusion

The movement to oppose the deregulation of synthetic additives was, without doubt, one of the largest and best-organized single-issue consumer campaigns of the postwar period. To the leaders of the movement, the authorization of the eleven additives symbolized a capitulation to foreign pressure that did not correspond to the nation's cultural values, domestic demand, or economic necessity. Critics contend that the movement's opposition to deregulation on the grounds that the additives might be unsafe was built on scientific quicksand; indeed, there is no conclusive evidence even today that the fears of the movement and the general public were scientifically sound. What is important in this case, however, is not so much the scientific validity of the movement's position as the perceptions of both consumer organizations and an attentive public that many of those additives were unfit for human consumption. And as the size and cohesiveness of the anti-deregulation campaign show, perceptions can be as potent a force as truth when it comes to galvanizing the public behind a political cause.[31]

The anti-deregulation movement was overpowered by a tightly knit governmental coalition backed by business interests and legitimized by foreign pressure. This coalition had complete control over the decision-making process and managed to reach a decision before the issue became mired in political controversy and party politics. Faced with the monolithic power of this coalition, the cohesiveness of the consumer coalition and the strong support of both local governments and public opinion proved inconsequential. In this respect, the anti-deregulation case is proof that the relative impact of an organized social movement on policy is ultimately determined not by the wealth and size of that movement but by the structure of the policymaking system and by the nature of the political alliances within that system.

As noted at the outset of this chapter, the failure of the anti-deregulation campaign marked the advent of a "winter period" (fuyu no jidai) in the postwar history of the organized consumer movement. Overwhelmed by the conservative, pro-business political atmosphere of the 1980s, consumer organizations suffered a crisis of confidence and a leveling off or decline in their membership levels. Many individual consumer organizations continued to fight for such food safety objectives as a ban on the use of chemical fertilizers and pesticides on agricultural products. Aside from these campaigns and a highly unsuccessful bid to block the introduction of the consumption tax in 1988, consumer activism became primarily a local affair as participation in national policy-related campaigns fell to a twenty-year low. Then in 1991, the deregulatory movement catapulted consumer organizations into the national political arena once again, this time to enact a product liability law.

8 The Right to Redress: The Movement to Enact a Product Liability Law

In October 1982, a Tōkyō housewife took a can of spray detergent to a particularly noxious case of mold and mildew on her bathroom walls. Pleased with the results, she remained loyal to the product for about a year. Then, one day, she began coughing and feeling a painful burning sensation in her throat while using the detergent and was eventually rushed to a hospital in severe respiratory arrest. Suffering permanent lung damage and chronic bronchitis, the housewife sued the manufacturer of the "mold killer" (*kabi kiraa*) in 1988 for 13 million yen in damages.

The Tōkyō District Court ruled on the case in March 1991 after tremendous outlays in both time and money by the plaintiff. While accepting the argument that the mold killer had caused her initial respiratory problems, the judges argued that the plaintiff had failed to establish a link between the product and her chronic bronchitis and awarded her a mere 700,000 yen (Hara 1992:34–36).

The mold killer case quickly became a cause célèbre in Japan just as the scandal-ridden LDP government was facing heightened demands from the electorate for more consumer-friendly policies. Consumer organizations and their allies in the legal and scholarly communities rallied behind the Tōkyō housewife in an effort to publicize the case as symbolic of all that was wrong with Japan's system of consumer redress: the failure of many manufacturers to accept responsibility for defective products, the heavy burden of proof placed on plaintiffs in product liability suits, and the inadequate settlements handed down through the country's various redress mechanisms. The system, advocates argued, had failed to guarantee the consumer's rights to product safety and redress and was in dire need of reform. And reform, they contended, was best achieved by passing a product liability law based on the concept of strict liability.

In this chapter, I trace the consumer movement's efforts to introduce a product liability (PL) law, starting in the early 1970s, when the concept was first debated in Japan, until its enactment in 1994 and implementation the following year. Although my main objective is to analyze the role and impact of consumer organizations in the consumer protection policymaking process, I also assess the myriad dimensions of the process itself: the influence of business groups over the deliberative process, the effects of a fragmented bureaucratic system on decision making, the role of ideas in the consumer protection policy process and their interaction with power configurations, and the impact of public opinion on policy outputs. The chapter concludes with a discussion of Japan's new strict liability administrative regime—a regime that symbolizes both the modest but significant improvements in national consumer protection policies following the end of one-party dominance and the lingering power of bureaucratic and business interests over Japanese consumer affairs.

Background

The Problem: Japan's Pre-1995 Redress System for the Victims of Defective Products

Consumer advocates interested in product liability during the early 1990s were concerned not so much about the problem of defective products in the marketplace—Japan was, after all, producing some of the world's safest and highest-quality products by the late 1970s—as deficiencies in the country's consumer redress. As the mold killer case so cogently illustrated, most of those deficiencies were rooted in the legal principles and institutional mechanisms making up that system.

Before 1995, a consumer seeking redress for economic or bodily damages suffered as a result of a defective product could do one or more of the following. First, he or she could contact the manufacturer or retailer directly and demand compensation. Although it is impossible to know exactly how many cases were handled through *aitai kōshō* (face-to-face negotiations with business), given the reluctance of firms to divulge information relating to the procedure, one reliable source estimated the total at roughly 70,000 cases per year.[1] About half of those were settled by the companies concerned (Kitamura 1992:20), usually in the form of product exchanges, free repairs, and/or small amounts of compensation.

Although many corporations went to great lengths during the 1970s and 1980s to improve their in-house claim management systems (Kitamura 1992:23), *aitai kōshō* attracted a great deal of public criticism. In an annual telephone poll organized by Nichibenren (Japan Federation of Lawyers' Associations) and consumer organizations, for example, many consumers complained about companies that had ignored their claims or accused them unfairly of mishandling products or misreading product warnings and directions. Even customers that did receive some form of redress expressed dissatisfaction with its form and amount, referring derogatorily to the often paltry sums awarded as *mimaikin* (money awarded to a sick person as a token of one's sympathy) or *isharyō* (consolation money).

Consumers who had fallen through the cracks of the *aitai kōshō* process and who had not yet "cried themselves to sleep" (*nakineirisuru*) could appeal to the Japan Consumer Information Center or a local consumer center either to intervene on their behalf or launch conciliation procedures (*chōtei*) between themselves and the targeted companies. Consumers could also apply to a number of ministerial programs at the national level designed to compensate the victims of defective products. Approximately 20 percent of cases not directly settled through *aitai kōshō* reached this stage (Kitamura 1992:21).

The ministerial programs received a great deal of attention from foreign scholars as an innovative way to deal with product-related accidents (see, e.g., Forbes 1987:178; Ramseyer 1996). The best-known of these programs was the SG Mark system administered under the Consumer Product Safety Law[2] by the Product Safety Association (Seihin anzen kyōkai), an organization affiliated with MITI. Under this system, an SG ("safety good") label was affixed to products that had been approved by the association, signifying to consumers that they had met certain safety standards. In the event of an accident involving one of the designated products that resulted in economic loss or injury, the user was entitled, on the basis of liability without fault, to compensation of up to 30 million yen (Nakamura, Tajima, and Yonekawa 1992:82), but only if it could be established that the accident had been caused by a product defect. The system was funded by participating manufacturers and importers and, as of 1992, covered a total of ninety-one products, including bicycle helmets, baseball bats, gas lighters, and baby carriages (*Yomiuri shimbun*, June 9, 1992). In addition to the SG Mark system, a number of similar programs were administered by the ministries or semigovernmental organizations to cover such items as fireworks (SF Mark), housing parts (BL [better living] Mark) and children's toys (ST Mark). Finally, the Ministry of Health and Welfare oversaw a program known as the Redress System for Damages Due to Medicinal Side Effects (Iyakuhin fukusayō higai kyūsai seido),[3] which was also funded by the companies concerned. All these programs, as we shall see later, are still in effect today under post-1994 product liability rules.

Although the mark systems were widely acknowledged for their positive contributions to the safety of Japanese products, consumer advocates during the 1980s and early 1990s viewed them as inherently flawed. They noted, for example, that since a very limited number of items had been incorporated into the programs, consumers burdened with defective products that did not carry the safety marks had to seek compensation by other means. Second, the organizations administering the programs were known to deny compensation to consumers on the grounds that the existence of defects had not been clearly established. Many of these decisions were criticized by advocates as arbitrary and unfair (Nakamura et al. 1992:83). The problem of proving the existence of defects may explain why as of October 1991, only 330 out of 705 accidents involving products carrying the SG mark had resulted in compensation (*Yomiuri shimbun*, June 9, 1992), a number that many advocates felt was far too low given the severity of the accidents in question. Finally, consumer advocates and their allies criticized the mark systems in principle for failing to hold companies legally liable for releasing defective products into the marketplace.

When all these avenues of recourse had been exhausted, the victims of defective products could sue the manufacturers for damages. But as proponents of a PL law were quick to point out, this was an almost impossible undertaking, for two sets of reasons. First, plaintiffs confronted the same procedural and financial barriers that functioned as disincentives for all forms of litigation in Japan. Those barriers included the lack of juries,[4] weak discovery provisions, the high cost of bringing suits to completion, the shortage of lawyers in Japan, bottlenecks in the court system, and the lack of a retainer fee system for PL counsel. Second, in order to win suits involving damages caused by defective products, consumers had to abide by article 709 of the Civil Code and prove (1) that manufacturers were negligent in the planning or manufacturing stages of the targeted products and (2) that the damages incurred were the direct result of product defects. To fulfill these legal obligations, consumers required detailed information about manufacturing processes and the technological composition of the products in question. But neither the Civil Code nor consumer-related statutes provided for consumer access to such information (Miyasaka et al. 1990b:31–42). Not surprisingly, only about 150 lawsuits involving defective products were tried in Japan between the turn of the century and July 1995. The United States, by contrast, had more than 13,000 product liability cases before the federal courts in FY1991 *alone* (Hamada 1996:12).

In some cases, plaintiffs have been exempted from this overwhelming burden of proof. The thalidomide disaster of the early 1960s, the SMON incident[5] involving central nervous system injuries caused by a diarrhea medicine tainted with quinoform, and the case of PCB-tainted Kanemi cooking oil that caused the so-called black pimple rash all were settled by the courts on the *presumption* that the manufacturers had been negligent and that the defective products in question were indeed the cause of death or physical handicaps. In none of these cases were the plaintiffs able to prove negligence. The sheer scope of the damages incurred and the fact that the cases had resulted in such resounding public outcries were what led to a departure from the traditional legal approach to negligence and ultimately to settlements in the plaintiffs' favor.

The victories for the plaintiffs notwithstanding, these cases highlighted a number of problems in Japan's system of product-related redress. First, the suits took as long as a decade or more to resolve and required enormous expenditures by the plaintiffs. Second, since most of the settlements were reached out of court, the question of who was to take legal responsibility for the disasters was never resolved. Finally, while something approaching strict liability had come to be accepted in lawsuits involving large numbers of plaintiffs, the burden of proof remained intact for cases with only one or a few plaintiffs.

It was in response to these perceived problems that Japanese scholars began to push for a law based on the principle of strict liability (*genkaku sekinin*) or liability without fault (*mukashitsu sekinin*), looking to the United States as a model.[6] The principle had first arisen in regard to defective products in the United States during the early to mid-1960s as the cumulative result of several years of case law. Briefly stated, strict liability requires plaintiffs to show that the products resulting in economic or bodily damage are defective. Plaintiffs are not required to prove that manufacturers were negligent in the planning or manufacturing stages of those products. Some of the burden of proof is thus transferred from consumers to manufacturers, who must prove that products were *not* defective at the time of their release into the marketplace in order to be exempted from liability. Since a similar law would help compensate for the Japanese consumer's lack of access to vital information about the manufacturing process, strict liability came to be defined by consumer advocates and their allies during their "issue definition" (*mondai teigi*) activities as a prerequisite for the consumer's rights to safe products and effective redress.

Ideas Without Broad Constituencies: The Pre-1985 Policy Process

The first decade of activism for strict liability was marked by a series of false starts. Scholars, lawyers, a handful of consumer advocates, and government officials discussed the idea during the early 1970s, but the political and economic conditions were such that a broad-based constituency either for or against enactment never materialized. As businesses strove to improve the quality of their products toward the end of the rapid-growth period and in the wake of the product-related disasters of the 1950s and 1960s, for example, many argued that the "problem" of defective products was not sufficiently serious to warrant a wholesale overhaul of product liability rules. Moreover, the fact that policymakers were far more concerned with sluggish economic growth rates than consumer safety after the 1973 oil shock decreased even further the chances of strict liability advancing to a priority position on the government agenda.[7] That said, pre-1985 discussions gave rise to some important ideas and interest-group alliances that influenced the future legislative process.

Scholars interested in product liability found a willing ally in the Economic Planning Agency (EPA), the agency responsible for the coordination of governmental consumer policy and the overseer of the Japan Consumer Information Center (Kokumin seikatsu sentaa). The Social Policy Council (Kokumin seikatsu shingikai), which is administered by the agency, began low-level discussions on the topic of consumer redress in 1973 and issued a report two years later that mentioned a strict liability law as a possible solution to the legal problems shouldered by the victims of defective products (Kitamura 1992:39). The report was the first formal statement issued by the bureaucracy on product liability reform.

The EPA took up the issue of reform for a number of reasons. The end of rapid economic growth, the rise of progressive local governments and the concomitant decline of LDP supremacy, the movement to strengthen the Antimonopoly Law, and the introduction of environmental and welfare legislation during the late 1960s and early 1970s had created a political environment amenable to the discussion of consumer protection issues like PL. There was, in short, a "policy window" in place that had appeared with little prompting from pressure groups aside from the demonstration effect of ideas generated by academic circles. Furthermore, the EPA, as the government's official consumer watchdog and an agency looking for an issue through which to distinguish itself vis-à-vis the more powerful economic ministries, was the logical agency to orchestrate the debate.

Encouraged by the Social Policy Council's final report on the topic, a study group on PL headed by Wagatsuma Sakae, a prominent civil law specialist from Tōkyō University and a former adviser to the Justice Ministry, released a general or "tentative" draft (yōkō shian) of a strict liability law. One of the most influential contributions to the debate and decidedly pro-consumer, the draft formed the basis of many subsequent proposals generated during the next two decades (Nihon keizai shimbunsha 1991:107) in much the same way that the JFTC's 1974 proposal for antitrust reform influenced the debate leading up to the 1977 amendments to the Antimonopoly Law.

Although the issue failed to achieve a higher level of priority on the government agenda, research on product liability continued between 1975 and 1985. The Social Policy Council released additional reports on the topic in 1976 and 1981 (Kitamura 1992:39); the EPA launched a series of surveys and studies on Japanese consumer redress systems and the possible impact of PL on industry (Kitamura 1992:39–40); and the Kōmeitō set up an intraparty "PL Law Study Group" (PL hōritsu no benkyōkai) in 1980 to look into the issue (interview, Hikasa, March 1993). Conspicuously absent from the debate during these early years, however, was participation by the ruling LDP and the major economic ministries. Business, for the most part, appeared uninterested in the debate and contributed virtually nothing to its development.

Consumer organizations observed these early deliberations from the sidelines. Although a small number of leaders recognized the potential impact of a PL law on the quality of consumer protection in Japan, the vast majority were still unfamiliar with the issue during the 1970s and early 1980s (interview, Andō, February 1993) and were preoccupied with antitrust and food safety issues. The debate was, after all, largely confined to academic circles and packaged in a way that was at times incomprehensible to activists with virtually no training in civil law. The political and economic environments, moreover, were not generating the kinds of opportunities that might encourage activism. The early 1980s were a period of economic retrenchment, resurgent conservatism in the political realm, movements toward administrative reform, and a declining interest in quality-of-life issues. The time was simply not ripe for investing scarce movement resources in a full-scale legislative movement.

The Turning Point: The European Community's Directive on PL and Japanese Domestic Trends

The turning point in the product liability debate in Japan was the July 1985 directive on product liability issued by the European Community's Council of Directors. The purpose of the directive was to eliminate the numerous disparities between the PL systems of the twelve member nations—disparities viewed as barriers to trade[8]—in preparation for union in 1992. Serving as a model for the PL statutes of member nations, the directive not only led to the unification of European Union statutes but also spurred the adoption of strict liability rules in the European Free Trade Association (EFTA), Australia, Brazil, China, and South Korea. By suggesting that liability without fault was an international trend that could no longer be ignored, these trends served as "focusing events" (Kingdon 1984:104) in the Japanese policy process—as powerful symbols, in other words, that helped focus the attention of both policymakers and the attentive public on PL reform.

The EC directive quickly became a reference point for actors in the policy process. Many Japanese found it particularly appealing because it gave member states the option of incorporating the following pro-business concessions into their respective legislation: (1) the exemption of primary agricultural products from the purview of the law, (2) the recognition of the "development risk" plea (kaihatsu kiken no kōben),[9] and (3) the imposition of ceilings on the amount of compensation that could be awarded to plaintiffs. One of the more controversial features of the directive that drew the opposition of Japanese consumer advocates was the requirement that plaintiffs prove the existence of product defects and the cause-and-effect relationships between those defects and the damages incurred.

Conditions in Japan during the mid- to late 1980s also stimulated the PL debate. First, the government was issuing a number of high-profile statements on consumer protection. In August 1989, following the Recruit stocks-for-favors scandal and in anticipation of the Structural Impediments Initiative (SII) talks that were to begin the following month, Prime Minister Kaifu Toshiki announced a "consumer declaration" (shōhisha sengen) that emphasized the important position of consumers in society (shōhisha jūshi). The government later introduced a series of policies, including the loosening of the Large-Scale Retail Store Law[10] and increases in public works spending, that were designed in part to meet the interests of consumers.

Comparable statements and policies continued into the 1990s. In May 1991, MITI recommended that consumption and other quality-of-life issues replace economic expansion as the primary goals of the government's economic policy. This message was seconded the following month in a report issued by the Ad Hoc Council for the Promotion of Administrative Reform (Rinji gyōsei kaikaku suishin shingikai) that called for more attention to "citizen lifestyles" (kokumin seikatsu) and the enactment of some kind of product liability law. Not to be outdone, the Miyazawa cabinet adopted that same month a highly publicized resolution to transform Japan into a "lifestyle superpower" (seikatsu taikoku).[11] Although many of these policies were often criticized by consumer organizations as little more than halfhearted responses to American demands for the development of a more consumer-friendly society in Japan (interview, Ohta, December 1993), they nevertheless lent an aura of legitimacy to strict liability as an integral part of consumer protection (interview, Kawaguchi, June 1993).

The movement toward deregulation served as an additional impetus behind the heightened deliberations on PL. As in other countries, consumer access to safe products in Japan had been achieved mainly through economic and social regulation. As pressures mounted for regulatory reform during the late 1980s and early 1990s, consumer advocates, their allies in the legal and academic professions, a number of opposition party politicians, and even a few government officials looked to a product liability law based on strict liability as one way to guarantee consumer access to safe products in the midst of the government's partial disengagement from the affairs of business. A PL law, we should note, would do much more than just provide for prompt and efficient compensation to the victims of defective products on those infrequent occasions when product-related accidents did occur; it would also serve a preventive function by presenting businesses with incentives—the clear demarcation of producer liability and the threat of costly lawsuits—to enhance the safety levels of their products *before* accidents occurred.

In sum, by the late 1980s, PL had become a potential solution to the problem of consumer redress as well as to international pressures for the harmonization of domestic laws and trade standards, to the government's professed commitment to building a more consumer-oriented society, and to the safety concerns of consumers in the wake of deregulation. It was now up to the supporters of PL to persuade their business-oriented opponents that strict liability was in everyone's best interest.

The Formation of the PL Promotion Faction

The development of a pro-PL movement began in the EPA and the academic community, expanded during the 1980s into Nichibenren and some of the opposition parties,[12] and then grew to encompass consumer organizations. This was not, however, a well-developed "policy community" marked by regular exchanges of information and intergroup strategizing. For one thing, the access of nongovernmental groups to the EPA was limited and sporadic. Of the five sets of actors that comprised the pro-PL movement, only the academics in their advisory capacity seemed to enjoy any semblance of regular contact with the agency. As for the opposition parties, the Socialist Party and the Kōmeitō carried out their respective deliberations on PL largely in isolation from both each other and other groups in the movement, although there was some intergroup communication at key junctures of the policy process. In keeping with movement precedent, however, the alliance between lawyers and consumer organizations was characterized by close and regular contact. Despite the fragmentation of the pro-PL movement, there was enough commonality of thinking among the constituent groups to earn them the label PL *suishinha*, or "PL promotion faction."

From 1989, in response to pro-consumer changes in the general political atmosphere, Nichibenren, the Tōkyō bengōshikai (Tōkyō Lawyers' Association), and the Socialist Party and the Kōmeitō floated model PL laws or, in the case of the parties, Diet bills, that defined the early positions of much of the PL promotion faction. Based on Professor Wagatsuma's 1975 recommendations, these proposals omitted the development risk plea and incorporated "presumption clauses" (*suitei kitei*) that released plaintiffs from the responsibility of proving the connection between a product defect and damages incurred.[13] The presumption clause was an important point of departure from the EC directive, which, according to many in the promotion faction, was not an appropriate model for Japan given the numerous barriers to litigation faced by Japanese plaintiffs (J. Kobayashi 1992:113).[14] Since the PL models produced by the promotion faction were generally deemed pro-consumer (*shōhisha yori*) and much harsher on business than the 1985 EC directive, they were severely criticized by business circles.

Hampered by their relatively meager human and financial resources and reluctant to commit to a full-blown legislative movement until a political window of opportunity had definitely been opened, consumer organizations did not jump onto the PL bandwagon until well after the reform movement had gained a firm footing in the legal and academic communities. By the late 1980s, however, key advocates at the national level were studying the issue, attending academic lectures, conferring with lawyers, and occasionally meeting with PL proponents in the opposition parties. One advocate in her fifties even went so far as to obtain a law degree from a prestigious Tōkyō university in order to master the legal nuances of product liability. For the most part, however, consumer organizations felt handicapped by their lack of legal expertise and formal access to the main policymaking fora and were thus forced to react to the debate and to support proposals generated elsewhere in the pro-PL movement. As during the movement to amend the Antimonopoly Law, the primary role of consumer organizations was to help define the issue and to distribute information produced by experts to an attentive public.

The Thirteenth Social Policy Council

The "signal" (Tarrow 1996:54) that proved pivotal to the full mobilization of consumer organizations in the PL promotion faction was Prime Minister Kaifu's establishment in December 1990 of the Thirteenth Social Policy Council (Kokumin seikatsu shingikai) under the chairmanship of Katō Ichirō.[15] The council was given a mandate to deliberate on the pros and cons of strict liability for two years, a move interpreted by consumer activists as a sign that product liability reform had achieved a significant position on the government agenda. But because of the council's institutional features, advocates failed to assume much more than a symbolic presence in the policymaking process.

The Institutional Context

According to the 1965 directive under which the Social Policy Council was established, its members were to reflect the opinions of "ordinary citizens." In practice, however, members have been drawn not only from consumer and other citizen organizations in which one would expect to find "ordinary citizens" but also from academia, the media, private and semigovernmental research organizations, and, most important, the business community.

Consumer advocates who sat on the Thirteenth Social Policy Council complained about a number of institutional features—many of them informal—which further weakened the council's mandate to incorporate the opinions of "the people" into the policy process. First, as one prominent consumer activist and frequent *shingikai* member put it, only those individuals whose opinions were "convenient" (*tsugō ga ii*) from the bureaucrats' point of view were allowed to serve on the council (interview, consumer activist, February 1993). This custom often discouraged activists from expressing their opinions for fear of losing these coveted positions, positions that, it must be remembered, constituted the movement's most valuable inroad into the national policymaking process. The heavy hand of the bureaucracy was also apparent in the way deliberations were carried out. The EPA, for example, set the council's agenda, banned the public from attending sessions, and prohibited members from discussing reports and reference materials with nonmembers. Finally, reports issued by the Social Policy Council were drafted by officials in the Citizens' Lifestyles Bureau rather than by the council members themselves, a practice that often resulted in documents that failed to reflect the different opinions of the members.

In an unprecedented move in the history of PL reform, the Thirteenth Social Policy Council established a high-profile working group on product liability in its Consumer Policy Subcommittee (Shōhisha seisaku bukai). The move was widely hailed as a sign of the government's enhanced commitment to reform (*Yomiuri shimbun*, February 1991; interview, Hara, February 1993). Chaired by Morishima Akio of Nagoya University, a prominent civil law and product liability expert, the committee consisted of four consumer representatives, nine individuals from the business community, and ten "individuals of learning and experience" (*gakushiki keikensha*) from academia, the media, and semiprivate research organizations, for a total of twenty-three members. The working group's primary task was to determine whether or not Japan actually needed a product liability law. Although the specific features of different PL regimes were discussed throughout the deliberations, the working group focused on this larger question in the hopes of uncovering a consensus either opposed to or in favor of the notion of strict liability. Accordingly, this stage of the policy process was referred to as the *rippōron* phase, or the "debate on whether or not to enact." In keeping with their long-standing views of the Social Policy Council, consumer advocates and the media[16] were harshly critical of the heavy representation of business interests in the working group, arguing that the makeup of the group would hamper efforts to carry out its mandate.

The Business Community

For all intents and purposes, the business community, as represented by its members on the Social Policy Council, was putting a very negative foot forward in 1991 and early 1992 on the issue of product liability reform. At one extreme were the pharmaceutical, household appliance, and automobile industries, which expressed outright opposition to the very idea of a new PL law based on the concept of strict liability. The products manufactured by these industries represented the leading edge of technological development and were consequently the target of the most complaints from consumers both at home and, more tellingly, in the United States. Industry representatives therefore feared that the enactment of a PL law would lead to an American-style run on the courts (*ranso*)[17] and a subsequent drain on company resources, not to mention a dampening of incentives to delve into new but potentially risky technologies (interview, Kumada, June 1993; see also Nihon keizai shimbunsha 1991:43–91). These and other industries were also worried that costs like higher product liability insurance fees would hurt the economy in the midst of a deepening recession and weaken the competitive edge of Japanese business in international circles (Morishima 1993a:726). During the *rippōron* phase of deliberations, these industries led the pack in extolling the virtues of such uniquely Japanese institutions as *aitai kōshō*, obligatory car testing (*shaken*) and insurance, the mark programs, and other alternatives to strict liability (Nihon keizai shimbunsha 1991:55–66).

Small and medium enterprises also opposed strict liability, although most were still unaware of the concept's legal meaning and economic implications. The Japan Chamber of Commerce and Industry (Nisshō), the political spokesperson for this sector, claimed that small manufacturers would be crippled by the heavy financial burdens imposed by product liability insurance and lawsuits and that the manufacturers of component parts would be held unfairly responsible for the defects of finished products (interview, Fujimori, June 1993).

These strong pockets of resistance notwithstanding, it appears that more and more firms viewed PL as inevitable at this time and were preparing for its arrival. According to a survey released by the *Nihon keizai shimbun* in March 1991, for example, 80 percent of 230 large companies surveyed stated that they anticipated the introduction of a PL law in the next five years (*Nihon keizai shimbun*, March 4, 1991). Many businesses were also taking steps to prevent future lawsuits by improving the safety of their products and were meeting regularly with competitors to discuss possible industrywide responses to issues related to consumer redress (*Asahi shimbun*, March 17, 1991). If given the choice, businessmen would have preferred to avoid the introduction of a product liability law altogether. But in light of international trends and mounting public support, even some firms that were publicly opposed to enactment were treating it as a foregone conclusion.

These sentiments were neatly illustrated for me during an impromptu conversation with a youngish businessman on a Tōkyō commuter train at the height of PL deliberations. Curious to learn what had brought me to Japan, this well-dressed businessman, who worked for a medium-size manufacturing company, was eager to talk about product liability when I told him the purpose of my research visit. Taking advantage of the situation, I immediately asked him about his company's position on PL reform:

> "Well," he replied, "Although some of our higher-ups in my company and our representatives in Nisshō hope that strict liability will never be enacted, we are preparing for it: investigating product liability insurance, making our products a bit safer—that sort of thing. We certainly don't have the power to influence the decision either way, so we may as well be prepared.
>
> "Personally, I support strict liability, and so does my wife, who reads about it a lot in the newspapers. As a consumer, I think it's only fair. Trouble is, I can't make my opinions known to my superiors because they'll only question my loyalty to the company. This is, after all, one of those issues in which consumers and businesses can't be expected to see eye to eye."

MITI

MITI also sent out some mixed signals on PL reform in 1991 and early 1992. On the one hand, MITI was determined to investigate PL once the issue had gained a foothold elsewhere in the policy process. Its reasons for doing so included, first, ongoing pressure from abroad to contribute more to the international harmonization of trade-related laws and product safety standards. Second, MITI was influenced by the fact that PL had become an international trend of the times. Direct foreign pressure (*gaiatsu*) on the topic was never a large factor,[18] but the force of foreign example, if we can refer to it as such, seemed to have swayed the ministry. Finally, MITI was intent on gaining control of a policy process that was centered elsewhere in the bureaucracy (*Nihon keizai shimbun*, June 12, 1991). A friend of consumers MITI was not; its interest in PL was, for the most part, rooted in image and power considerations.

The fact that MITI did not have the consumer interest at the top of its agenda was underscored by its cautious stance on product liability, which was in turn a reflection of its determination to prevent the introduction of a PL law that would dampen productivity (*Nihon keizai shimbun*, June 6, 1991). The ministry's go-slow approach was heavily conditioned by a close and well-institutionalized relationship with the business community. As governmental deliberations on PL progressed, high-level officials from the Consumer Economics Bureau (Shōhi keizai kyoku)[19] of the Industrial Policy Section (Sangyō seisakuka) frequently made the rounds of business groups to inform them of major decisions and the overall direction of policymaking on PL. Officials from industry-specific sections in the ministry, moreover, went to great lengths to keep the industries in their respective jurisdictions updated on various developments in the policymaking sphere (interview, Tagaya, March 1994). This constant communication between the ministry and business clarified to MITI the trepidations of the business community concerning product liability reform.

Pressure from the business community appeared to have had a major impact on MITI. In August 1991, for example, the ministry refused to publicize the results of a study carried out by its Consumer Economics Bureau on the effectiveness of consumer redress mechanisms in individual companies. Analysts speculated that since the survey had uncovered a number of weaknesses in Japanese consumer redress mechanisms, publicizing the report would have compelled the ministry to take a stronger stand against business opposition to PL (*Nihon keizai shimbunsha* 1991:97). Clearly, MITI was not about to take a proactive stance on PL until the business community was more firmly on board.

The Liberal Democratic Party (LDP)

The Liberal Democratic Party was also heavily influenced by key business spokespersons and determined to put a brake on outside demands for a consumer-friendly product liability law. Recognizing that the public would hold it to its commitment to promote a more consumer-oriented society, the party established in 1991 the Subcommittee on Product Liability Systems (Seizōbutsusekikinseido ni kansuru shōinkai) under the Research Commission on Economics and Commodity Prices (Keizai bukka mondai chōsakai) of the Policy Affairs Research Council. Headed initially by Hayashi Yoshirō, who later went on to become finance minister, the committee of thirty-one members carried out research on PL and heard from concerned parties throughout the polity. In only one of those early sessions, however, did consumer representatives and lawyers have a chance to voice their positions (Jiyūminshutō 1992b).

Although the party tried to influence policymaking at this early stage, it was not as influential as MITI in defining the course of the debate. Since PL was not a great vote getter, only a few LDP Diet members were actually paying attention to the issue. Of those who were interested in strict liability, moreover, many opposed the concept altogether as a result of their close links to the small- and big-business communities. Finally, the LDP lacked expertise on product liability and thus took a back seat to MITI in terms of defining — or at least reacting to — the debate. On several occasions, the LDP's public position reflected almost verbatim the demands of the business community. In September 1991, for example, Keidanren issued a negative report on PL and appealed (*mōshiire*) to the LDP to exercise restraint on decisions pertaining to the topic (*Chūnichi shimbun*, October 15, 1992). Keidanren's position was later incorporated into the interim report of the party's Subcommittee on Product Liability Systems that was released the following month.

The Mobilization of Consumer Advocates

As it became increasingly apparent that the formal and informal dimensions of the PL policy process would be closed to consistent and effective participation by representatives of the consumer interest, consumer advocates, lawyers, and a number of influential scholars launched an extrainstitutional offensive against the pro-business camp.

From May 1991, consumer advocates established the PL renrakukai (Shōhisha no tame no seizōbutsusekininhō no settei wo motomeru zenkoku renrakukai, or All-Japan Liaison Committee to Demand the Establishment of a Product Liability Law for Consumers) and nine regional chapters under the auspices of Shōdanren.[20] The primary purpose of the PL renrakukai was to facilitate strategic networking in the organized consumer movement and between the movement and other actors in the PL promotion faction. The organization served, for example, as a conduit for conveying information between members of governmental *shingikai* and other leaders at the national level, as a channel for national leaders to coordinate strategy with grassroots activists, and as a mechanism for grassroots groups to convey their opinions and important information to the center. Based on my observations of past consumer campaigns, I would argue that the PL renrakukai was one of the best-organized consumer networks in the history of the postwar consumer movement.

Strategically, the renrakukai orchestrated a number of activities designed to mobilize public opinion, convey that opinion to policymakers, and, in the process, poke holes in the arguments of the pro-business camp. In order to mobilize and channel public opinion, it coordinated countless petition drives; sponsored symposia, lectures, study groups, and mass rallies; and pressured local assemblies into adopting pro-PL resolutions (PL renrakukai 1997:10). Most of the symposia and lectures were conducted by prominent allies from the legal and academic communities and were carried out in local consumer centers, many of which also supplied renrakukai activists with facilities for their intragroup meetings.[21]

Some of the tactics that were employed by the renrakukai were unique to the PL campaign. The most noteworthy was the defective products hotline (*kekkan shōhin 110 ban*),[22] an annual three-day telephone service launched in 1990 by Nichibenren that in subsequent years included the participation of Shufuren and other organizations from the renrakukai. The hotline, which was at one point available in thirty-three locations around the country, gave average consumers an opportunity to inquire about product liability and, more important, to talk about their own experiences with defective products and consumer redress systems.

The PL hotline was an ingenious program that killed two birds with one stone. First, since the event was well covered by virtually all the major newspapers, it proved to be an effective mechanism for reaching the citizenry and educating them about product liability and their rights as consumers. To date, "issue definition" in the product liability case had proved to be particularly challenging for consumer representatives and their allies; PL was, after all, a highly technical issue lacking in political urgency and appeal. The problem was compounded by the nature of the term itself. A mouthful in Japanese (seizōbutsusekinin), let alone English, "product liability" was the source of considerable confusion even as late as 1993 among local consumer leaders (interview, Tanaka, May 1993). The use of the acronym "PL" helped simplify matters somewhat, although many citizens mistakenly associated it with a high school of the same name that was well known for its baseball team (interview, Tanaka, May 1993).

Second, the PL hotline was one of several tactics that enabled Nichiben-ren and consumer leaders to gather rough but compelling statistics about the perceived inadequacies of extant systems of consumer redress.[23] The renrakukai then used these statistics to counter pro-business arguments that the problems of defective products and consumer redress were minor and that existing institutions were capable of adequately dealing with them (Nakamura et al. 1992:23–25). Other means used by the pro-consumer camp to discredit their opponents included the dissemination of survey results that exposed the numerous barriers to litigation under the existing PL regime[24] and the distribution of well-researched studies—many of them paralleled by comparable EPA reports—highlighting the distinctive institutional features of the Japanese court system that would prevent the country from succumbing to an American-style "product liability crisis."

Efforts by the PL renrakukai and its allies to mobilize public opinion and expose the weaknesses of the arguments emanating from the pro-business camp were favorably conveyed to the public by Japan's national and regional newspapers. Product liability was being covered by all the major national dailies—albeit not as a headline issue—with the Mainichi shimbun taking the most pro-consumer stance. The regional papers, meanwhile, were faithfully charting the activities of consumer advocates in their respective areas and, I would argue, were even more pro-consumer than their national counterparts.[25] All newspapers, to varying degrees, were critical of the business community and MITI and stressed the need for enhanced consumer protection in Japan through the enactment of a product liability law. Over time, a number of editors established close relations with activists in the PL promotion faction. A few of the lawyers, for example, were frequently contacted by newspapers for input into editorials and their feedback on the accuracy of articles relating to product liability (interview, source withheld).

Stalemate

At the end of the day, the PL renrakukai and its allies proved powerless against the stubborn resistance of the business community to product liability reform. In October 1991, in a move reminiscent of Prime Minister Miki's roundtable on antitrust reform, the Social Policy Council postponed submitting a definitive statement on the issue of reform for another year, citing a lack of consensus (interview, Kawaguchi, June 1993; Keizaikikakuchō 1991a). Despite the fact that two-thirds of the members of the working group had pressed for speedy enactment, the report emphasized the potential of existing consumer redress systems to solve the problems connected to accidents caused by defective products. As might be expected, the interim report met with scathing criticism from consumer organizations and the legal community and approval from Keidanren (Nihon keizai shimbunsha 1991:101: *Asahi shimbun*, October 12, 1991).

The stalemate between the consumer and business camps in the Social Policy Council continued into 1992 and eventually spilled outside the confines of the council. The events that subsequently transpired from the spring of 1992 show the important role played by public opinion in the debate.

Sometime in late 1991 or early 1992, Professors Katō and Morishima — both moderate proponents of a product liability law—privately contacted key politicians in the Kōmeitō and urged them to immediately submit a PL bill to the Lower House in the hopes of attracting public attention to the debate and breaking the impasse in the Social Policy Council. The party, which was in the midst of drafting such a bill, complied in May 1992 (interview, Hikasa, March 1993), and the Socialist Party followed suit in the Upper House in June.[26] Both bills included presumption clauses and did not provide for the risk development plea. But as often happens with private members' bills, both bills failed to reach the deliberation stage.

Neither party expected their bills to pass. They did, however, hope that they would have an indirect impact on the direction of deliberations in the Social Policy Council by strengthening the public's interest in the issue. And this is precisely what happened. From the summer of 1992, newspaper articles on PL were written much more regularly; books on the subject rapidly appeared in bookstores; and public lectures sponsored by universities and other public and private organizations began to proliferate around the country. Consumer organizations, for their part, rode this wave of heightened interest in PL by intensifying their efforts to mobilize public opinion at the grassroots level in favor of reform. Business representatives, meanwhile, refused to discuss their positions with either journalists or consumer advocates (interviews, *Nihon keizai shimbun* staff writer, November 1992; Hara, February 1993). Keidanren justified its own reticence with the argument that it "had not yet established an official position" on the subject (interview, Keidanren official, May 1993).

In October 1992, the Thirteenth Social Policy Council succumbed to the stalemate by releasing a final report that deferred for another year the decision on whether or not to enact a product liability law. The council was formally disbanded and the task of deliberating on PL was left to the Fourteenth Social Policy Council.

The inability of the Thirteenth Social Policy Council to come to a formal decision on PL struck many onlookers as highly suspicious, particularly in light of the LDP government's professed plans to build a more consumer-oriented society and the fact that a majority of council members supported enactment. How can we explain this? Why did the bureaucratic architects of the Social Policy Council report in the Economic Planning Agency act against the wishes of both the council and public opinion?

The official explanation was that a consensus on PL had not yet been reached (interview, Kawaguchi, June 1993). Given what we know about the various players in this drama, however, "consensus" was simply a euphemism for the support of the business community. But this only begs another question: if, as the survey statistics quoted earlier suggest, the business community was viewing strict liability as an inevitability, why was it so reluctant to publicly endorse reform?

The answer, I believe, had a lot to do with the terms of the PL debate in 1991 and 1992. Consider the various bills and proposals that were circulating at the time. Drafted by actors in the pro-consumer camp, these bills, with their presumption clauses and lack of development risk pleas, were all very tough on business, at least much more so than comparable laws in western Europe. Had the kind of law advanced by the pro-consumer camp been enacted in Japan, businesses would have lost out not only financially — strict liability without built-in protections for business can, as many American firms have found out the hard way, raise costs and drain profits[27] — but also in terms of their overall power relationship with consumers.

Many business representatives still believed during the early 1990s that the task of consumer protection was best left to the initiatives of business and the bureaucracy (interviews, Fujimori, June 1993; Keidanren official, May 1993), a paternalistic approach that had fared well with businesses in the past but could not have survived in a PL system that strengthened the legal powers of individual consumers. And the PL proposals floating about in 1991/92 did precisely that by lessening the burden of proof shouldered by consumers and by virtually eliminating opportunities for firms to exempt themselves from liability. Business, I contend, felt much more threatened by these proposals than by the concept of strict liability per se. Thus, their drag on Social Policy Council deliberations should be interpreted not as a vote against the principle of strict liability but, rather, against the *kind* of strict liability regime advocated by the PL promotion faction. Consequently, business representatives refused to endorse a decision to enact until the details of the law had been settled.

These observations have important implications for the impact of consumer organizations and their allies on the consumer protection policy process. The evidence presented earlier suggests that when the debate was centered in the Thirteenth Social Policy Council, the PL promotion faction—working both inside and outside the council—was able to put business representatives on the defensive by determining many of the terms of that debate. If this is indeed true, then the two-year stalemate should be interpreted as a sign of consumer as well as business influence. Unfortunately for the movement, however, that influence declined during the next leg of deliberations.

Voices from Heaven: The Stalemate Dissolves

One reason that consumer influence waned after the autumn of 1992 was that the institutional configurations of PL policymaking changed in a way that enabled business interests to regain the upper hand. Since businesses refused to support enactment until the details of a new PL law had been settled, the focus of deliberations in the Fourteenth Social Policy Council formally shifted from an emphasis on whether or not to enact a law (*rippōron*) to discussions of what the contents (*nakami*) of such a law should be. In order to carry out those discussions, the policymaking process was decentralized to embrace all the ministries that would have a hand in implementing a strict liability law. Puzzled onlookers looked to these developments as a "voice from heaven" (*ten no koe*) or water suddenly overflowing a dam (Y. Kitagawa and Z. Kitagawa 1993:7), the implication being that enactment had suddenly become a foregone conclusion. While it is certainly true that Japan appeared closer to enactment than ever before, the subsequent deliberations show that as the policy process was decentralized and the leverage of the PL promotion faction over formal decision making declined, consumers still had a great deal to lose.

Shingikai *Deliberations*

Unlike the Thirteenth Social Policy Council, there was no working group under the Consumer Policy Committee (Shōhisha seisaku bukai) of the Fourteenth Social Policy Council[28] to deliberate exclusively on product liability. PL was, however, the main topic of discussion in the committee, which consisted of three consumer activists, a representative from NHK, eight members from the business community, and four scholars. One consumer advocate on the committee, a prominent leader of the PL renrakukai, had also served on the Thirteenth Social Policy Council.

During the deliberations, the EC directive was promoted by both the EPA and other members of the Hosokawa government as the most viable model for Japan, a move that eventually discredited the feasibility of the various proposals drafted by the PL promotion faction. To add punch to the directive, the EPA invited Hans Claudius Taschner to speak before the council. Dr. Taschner was a specialist in civil and economic law and citizen rights in the Directorate-General of the Commission of the European Communities and a drafter of the 1985 directive. In addition to explaining the directive to the members of the Social Policy Council, Dr. Taschner also spoke to groups of consumers and businessmen and urged them to find a compromise solution to their long-standing impasse. Many in the business community seemed willing to consider the directive, given its built-in protections for business. Consumer organizations, however, were far more critical of the European model on the grounds that it did not make sufficient allowance for Japanese legal and political institutions that put consumers at a disadvantage vis-à-vis business.

As often happens during Social Policy Council deliberations, consumer representatives complained that their voices had been stifled by the nature of the proceedings. In the summer of 1993, for example, the council held hearings with members of Keidanren, Nichibenren, and the PL renrakukai. The participants were given fifteen minutes each to state their cases, with the Keidanren representative expressing a predictably cautious attitude. Although consumer organizations welcomed the chance to participate in the hearings, they complained about the time restrictions and the rigid structure of the proceedings which, they argued, prevented them from freely expressing their opinions (interview, consumer activist, February 1994).

Compared with many of the other ministries, however, the Social Policy Council was a paragon of openness. Several ministries, including MITI, the Ministry of Health and Welfare, and the Ministry of Agriculture, Forestry and Fisheries pulled out all the stops and established *shingikai* whose makeup was comparable to that of the Social Policy Council. Since all these *shingikai* included consumer representatives, several of whom were sitting on two or three ministerial PL-related *shingikai* simultaneously, the PL promotion faction was able to voice consumer-related demands to the various powers that be. In many instances, however, advocates complained that their demands and suggestions had been all but ignored. This was particularly true in the case of MITI's Industrial Structure Council, whose Committee on General Product Safety (Sōgō seihin anzen bukai) had been deliberating on PL since 1991. The four consumer representatives on this thirty-six member committee viewed their participation largely as an empty formality and frequently criticized the overwhelming influence of business representatives. As for the Ministries of Construction, Transportation, and Justice—none of which had established formal committees to debate the issue—informal deliberations on product liability were held between officials and representatives of the industries in their respective jurisdictions with virtually no opportunities for input from consumer advocates.

In late 1993, the Social Policy Council compiled a final report based on the recommendations of the ministries and submitted it to the prime minister. The report was endorsed in mid-December by the cabinet's Consumer Protection Council (Shōhisha hogo kaigi), thereby marking the government's formal decision to enact a product liability law based on the concept of strict liability.The report attested to the strength of the pro-PL movement by strongly recommending the enactment of a product liability law. With regard to the content of legislation, however, it met all the major demands of the business community, including the omission of a presumption clause, inclusion of the development risk plea, and limits on liability. Critics, including consumer representatives, condemned the document for departing from the spirit of the EC directive by failing to make allowances for special features in the Japanese legal system that put a heavy burden of proof on plaintiffs in civil lawsuits.

Enactment

Enter the Political Parties

Shortly after the Fourteenth Social Policy Council disbanded, the constituent parties of the new Hosokawa coalition government set up a "PL project team" to look further into the issue and to "forge a political consensus" on product liability in preparation for the drafting stage of the legislative process (interview, H. Itō, February 1994). The twenty-one member team (*Nihon shōhi keizai*, March 7, 1994), which included a number of former lawyers and even the odd citizen activist, met weekly for about three months, with section chiefs from the relevant ministries in regular attendance (interview, Edano, March 1994). From the standpoint of consumer protection policymaking—and in marked contrast to the antitrust and additives cases—it was an unusual show of political party power over a process that was normally centered in the bureaucracy.

The project team was committed to forging a workable compromise between the polarized demands of consumer and business representatives. At one of several meetings between the team and PL renrakukai leaders, for instance, a team representative urged consumer activists to soften their positions toward business. A law that fulfilled "100 percent" of consumer demands would have been ideal, he argued, but it was not politically feasible; legislation that met "60 percent" of those demands should therefore be welcomed as a step forward for consumer protection in Japan. By this point in the policy process, however, it was clear that the PL renrakukai and its allies were no longer speaking with a single voice. While all supported the enactment of a strict liability law, a number of scholars and even a few consumer organizations distanced themselves from the others and expressed their support for an EC-style law.[29]

While more and more businesses were accepting product liability legislation as a logical antidote to deregulation (*Mainichi shimbun*, January 21, 1994), a few business leaders threatened to withdraw their support for enactment altogether if the following conditions were not met: (1) incorporation of the development risk plea, (2) omission of a presumption clause, (3) establishment of the term of liability to ten years (as opposed to twenty years, as demanded by the consumer camp), and (4) detailed codification of the concept of product "defect" (*Mainichi shimbun*, January 21, 1994). All these conditions had been cited in the Fourteenth Social Policy Council's final report, but business leaders continued to push their demands for fear that ongoing pressures from the pro-consumer camp in a context of political party instability would result in an alteration of the final legislative product.

Consumer activists, meanwhile, shifted their tactics to take advantage of that instability. To date, most of their activities had focused on mobilizing public opinion at the local level. Once the PL project team assumed the initiative in the debate, the PL renrakukai and its allies launched an intensive lobbying campaign. Members of the renrakukai made the rounds of Diet members from both houses, urging them to support a PL law that met the needs of consumers (interview, Ohta, December 1993). They also conducted surveys of the political parties to gauge their positions on the content of the law (*Nikkei ryūtsū*, December 2, 1993). A few of the activists, including one prominent lawyer, even managed to establish informal links with a few key bureaucrats (interview, source withheld), links that provided the renrakukai as a whole with important insider information. Clearly, consumer politics in Japan looked to be in the midst of a change. In contrast to the past when consumer representatives had been granted audiences with conservative politicians only rarely (interview, Miyamoto, February 1994), they now enjoyed a much more meaningful dialogue with policymakers (interviews, Edano, March 1994; H. Itō, February 1994).

Once the ball bounced back into the bureaucracy's court and the drafting stage was set in motion, however, consumer lobbying proved fruitless. Centered in the EPA and with input from section chiefs (*kachō*) from all the major economic ministries, the process, which lasted for about six weeks in the spring of 1994, was completely closed to input from consumer representatives and shrouded in a veil of secrecy.[30] Officials justified their actions at the time on the grounds that opening the process to public input would obstruct the often tricky process of interministerial coordination (interview, Ministry of Transportation official, March 1994). The bill that finally emerged incorporated all the recommendations of the final report of the Fourteenth Social Policy Council mentioned earlier. Not surprisingly, it met with the approval of both the LDP and the business community (interview, Machimura, April 1994).

In June 1994, the bill was passed unanimously by both houses of the Diet. It contained very few surprises.[31] On two important points, however, the consumer interest managed to reassert itself as a result of pressure from within the Diet by members of the PL project team. First, following an intense Upper House battle over the subjection of blood products to the purview of the law,[32] the forces in favor of inclusion eventually won out (Kawaguchi 1994:47). Second, and largely in response to demands emanating from the Justice Ministry, as well as from lawyers, consumer organizations, and many academics, the concept of product defect was defined very loosely in order to give the courts adequate leeway in interpreting product liability cases (Kawaguchi 1994:47). These hard-won victories of the pro-consumer camp were a rare instance in which consumer representatives had a significant, albeit indirect influence over the actual details of public policy. The victories also symbolized the determination of the Hosokawa government to assert its commitment to the consumer. In all other respects, however, the legislation reflected the wishes of politically entrenched business interests.

Why Now?

The question that we must now answer is, if business wanted to stick with the old PL regime, why did it ultimately support the new strict liability law?

One reason was that it had a lot to lose by the end of the deliberative process. The PL renrakukai and its allies had orchestrated such an onslaught of public opinion on the policy process that to say no to PL reform would have made the business community appear anticonsumer, and that would have been bad for business in the context of the recession and increasing governmental attention to the affairs of consumers. By the eve of enactment, the PL renrakukai had overseen more than 320 locality-specific *ikensho* campaigns, each involving literally hundreds—sometimes thousands—of citizens sending waves of postcards to bureaucrats and politicians demanding the early enactment of a product liability law (PL renrakukai 1997:259–62). The renrakukai also orchestrated petition drives by 1,713 consumer organs across the country, and the results—about 3.5 million signatures—were presented by consumer representatives to the various PL-related *shingikai* (PL renrakukai 1997:249–58). In addition, more than 300 localities were pressured by renrakukai chapters to adopt resolutions favoring enactment (PL renrakukai 1997:12); a number of demonstrations were organized in and around Nagatachō; and countless appeals and "written demands" (*yōbōsho*) were showered on policymakers. Although not as large as the public backlash directed at the government over the deregulation of synthetic additives, it was a well-organized public opinion campaign that should be credited, along with the force of foreign example, for inducing a divided conservative coalition into supporting the law.

Credit must also be given to the Hosokawa government. Shortly after assuming office, Prime Minister Hosokawa Morihiro openly declared his support for a PL law as a fundamental step toward a more consumer-oriented society. His cabinet reflected these priorities. Kumagai Hiroshi, the new minister of international trade and industry, for example, was far more favorably disposed toward enactment than his predecessors had been, and the same can be said for several of his cabinet colleagues. But even though these individuals helped win over pockets of resistance to strict liability rules, the fact remains that most of the agreements among the various actors of the pro-business camp had been reached *before* the LDP fell from power (interview, Machimura, April 1994). The Hosokawa government did not formulate these agreements; it inherited them.

A more persuasive explanation of the business community's capitulation to demands for PL reform is that businesses had been granted many of the same limits on producer liability that had been secured by European businesses, limits that were designed to prevent a U.S.-style "product liability crisis" and that meshed well with the country's bureaucracy- and business-centered approach to consumer protection. In addition to the demands noted earlier, those limits included exemptions for farmers and the manufacturers of component parts; limits of repose;[33] a ban on punitive damage awards; and, in a marked departure from the EC directive, the exemption of unprocessed agricultural products from the law's purview (Marcuse 1996:384).

Welcome though these concessions may have been, they nevertheless beg the most important question of all: if European-style limits on producer liability were all it took to obtain the support of Japanese business for a new strict liability law, why did the business community take so long to agree to these concessions? Based on observations of the post-1994 product liability regime, the most probable answer is that businesses and their allies in the bureaucracy and the LDP were buying time in order to reform or introduce institutions that would both minimize the negative impact of strict liability rules on producers and preserve the long-standing power configurations of Japan's distinctive consumer protection regime.

The New PL Regime: A Half Step Forward for Consumers

These objectives were achieved through the reform and expansion of the nonstatutory governmental, semigovernmental, and business-centered mechanisms for consumer redress that had kept consumers out of the courts in the past and that will continue to do so under strict liability rules.[34] Although these mechanisms were not addressed by the new Product Liability Law, they had been the topic of ministerial *shingikai* deliberations.[35] They were also the subject of supplementary resolutions released by the commerce committees (*shōkō iinkai*) of both Diet chambers in June 1994. As the following overview reveals, these mechanisms help businesses as much as — if not more than — consumers.

Alternative Dispute Resolution Facilities (ADR)

As before, the majority of product liability complaints will be handled privately between consumers and businesses through *aitai kōshō* procedures that will now be carried out in conformity with strict liability rules. In fact, the media have reported noticeable improvements in the responses of individual firms to complaints from their customers since the law's enactment (see, e.g., *Mainichi Daily News*, December 6, 1995; *Japan Times*, March 5, 1996). Business efforts to improve these procedures are no doubt motivated by a desire to avoid the dubious distinction of becoming the target of one of the country's first strict liability lawsuits.

As an alternative to the courts, the government-administered mark programs have been maintained and reformed under the new strict liability regime. Since the law was enacted, ceilings on the amounts of damages awarded to consumers have been raised (*Mainichi Daily News*, March 5, 1996), and more and more products are coming under the aegis of the programs. It remains to be seen, however, whether information pertaining to claims lodged with the ministries will be readily made available to the public.

In the event that *aitai kōshō* or the mark programs fail to resolve product-related disputes, the consumer can submit the case to a third-party or "alternative dispute resolution" (ADR) organization. The neutrality of these organizations is in question, however, given the role of both state and business interests in their proceedings.

Among the most important institutional venues for ADR are the local governmental "complaint-processing committees" (*kujō shori iinkai*) which have been in place for decades but rarely used. Local governments, in accordance with guidelines issued by the Economic Planning Agency, have significantly reformed these organizations and are setting up new ones around the country. The panels normally consist of lawyers or former judges, consumer representatives, "individuals of learning and experience" (*gakushiki keikensha*), and technical experts dispatched on demand by the Economic Planning Agency (Kōmura 1995:3). Like comparable local panels that deal with pollution-related disputes (see, e.g., Upham 1987:ch. 2), these committees appear to operate in a fair and impartial fashion (Yanagi 1995:27–30). In two important respects, however, the committees' procedures could weaken the letter of the law. First, a commitment to compromise solutions, as opposed to the more adversarial "winner-take-all" approach of the courts, may, in some cases, enable the manufacturers of defective products to escape their ultimate legal responsibilities. Second, public access to information pertaining to defective products may be hampered by the committees' commitment to protect not only the personal privacy of plaintiffs but also the right of firms to protect their trade-related secrets.

A much more controversial venue for third-party dispute settlement is the Product Safety Association (Shōhin anzen kyōkai), the organization that administers the SG Mark program. The association recently opened a product liability center to solicit inquiries and complaints from consumers pertaining to a wide range of products and to provide mediation (*assen*) services between consumers and businesses engaged in *aitai kōshō*. As a last resort, consumers can submit their claims to a mediation panel consisting of a former judge or legal specialist, a consumer consultant, and a technical specialist. Consumers must pay a small fee for this service unless the product in question is part of the SG Mark program, and the products covered are restricted to those produced by companies affiliated with the association (Seihin anzen kyōkai 1995). Like the local complaint-processing committees, the procedures are closed to public scrutiny, and information pertaining to specific cases will be publicized only if it is deemed by the association to have a bearing on public safety. Unlike the complaint-processing committees, however, the procedures may not always be carried out in a fair and impartial fashion, given the Product Safety Association's organizational connection to MITI and its long-established reputation for being pro-business.

An even more controversial set of organizations is the dozen or so product liability centers established at the industry level to deal exclusively with specific product types. These centers administer panels consisting of technical, legal, and consumer experts who offer mediation services to consumers and manufacturers, but their ability to work in a fair and neutral manner is somewhat suspect. For starters, many of these centers are part of organizations with clear ministerial connections. The center that oversees electrical home appliances, for example, is part of the Electric Home Appliances Association (Kaden seihin kyōkai), a special corporation (*zaidanhōjin*) connected to MITI. Dispute resolution services for conflicts involving housing parts, moreover, are carried out by a product liability center in the "Better Living" organization, an organ affiliated with the Ministry of Construction. Business interests also permeate the affairs of these purportedly "neutral" centers. The selection of members for the mediation panels, for example, is often vetoed by concerned manufacturers, and many—if not most—of the consultants in the centers are lent temporarily by the very manufacturers targeted by consumer complaints (*Nihon keizai shimbun*, July 19, 1995). Finally, the centers are under no obligation to make the details of product-related claims open to the public, much to the disappointment of both lawyers and consumer representatives (*Japan Times*, January 5, 1996).

The institutionalization of noncourt dispute resolution procedures will provide undeniably useful services to consumers in a legal system that precludes quick and easy access to the courts. At the same time, however, the institutional structure of these organizations gives both the state and business interests the ability to resolve product liability cases away from the public eye and without allocating legal liability. (Although as of this writing fewer than twenty product liability lawsuits have been filed since the law was implemented, consumers do have the option of litigating when they are dissatisfied with the results of mediation.) The fact that mediation is conducted behind closed doors, however, will make it difficult for consumers to judge whether the procedures have been carried out fairly and if the damages awarded are comparable to what would be obtained in the court system.

Product Liability Discovery Services

Another focus of controversy since the law was enacted has been the burden of proof shouldered by consumers in proving the existence of product defects and the causal relationship between defects and damages incurred in the absence of a presumption clause and pretrial discovery provisions in the court system. This burden will be particularly onerous for technologically sophisticated products like pharmaceuticals, automobiles, and even consumer electronics. The Japanese government has set up a number of organizations to facilitate citizen access to information that will lessen this burden of proof—organizations that were discussed and recommended along with the third-party dispute resolution bodies in *shingikai* reports and Diet resolutions.

Most of these "discovery organs" (*genin kyūmei kikan*, lit. "facilities for uncovering causes" of product-related accidents), which carry out product testing and other research designed to determine the causes of product-related accidents, are based in the national ministries and special corporations connected to the bureaucracy. According to a publication on the subject released jointly by seven agencies and ministries in June 1995, there are twenty-one governmental or semigovernmental facilities that carry out such functions (Keizaikikakuchō 1995), most of which have branch offices around the country. For example, the Japan Consumer Information Center, which falls under the jurisdiction of the Economic Planning Agency, has well-equipped facilities for product-related research, as do a number of local consumer centers. Most facilities specialize in research pertaining to one or a few product lines, and many of them supply noncourt dispute resolution services upon request.

As with the new ADR facilities, these information-gathering organizations provide invaluable services to consumers who do not have easy access to business-related information and in the absence of a small-claims court system. At the same time, however, the fact that many of these organizations are controlled or influenced by the bureaucracy or business interests renders their alleged neutrality dubious and the possibility for arbitrary decision making quite high.

Conclusion

The movement to enact a product liability law was a rare and remarkable case in which a diverse assortment of both national and local consumer organs was able to mobilize a substantial cross section of public opinion in favor of product liability reform. In the context of uncertainty and conflict in the pro-business camp, that movement helped persuade policymakers to push strict liability through the policy process. With a few important exceptions, however, the PL promotion faction had very little influence over the kind of strict liability regime that was eventually introduced.

Clause for clause, Japan's product liability law closely resembles western European laws. In the manner in which it is being implemented, however, Japan has parted company from its European counterparts. As critics are quick to point out, many of the noncourt dispute resolution procedures and information services are carried out by the bureaucracy or business organizations—services that in the United States and many European countries are normally performed by lawyers, the courts, or "neutral" private organizations (Urakawa 1995:37). Accordingly, consumer representatives and other critics of the system have branded the new law as "less than the EC" (EC *ika*) directive.

Japan's new product liability system has important implications for the protection of consumer rights. While Japanese consumers are certainly better off under this new system than ever before in terms of access to safe products and more effective redress systems, these benefits are enjoyed not as individual rights but, rather, as benefits bestowed by businesses and bureaucrats. Although consumer organizations are to be credited for the fact that Japan even has a strict liability law, no amount of public pressure could have enticed pro-business interests into instituting a product liability regime that empowers consumers over business in legal or political terms. The best they could do was to improve the overall lot of consumers within preexisting power arrangements that encourage citizen dependence on governmental and business authorities for consumer protection. As such, the story of product liability reform attests to the lingering strength of the bureaucracy and business interests after the era of one-party dominance.

The Right to Be Heard: The Past, Present, and Future of the Japanese Consumer Movement

In June 1999, in preparation for the final chapter of this book, I traveled to Tōkyō for a round of follow-up interviews. Although I had arrived with an inkling that the organized consumer movement was once again in flux, I was unprepared for the actual extent of those changes. Japanese consumer organizations, I think it fair to say, are in the midst of yet another "formative moment" in their postwar history, a moment that may be no less significant than the ones experienced during the immediate postwar period and following the 1968 enactment of the Consumer Protection Basic Law.

An interview with one of the country's leading consumer advocates brought the magnitude of these changes home to me. Shimizu Hatoko, a niece of Oku Mumeo, now in her mid-seventies, participated in the founding of Shufuren, served as one of its presidents, and continues to work full time for the organization. A woman of boundless energy and undying commitment to the consumer cause, Mrs. Shimizu was a leading consumer advocate in each of the three consumer campaigns chronicled in this volume. The last time I spoke with her was in February 1993, when the uncertain future of the proposed Product Liability Law was hanging heavily over the organized movement. As might be expected in such circumstances, our conversation revolved around the power of business interests in the consumer protection policymaking system and the concomitant barriers confronted by consumer activists seeking to influence the direction of public policy. What I remember most about that meeting was the profound sense of frustration with the political system that lurked behind Mrs. Shimizu's remarks, frustration that bubbled to the surface toward the end of our discussion when she suddenly paused, raised her hands in a gesture of helplessness, and asked rhetorically, "Just whose side is the government on, anyway?"

After six years, the contrast in Mrs. Shimizu's outlook on "the system" could not have been more pronounced. As soon as we sat down in the reception area of Shufuren's brand new headquarters in the Chiyoda ward of Tōkyō, an elated Mrs. Shimizu directed my attention to the many changes that had taken place in the consumer protection realm since our last meeting. "The setup (*shikumi*) of consumer policymaking is changing," she announced. "There are now more opportunities for consumers to voice their concerns to the government; the policy process is more open; several consumer-related laws have been strengthened; and more legislative changes are pending." She spent the next two and a half hours recounting the details of those changes to her all too willing student.

Although other activists in the movement may be less sanguine about the state of Japanese consumer politics, most agree that because of the political, policy, and institutional changes that resulted from the LDP's temporary fall from power in 1993, the likelihood of being "turned away at the gate" (*monzenbarai*) of the national policymaking system has declined. My purpose in this chapter is to explore these recent developments and to assess their significance for consumer organizations and their professed right to be heard and for the representation of diffuse societal interests more broadly. Before doing so, however, I shall briefly recapitulate the findings of this study, for in order to determine where Japanese consumer organizations are heading, we need to be certain of where they have been.

The Past: Consumer Activism from a Comparative Perspective

The story of consumer participation in the national consumer policy process between 1968 and the enactment of the 1994 Product Liability Law is in many ways one of governmental control over the nature and extent of that participation. Although the Consumer Protection Basic Law and supporting statutes and policies provided for consumer representation in decision-making institutions, many of the pro-producer customs that infused the day-to-day workings of those institutions weakened the political impact of consumer voices. It was, quite simply, a classic example of the elite manipulation of formal and informal institutions designed to channel and manage societal participation, comparable to what Frank Upham found in his pathbreaking study of Japanese environmental, gender, and minority politics (Upham 1987:29).

As previous chapters have shown, however, advocates managed to partially circumvent the institutional barriers to consumer activism at the national level by turning to the localities. Local and prefectural governments were key to consumer activism in that they provided advocates with the political and economic resources that enabled movement strategizing vis-à-vis the center. Many of those strategies, as we have seen, focused on the activation or manipulation of local public opinion. When pro-business alliances were characterized by consensus, pressure from below had little impact on policy outputs. But when those alliances were fraught with conflict and indecision, public pressure could prevent the policy process from succumbing to stalemate and function as a swing vote in favor of consumer-oriented reform.

The distinctive qualities of postwar Japanese consumerism become particularly apparent when measured against the experiences of the environmental movement. Although the two movements have overlapped in regard to personnel and the nature of their respective policy priorities, institutionally they differ in at least two important respects. First, consumer organizations have enjoyed more routinized access to the national policy process than their environmental counterparts have, particularly during the 1960s and 1970s when the two movements were at their political peak. As McKean (1981), Upham (1987), and Broadbent (1998) all have shown, the organizational expressions of the environmental movement were confined mainly to the local level, a phenomenon, as we noted in an earlier chapter, that can be at least partially explained by the institutional opportunities of the eras in which those organs were first established. For consumer representatives, access to the national policy process—no matter how symbolic it may have been—served as an incentive to participate in national legislative and policy-related movements and to build sophisticated organizational networks designed to facilitate that participation. Environmental groups, on the other hand, remained largely focused on politics at the grassroots level, although this has been changing in recent years.

Second, the relationship of consumer organizations with the localities has differed from that of their environmental counterparts. Whereas past studies suggest that environmental groups focused mainly on the courts, local assemblies, and local elections during the 1960s and early 1970s as the primary targets of their political activism, the representation of consumer interests occurred mainly between local elections and in the context of long-term relationships between activists (both national and local) and local officials. Institutional factors largely explain this discrepancy. Specifically, the local bureaucracy has been more extensive in the consumer realm, embracing, as we have seen, a sophisticated network of semigovernmental consumer centers that have had no counterpart in environmental politics. These centers have served as fora for close relationships between consumer advocates and local governmental officials. Although the functional raison d'être and/or political independence of many representative organs eroded after these centers were established, there remained a strong and independent core of local and national advocates who continued to exercise some influence over local policymaking.

As a result of these institutional discrepancies, consumer organizations pursued tactics different from those of citizen groups during the heyday of environmental activism. Environmental groups, for example, which were almost completely marginalized in the national decision-making system, relied regularly on protest and, in some cases, the selective use of violence (Upham 1987:55) to get their political points across. Most consumer organizations, by contrast, downplayed protest in their determination to either obtain or maintain a hearing in the policy process and completely avoided the use of violence.

Consumer representatives were also more reluctant than environmental groups were to engage in litigation. One reason for this has been the nature of the rules governing consumer lawsuits. While environmental litigant groups were usually composed of persons who themselves had suffered the effects of environmental degradation, for instance, their consumer counterparts often consisted of advocates who sued on behalf of a broader constituency. As the evidence presented in this volume attests, Japanese judges did not normally recognize the standing of such groups to sue. We should also note that consumer issues rarely stirred up the kind of political ferment that encouraged judges in large environmental suits to suspend many of the judicial rules and regulations that might have prevented litigants from achieving their court-related goals.

The strategic choices of Japanese consumer organizations differed not only from those of environmental activists but also from those of their counterparts in the United States. Again, institutional factors contributed to many of these discrepancies. The presidential system, party competition, separation of powers, decentralization of Congress, and an accessible judicial system, for example, opened up multiple access points for consumer advocates into the American political process during the 1960s and 1970s. The presence of multiple access points in turn explains why advocates implemented a much wider range of tactics than did British or Japanese advocates, tactics that included litigation and alliances with politicians, presidential advisers, and regulatory bureaucrats.

The strategic similarities between the British and Japanese advocacy movements, by contrast, are striking. For example, although party competition encouraged British advocates to ally with politicians from time to time, both British and Japanese advocates tended to focus on bureaucracies as the main targets of their political activism, a custom that is to be expected in parliamentary systems. The Japanese parted company from the British, however, in their actual influence on bureaucratic decision making at the national level. For while British consumer representatives had meaningful influence over policy as a result of their relatively secure position in a semicorporatist system of consumer protection policymaking, advocates were effectively sidelined in the Japanese case by the pro-business norms and customs governing bureaucratic deliberative procedures. The exclusionary nature of the Japanese corporatist policymaking system at the national level encouraged advocates to look to the localities as alternative fora of interest articulation.

These differences notwithstanding, consumer organizations in Japan, the United States, and Britain all emphasized the activation or manipulation of public opinion as a key component of their strategic arsenals. Public opinion is important to consumer advocates for at least two reasons, not the least of which is the simple fact that consumer movements, like their environmental counterparts, are in the business of extracting public goods from governments—public goods that appear more legitimate to policymakers the more the public supports them. Resource deficiencies within the organized movement have enhanced the importance of public opinion for consumer advocates even further. Since consumer representatives in all advanced industrial democracies often lack the money, personnel, or strategically placed allies to overcome business opposition and to influence policymakers directly, they must do so indirectly by appealing for support to the ultimate beneficiaries of public goods.

The extent to which consumer representatives focused on mobilizing public opinion, however, differed according to the institutional context of movement activism. In the United States, where the level of consumer ac-

cess to policymaking usually fluctuates, the movement's emphasis on mobilizing public opinion varied according to the level of mobilization of business organizations. When business was weakly organized during the 1960s
and early 1970s, for example, consumer organizations behaved more like
interest groups than social movement organizations in that they concentrated more on lobbying than on manipulating public opinion. Following
the business backlash of the late 1970s and 1980s and the concomitant
narrowing of entry points into the policy process, however, consumer representatives turned increasingly to the grassroots public for support. In Britain, meanwhile, the institutional positioning of consumer representatives at
the heart of the governmental decision-making process enabled those representatives to influence policy from within, thereby diminishing the need
to appeal to public opinion. In Japan, by contrast, consumer activists stressed
the activation and manipulation of public opinion more than in the United
States or Britain, because of their weak presence in national decision-making
circles and their concomitant reluctance to use protest tactics that might
weaken that position even more.

How, then, did the strategies of consumer organizations in their respective
institutional contexts influence the consumer protection policymaking process? In the United States during the 1960s and early 1970s, the relatively
open institutional context of consumer protection policymaking and the
consumer movement resource configurations that were conditioned by that
context enabled consumer representatives to perform a wide range of functions, including agenda setting, policy formulation, and watchdog duties.
With the mobilization of business interests during the late 1970s and 1980s,
however, the influence of consumer organizations waned in all respects.
Britain's larger consumer organizations also influenced agenda setting and
policy formulation, although not quite as effectively as American advocates
did. This was largely due to the more entrenched position of business interests in the British policy process. We should note, however, that because of
their institutionalized presence in that process, British consumer organizations were also better positioned than their American counterparts to perform both consultative functions for other policymakers and watchdog functions during the implementation stage of the policy process.

Compared with Anglo-Saxon organizations, Japanese consumer organizations before the early 1990s had less influence over agenda setting and
policy formulation and performed only limited consultative and watchdog
functions. This can be explained with reference to their relatively weak pres-

ence in the national policy process, their consequently narrower resource base, and the power of business representatives in the Japanese political system. But even though consumer representatives had little direct influence over agenda setting, the evidence presented in this volume suggests that consumer activism orchestrated from the local level contributed to a climate of public opinion in favor of governmental action on pro-consumer issues. Without that broad climate of opinion, governmental authorities would have had fewer incentives to address those issues, particularly given their long-standing bias toward business interests.

Though significant, the impact of Japanese consumer activism on policy formulation should not be exaggerated. First, it is important to keep in mind one of the central arguments of this study, namely, that consumer advocates in Japan can influence the general direction of policy formulation only when pro-business alliances are disorganized. When that alliance is tightly knit and based on common objectives, consumers have much less impact on that process.

Second, a word about the influence of Japanese activists over the actual *content* of specific policies. For relatively straightforward issues like the establishment of quality and safety standards for specific product lines, consumer organizations occasionally helped establish some of the specific details of those standards. The fact that business groups themselves often supported stricter standards as a mechanism for curbing "excessive" competition in the marketplace and were relatively supportive of movement initiatives is, of course, a major source of movement "influence" in this regard. As exemplified by the juice-bottling industry's reluctance to accept stricter labeling guidelines, however, consumer advocates had little impact on product standards in the face of business opposition unless relevant government authorities broke with the producer camp and sided with consumers.

For legally complicated and politically contentious issues like antitrust and product liability—issues that pitted consumer interests and their producer and government adversaries against one another—policy specifics were normally decided by bureaucrats in alliance with conservative politicians and business representatives. That said, even in relatively hostile political environments, consumer organizations were important in that they helped keep policy proposals on the government agenda during periods of political stalemate, when the likelihood of their being abandoned by governmental and business actors was particularly high. Consider, for example, the role played by consumer organizations between 1973 and 1977 in holding a succession of LDP cabinets to their professed commitment to antitrust reform, and during the early 1990s, when business groups tried hard to stall product liability policymaking. As Japanese observers have often remarked, for all their flaws, the antitrust reforms and the PL law might never have been introduced had it not been for the relentless pressure of the organized consumer movement.

These findings point to several conclusions about the representation of diffuse societal interests in Japan. First, and most obviously, they reinforce what we have always known about Japan, namely, that it is a country in which business interests have far more say over public policy than they do in many other advanced industrial democracies. Before we jump to the simplistic conclusion that these actors are omnipotent, however, we must remember that even though consumer leaders have felt perennially handicapped in relation to business interests and have suffered numerous defeats in the policy process, the fact remains that they, together with their allies elsewhere in the political system, have managed to wrest noteworthy concessions from their adversaries. Consumer voices *do* get a hearing in the mainstream policy process in Japan, although not in the manner intended by the national powers that be.

On that note, the history of consumer participation in the Japanese policy process speaks volumes about alternative avenues of interest articulation that are often overlooked by Japan scholars. The localities are certainly the most conspicuous example. Through the 1968 Consumer Protection Basic Law, the central government entrusted the localities with administering national consumer protection policies and gave them the authority to enact ordinances dealing with consumer issues specific to their jurisdictions. A subsequent law provided for the expansion of the local consumer centers. It is unlikely, however, that the government intended that these local institutions be used for alternative political purposes, but that is precisely what happened. Both national consumer organizations and local consumer groups, as we have seen, used their expanding linkages to the localities to influence policies at both the local level and the center.

The localities themselves, moreover, used their authority to innovate in the consumer policy realm and, in the process, to flex their political muscles by enacting progressive consumer ordinances in alliance with consumer representatives or issuing resolutions for or against policy proposals at the center. These findings complement those of Muramatsu (1997) and Steiner, Krauss, and Flanagan (1980a) on the relationship between the politicization of local government and the expansion of local autonomy; Reed's discussion (1986) of local policy innovation in the environmental realm; and patterns of center-local competition described by Samuels (1983). My study goes one step beyond these analyses of the relationship among citizen activism, the localities, and national policy, however, in that it emphasizes the role of local bureaucracies, in addition to legislative assemblies, as important and effective targets of citizen activism in the national, as well as the local, policy process.

In sum, this study shows that the demands of diffuse societal interests can be reasonably well articulated in Japan's public policy process not only through the ballot box or traditional modes of protest but also through local institutions intended to carry out administrative functions. This in turn has implications for our understanding of how public-interest policies are hammered out. As noted in the introduction, the story of postwar consumerism indicates that the public-interest policy process is not always controlled by bureaucrats, although bureaucrats are certainly important; nor is it simply the product of crisis and compensation dynamics in the ruling conservative party (see Calder 1988), although the LDP is more likely to grant concessions to consumers during periods of scandal and relative political decline. The evidence presented in this volume also parts company from Margaret McKean's model of public-interest policymaking in which bureaucrats, conservative politicians, and business representatives are motivated by a long-term time horizon and a number of other incentives to respond to societal pressure for policy-related benefits. According to McKean, those benefits are usually bestowed in anticipation of citizen mobilization (1981:97). By contrast, my findings underscore a higher level of organization and sophistication among diffuse society interests than McKean acknowledges, as well as more protracted conflict between those interests and political authorities. Clearly, Japan's corporatist and "exclusionary" national policymaking system is more vulnerable to pluralist pressures from below than conventional wisdom or many academic models would lead us to believe.

Ironically, many of Japan's seasoned consumer activists would take issue with this conclusion. After the 1994 enactment of the Product Liability Law, for example, movement leaders could barely muster the energy to celebrate. The fact that the law had been "deboned" (*honenuki*) by the institutions designed to implement its provisions was certainly one source of their discontent. More important, however, was their disappointment with the policy process itself. To them, the years preceding enactment had been filled with instances of bureaucratic control over *shingikai* deliberations, of the refusal of business representatives to even meet with consumer advocates, and of a dearth of consumer sympathizers in the LDP. As far as consumer advocates were concerned, they had been turned away at the gates (*monzenbarai*) of national power, a state of affairs, they believed, that did not speak well for the consumer's right to be heard or, more broadly, for democracy.

The Present: A New Era of Consumer Politics?

As Mrs. Shimizu so eloquently noted, however, signs of change are in the air, so much so, in fact, that the era of "post-1968 consumer politics" may be drawing to a close. What follows is an overview of some of the changes that have taken place in both the institutional context of Japanese consumer protection policymaking and the nature and impact of consumer movement activism. Taken together, these changes represent further expansions in the institutional boundaries of consumer politics, which may render the Japanese consumer protection policymaking system even more vulnerable to pluralist pressures from below than before.

Political and Institutional Change

As with past turning points in the Japanese consumer movement's development, contemporary trends in the institutional context of consumer politics are taking place against a backdrop of broad economic change. The most conspicuous economic development for consumers has been, of course, the lingering recession of the 1990s and its negative impact on spending. In marked contrast to the spending boom of the mid- to late 1980s, consumers have grown much less willing to pay exorbitant prices for high-status goods and services and have developed a fondness for bargains and discount shops. In 1997, these trends contributed to a growing public intolerance of price fixing that eventually culminated in the removal of cosmetics and general pharmaceutical products from the Japan Fair Trade Commission's list of products approved for resale price maintenance (*saihanbai kakaku iji*).[1]

Superimposed on these short-term Japanese buying habits have been dramatic changes in broad consumption patterns resulting from the diversification of product lines and the development of smaller niche markets, the proliferation of luxury goods, the exponential growth of the financial services industry, the introduction of new businesses offering care for the elderly, the development of electronic commerce ("e-commerce"), and so on. As illustrated by public inquiries to local consumer centers, the problems now confronting consumers have shifted accordingly. In 1971, the majority of complaints pertained to the safety and quality of consumer products, whereas in 1997, most of them had to do with problems resulting from unfair business practices and consumer contracts (Ikemoto 1999:29). These developments have influenced the kinds of issues espoused by consumer advocates. Put simply, *what* consumers purchase has become far less problematic for the organized movement than *how* those purchases are made.

Broad political developments have also had an impact on consumer politics during the 1990s. With the end of one-party dominance in 1993[2] and the ascension to power of a series of coalition governments, Japanese politics have grown increasingly fragmented and fluid (Pempel 1998:167). In the political-economy realm, political instability has contributed to a degree of policymaking inertia regarding many of the issues that are foremost in the minds of decision makers, with banking reform being the most conspicuous case in point. For the organized consumer movement, however, instability has had some positive side effects.

For example, the strong government-business relationship that stifled consumer voices in the past has weakened. As a result, post-1993 governments—starting with Hosokawa Morihiro's seven-party coalition government and including the LDP cabinets of the late 1990s—have paid more attention to broad consumer needs than ever before. For the Hosokawa and Hata governments, sympathy for the consumer appeared to reflect a genuine policy preference. But for subsequent LDP governments, this kind of behavior can be attributed to electoral uncertainty, the party's tenuous hold on Diet proceedings, and the concomitant need to cooperate more closely with the more "pro-citizen" opposition parties.

Recent political changes have also affected the role of politicians in consumer protection policymaking. Specifically, increases—albeit small—in party competition levels have motivated politicians to listen more closely to nonbusiness lobbyists, a trend, as we saw in the chapter on product liability reform, that became evident as early as late 1993 and early 1994. Although none of the parties has made consumer policies an integral part of its party platform, more and more politicians—particularly from the nonconservative parties—have made a name for themselves by standing up for such quality-of-life concerns as consumer protection, human rights, environmentalism, and good governance. In the past, most such politicians were members of the House of Councillors,[3] whereas today, many of them are elected to the more powerful House of Representatives on proportional representation (PR) tickets. The partisan backgrounds of these pro-citizen politicians have also changed. Until recently, those politicians hailed primarily from the Japan Social Democratic Party, the Japan Communist Party, and the Kōmeitō or ran on independent tickets. Today, nearly all the parties, with the notable exception of the LDP, have at least a few budding consumer specialists in their midst. According to consumer activists, the Democratic Party has been leading the pack in this regard (interviews, June and July 1999). Although the party still lacks a comprehensive consumer platform, the number of Democratic Party politicians who have taken up the consumer banner surpasses that of any other party.

Ishige Eiko and Haraguchi Kazuhiro, Lower House Diet members from the Democratic Party, embody many of the characteristics of this new breed of "citizen politician." Mrs. Ishige was elected to the Diet for the first time in 1996 as the second-ranking candidate on the Democratic Party list in a proportional representation district.[4] Her ranking highlights the potential of the new PR system to magnify the importance of consumer and other public-interest issues in national electoral politics. A former housewife, Mrs. Ishige speaks out for rights for the handicapped as well as consumer issues and was a leading proponent of the recently enacted nonprofit organization and information disclosure laws (interview, Ishige, July 1999). Mr. Haraguchi, a psychologist by training who was also elected on a PR ticket, is equally devoted to citizen issues. Both he and Mrs. Ishige are actively involved in the recently established Diet members' Roundtable on Citizen Policies (Shimin seisaku giin kondankai), a nonpartisan coalition of legislators that serves as an important access point for citizen groups to the policy process. Mr. Haraguchi relayed his political motivations to me in a recent interview:

> I'm very interested in citizen groups—consumer, environmental, human rights, et cetera. Even today, Japanese citizens depend far too heavily on government to get things done. I'd like to use my position to change that old penchant for leaning on the government and to encourage citizens to function more independently in the political system. For these reasons, I work closely with citizen groups and was a strong supporter of the Nonprofit Organization Law.
>
> (interview, Haraguchi, July 1999)

Another political development that has had an impact on the institutional context of consumer politics is progress—albeit limited—in the sphere of regulatory reform[5] and the opening up of the bureaucracy to greater outside input. Generally, regulatory reform has been accompanied by a shift in the government's basic consumer policy from a focus on consumer protection as a responsibility of government to the encouragement of the "self-responsibility" (*jiko sekinin*) of consumers in a freer market setting. In the past, consumer advocates opposed the very idea of deregulation without better legal protections for consumers. Today, they are softening their opposition to regulatory reform as shifts in government policy toward the consumer contribute to legislative and institutional changes designed to give the consuming public the means to survive in a more competitive market.

Starting in 1995, for instance, the veil of secrecy shrouding *shingikai* proceedings has gradually been lifted. In keeping with the long-standing demands of Shufuren and other consumer organizations, bureaucrats have opened council meetings to outside observers who apply for admission and have made *shingikai* documentation more readily available to the public. Although consumer representatives complain that *shingikai* reports are still poor reflections of prevailing patterns of opinion among council memberships, these changes have been welcomed by those who equate greater *shingikai* openness with more opportunities for consumers to express their interests to the bureaucracy (interviews, consumer advocates, June and July 1999).

Consumers will be further empowered when the May 1999 Information Disclosure Law goes into effect in 2001. Under the new law, all government documents, with a few notable exceptions,[6] will be subject to disclosure, thereby giving citizens greater access to information pertaining to the goods and services they consume. A number of consumer activists have revealed to me that they will use information obtained under national and local disclosure rules to pressure governmental officials on such topics as product safety and governmental corruption.

Another bureaucratic change that will partially empower consumers is the establishment of the so-called public comment system. The system, which was introduced by most national ministries and agencies in 1999, enables ordinary citizens to comment on policy proposals over the Internet. It is not without flaws. Critics complain, for instance, that only a small number of policy areas have been declared open to commentary and that there is no guarantee that citizen input will be incorporated into the formal policy process. Nevertheless, advocates praise the procedure as an epoch-making change in bureaucratic attitudes toward the opinions of private citizens (Hiwasa 1999:35; *Shufuren dayori*, July 15, 2000).

Finally, changes are also taking place at the local level. Many consumer centers, for instance, are being reorganized in response to the changing needs of consumers in the context of the government's emphasis on regulatory reform and the "self-responsibility" (*jiko sekinin*) of consumers. In order to give consumers the resources they need to navigate the country's increasingly free markets, both consumer centers and the Japan Consumer Information Center (Kokumin seikatsu sentaa) are expanding their consultative and educational services and taking steps to make consumer-related information more accessible to consumers both in bookstores and over the Internet.

Local consumer centers are also collaborating with citizen groups on consumer self-help projects and are encouraging the formation of consumer group networks (interview, Tōkyō Consumer Center official, December 1997). In 1996, Tōkyō consumer centers helped organize the "Green Consumers Tōkyō Network," an alliance of consumer and environmental groups, businesses, local governmental officials, and other concerned citizens promoting environmentally friendly consumption patterns among residents in the Tōkyō metropolitan area (Shimada 1999:20). It is a project highly reminiscent of the kind of collaboration among business, government, and consumer activists that took place during the early postwar period, but with an important difference. Whereas early cooperation was pursued by activists as part of a broader effort to build comprehensive consumer protection programs at the governmental level, it is now designed to facilitate the movement from "consumer protection" as a regulatory responsibility of government to a more free-market system based on consumer self-responsibility.

The Consumer Movement's Response

Consumer centers in Tōkyō and elsewhere did not invent the notion of consumer networking; instead, they are complementing an accelerated trend in the organized consumer movement that in turn can be viewed as a strategic response to many of the broad socioeconomic, policy, and institutional changes just described. As the act of consumption grows more complicated and the role of government as the ultimate overseer of consumer protection diminishes, consumer organs emphasize the importance of "the

dissemination of information" not only as a tactic during legislative campaigns but also as a means to help "self-responsible" consumers make wise
choices in the marketplace. Given the resource constraints that plague consumer organs—constraints that have only intensified as a result of the recession—activists have become more willing to ally with a broader range of
citizen and professional groups, to pool resources during consumer campaigns, and to divide the task of generating information according to group
expertise.

Many consumer organs are establishing new organizations to facilitate
consumer networking. Shōdanren, for example, recently launched the Research Committee on Laws Relating to Consumers (Shōhisha kanren hō
kentō iinkai), a committee consisting of both Shōdanren members and nonmembers that serves as both a communication and networking forum for
activists and, since several members sit concurrently on *shingikai*, a pipeline
to the bureaucratic deliberative process (Hiwasa 1999:35). As such, the committee performs organizational and informational functions similar to those
of the issue-specific consumer liaison committees (*renrakukai*) mentioned
in earlier chapters, but on a broader and more permanent basis.

Consumer advocates are adopting state-of-the-art technology to facilitate
their networking efforts. The fax machine, for example, has become a technological staple for many consumer organizations that heretofore had relied
on newsletters and pamphlets to get their messages across. Shōdanren, for
one, has a comprehensive fax service to send consumer-related information
to citizens around the country (Hiwasa 1999:37). Some consumer organizations also use the Internet. Shufuren was one of the first consumer organizations to set up its own web page, which it uses to pass on information
about its various activities to a broad readership. For financial and personnel
reasons, however, many other organizations have been reluctant to com-
puterize.

In addition to enhanced consumer networking and in response to
changes in the political party system, consumer organizations are devoting
more time to lobbying politicians. Activists sense that politicians are more
willing to at least listen to the consumer point of view, now that they are less
beholden to special interests than they were during the era of one-party
dominance.

While attention to lobbying as a movement tactic has increased somewhat, litigation rates have remained more or less unchanged. In 1996, the
Diet passed a series of amendments to the 1890 Code of Civil Procedure

(Minjisoshōhō) that were designed to make the country's civil court system less time-consuming and expensive, particularly for small-claims cases.[7] One of the more noteworthy amendments introduced at the insistence of the opposition parties was the stipulation that bureaucrats would no longer have the authority to refuse to comply with court orders demanding the release of bureaucratic documents for trial purposes (Tsuruoka 1996:44–47). In theory, this provision is important to product liability cases, many of which depend on access to product-related information held by governmental agencies. In practice, however, the structure of the PL regime, as we saw in the last chapter, prevents most product liability cases from ever reaching the courts. It is unlikely, moreover, that the amendments will lead to an upsurge in consumer litigation as a political tactic because they do not include changes in the standing to sue. Generally, consumer organizations will continue to use litigation only in exceptional political circumstances.

What do the strategic responses of consumer representatives to these policy and institutional changes say about the movement's current participation in the national policymaking process? First, enhanced emphasis on lobbying may be indicative of both small increases in legislative influence over the direction of consumer policy and a partial reorientation of consumer activism away from the localities and toward national politics. Whether or not these trends continue, however, depends greatly on future alignments in the political party system and further openings in the national bureaucracy.

Second, I think it fair to conclude that the leverage of consumer organizations and citizen groups more generally has increased in both the agenda-setting and policy-formulation stages of the policy process. Activists, for example, played a major role in the recent strengthening of laws regulating payment plans based on installments (Wappu hanbaihō) and door-to-door sales practices (Hōmon hanbaihō). The legislative process surrounding the enactment of the Information Disclosure Law is an even more telling illustration of the impact of "citizen power" in the 1990s.[8] Since 1993, networks of consumer and citizen groups helped elevate the issue onto the national political agenda by filing for the disclosure of information pertaining to corrupt local bureaucratic practices, testing the redress mechanisms of local governments when their requests were refused, and even resorting to the courts. Over time, their campaign heightened the public's awareness of governmental corruption, problems inherent in local and prefectural disclosure ordinances, and the need for a comprehensive national disclosure law. In response to intense media and public pressure, the LDP finally presided over the enactment of the disclosure law in the spring of 1999. Widely hailed as a rare piece of "citizen legislation," the disclosure law meets many of the demands of consumer and citizen advocates[9] and, in an interesting and surprising twist, actually surpasses many of the disclosure standards set by the prefectural and city ordinances (see Maclachlan 2000).

Finally, and in part as a response to the gradual deregulation of the country's consumer administrative apparatus, there are clear signs that Japanese consumer organizations are taking on more watchdog functions toward both business and the bureaucracy. Leaders in many of the nation's large consumer organizations, for example, are paying close attention to the myriad ADR facilities that help resolve product liability disputes, and a number of advocates sit on the ADR panels of industry-specific "PL centers." Second, networks of consumer organs are being formed to facilitate the activation of the country's new information disclosure statute. Third, consumer organizations, most of which were dormant during the legislative phase of the 1997 law designed to provide long-term care insurance for the elderly (*kaigo hoken*),[10] are now taking steps to ensure that consumers are treated fairly by private businesses that provide home-care services. To that end, they have been working informally with the Japan Consumer Information Center and local consumer centers.

Lingering Signs of Uncertainty

These positive changes notwithstanding, Japan's system of consumer protection policymaking and administration has also suffered a few setbacks over the past decade. In response to the ongoing recession and regulatory and administrative reform, for instance, national budgetary outlays for consumer centers have been slashed and several centers — including the Kanagawa Consumer Center, one of the oldest and most respected of such institutions — have been shut down (*Tōkyō shimbun*, September 22, 1998). Critics argue that these cutbacks could not have come at a more inopportune time, now that the centers' consumer consultation and alternative dispute resolution functions are expanding (Ikemoto 1999:29–31; Oikawa 1999:10) and demands for more consumer-related information in the context of regulatory reform are increasing. Accordingly, many consumer advocates and officials in the Japan Consumer Information Center are pushing for the establishment of more centers in the future (*Asahi shimbun*, November 22, 1999).

A cloud of uncertainty has gathered over the national consumer bureaucracy as well, now that the number of ministries and agencies has been reduced. With the abolition of the Economic Planning Agency and the absorption of many of its functions—including consumer-related ones—by the newly instituted cabinet office, the level of governmental involvement in consumer affairs is expected to decline. Although the erosion of bureaucratic functions regarding consumer protection is to be expected in an atmosphere of regulatory reform, consumer activists would like to see a concomitant increase in the government's watchdog role over business-consumer relations. To that end, activists argue, Japan is in more need than ever before of an independent consumer agency—or, at the very least, an expansion in the number of local consumer centers.

Last but not least, consumers must also contend with the lingering power of business in the policy process, as the recent movement to enact a consumer contract bill showed. Widely supported as a crucial legal protection for consumers in the context of deregulation, the law was an important focus of consumer activism after the enactment of the Product Liability Law in 1994. Although finally passed in April 2000, the bill's future was very uncertain for much of 1998 and 1999 as business representatives criticized the provisions for putting too much power in the hands of consumers. Consequently, the law contains several stipulations that advocates and their allies in the legal profession find unacceptable. Critics contend, for instance, that the law does not do enough to protect consumers who have been subjected to aggressive door-to-door canvassing and phone sales. They also complain that it does not force sellers to provide their customers with complete information pertaining to particular contracts.[11] Although activists welcome the law as an important step forward for consumers—particularly since it gives them the legal means to terminate contracts under specified conditions— they have branded it as sorely in need of amendment.

The consumer contract case should serve as a cautionary tale for those who paint too rosy a future for Japanese consumers. In many ways, the Consumer Contract Law, the Product Liability Law, and the Information Disclosure Law are important milestones in the history of consumer protection insofar as they provide significant civil law protections for consumers in an age of regulatory reform. The policymaking process preceding the contract law's enactment, however, strongly suggests that despite all the positive changes noted earlier in this chapter, Japan's system of consumer policymaking is still subject to the whims of the business community. One casualty of this carryover from the post-1968 system of consumer protection policymaking is the failure of any of the above-mentioned laws to acknowledge specific consumer rights. This is a crucial precondition, many believe, for achieving equality between consumer and business interests. In short, although trends are certainly heading in the right direction, much remains to be done before Japan can be rightfully deemed a consumer-oriented society.

The Future: The Changing Nature of Consumerism in Japan

As we observed in chapter 1, the organizational expressions of a social movement may not always conform to the "opinions and beliefs" that define that movement for a particular population. The more that social movement organizations diverge from those opinions and beliefs, moreover, the lower their chances will be of long-term survival. Some contend that Britain's Consumers' Association may be jeopardizing its future as it clings to old recipes for consumer activism, neglects some of the issues that are of concern to contemporary consumers, and fails to attract new followers. In the United States, by contrast, consumer organizations appear to be more adept at responding to the changing nature of consumerism as they search for new political opportunities at the local level, adopt new objectives, and struggle to expand their bases of support.

Japan's leading consumer organizations stand at a similar crossroads as they celebrate more than half a century of political activism. And it has been half a century of achievement: Japanese products are now much safer than they were thirty years ago; consumers have access to far more information about the products they consume than they did in the past; consumer access to a range of product choice at reasonable prices—while far from perfect— has certainly expanded; and the country's consumer redress mechanisms have improved. Their myriad disappointments notwithstanding, Japanese consumer organizations have presided over far-reaching change. Whether or not these organizations survive well into the twenty-first century depends on how well they adapt to changing perceptions about consumerism in Japanese society.

Although some of the larger consumer organizations are struggling with financial problems[12] and declining memberships,[13] the organized movement as a whole appears to be following its American counterpart in adapting its strategies to new institutional contingencies and redefining the relationships and objectives that make up its organizational raison d'être. The task of organizational redefinition has in turn meant a reassessment of movement conceptualizations of what it means to be a consumer. In the 1940s and 1950s, the juxtaposition of consumer and producer identities under a common conceptual aegis was a creative response to both parties' interest in economic recovery in the wake of wartime destruction, as well as to the eventual predominance of producers in Japanese politics in the context of rapid economic growth. Against that broad political and economic backdrop, consumer activists cooperated with small producers toward common goals while encouraging consumers-as-citizens-of-Japan (*kokumin*) to "buy Japanese" and, as members of civil society (*shimin*), to oppose big-business transgressions of basic consumer interests.

Today, the balance among the various dimensions of the postwar consumer identity has shifted in response to a changing political and economic context. Selective cooperation with producers, for example, is now driven by the need to find alternative approaches to consumer protection as the state slowly retreats from the internal affairs of business. Meanwhile, the *shimin* dimension of the consumer identity has been strengthened as consumers confront issues that go beyond the mere consumption of goods and services, issues like good governance, citizen rights, political participation, and environmentalism.

This emphasis on the *shimin* dimension reflects the priorities championed by the country's leading consumer advocates at the end of the century. Advocates are quick to point out, for example, that the country has not done enough to recognize consumer rights and to expand civil law provisions for greater access to the information and legal protections required by consumers in a deregulated and increasingly complex economy (see, e.g., Ochiai 1999). The campaigns to enact product liability, information disclosure, and consumer contract laws were certainly manifestations of these priorities. Other objectives that activists are now pushing include measures to protect individual consumer privacy, to protect consumers in the financial services industry,[14] and to reform the judicial system.[15]

This interest in citizenship has also spurred movement organizations to expand their bases of support. Shōdanren, for example, has increased its membership from about a dozen to forty or so organizations,[16] many of which look more like civil rights or environmental groups than consumer organs. Shufuren, meanwhile, is cooperating with a much wider spectrum of citizen groups as it strives to achieve its political objectives (*Asahi shimbun*, January 11, 1998) and is working to create a more effective division of labor between itself and those groups (interview, Shimizu, July 1999). Shufuren is also trying to shed its image as a "housewives'" organization, by admitting men into its ranks.[17] In 1997, it held a contest to name its new headquarters[18] which were due to open in time for the association's fiftieth anniversary the following year. The winner: a fifty-year-old businessman! The new name: "Plaza F," the F standing for such concepts as friend, faith, free, female, and future (Shufurengōkai 1998:89).

As Japan's aging consumer organizations redefine themselves, a new breed of consumer groups—and I am using the term very loosely here—is appearing in cities around the country. Small and grassroots in orientation, many of these groups are led by relatively young, well-educated men and women who mix consumer-related issues with environmentalism, human rights concerns, and good governance. They were active in the movement to enact and monitor the product liability law (see Madge 1999) and in the information disclosure and nonprofit organization campaigns. Their numbers, moreover, are slowly increasing under the new NPO Law (Pekkanen 2000), which has made it easier for citizen groups to obtain nonprofit status from the government. In many ways, these groups have acquired the trappings of new social movements, particularly with respect to their concern for quality-of-life issues and adherence to democratic decision-making norms.

As Mrs. Shimizu pointed out to me in our interview in the summer of 1999, this new grassroots phenomenon may be the harbinger of the end of advocacy politics led by housewives in large national and regional consumer organizations and the beginning of a more mass-based, grassroots approach to consumerism. Mrs. Shimizu seemed pleased with this development, as she noted the strong sense of political efficacy among many of these grassroots leaders and the fact that they were men as well as women and young instead of middle aged and elderly. I, on the other hand, was taken aback by her attitude, since these new grassroots groups could very well reduce the role of her own organization in Japanese consumer politics. But after pondering this point for a moment, I soon recognized the error in my thinking. Whether or not organizations like Shufuren survive intact over the long term, I realized, was beside the point; what mattered was the fact that more and more Japanese consumers have been standing up for their professed right to be heard. Japan's postwar consumer organizations, it seems, are finally succeeding in fulfilling one of their most important objectives: fashioning a strong consumer-as-citizen consciousness in the public at large. It is a development that bodes well not only for the future of consumer protection but also for Japanese democracy.

Notes

Introduction

1. Literally, "a temple for seeking refuge."

2. Demands for a consumer *kakekomidera* have ranged from requests for the introduction of facilities in preexisting ministries and agencies to deal with consumer-related issues, to the establishment of a specific ministry or agency for consumer affairs.

3. I use the term *consumer group* to refer to small, fluid consumer organs at the local level and reserve *consumer organization* for the larger, more tightly organized entities that focus on prefectural and national politics.

4. Consumer advocates are self-designated representatives of broad consumer constituencies who campaign for public goods in a particular political system. In Japan, a number of advocacy organizations are sponsored by business interests. Unless otherwise specified, I do not include these organizations in my analysis.

   Private organizations that specialize in consumer advocacy should also be distinguished from grassroots consumer groups consisting of concerned citizens who perform consumer-related functions exclusively for themselves or their immediate communities. These groups include self-help groups designed to increase awareness of smart shopping techniques, local recycling groups, and purchasing clubs.

5. See chapter 1 for a discussion of the "consumer interest."

6. In order to assess the nature of the conflict between consumer and producer interests, I have excluded cases like the anticonsumption tax campaign in which consumers and producers (small businessmen, in the tax case) joined together in pursuit of common goals. The antitax campaign is also problematic for my purposes because it does not reflect the "consumer interest" as defined

by Japanese activists. As several movement insiders revealed to me, many activists believed the tax to be in the long-term best interests of consumers in a
rapidly aging society and therefore participated in the campaign only for the
sake of movement solidarity.

1. Toward a Framework for the Study of Consumer Advocacy

1. Although the scope and meaning of the term is subject to debate among scholars, *consumerism* is often used interchangeably with *consumer movement* to refer
   to a particular type of social movement (see Brown 1996:77–78; Mayer 1989:
   3–5).
2. For further analysis of the controversies surrounding the concept of the "consumer interest," see Forbes 1987:ch. 1.
3. Consumers International is an international network of national consumer organizations from both advanced and lesser-developed economies.
4. For a discussion of "political entrepreneurs" in social movement organizations,
   see McCarthy and Zald 1977, Oberschall 1973, and Walsh 1978.
5. As stated by the British government in its 1962 *Final Report of the Committee
   on Consumer Protection* (the Molony Report), "the consumer is everybody all
   the time" (quoted in Wraith 1976:9).
6. Environmental activists are also concerned with issues that transcend socioeconomic boundaries. However, since pollution and other forms of environmental degradation can have a severe and immediate impact on both the eco-
   system and human health, they are more likely than consumer-related issues
   to spark strong grievances that motivate individuals to mobilize in pursuit of
   collective goals.
7. For a detailed discussion of the conflict between producer and consumer interests at the individual level, see D. Vogel and Nadel 1976.
8. As one British scholar noted, "Consumers are more obviously mobilized around
   their roles in the division of labor, typically as members of occupational groups,
   trade unions or professional associations which overwhelmingly determine
   their social and political organization" (Hornsby-Smith 1986:303).
9. By implication, the functions of advocacy organizations may diminish and
   those of educational organs expand as advanced industrial democracies shift
   from a system of consumer protection based on governmental regulation to one
   based on the self-responsibility of well-informed consumers.
10. Many of Japan's small, local consumer groups and the Seikatsu Club Consumer
    Cooperative are exceptions to this general trend. Both the Seikatsu Club and
    its electoral wing, the Seikatsusha Network, are characterized by democratic
    participation by rank-and-file members in decision making. Since the club does
    not participate in national policymaking processes, I have not included it in

my analysis. For more on the Seikatsu Club, see Gelb and Estevez-Abe 1998 and LeBlanc 1999.

11. For an in-depth analysis of the criteria for a successful boycott, see Friedman 1999.

12. The Seikatsusha Network is, of course, an important exception to this rule. But as Robin LeBlanc (1999:ch. 5) shows, even the "netto" has trouble recruiting Seikatsu Club members into electoral politics.

13. The leading works in the resource mobilization tradition include McCarthy and Zald 1977, Jenkins and Perrow 1977, Oberschall 1973, and Wilson 1973.

14. Examples of the classical approach include Davies 1969, Kornhauser 1959, and Smelser (1959).

15. The resource mobilization perspective has been adopted by several scholars to explain the initial formation of social movements in Japan. Margaret A. Mc-Kean argues that the proliferation of environmental organizations during the 1960s and early 1970s was a direct function not of any growing sense of isolation or alienation among individuals but, rather, of "rational attempts by [aggrieved groups] to mobilize hidden resources" in specific communities (McKean 1981:160). Krauss and Simcock explain the "rapid and spectacular spread" of environmental citizen groups in a similar vein, paying particular attention to "the availability of an extensive web of community and associational organizations at the local level" (Krauss and Simcock 1980:207–8).

16. "Historical precedents for social mobilization" include the demonstration effects of social movements that have organized in the past.

17. The historical institutionalist school of thought is a very diverse one and is by no means fully represented in this book. Works in this tradition that have informed this study include Dunlavy 1993, Hall 1986, Hattam 1993, Immergut 1992a, Steinmo 1993, and Steinmo, Thelen, and Longstreth 1992.

18. For a detailed overview of different conceptualizations of "institution," see Steinmo et al. 1992.

19. I prefer the *historical* institutional approach to the *rational-choice* version as an analytical framework for studying social movements, for three reasons. First, social movement activists do not always act rationally. As historical institutionalists have observed, many activists respond subconsciously to institutional norms and historical precedents in ways that are not always in their best interests. The national choice approach is further weakened by the fact that advocates rarely act on the basis of perfect information. In fact, many movement organizations are frequently denied access to crucial information not only by other societal actors but also by governments. Finally, as Steinmo et al. point out, the rational-choice approach tends to address the preferences and objectives of societal actors as givens rather than as variables that need to be explained. The historical institutional approach, I believe, with its historical focus and inductive methodology, is better poised to explain the seemingly irrational

objectives of specific social movements. For more on the differences between these and other strains of the "new institutionalism" approach, see, e.g., Hall and Taylor 1996, Koelble 1995, March and Olsen 1989, and Steinmo et al. 1992:ch. 1.

20. Frank K. Upham's analysis of the effects of legal structures on political conflict and social change in Japan is written at least in part in this tradition. According to Upham, institutions—in this case, laws and judicial structures—can have a major impact on the fora of particular political conflicts, the manner in which societal actors organize themselves, and the development of political alliances (Upham 1987:4). Jeffrey Broadbent also incorporates an institutional focus into his multifaceted treatment of the environmental movement (Broadbent 1998).

21. Notable exceptions to this norm include Kitschelt's research on the antinuclear movement.

22. In a similar fashion, March and Olsen argue that "the primary source of the institutionalist challenge is empirical" (March and Olsen 1984:741).

23. Kitschelt, writing from the POS perspective, addresses policies, but mostly in terms of the state's capacity to implement them, a variable that he argues can "determine the overall responsiveness of politics to social movements" (Kitschelt 1986:63).

24. Theorists writing from a social movement perspective who analyze the impact of policies on social movement behavior include Andrain and Apter 1995 and Duerst-Lahti 1989.

25. Georgia Duerst-Lahti (1989) argues along similar lines in her study of the government's impact on the development of the women's movement in the United States. Duerst-Lahti shows how changes in government policy toward women led to the introduction of a number of federal institutions that gave female activists incentives to mobilize into a nationwide political movement. One implication of these findings is that networks of social movement organizations often follow rather than precede state initiatives in a particular policy area. As subsequent chapters illustrate, comparable patterns can be found in the case of organized consumer movements.

2. Consumer Advocacy in the United States and Britain

1. Definitive works on the American consumer movement include Aaker and Day 1974, Berry 1977, Bloom and Smith 1986, Maney and Bykerk 1994, Mayer 1989, and Nadel 1971.

2. Notable exceptions to this norm include Asch 1988.

3. Some of the criticisms posed by Kallet and Schlink (1933) appear quaint in retrospect. In chapter 2, for instance, the authors describe the many dangers posed to the human digestive system by eating Kellogg's All Bran and raw fruits and vegetables (pp. 19–24).

4. Among the senators who embraced the consumer cause were Ed Muskie, Edward Kennedy, Estes Kefauver, Warren Magnuson, Mike Mansfield, John Moss, Philip Hart, Abraham Ribicoff, and Benjamin Rosenthal.

5. Most of these measures were regulatory in scope and included the Cigarette Labeling and Advertising Act (1965), the Fair Packaging and Labeling Act (1966), the National Traffic and Motor Vehicle Safety Act (1966), and amendments to the Food, Drug, and Cosmetics Act (1962) and the Flammable Fabrics Act (1967).

6. For more on the organized movement's power of persuasion, see Nadel 1971:211.

7. Today, there are almost 5 million paid subscribers to *Consumer Reports*. Consumers Union amasses about $100 million in total revenue, most of it coming from sales of this and other publications. Private, noncorporate donations also are a large revenue source (Karpatkin 1997a:183–84).

8. Many consumer organizations refuse to accept governmental financial assistance. Consumers Union, for instance, stopped accepting government grants for specific projects during the 1970s in an effort to preserve its political independence and to prevent conflicts of interest (interview, James, May 1999).

9. Dan Burt's organization, for example, argued that Nader stood at the head of a "huge lobbying and opinion-marketing conglomerate" that resisted the very kinds of organizational accountability that Nader was demanding of industry (Burt 1982).

10. For more on the proposed agency, see Herrmann and Mayer 1997:593.

11. Consumer organizations do not speak with a unified voice on free trade issues. Whereas Nader's network has opposed NAFTA and the GATT for their potentially negative effects on the environment and domestic employment, for example, Consumers Union has come out in support of free trade on the grounds that it promotes economic development in Third World countries (interview, James, May 1999).

12. The number of autonomous local groups in the movement rose from a mere thirty-eight in 1969 to nearly 400 in 1983 (Brobeck 1997:532). In addition, Nader's network of public-interest research groups (PIRGs) expanded during the 1980s. PIRGs are nonprofit, state-level organizations that concentrate not only on consumer protection but also on issues relating to governmental reform and environmentalism (Mierzwinski 1997).

13. The British cooperative movement, the first of its kind in the world, served as the leading representative of consumer interests until the early postwar period. Although a few cooperative leaders continue to sit on governmental committees, the functions of consumer advocacy are now largely carried out by other organizations. For excellent analyses of consumer cooperation in Britain and elsewhere, see Furlough and Strikwerda 1999.

14. The bulk of NCC funding comes in the form of grants-in-aid from the Department of Trade and Industry.

15. Unlike *Consumer Reports, Which?* is available only to subscribers.
16. The CA now has roughly 800,000 members, two-fifths that of Consumers Union.
17. This total makes the CA the second richest consumer organization in the world, after Consumers Union.
18. Local consumer groups are affiliated with the National Federation of Consumer Groups.
19. The NCC, unlike other consumer organizations in Britain or, for that matter, the United States and Japan, has its own press office.
20. Britain's incomes and pricing policies were aimed primarily at curbing inflation.
21. For a discussion of the processes of "re-regulation," see S. Vogel 1996.
22. This is, of course, a play on Pempel and Tsunekawa's term "corporatism without labor" (Pempel and Tsunekawa 1979).

3. The Politics of an Emerging Consumer Movement

1. Even though I use the well-known term *Reverse Course* for the sake of convenience, I take it with a grain of salt. This phase of the Occupation, which began around 1947/48, did *not*, as the term implies, usher in a wholesale unraveling of earlier democratic reforms. Rather, it should be interpreted as a reorientation of Occupation policy away from democratization and toward the reinvigoration of the postwar Japanese economy.
2. For more on the economic conditions facing Japanese citizens in the immediate aftermath of World War II, see Dower 1999:89–97.
3. The name of the group was the Women's Committee for Postwar Policies (Sengo taisaku fujin iinkai), a precursor of the Japan League of Women Voters (Nihon fujin yūkensha dōmei).
4. For prewar examples of direct confrontation between consumers and public authorities, see Lewis 1990.
5. A *furoshiki* is a large, square cloth used for wrapping and carrying small parcels.
6. The expression *kome yokose* apparently appeared for the first time in the journal *Sekki*, the precursor to *Akahata*, the official newspaper of the Japan Communist Party. Originally devised as an appeal to the government to issue more adequate rice rations to hungry workers, the expression was eventually adopted as a slogan by many early consumer activists who were protesting inefficiencies in the rice-rationing system (K. Kobayashi, June 1993:41). The inclusion of the term *furoshiki* in the slogan Give Us Back Our Rice *furoshiki* movement signals the leading role of housewives-as-consumers in this early postwar consumer campaign. For more on this subject, see Yamamoto 1976.

7. The movement reached a peak on May 19, 1946, when a demonstration of more than 30,000 labor unionists, left-wing political activists, and consumers was carried out in front of the Imperial Palace in Tōkyō. Known as the Give Us Our Rice Mayday, the incident was criticized by General Douglas Mac-Arthur as a threat to domestic peace (NHSK 1980:17).

8. I have yet to see evidence that the designation was consciously modeled after the New York prototype.

9. According to Oku Mumeo, one out of every five or six matches in a five-yen box was defective (Oku 1988:176).

10. See Oku 1988. For more on Oku's life and career, see Oku 1988, Tokuza 1999, and Narita 1998.

11. The rice paddle was chosen as the official symbol of Shufuren because it symbolized the woman's caretaker role in the family, the problems encountered by Japanese housewives as both women and consumers, and the kitchen as the basic building block of the contemporary consumer movement. Large cardboard replicas of the rice paddle covered with political demands ("Stop Price Fixing!), angry pronouncements ("Goodbye Tanaka Cabinet!"), and slogans ("Turned Away at the Gate") are often held aloft in street demonstrations.

12. Chifuren was particularly active during the early postwar period in opposing proposed changes to constitutional provisions pertaining to women.

13. Chifuren eventually withdrew from the antinuclear movement after the movement became heavily politicized (KSS 1997:70).

14. The Tōkyō chapter of the federation, led by Tanaka Satoko, has been particularly active in the consumer advocacy realm.

15. A consumer cooperative is a nonprofit organization in which members serve as both consumers and suppliers of capital. For an excellent history, in Japanese, of the Japanese cooperative movement, see Yamamoto 1982.

16. Seikyōren, with 674 member organizations, is the wealthiest consumer-related organization in Japan. In 1990, it took in roughly 700,800,000 yen from its affiliates (Keizaikikakuchō 1991c:82).

17. Established in 1965, the Seikatsu Club had more than 55,000 members in 1992. The club promotes participatory democracy in both the cooperative setting and local government and is a strong advocate of environmental protection (Tōkyō Initiative on International Cooperative Alliance 1992). For more on the history and significance of the club, see Gelb and Estevez-Abe 1998 and LeBlanc 1999:ch. 5.

18. Article 5 of chapter 1 states: "The Cooperative Society shall not be established covering a wider area than that of a prefecture " (Ministry of Health and Welfare 1989:2).

19. According to statistics compiled by Kurimoto Akira, the Japanese movement is larger than those of Austria, Denmark, Germany, Italy, Sweden, and the U.K. in terms of total membership. However, Japanese co-ops comprise only 2.5

percent of market share, a very small proportion compared with Sweden's 15.2 percent (Kurimoto 1992:224).

20. Japanese consumer cooperatives have assumed more consumer advocacy functions than their American and British counterparts have. The British co-ops, as we noted in the last chapter, were widely recognized as the country's leading advocates until 1957, when the Consumers' Association assumed this distinction.

21. Although the Co-op Law has been updated several times, its most controversial provisions remain intact.

22. In a 1983 survey, for example, only 2 percent of the members of forty-two cooperatives indicated that they had joined for political reasons (Kilburn and Nomura 1986:53).

23. The only other private entity engaged in extensive consumer product testing after the war was the magazine *Kurashi no tetchō*. The magazine is still published today. Shufuren's testing facilities, on the other hand, are no longer operating.

24. For a history of prewar and wartime Japanese savings campaigns that also touches on early postwar trends, see Garon 2000.

25. See chapter 4 for a discussion of the lifestyle schools. For a more in-depth analysis of the New Life movement, see Garon 1997.

26. For a history of moral suasion campaigns based on partnerships between citizens and governmental authorities, see Garon 1997.

27. Shufuren has tried on several occasions to obtain foundation (and hence tax-exempt) status as a means to enhance the independence of its financial base, but it could never raise the principal required for such status.

28. For example, Oku Mumeo and Higa Masako, the leaders of Shufuren and the Kansai shufuren, respectively, were well-known adversaries. Some observers in the movement chalked their differences up to the conflicting temperaments of Tōkyōites and Ōsaka natives (K. Kobayashi, June 1994:46).

29. From this perspective, consumption refers simply to the act of using the fruits of production to satisfy wants. A consumer, then, is someone who performs this act.

30. For a comprehensive history and competing definitions of the concept of *seikatsusha*, see Amano 1996. Shimizu Makoto, a scholar of consumer law, tends to avoid the term *seikatsusha* yet assigns the conceptual identities of that term — consumer, producer, citizen (*shimin* and *kokumin*) — to his definition of *shōhisha* (consumer). Shimizu's multifaceted definition of *shōhisha*, which he applies to contemporary Japan, mirrors the conceptual approach of early postwar consumer activists, an approach that still holds sway today in the movement (see Shimizu 1994).

31. The term *seikatsu* (lifestyle), by contrast, was widely used both in the organized consumer movement and by other societal and government actors. For more on the use of this term during the interwar period, see Garon 2000.

32. The determination of many women to take an integrative approach to the politics of consumption—one that would not infringe on the priorities of family life—was symbolized at the micro level by Oku Mumeo's habit of calling on the homes of Shufuren activists to personally thank their families for allowing her to take them away from their housewifely duties (Oku 1988:182–83).

33. Both the American and British movements did, however, ally with other economic groups. As noted in chapter 2, the British consumer cooperative movement was closely associated with the labor movement, and Ralph Nader's network of organizations has allied with the AFL-CIO. That said, American and, to a lesser extent, British consumer advocates have been far more willing to draw a line in the sand between citizens as "consumers" and other economic groups in the polity than Japanese advocates have.

4. Consumer Politics Under Early One-Party Dominance

1. For a comprehensive analysis of changing Japanese consumption patterns since the Meiji Restoration (1868), see Partner 1999.

2. The expression "extravagance is the enemy" never really disappeared from the postwar lexicon. As Garon notes, many Japanese still endorsed it toward the end of the twentieth century in their efforts to save (Garon 2000).

3. For more on these and similar incidents, see Morishima and Smith 1986 and Reich 1984.

4. For more on patterns of local intergovernmental relations, see Samuels 1983:17–32.

5. For several years, British consumer-related administrative functions were concentrated in the Department of Prices and Consumer Protection. After the department was abolished, those functions were assumed by the minister for consumer affairs and small firms, a junior-ranking position in the Department of Trade and Industry. Many British consumer advocates believe that the consumer-related functions of the bureaucracy should be expanded.

6. Many of these groups, of course, did not last beyond the Occupation.

7. Of the 357 groups established between 1965 and 1969, for example, four were national groups, twenty-nine were prefectural in scope, and the remaining 324 were local (Keizaikikakuchō 1997:9).

8. Each school consists of about 100 housewives (Osami 1995:8).

9. In 1995, for example, membership in the lifestyle schools totaled a mere 64,000. Participation in the schools reached a postwar high of 105,000 in 1974/75 (Keizaikikakuchō 1997:5).

10. Shufuren's Takada Yuri was one such representative.

11. The center's regional programs were mainly targeted toward the *fujinkai* (Zenchifuren 1986:27).

12. According to at least one reliable source, members of consumer-related organizations affiliated with MITI are occasionally warned by ministry officials to refrain from politicized consumer movement activities. This kind of "administrative guidance" is often heeded by those organizations because MITI is a very important source of funding (interview, source withheld, February 1994).

13. The Consumption Science Center is licensed by the Economic Planning Agency. Shufuren does not hold this kind of legal status.

14. In 1980, Shōkaren concluded on the basis of taste tests conducted on various brands of imported and domestic rice that high prices did not necessary signify high quality. After informing the public that California brands were of very high quality and competitively priced, Shōkaren's offices were flooded with inquiries from consumers who wanted to know how to obtain them.

15. The Japan Automobile Users' Union, a relatively small and highly specialized consumer organization that supervises the automobile industry, consists almost entirely of men. It is not normally a player in broad political advocacy movements.

16. Many activists believe that this weak sense of civic consciousness prevented a more rapid expansion of consumer organizations over the years (Inaba et al. 1979:7).

17. As Feldman argues, the public assertion of rights normally occurs during conflicts in which the desire to maintain a "superficially harmonious" relationship with one's opponents is discarded (Feldman 2000:5).

18. An awareness of individual rights among ordinary Japanese citizens appears to have progressed far more on issues like environmentalism and health care, issues that tend to have a much greater impact on the health and welfare of individuals. For more on the development of rights consciousness in the health-care realm, see Feldman 2000.

19. John O. Haley points out that the notion of rights, which he defines as "the claims of individuals to protection by specific procedures and remedies," is a characteristic of Roman law. In Japan and other East Asian countries, the delineation of *duties* is often the main mechanism through which legal rules are enforced. So, while Japan's approach to consumer protection may differ from that of its Western counterparts, it fits in well with Asian legal norms (Haley 1991a:11).

20. The law has often been criticized by many Americans for prohibiting the provision of free gifts or services in excess of 10 percent of the value of the product or service purchased. This would, in theory, hurt imports, whose prices are not always competitive with those of domestic products.

21. In September 1960, the Ikeda cabinet announced a "consumer price policy" (*shōhisha bukka taisaku*) designed to ensure the proper application of the Antimonopoly Law and to specify governmental measures to adjust supply to demand. The government also introduced a number of more specific measures

to control the prices of such basic commodities as milk, meat, and vegetables (NHSK 1980:54).

22. Nakamura Kii noted that the boycott was one of the very few occasions when the media aggressively pursued consumer activists, rather than the other way around (interview, K. Nakamura, April 1994).

5. The Post-1968 Consumer Protection Policymaking System

1. The agency was headed at the time by Miyazawa Kiichi.
2. Sunada was one of the only postwar conservative politicians who openly championed consumer issues. Although he occasionally made appearances at national consumer rallies sponsored by Shōdanren, Sunada's relationship with consumer organizations was apparently not a close one (Shōdanren 1987b:15).
3. For more on this trend, which intensified during the 1970s, see Krauss 1984.
4. For information on the 1961 Agricultural Basic Law, see Calder 1988:264–66. For analyses of the 1967 Basic Law on Environmental Pollution, see McKean 1981:20 and Broadbent 1998:114, 120–22, 128, 132.
5. The reference to free and fair competition alludes to the proper implementation of the Antimonopoly Law.
6. For a discussion of the impact of *tatewari gyōsei* on consumer policymaking, see chapter 4.
7. The "Japan Consumer Information Center" was the official Japanese translation of Kokumin seikatsu sentaa. In late 2000, the center changed its English name to National Consumer Affairs Center.
8. In 1999, there were 359 consumer centers in Japan (Keizaikikakuchō 1999:17).
9. This is a complaint shared by nearly all the consumer advocates I interviewed who had served on national *shingikai*.
10. See Upham's discussion of pollution complaint counselors and prefectural pollution review boards (Upham 1987:56–58).
11. Ordinance to Prevent Damages Caused by Lifestyle Commodities, to Rationalize Business Practices Pertaining to Labeling, etc., and to Provide for the Relief of Consumer Damages (Tōkyōto seikatsu busshi no higai no bōshi, hyōji nado no jigyō kōi no tekiseika oyobi shōhisha higai no kyūsai ni kansuru jōrei).
12. More specifically, the Local Autonomy Law encourages local self-government as a key to democratization and the development of local administrations that reflect public opinion (Samuels 1983:xx).
13. In the spring of 1994, for instance, I was amazed to find consumer leaders in the movement to enact a product liability law devoting the bulk of their time during public meetings to defining basic legal terms, even though the bureaucracy, which was in the midst of drafting a bill, had moved well beyond that stage.

14. Since class action suits are not permitted in Japan, activists file suit as groups of plaintiffs.
15. In this regard, consumer organizations were behaving like other social movements in Japan. For an analysis of the significance of litigation for the assertion of rights by social movements, see Feldman 2000.
16. For general analyses of the institutional barriers to litigation in Japan, see Haley 1978 and Yamanouchi and Cohen 1991.
17. There are relatively few examples of local governmental support for lawsuits involving small claims and large numbers of plaintiffs, in part because such suits are not often filed in Japan.
18. Shufuren, for instance, received some support from the Tōkyō metropolitan government for its lawsuits against the alleged kerosene cartel during the 1970s and 1980s.
19. For more on the internal functions of protest in Japan, see Pharr 1990:ch. 6.
20. The product boycott—the quintessential form of market-oriented protest for consumer advocates—was not a large part of the organized movement's strategic arsenal after the 1970/71 color TV boycott. There are at least two reasons for this. First, boycotts are extremely labor intensive and difficult to carry out in the best of times. With the decline of mass production and the development of small-niche markets, they have become even more difficult to organize. Second, boycotts were most appropriate during the high-growth era, when consumers were bombarded with unsafe products. Once the flood of defective products into the marketplace slowed, however, boycotts lost much of their strategic appeal.
21. For more on the Information Disclosure Law, see chapter 9.
22. For an up-to-date analysis of the role of the reporters' clubs in Japanese politics, see Freeman 2000.

6. The Right to Choose

1. George Fields, for example, points out that "there is virtual silence [on the part of consumer advocates] when the biggies fix prices" (Fields 1989:133).
2. The so-called per se illegal principle is a defining feature—in theory, at least—of American antitrust policy. In British and many European antitrust systems (with the notable exception of Germany), it is the *effects* of monopoly and collusive business practices, rather than the phenomena themselves, that are the main targets of regulation.
3. These laws targeted, for example, the export and import sectors, the ammonium sulfate industry, the coal and machine tool industries, and textiles (Misono 1987:95–97).
4. This is the official "tentative" translation of the Japan Fair Trade Commission.

5. For summaries of these different points of view, see, for example, Hosokawa June 1996:1–21 and September 1996:29–46; Yamane, Seryō, and Mori 1998:67–82.
6. The membership of the council consisted of three scholars, one media representative, and eleven representatives from the business community.
7. Japanese consumer advocates view premiums as an enticement for consumers to buy overpriced products.
8. Illegal RPM setups were often referred to as "black market resale price maintenance systems" (*yami saiban seidō*).
9. The JFTC ruled that under the Law to Prevent Unjustifiable Premiums and Misleading Representations, qualified complainants must suffer damages as a result of violations to the law. In the eyes of the commission, Oku Mumeo, who filed the complaint on behalf of Shufuren, had incurred no such damages (*Shufuren dayori*, April 15, 1973).
10. The Sendai High Court ruled in favor of the consumers in 1985, but its decision was overturned by the Supreme Court.
11. Iyori notes, for example, that only seven suits were filed under the provisions of article 25 of the AML between 1947 and 1984. In the United States during the early 1980s, more than 1,000 private antitrust actions were filed each year (Iyori 1986:75, n. 21).
12. This certainly seemed to be the case in the "Big Four" environmental cases and the suits involving damages incurred by consumers of tainted foods and medicines.
13. For more on the impact of litigation on rights awareness in the general public, see Feldman 2000.
14. Of the thirteen members of the JFTC study group, ten were from the academic community, two from the media, and one from a semiprivate research organization (Misono 1987:256, n. 7).
15. Under the existing law, a consumer had the power to request a JFTC investigation of an alleged AML violation, but the commission was not obligated to alert him or her of its findings. Consumer representatives and many scholars and opposition party politicians wanted this changed.
16. Article 25 of the AML stipulates that consumers can sue companies—on the basis of strict liability—for damages caused by violations of the AML. Article 26, however, states that lawsuits cannot be launched until after the JFTC has ruled on the case. Consumer advocates supported an amendment to the law that would permit citizens to file such suits independently of JFTC investigations.
17. In my interviews with advocates on the AML and other consumer issues, most were very forthcoming in expressing their disappointment in Nakasone's stance toward consumers as both head of MITI and prime minister. One advocate, at the mere mention of his name, growled, "That man! Oooooh, he infuriates me!"

18. The items that took precedence over the AML reform bill included revision of the political finance and election laws and the ratification of both the Sino-Japanese Friendship Treaty and the Nuclear Nonproliferation Treaty.
19. The only other issue of concern to the consumer movement that received comparable attention at election time was the controversial consumption tax.

7. The Right to Safety

1. Takeuchi Naokazu, the founder of Japan Consumers Union (Nihon shōhisha renmei), is the most prominent proponent of this position.
2. This term is often used in the Japanese literature to refer to the decline of movement growth rates during the 1980s, the aging of movement leaders, and the movement's failure to prevent the introduction of a general consumption tax.
3. In regard to the number of participants, the anti-deregulation movement is surpassed only by the movement to oppose the introduction of a general consumption tax, which occurred later in the decade.
4. For a comparison of governmental approaches to regulation and deregulation in Japan and the West, see Maclachlan 1999.
5. The commuter's patronage of small, often dirty, noodle stands located next to train stations is, of course, an exception to this general tendency.
6. That number shrank during the early 1970s when several of those additives were discovered to be carcinogenic.
7. The Morinaga Milk incident of 1955 involved a powdered milk formula that had been tainted with arsenic.
8. The so-called Kanemi oil incident. For more on this story, see Reich 1984.
9. David Vogel suggests that food processors "did not oppose this policy change" (D. Vogel 1992:129). Although this was no doubt true if we are to measure "opposition" according to the public pronouncements of business, consumer activists have stated to me that opposition was carried out quietly behind the scenes so as to avoid a public backlash.
10. Unless otherwise specified, the following two paragraphs are based on NHSK 1980:133–36.
11. The cyclamate boycott also proved to be an important dry run for the much more effective color TV boycott that was carried out the following year.
12. David Vogel points out that depending on how they are defined, between 50 and 200 additional synthetic additives are permitted for use in the United States (D. Vogel 1992:123).
13. Britain's regime was the most permissive in the European Union before harmonization, a process that increased the number of approved additives on the continent to 412. Germany, for instance, had authorized 150 synthetic additives, and Greece only 120 (D. Vogel 1995:51–52).

14. The law was strengthened in response to both the Kanemi oil disaster and the SMON incident involving tainted diarrhea medicine.

15. For a detailed analysis of mounting trade frictions between the United States and Japan over Japan's strict food regulatory regime, see D. Vogel 1992.

16. The irony here is, of course, that natural additives also have the potential to damage the health of consumers.

17. One of the most prominent proponents of this position has been Takeuchi Naokazu, president of Consumers Union. Unlike the United States, natural additives are not subject to regulation in Japan.

18. As David Vogel points out, this latter requirement distinguishes Japan's regulatory system governing food additives from that of the United States (D. Vogel 1992:121).

19. For a comparative analysis of the theories of deregulation, see S. Vogel 1996: ch. 1.

20. In the United States, for example, American policymakers were questioning the validity of the 1958 amendment to the Food, Drug, and Cosmetics Act (the "Delaney Clause") which prohibits the use of additives suspected of having even trace levels of carcinogenic properties. The clause was criticized as excessive and outdated, given the availability of new, sophisticated technology capable of determining the exact levels at which synthetic additives can be safely consumed by human beings.

21. Consumer activists, relying on scientific studies conducted in Japan, argued that the substance may have had carcinogenic properties (KSS 1997:155).

22. In use in Japan since 1954, BHA is found in such products as margarine, cooking oil, and instant noodles.

23. During the early 1990s, for example, consumer advocates solicited American support for a Japanese strict liability law.

24. The most publicized experiments were those conducted by Professor Itō Nobuyuki of Nagoya City University's Medical Department (*Mainichi shimbun*, February 1, 1983).

25. In 1981, the Ministry of Health and Welfare announced an "interim five-year plan for the administration of food additives" (Shokuhin tenkabutsu gyōsei chūki gokanen shikaku) that highlighted the need to deregulate additives in the interest of the international harmonization of food safety standards.

26. Partly in response to mounting American pressure to open Japanese markets, Keidanren supported the authorization of additives that were in use in foreign countries (*Mainichi shimbun*, July 13, 1983).

27. A summary of the questions and responses was reprinted in *Shufuren dayori* (June 15, 1983). Details presented in this and the two following paragraphs are from this source.

28. The media's interest in the consumer movement's position on additives was conditioned by the nature of the issue. John C. Campbell notes with reference

to policymaking regarding the elderly that "a proposal will be attractive to the media . . . if it is easily understandable (not highly technical), human and concrete (not abstract), in line with conventional social values (does not make people uncomfortable) and benefits the public as a whole (not special interests)" (Campbell 1996:193). These same criteria were also in place during the antiregulation campaign.

29. "Shokuhin tenkabutsu kyūzō naze?" [Why the sudden increase in food additives?] *Mainichi shimbun*, July 1983.

30. Shufuren, for instance, complained that the parties were much too slow in following the procedures for accepting petitions from consumer organizations and deliberating on whether or not to pass resolutions on the basis of those petitions (*Shufuren dayori*, February 15, 1984).

31. As I write this, I am reminded of the ongoing consumer backlash in Europe against the import of genetically engineered agricultural produce from the United States. Like their Japanese counterparts in 1983/84, European consumers base their opposition on fear rather than fact, for there is no conclusive evidence that these products pose a threat to the health of consumers. Much to the chagrin of American producers, however, that fear has evolved into an effective trade barrier and threatens to form the basis of a transatlantic trade war. These developments also lead me to question David Vogel's position that the politics of food safety regulation in Japan are "unique" (See D. Vogel 1992:124).

8. The Right to Redress

1. These statistics were compiled by Kitamura Haruo, former director of the Japan Consumer Information Center (Kitamura 1992:20).

2. In addition to establishing the SG Mark system, the 1973 Consumer Product Safety Law sets a number of product safety standards and provides for stricter governmental regulation of product safety (see Morishima and Smith 1986: 519–20).

3. This program was introduced in 1979 under the Drug Side Effects Injuries Relief and Research Promotion Fund Act (see Tejima 1993).

4. Compared with judges, juries tend to be more sympathetic to (and hence generous with) plaintiffs who have suffered damages caused by defective products.

5. In the SMON (Subacute-meylo-optico-neuropathy) case, about 6,000 victims in fifteen districts filed suit against the government. As Morishima notes, the main purpose of those cases was not to receive monetary compensation but, rather, to point out the weaknesses in the government's regulation of medicinal products (Morishima 1993a:723).

6. The concept of strict liability does have historical precedence in Japan. In 1955, for example, it was incorporated into the Automobile Compensation Law, which holds car owners strictly liable for damages caused by traffic accidents and establishes a system of compulsory automobile insurance (Morishima 1993a:723; see also Morishima and Smith 1986).

7. For more on how "problems" are addressed in the agenda-setting stage of the policymaking process, see Kingdon 1984:95–121.

8. The EC viewed a uniform products liability standard as a necessary step toward (1) the equalization of competition among member countries, (2) the promotion of the free flow of goods across borders, and (3) the promotion of the "equal protection of the consumer" (Nilles 1985:744).

9. The development risk plea enables manufacturers to avoid liability if they can prove they were incapable of predicting the occurrence of product defects on the basis of existing technological knowledge. Also known as the state-of-the-art plea, the provision was viewed by supporters as necessary to the survival of the high tech, pharmaceutical, and other industries that produce inherently risky products. Of the EU countries that have enacted PL laws, only Luxembourg, Finland, and Norway have ruled against the plea.

10. Although the loosening of the Large-Scale Retail Store Law technically increases the consumer's access to a wider range of products, the move met with opposition from activists who sought to protect small retailers from competition from larger retailers. For more on the law and its consequences, see Upham 1993.

11. The "Lifestyle Superpower" plan was a five-year economic plan introduced by Prime Minister Miyazawa in 1992 that had five interrelated objectives: (1) shorter working hours; (2) affordable housing; (3) improved social infrastructure; (4) harmonious external relations, achieved in part through a reduction of Japan's trade surplus, which would involve the stimulation of domestic demand; and (5) meaningful international contributions ("Tomorrow's 'Lifestyle Superpower' " 1992).

12. Among the opposition parties, only the Kōmeitō and the Japan Social Democratic Party had been active promoters of PL reform. The Japan Communist Party supported reform but did little to promote it openly until toward the end of the legislative process. The Democratic Socialist Party, meanwhile, expressed reservations about strict liability in response to the wishes of the auto workers' unions.

13. Advocates in the legal community argued that given the barriers to information confronted by plaintiffs in civil suits, a product liability law without a presumption clause would defeat one of the key purposes of the law: lessening the heavy burden of proof shouldered by plaintiffs (M. Nakamura 1993).

14. The PL promotion faction failed to note that European plaintiffs face similar—although perhaps not as severe—barriers to litigation.

15. Katō, professor emeritus of Seijō University and a former president of Tōkyō University, is a highly respected legal scholar and expert on consumer-related issues.

16. For example, the NHK, Japan's leading television broadcasting corporation, aired a fascinating documentary that was highly critical of the council's role in articulating the interests of average Japanese citizens (see NHK 1993).

17. *Ranso* is composed of the characters for "riot" or "disturbance" (*ran*) and "to sue" (*so*). The term was used frequently by PL critics who regarded American-style PL rules as far too tough on business.

18. Product liability was apparently discussed briefly during the SII talks of 1989/90 but was not incorporated into the final report. Sources connected to the American embassy told me in early 1994 that the U.S. government had directed embassy officials to refrain from voicing a position on Japanese policymaking surrounding product liability for fear that it would spark Japanese resentments that might hamper the "framework talks" between the two countries. They also revealed that the embassy was ambivalent about Japanese PL reform, since some U.S. businesses were complaining that the introduction of strict liability rules would constitute another nontariff barrier to imports.

19. The bureau both formulates and coordinates MITI's consumer policy.

20. Leading members of the PL Renrakukai included advocates from Shufuren, Chifuren, Shōkaren, Consumers Union, and the consumer cooperatives.

21. Most of the Renrakukai meetings I sat in on, for example, were held at the large consumer center located at Iidabashi Station in Tōkyō. I was surprised at the extent to which movement activists felt so at home in these facilities and at the level of communication between activists and center officials.

22. In Japan, 110 denotes a toll-free telephone number, similar to 1-800 in North America.

23. According to hotline organizers, most of the 715 consumers who used the service in 1990 expressed intense dissatisfaction with the *aitai kōshō* process and a general lack of awareness of alternative avenues of redress (M. Nakamura, Tajima, and Yonekawa 1992:23–25).

24. One such questionnaire distributed in Nichibenren, for instance, revealed that of the 250 cases involving defective products handled by lawyers in 1989, 166, or 66 percent, never made it past the consultation stage. Of the remaining eighty-four cases, fifty-four were resolved through out-of-court settlements, and only thirty were either before the courts or had reached in-court settlements. During the entire year, only four lawsuits resulted in victories for consumers. In this and subsequent studies conducted by Nichibenren, difficulties in proving negligence on the part of the manufacturer were cited as the main reason most of the cases never advanced beyond the consultation stage (M. Nakamura et al. 1992:26–30).

25. Both the *Hokkaidō shimbun* and the *Chūnichi shimbun*, for example, reported

regularly on the activities of consumer organizations and supported consumer proposals for a product liability law.

26. It is unclear whether such actions by the Socialist Party were carried out on the party's own initiative or in response to urging from members of the Social Policy Council.

27. A PL law that includes incentives for the courts to play a major role in settling product liability disputes would result in increased legal expenditures for businesses. A law without the development risk plea, moreover, would dampen incentives to innovate by holding firms legally liable for damages caused by state-of-the-art technologies and medicines.

28. Once again, Professor Katō Ichirō was appointed chairman of the council and Professor Morishima Akio head of the Consumer Policy Subcommittee.

29. The Nippon Association of Consumer Specialists (NACS), for example, was the only consumer-oriented organization in the PL Renrakukai that had drafted its own model law. NACS is an association of advisers and consultants licensed by MITI and the Shōhisha kyōkai, respectively, who are hired by both companies and local consumer centers to advise consumers. The NACS model met many of the demands of the business community. It was also opposed by a number of other consumer advocates on the grounds that it did not do enough for consumers in a court of law.

30. Indeed, the public was not even informed that the Economic Planning Agency was the center of gravity in the drafting process until after the bill had been drawn up.

31. For analyses of the statute itself, see Madden 1996, Marcuse 1996, and Takahashi 1996.

32. The battle pitted conservative politicians representing the medical lobby against those in the coalition parties who viewed inclusion as a symbol of the government's commitment to the consumer welfare.

33. A time limit on producer liability is set at three years from the time that a consumer or his or her lawyer becomes aware of product-related damages. In addition, manufacturers are liable for only ten years following the release of a product into the marketplace.

34. For a comprehensive analysis of those mechanisms, see Maclachlan 1999.

35. MITI's Industrial Structure Council, for example, had established a subcommittee to deal exclusively with these third-party redress mechanisms.

9. The Right to Be Heard

1. Only books remain on the government's official list.

2. For in-depth analyses of the political developments of the 1990s, see Curtis 1999 and Pempel 1998.

3. For a profile of one such politician before the LDP's downfall, see LeBlanc 1999.
4. Mrs. Ishige was ranked second only to Kan Naoto, the president of the Democratic Party at the time.
5. For an excellent analysis of Japan's deregulatory process, see S. Vogel 1996.
6. The Information Disclosure Law exempts several categories of bureaucratic information from disclosure, such as information that, if disclosed, would violate business secrets or the privacy of individuals and that pertain to foreign affairs and national security. Information generated by semigovernmental corporations will also be exempted from the law, although this provision is now under review. For more on the disclosure law and its legislative history, see Maclachlan 2000.
7. The legislative process formally began in 1990, when the Legislative Advisory Council took up the issue in response to long-standing pressure from citizen groups, the corporate sector, and the legal profession. The 1996 changes constitute the first time the code was significantly amended since 1926 (see Oda 1996:457–58).
8. For more on that process, see Maclachlan 2000.
9. For comparable trends in the NPO case, see Pekkanen 2000. Although consumer organizations supported the movement to enact the Nonprofit Organization Law, they were not major players. Ironically, virtually no consumer advocacy organizations have filed for NPO status since the law was enacted, although several new, local, issue-specific groups have taken advantage of the new provisions (interviews with consumer advocates, October 2000).
10. Consumer organizations viewed the new *kaigo hoken* law as primarily a "welfare" issue that did not warrant the expenditure of scare movement resources (interview, Shimizu, July 1999). For more on the *kaigo hoken* system, see Campbell 2000.
11. The law merely requires businesses to "do their best" (*doryoku suru*) to provide such information to consumers (*Nihon keizai shimbun*, April 12, 2000).
12. Many of the consumer cooperatives, for instance, have been grappling with financial difficulties as result of the recession. Co-op prices tend to be higher than those of mainstream retailers because of smaller economies of scale and the sale of organic (read costly) food products.
13. Chifuren, for instance, has lost many of its members over the last few years and is struggling to strengthen its presence in the cities (*Asahi shimbun*, June 5, 1998).
14. In late 1998, the Finance Ministry began deliberations on a financial services law that would protect consumers (*Asahi shimbun*, December 9, 1998).
15. Many advocates, for instance, are responding to bureaucratic deliberations on the question of judicial reform by clamoring for the introduction of a jury

system that, they believe, will make the courts more sympathetic to the particular concerns of consumers (*Shufuren dayori*, October 15, 2000).

16. In contrast to the early years of Shōdanren's existence, labor unions are no longer members of the organization.

17. As of this writing, however, only four or so men have joined the association.

18. The old headquarters were known as the Housewives' Hall (*Shufu kaikan*), a rather progressive-sounding name in the 1950s when women were still very marginalized politically. The new building has provided the cash-strapped association with additional sources of revenue, as several floors are rented out not only to citizens in search of meeting and wedding reception facilities but also to other consumer organizations, including Seikyōren, the national umbrella organization for consumer cooperatives, and Shōdanren. The last two organizations used to occupy separate facilities before financial constraints forced them to seek new accommodations.

Bibliography

Books and Articles

Aaker, David A., and George S. Day, eds. 1974. *Consumerism: Search for the Consumer Interest*. 2d ed. New York: Free Press.

Allinson, Gary D., and Yasunori Sone, eds. 1993. *Political Dynamics in Contemporary Japan*. Ithaca, N.Y.: Cornell University Press.

Amano, Masako. 1996. *Seikatsusha to wa dare ka* (Who is the seikatsusha?). Tōkyō: Chūkōshinsho.

Andrain, Charles F., and David E. Apter. 1995. *Political Protest and Social Change: Analyzing Politics*. New York: New York University Press.

Anzen shokuhin renrakukai. 1980. *Anzen na shokuhin wo motomete* (Demanding safe food products). Tōkyō: San'ichi shōbo.

Apter, David E., and Nagayo Sawa. 1984. *Against the State: Politics and Social Protest in Japan*. Cambridge, Mass.: Harvard University Press.

Asaoka Mie. 1992. *Tōron! PLhō: Kekkan shōhin to seizōbutsusekinin* (Debate! The PL law: Defective products and product liability). Tōkyō: Kamogawa shuppan.

Asch, Peter. 1988. *Consumer Safety Regulation: Putting a Price on Life and Limb*. New York: Oxford University Press.

Ashford, Nigel, and Grant Jordan, eds. 1993. *Public Policy and the Impact of the New Right*. London: Printer Publishers.

Atsuya Jōji. 1986. *Dokusenkinshihō nyūmon* (An introduction to the antimonopoly law). Tōkyō: Nihon keizai shimbunsha.

Berger, Suzanne, ed. 1981. *Organizing Interests in Western Europe: Pluralism, Corporatism, and the Transformation of Politics*. Cambridge: Cambridge University Press.

Berry, Jeffrey M. 1977. *Lobbying for the People: The Political Behavior of Public Interest Groups*. Princeton, N.J.: Princeton University Press.

———. 1978. "On the Origins of Public Interest Groups: A Test of Two Theories." *Polity* 10, no. 3: 379–97.

———. 1999. *The New Liberalism: The Rising Power of Citizen Groups*. Washington, D.C.: Brookings Institution Press.

Bestor, Theodore C. 1989. *Neighborhood Tokyo*. Stanford, Calif.: Stanford University Press.

Blanke, Doug. 1997. "State Attorneys General." In *Encyclopedia of the Consumer Movement*, ed. Stephen Brobeck, pp. 538–42. Santa Barbara, Calif.: ABC-Clio.

Bloom, Paul N., and Stephen A. Greyser. 1981. "The Maturing of Consumerism." *Harvard Business Review* 59 (November/December): 130–39.

Bloom, Paul N., and Ruth Bilk Smith, eds. 1986. *The Future of Consumerism*. Lexington, Mass.: Lexington Books.

Bollier, David. 1989. *Citizen Action and Other Big Ideas: A History of Ralph Nader and the Modern Consumer Movement*. Washington, D.C.: Center for the Study of Responsive Law.

Brand, Karl-Werner. 1990. "Cyclical Aspects of New Social Movements: Waves of Cultural Criticism and Mobilization Cycles of New Middle-Class Radicalism." In *Challenging the Political Order: New Social and Political Movements in Western Democracies*, ed. Russell J. Dalton and Manfred Kuechler, pp. 23–42. New York: Oxford University Press.

Broadbent, Jeffrey. 1998. *Environmental Politics in Japan: Networks of Power and Protest*. Cambridge: Cambridge University Press.

Brobeck, Stephen. 1991. "Economic Deregulation and the Least Affluent: Consumer Protection Strategies." *Journal of Social Issues* 47, no. 1: 169–91.

Brobeck, Stephen. 1997. "State and Local Consumer Organizations." In *Encyclopedia of the Consumer Movement*, ed. Stephen Brobeck, pp. 527–38. Santa Barbara, Calif.: ABC-Clio.

Bronfenbrenner, Martin, and Yasukichi Yasuba. 1987. "Economic Welfare." In *The Political Economy of Japan*. Vol. 1, *The Domestic Transformation*, ed. Kozo Yamamura and Yasuba Yasukichi, pp. 93–136. Stanford, Calif.: Stanford University Press.

Brown, Colin. 1996. "Defining Consumerism." *Consumer Policy Review* 6, no. 2: 77–78.

———. 1997. "Greater Democracy, Better Decisions." *Consumer Policy Review* 7, no. 5: 170–73.

———. 1998. "Consumer Activism in Europe." *Consumer Policy Review* 8, no. 6: 209–12.

Burt, Dan M. 1982. *Abuse of Trust: A Report on Ralph Nader's Network*. Chicago: Regnery Gateway.

Button, Kenneth, and Dennis Swann, eds. 1989. *The Age of Regulatory Reform*. Oxford: Clarendon Press.

Calder, Kent E. 1988. *Crisis and Compensation: Public Policy and Political Stability in Japan, 1949–1986*. Princeton, N.J.: Princeton University Press.

Cammack, Paul. 1992. "The New Institutionalism: Predatory Rule, Institutional Persistence, and Macro-Social Change." *Economy and Society* 21, no. 4: 397–429.

Campbell, John C. 1984. "Policy Conflict and Its Resolution Within the Governmental System." In *Conflict in Japan*, ed. Ellis S. Krauss, Thomas P. Rohlen, and Patricia G. Steinhoff, pp. 294–334. Honolulu: University of Hawai'i Press.

———. 1989. "Bureaucratic Primacy: Japanese Policy Communities in an American Perspective." *Governance* 2 (January): 5–22.

———. 1992. *How Policies Change: The Japanese Government and the Aging Society*. Princeton, N.J.: Princeton University Press.

———. 1996. "Media and Policy Change in Japan." In *Media and Politics in Japan*, ed. Susan J. Pharr and Ellis S. Krauss, pp. 187–212. Honolulu: University of Hawai'i Press.

———. 2000. "Changing Meanings of Frail Old People and the Japanese Welfare State." In *Caring for the Elderly in Japan and the U.S.: Practices and Policies*, ed. Susan Orpett Long, pp. 84–99. London: Routledge.

Caves, Richard, and Masu Uekusa. 1975. "Industrial Organizations." In *Asia's New Giant*, ed. Hugh Patrick and Henry Rosovsky, pp. 459–523. Washington, D.C.: Brookings Institution Press.

Chihō shōhisha gyōsei suishin iinkai. 1990. *Chihō shōhisha gyōsei no aratana tenkai* (New developments in local consumer administration). Tōkyō: Daiipposhi shuppan.

Cobb, Roger W., and Charles D. Elder. 1972. *Participation in American Politics: The Dynamics of Agenda-Building*. Baltimore: Johns Hopkins University Press.

Cohen, David, and Karen Martin. 1985. "Western Ideology, Japanese Product Safety Regulation and International Trade." *University of British Columbia Law Review* 19, no. 2: 315–74.

Cohen, Jean L. 1985. "Strategy or Identity: New Theoretical Paradigms and Contemporary Social Movements." *Social Research* 52, no. 4: 663–716.

Cowhey, Peter F., and Mathew D. McCubbins. 1995. *Structure and Policy in Japan and the United States: The Political Economy of Institutions and Decisions*. Cambridge: Cambridge University Press.

Crenson, Matthew A. 1971. *The Unpolitics of Air Pollution: A Study of Non-Decision Making in the Cities*. Baltimore: Johns Hopkins University Press.

Cullum, Philip. 1997. "A Right to Be Heard?" *Consumer Policy Review* 7, no. 5: 174–79.

Curtis, Gerald L. 1988. *The Japanese Way of Politics*. New York: Columbia University Press.

———. 1999. *The Logic of Japanese Politics: Leaders, Institutions, and the Limits of Change*. New York: Columbia University Press.

Dalton, Russell J., and Manfred Kuechler, eds. 1990. *Challenging the Political Order: New Social and Political Movements in Western Democracies.* New York: Oxford University Press.

Davies, James C. 1969. "The J-Curve of Rising and Declining Satisfactions As a Cause of Some Great Revolutions and a Contained Rebellion." In *Violence in America: Historical and Comparative Perspectives*, ed. Hugh Davis Graham and Ted Robert Gurr, pp. 690–730. Washington, D.C.: U.S. Government Printing Office.

Davis, Joseph W. S., ed. 1996. *Dispute Resolution in Japan.* The Hague: Kluwer Law International.

Derthick, Martha, and Paul J. Quirk. 1985. *The Politics of Deregulation.* Washington, D.C.: Brookings Institution Press.

DeVos, George, ed. 1984. *Institutions for Change in Japanese Society.* Berkeley, Calif.: Institute of East Asian Studies, University of California.

Domon Takeshi. 1989. "Jidai no piero: Nihon no shōhisha dantai" (The era's clowns: Japanese consumer organizations). *Chūō kōron*, November, pp. 218–25.

Donahue, Kathleen. 1999. "From Cooperative Commonwealth to Cooperative Democracy: The American Cooperative Ideal, 1880–1941." In *Consumers Against Capitalism? Consumer Cooperation in Europe, North America, and Japan, 1840–1990*, ed. Ellen Furlough and Carl Strikwerda, pp. 115–34. Lanham, Md.: Rowman & Littlefield.

Douglas, Mary, and Aaron Wildavsky. 1982. *Risk and Culture: An Essay on the Selection of Technical and Environmental Dangers.* Berkeley and Los Angeles: University of California Press.

Dower, John W. 1999. *Embracing Defeat: Japan in the Wake of World War II.* New York: Norton.

Downs, Anthony. 1972. "Up and Down with Ecology: The Issue Attention Cycle." *The Public Interest* 28 (Summer): 38–50.

Duerst-Lahti, Georgia. 1989. "The Government's Role in Building the Women's Movement." *Political Science Quarterly* 104 (Summer): 249–68.

Dunlavy, Colleen. 1993. *Political Structure and Industrial Change: Early Railroads in the United States and Prussia.* Princeton, N.J.: Princeton University Press.

Eckstein, Barbara. 1990. "Rethinking Social Movement Theory." *Socialist Review* 20, no. 1: 35–65.

Edelman, Murray. 1964. *The Symbolic Uses of Politics.* Champaign-Urbana: University of Illinois Press.

Edelman, Peter B. 1988. "Japanese Product Standards As Non-Tariff Trade Barriers: When Regulatory Policy Becomes a Trade Issue." *Stanford Journal of International Law* 24, no. 2: 389–446.

Evans, Phil. 1996. "The End of Resale Price Maintenance?" *Consumer Policy Review* 6, no. 6: 205–9.

Eyestone, Robert. 1978. *From Social Issues to Public Policy.* New York: Wiley.

Feldman, Eric A. 2000. *The Ritual of Rights in Japan: Law, Society, and Health Policy.* Cambridge: Cambridge University Press.

Fields, George. 1989. *Gucci on the Ginza.* Tōkyō: Kodansha International.

Finch, James E. 1985. "A History of the Consumer Movement in the United States: Its Literature and Legislation." *Journal of Consumer Studies and Home Economics,* no. 9: 23–33.

Fise, Mary Ellen R. 1997. "Consumer Product Safety Commission." In *Encyclopedia of the Consumer Movement,* ed. Stephen Brobeck, pp. 164–67. Santa Barbara, Calif.: ABC-Clio.

Fleming, Michael, and Kenneth Button. 1989. "Regulatory Reform in the U.K." In *The Age of Regulatory Reform,* ed. Kenneth Button and Dennis Swann, pp. 79–103. Oxford: Clarendon Press.

Flynn, Norman. 1989. "The 'New Right' and Social Policy." *Policy and Politics* 17, no. 2: 97–109.

Forbes, J. D. 1985. "Organizational and Political Dimensions of Consumer Pressure Groups." *Journal of Consumer Policy* 8, no. 1: 105–31.

———. 1987. *The Consumer Interest: Dimensions and Policy Implications.* London: Croom Helm.

Freeman, Jo. 1979. "Resource Mobilization and Strategy: A Model for Analyzing Social Movement Organization Actions." In *The Dynamics of Social Movements,* ed. Mayer N. Zald and John D. McCarthy, pp. 167–90. Cambridge, Mass.: Winthrop Publishers.

Freeman, Laurie Anne. 2000. *Closing the Shop: Information Cartels and Japan's Mass Media.* Princeton, N.J.: Princeton University Press.

Friedman, Monroe. 1991. "Research on Consumer Protection Issues: The Perspective of the 'Human Sciences'." *Journal of Social Issues* 47, no. 1: 1–19.

———. 1999. *Consumer Boycotts: Effecting Change Through the Marketplace and the Media.* New York: Routledge.

Furlough, Ellen, and Carl Strikwerda, eds. 1999. *Consumers Against Capitalism? Consumer Cooperation in Europe, North America, and Japan, 1840–1990.* Lanham, Md.: Rowman & Littlefield.

Gamson, William A., and David S. Meyer. 1996. "Framing Political Opportunity." In *Comparative Perspectives on Social Movements: Political Opportunities, Mobilizing Structures, and Cultural Framings,* ed. Doug McAdam, John D. McCarthy, and Mayer N. Zald, pp. 275–90. Cambridge: Cambridge University Press.

Garon, Sheldon. 1997. *Molding Japanese Minds: The State in Everyday Life.* Princeton, N.J.: Princeton University Press.

———. 2000. "Luxury Is the Enemy: Mobilizing Savings and Popularizing Thrift in Wartime." *Journal of Japanese Studies* 26, no. 1: 41–78.

Gelb, Joyce, and Margarita Estevez-Abe. 1998. "Political Women in Japan: A Case Study of the Seikatsusha Network Movement." *Social Science Japan Journal* 1, no. 2: 263–79.

Gerston, Larry, Cynthia Fraleigh, and Robert Schwab. 1988. *The Deregulated Society*. Pacific Grove, Calif.: Brooks-Cole.

Gregg, Barbara B. 1997. "State and Local Consumer Affairs Offices." In *Encyclopedia of the Consumer Movement*, ed. Stephen Brobeck, pp. 527–31. Santa Barbara, Calif.: ABC-Clio.

Groth, David Earl. 1996. "Media and Political Protest: The Bullet Train Movements." In *Media and Politics in Japan*, ed. Susan J. Pharr and Ellis S. Krauss, pp. 213–41. Honolulu: University of Hawai'i Press.

Grubel, Ruth. 1999. "The Consumer Coop in Japan: Building Democratic Alternatives to State-Led Capitalism." In *Consumers Against Capitalism? Consumer Cooperation in Europe, North America, and Japan, 1840–1990*, ed. Ellen Furlough and Carl Strikwerda, pp. 303–30. Lanham, Md.: Rowman & Littlefield.

Gusfield, Joseph. R. 1981. "Social Movements and Social Change: Perspectives of Linearity and Fluidity." In *Research in Social Movements, Conflict, and Change*. Vol. 4., ed. Louis Kriesberg, pp. 317–39. Greenwich, Conn.: JAI Press.

Haley, John O. 1978. "The Myth of the Reluctant Litigant." *Journal of Japanese Studies* 4 (Summer): 359–90.

———. 1987. "Government by Negotiation: A Reappraisal of Bureaucratic Power in Japan." *Journal of Japanese Studies* 13 (Summer): 343–57.

———. 1991a. *Authority Without Power: Law and the Japanese Paradox*. New York: Oxford University Press.

———. 1991b. "Japanese Antitrust Enforcement: Implications for United States Trade." *North Kentucky Law Review* 339. Reprinted in Kenneth L. Port, ed., *Law and the Legal Process in Japan*, pp. 409–17. Durham, N.C.: Carolina Academic Press, 1996.

Hall, Peter A. 1986. *Governing the Economy: The Politics of State Intervention in Britain and France*. New York: Oxford University Press.

———. 1989. *The Political Power of Keynesian Ideas*. Princeton, N.J.: Princeton University Press.

———. 1993. "Policy Paradigms, Social Learning, and the State." *Comparative Politics* 25, no. 3: 275–96.

Hall, Peter A., and Rosemary C. R. Taylor. 1996. "Political Science and the Three New Institutionalisms." *Political Studies* 44, no. 5: 936–57.

Hamada, Koichi. 1996. "Consumers, the Legal System and the Product Liability Reform: A Comparative Perspective Between Japan and the United States." Paper presented to the Micro-Economic Reform and Deregulation in Japan conference, Columbia University, New York, March 22–23.

Hamada, Koichi, Hideto Ishida, and Masahiro Murakami. 1986. "The Evolution and Economic Consequences of Product Liability Rules in Japan." In *Law and Trade Issues of the Japanese Economy: American and Japanese Perspectives*, ed.

Gary R. Saxonhouse and Kozo Yamamura, pp. 83–106. Seattle: University of Washington Press.

Hambleton, Robin. 1988. "Consumerism, Decentralization and Local Democracy." *Public Administration* 66 (Summer): 125–47.

Hara Sanae. 1992. *Kekkan shōhin to kigyō sekinin* (Defective products and the responsibilities of business). Tōkyō: Iwanami shoten.

Haruhi Yutaka. 1976. *Shōhisha wa jakusha* (Consumers are the weak). Tōkyō: Daigaku kyōikusha.

Hattam, Victoria C. 1993. *Labor Visions and State Power: The Origins of Business Unionism in the United States.* Princeton, N.J.: Princeton University Press.

Hayao, Kenji. 1993. *The Japanese Prime Minister and Public Policy.* Pittsburgh: University of Pittsburgh Press.

Herrmann, Robert O. 1974. "The Consumer Movement in Historical Perspective." In *Consumerism: Search for the Consumer Interest.* 2d ed., ed. David A. Aaker and George S. Day, pp. 10–18. New York: Free Press.

———. 1980. "Consumer Protection: Yesterday, Today, and Tomorrow." *Current History* 78, no. 457: 193–96, 226–27.

Herrmann, Robert O., and Robert N. Mayer. 1997. "The U.S. Consumer Movement: History and Dynamics." In *Encyclopedia of the Consumer Movement*, ed. Stephen Brobeck, pp. 584–601. Santa Barbara, Calif.: ABC-Clio.

Hiwasa Nobuko. 1999. "Shōhisha no jiko sekinin to shōhisha dantai no yakuwari" (The self-responsibility of consumers and the role of consumer organizations). *Kokumin seikatsu* 29, no. 5: 34–37.

Hokkaidō shimbunsha seikatsubu. 1991. *Shōhin no anzen wa mamorareteiruka: Seizōbutsusekinin to shōhisha hogo* (Is product safety being guaranteed? Product liability and consumer protection). Sapporo: Hokkaidō shimbunsha.

Holsworth, Robert D. 1980. *Public Interest Liberalism and the Crisis of Affluence: Reflections on Nader, Environmentalism, and the Politics of a Sustainable Society.* Boston: Hall.

Hornsby-Smith, Michael P. 1986. "The Structural Weaknesses of the Consumer Movement." *Journal of Consumer Studies and Home Economics*, no. 9: 291–306.

Hosokawa Kōichi. 1996. "Dokkinhō ni miru 'shōhisha no rieki' gainen ni tsuite" (The concept of consumer interests from the perspective of the antimonopoly law). *Kokumin seikatsu kenkyū* 36, no. 1: 1–21, and 36, no. 2: 29–46.

Howells, Geraint. 1993. *Comparative Product Liability.* Aldershot: Dartmouth Publishing.

Huddle, Norie, and Michael Reich. 1987. *Island of Dreams.* Rev. ed. Cambridge, Mass.: Schenkman.

Ikemoto Seiji. 1999. "Shōhisha higai to shōhi seikatsu sentaa no yakuwari" (Consumer damages and the functions of consumer lifestyle centers). *Kokumin seikatsu* 29, no. 5: 28–33.

Imamura Shigekazu. 1993. *Dokusenkinshihō nyūmon* (An introduction to the antimonopoly law). Tōkyō: Yūhikakusha.

Imamura Shigekazu, Kanazawa Yoshio, Shōda Akira, and Yoshinaga Eisuke, eds. 1982. *Dokusenkinshihō kōza 4* (Lectures on the antimonopoly law 4). Tōkyō: Shōji hōmu kenkyūkai.

Immergut, Ellen. 1992a. *Health Politics: Interests and Institutions in Western Europe.* Cambridge: Cambridge University Press.

———. 1992b. "The Rules of the Game: The Logic of Health Policy-Making in France, Switzerland, and Sweden." In *Structuring Politics: Historical Institutionalism in Comparative Analysis,* ed. Sven Steinmo, Kathleen Thelen, and Frank Longstreth, pp. 57–89. Cambridge: Cambridge University Press.

Inaba Michio, Ono Shōji, Shōda Akira, Nakamura Kii, and Hanahara Jirō. 1979. "Shōhisha mondai no arikata" (The nature of consumer issues). *Jurisuto zōkan sōgō tokushū* 13 (January): 6–25.

Inamura, Anne E. 1987. *Urban Housewives: At Home and in the Community.* Honolulu: University of Hawai'i Press.

Inamura, Anne E., ed. 1996. *Re-Imaging Japanese Women.* Berkeley and Los Angeles: University of California Press.

Inoguchi Takashi. 1982. *Gendai nihon no seiji keizai* (The political economy of contemporary Japan). Tōkyō: Tōyō keizai shimpōsha.

Ishida Akira, Kaneko Akira, Shiotani Takahide, Morishima Akio, and Yoshioka Hatsuko. 1993. "Shōhisha hogo no genjō to shōhisha no kenri" (The state of consumer protection and consumer rights). *Jurisuto* 1034 (November 15): 8–23.

Ishida Hidetō. 1994. *Dokusen seisaku kyōka no nami wo norikiru* (Riding the wave of stronger antitrust policy). Tōkyō: Chūō keizaisha.

Ishida, Takeshi. 1993. *Japanese Political Culture: Change and Continuity.* New Brunswick, N.J.: Transaction Books.

Isozaki Shiro, Nozawa Seiichi, Nakai Jirō, and Watanabe Zenjiro. 1976. *Shōhisha undō shiryō* (Documents on the consumer movement). Tōkyō: Daiyamondosha.

Itō Takatoshi. 1992. *Shōhisha jūshi no keizaigaku: Kiseikanwa wa naze hitsuyōka* (The economics of emphasizing consumers: Why is deregulation necessary?). Tōkyō: Nihon keizai shimbunsha.

Iwadare, Hiroshi. 1991. "Consumer Cooperatives in the Spotlight." *Japan Quarterly,* October-December, pp. 429–35.

Iyori, Hiroshi. 1986. "Antitrust and Industrial Policy in Japan: Competition and Cooperation." In *Law and Trade Issues of the Japanese Economy: American and Japanese Perspectives,* ed. Gary R. Saxonhouse and Kozo Yamamura, pp. 56–82. Seattle: University of Washington Press.

Japan Consumer Information Center. 1989. *Consumer Policy in Japan.* Tōkyō: Japan Consumer Information Center.

Jenkins, Joseph Craig, and Charles Perrow. 1977. "Insurgency of the Powerless: Farm Worker Movements (1946–1972)." *American Sociological Review* 42, no. 2: 249–68.

Jiyūminshutō. 1991. *Wagatō no honnen no hōshin* (Our party's policies for the current year). Tōkyō: Jiyūminshutō.

———. 1992a. *Wagatō no honnen no hōshin* (Our party's policies for the current year). Tōkyō: Jiyūminshutō.

———. 1992b. *Keizai bukka mondai chōsakai: Seizōbutsusekinin seido ni kansuru koiinkai kaigiroku* (Investigative council on economics and prices: Minutes of the subcommittee on product liability systems). Tōkyō: Jiyūminshutō.

Johnson, Chalmers. 1982. *MITI and the Japanese Miracle*. Stanford, Calif.: Stanford University Press.

Jordan, Grant. 1993. "The New Right and Public Policy: A Preliminary Overview." In *Public Policy and the Impact of the New Right*, ed. Nigel Ashford and Grant Jordan, pp. 1–18. London: Printer Publishers.

Jordan, Grant, and Jeremy Richardson. 1982. "The British Policy Style or the Logic of Negotiation?" In *Policy Styles in Western Europe*, ed. Jeremy Richardson, pp. 80–110. London: Allen & Unwin.

Jussaume, Raymond A., and D. H. Judson. 1992. "Public Perceptions About Food Safety in the United States and Japan." *Rural Sociology* 57, no. 2: 235–49.

Kabashima, Ikuo, and Jeffrey Broadbent. 1986. "Referent Pluralism: Mass Media and Politics in Japan." *Journal of Japanese Studies* 12 (Summer): 329–61.

Kaigai shimin katsudō jōhō sentaa. 1989. *Rarufu Needa wa ima* (Ralph Nader is now). Tōkyō: Kaigai shimin katsudō jōhō sentaa.

———. 1992. *Jōhōkōkaihō—Seizōbutsusekininhō wo motomeru* (Demanding information disclosure and product liability laws). Tōkyō: Kaigai shimin katsudō jōhō sentaa.

Kallet, Arthur, and F. J. Schlink. 1933. *100,000,000 Guinea Pigs: Dangers in Everyday Foods, Drugs, and Cosmetics*. New York: Vanguard Press.

Kamiyama Michiko. 1992. *Shokuhin tenkabutsu no anzen kijun ga yureteru* (Safety standards for food additives are being shaken). Tōkyō: Nihon seikatsu kyōdō kumiai rengōkai.

———. 1993. *Shokuhin anzen e no puropōzu* (A proposal for food safety). Tōkyō: Nihon hyōronsha.

Kaneko Akira. 1974. "Shōhisha higai to fuman moshitate" (Consumer damages and statements of dissatisfaction). *Hōritsu no hiroba* 27, no. 12.

———. 1996. "Shōhisha no ishiki to jōhō katsudō" (Consumer consciousness and information activities). *Kokumin seikatsu*, May, pp. 16–22.

Karpatkin, Rhoda H. 1997a. "Consumers Union." In *Encyclopedia of the Consumer Movement*, ed. Stephen Brobeck, pp. 182–87. Santa Barbara, Calif.: ABC-Clio.

———. 1997b. "State and Local Consumer Organizations." In *Encyclopedia of the Consumer Movement*, ed. Stephen Brobeck, pp. 183–84. Santa Barbara, Calif.: ABC-Clio.

Kataoka Hiromitsu. 1992. *Kokumin to gyōsei* (The people and the bureaucracy). Tōkyō: Waseda daigaku shuppanbu.

Katō Ichirō. 1991. *Seizōbutsusekinin to watashitachi* (Product liability and us). Tōkyō: Kokumin seikatsu sentaa.

Katō Ichiro and Takeuchi Akio. 1984. *Shōhishahō kōza: Sōron* (Lectures on consumer law: General arguments). Tōkyō: Nihon hyōronsha.

Katsube Kinichi. 1979. "Seikyō undō no rekishiteki kōsatsu to kadai" (The historical study and topics of the consumer cooperative movement). *Jurisuto zōkan sōgō tokushū* 13 (January): 54–59.

Katz, Richard. 1998. *Japan, the System That Soured: The Rise and Fall of the Japanese Economic Miracle.* New York: Sharpe.

Katz, Robert M., ed. 1976. *Protecting the Consumer: Private Initiative and Public Response.* Cambridge, Mass.: Ballinger.

Katzenstein, Mary Fainsod, and Carol McClurg Mueller, eds. 1987. *The Women's Movement of the United States and Europe: Consciousness, Political Opportunity, and Public Policy.* Philadelphia: Temple University Press.

Katzmann, Robert A. 1980. "The Federal Trade Commission." In *The Politics of Regulation,* ed. James Q. Wilson, pp. 152–87. New York: Basic Books.

Kawaguchi Yasuhiro. 1994. "Seizōbutsusekininhō no seiritsu ni tsuite" (On the establishment of a product liability law). *Jurisuto* 1051 (September): 45–52.

Keiser, K. Robert. 1980. "The New Regulation of Health and Safety." *Political Science Quarterly* 95, no. 3: 479–91.

Keizaikikakuchō. 1991a. *Kokumin seikatsu shingikai shōhisha seisaku bukai chūkan hōkoku: Sōgōteki na shōhisha higai bōshi, kyūsai no arikata ni tsuite* (Interim report of the Social Policy Council's Consumer Policy Division: Comprehensive consumer protection and relief). Tōkyō: Keizaikikakuchō.

———. 1991b. *Seizōbutsusekininhō no ronten* (The debate over a product liability law). Tōkyō: Keizaikikakuchō.

———. 1991c. *Shōhisa dantai no kōyō: Heisei 3 nendo* (A handbook of consumer organizations: 1991). Tōkyō: Keizaikikakuchō.

———. 1993a. *Handobukku shōhisha '93* (The consumer handbook, 1993). Tōkyō: Keizaikikakuchō.

———. 1993b. *Seizōbutsusekinin seido dōnyū no eikyō* (The effects of introducing a product liability system). Tōkyō: Keizaikikakuchō.

———. 1995. *Seizōbutsusekininhō ni kakaru kanren shisaku ni tsuite* (Policies relating to a product liability law). Tōkyō: Keizaikikakuchō.

———. 1997. *Heisei 8 nendo: Shōhisha dantai kihon chōsa kekka* (1996: Results of the basic survey of consumer organizations). Tōkyō: Keizaikikakuchō.

———. 1999. *Handobukku shōhisha '99* (The consumer handbook, 1999). Tōkyō: Keizaikikakuchō.

Kensetsushō. 1993. *Seizōbutsusekininseido ni kansuru kensetsushō no kangaekata: Heisei 5 nen 11 gatsu 17 nichi kokumin seikatsu shingikai shōhisha seisaku bukai hiaringu no naiyō* (The Construction Ministry's position on product liability systems: Contents of the November 17, 1993, hearings of the Social Policy Council's Consumer Policy Committee). Tōkyō: Kensetsushō.

Kielbowicz, Richard B., and Clifford Scherer. 1986. "The Role of the Press in the Dynamics of Social Movements." In *Research in Social Movements, Conflict and Change*. Vol. 9, ed. Kurt Lang, Gladys Engel Lang, and Louis Kriesberg, pp. 72–89. Greenwich, Conn.: JAI Press.

Kikuchi Motoichi. "Saihanbai kakaku iji to shōhisha no songai baishō seikyūken" (Retail price maintenance and the right of consumers to demand damages). *Jurisuto* 653 (December 15): 94–100.

Kilburn, David, and Naoko Nomura. 1986. "Japan's Consumer Voices Are Increasingly Important." *Journal of the American Chamber of Commerce in Japan*, December, pp. 52–66.

Kimoto Kinya. 1981. *Dokusenkinshihō* (The antimonopoly law). Tōkyō: Shin Nihon shuppansha.

———. 1986. *Gendai shōhishahō no kōzō* (The structure of contemporary consumer law). Tōkyō: Shinhyōron.

———. 1993. "Shōhisha gyōsei no gendaiteki igi to yakuwari" (The contemporary meaning and functions of consumer administration). *Kokumin seikatsu* 23: 8–15.

Kimoto Kinya, Takase Masao, Shōda Akira, and Takahashi Iwakazu. 1993. *Gendai keizaihō no kōza, 8: Kyōdō kumiai to hō* (Lectures on contemporary economic law, vol. 8: Cooperatives and the law). Tōkyō: Sanseidō.

Kingdon, John W. 1984. *Agendas, Alternatives, and Public Policies*. Boston: Little, Brown.

Kirkpatrick, Maurine A. 1975. "Consumerism and Japan's New Citizen Politics." *Asian Survey* 15: 234–47.

Kitagawa Yoshihiro and Kitagawa Zentaro. 1993. "Shōhisha to kigyō no 'atarashii jidai' ni mukete" (Facing a "new age" for consumers and business). *ESP* 10, no. 258: 6–19.

Kitamura Haruo. 1992. PLhō kō kangaeyō: Seizōbutsusekinin wa sekai no jōshiki (Let's think about the PL law this way: Product liability makes good international sense). Tōkyō: Daiyamondosha.

Kitazawa Zentarō. 1979. "Shōhisha hogo no hōritsu" (Consumer protection law). *Jurisuto zōkan sōgō tokushū* 13 (January): 38–43.

Kitschelt, Herbert. 1986. "Political Opportunity Structures and Political Protest: Anti-Nuclear Movements in Four Democracies." *British Journal of Political Science* 16, no. 1: 57–85.

Knoke, David, ed. 1990. *Political Networks: The Structural Perspective*. Cambridge: Cambridge University Press.

Kobayashi Hideyuki. 1993. *Seizōbutsusekininhō: Rippōka to taisaku* (The product liability law: Enactment and countermeasures). Tōkyō: Chūō keizaisha.

Kobayashi Hideyuki, ed. 1994. *Seizōbutsusekininhō taikei* (A history of the product liability law). Tōkyō: Kobundō.

Kobayashi Jutoku. 1992. PL–seizōbutsusekinin–nyūmon: Nihon kigyō no aratana kadai (An introduction to PL-product liability: A new topic for Japanese business). Tōkyō: Jitsugyō no nihonsha.

Kobayashi Kyōichi. 1994–96. "Nihon no shōhisha undōshi" (The history of the Japanese consumer movement). *Gekkan shōhisha* (parts 13 through 28: April 1994–December 1996).

Koelble, Thomas A. 1995. "The New Institutionalism in Political Science and Sociology." *Comparative Politics*, January, pp. 231–43.

Kokumin keizai kenkyūkyōkai. 1991. *Amerika kigyō no* PL *yobō taisaku jittai chōsa hōkoku* (Report on a survey of the state of product liability prevention policies of American companies). Tōkyō: Kokumin keizai kenkyūkyōkai.

Kokumin seikatsu sentaa (KSS). 1983. *Shōhisha no kenri: Daisankai shōhisha mondai zenkoku shimpojiumu no kiroku* (Consumer rights: Minutes of the Third All-Japan Symposium on Consumer Issues). Tōkyō: Kokumin seikatsu sentaa.

——. 1990. *Kokumin seikatsu sentaa nijū nenshi* (A twenty-year history of the Japan Consumer Information Center). Tōkyō: Kokumin seikatsu sentaa.

——. 1993. *Shokuseikatsu no shōhisha mondai* (Consumer issues relating to food lifestyles). Tōkyō: Kokumin seikatsu sentaa.

——. 1994. *Kurashi no henkaku wo mezashite* (Toward changing livelihoods). Tōkyō: Tōkyōto shōhisha sentaa.

Kokumin seikatsu sentaa (KSS), ed. 1996. *Shōhisha undō 50 nen: 20 nin ga kataru sengo no ayumi* (Fifty years of the consumer movement: Postwar history as recounted by twenty individuals). Tōkyō: Domesu shuppansha.

——. 1997. *Sengo shōhisha undōshi* (The history of the postwar consumer movement). Tōkyō: Kokumin seikatsu sentaa.

Kōmura Masahiko. 1995. "Seizōbutsusekininhō no shikō wo mukaete" (Facing the implementation of the product liability law). ESP, July: 2–3.

Kornhauser, William. 1959. *The Politics of Mass Society*. Glencoe, Ill.: Free Press.

Kōseishō. 1993. *Seizōbutsusekininseido nado tokubetsu bukai hōkokusho* (Report of the special committee on product liability systems and related topics). Tōkyō: Koseishō.

Kotani Masamori and Yasuda Yoshiaki, eds. 1980. *Gendai nihon no shōhisha mondai* (Consumer issues of contemporary Japan). Tōkyō: Mineruba shōbo.

Krasner, Stephen D. 1984. "Approaches to the State: Alternative Conceptions and Historical Dynamics." *Comparative Politics* 16 (January): 223–46.

Krauss, Ellis S. 1984. "Conflict in the Diet: Toward Conflict Management in Parliamentary Politics." In *Conflict in Japan*, ed. Ellis S. Krauss, Thomas P. Rohlen, and Patricia G. Steinhoff, pp. 243–93. Honolulu: University of Hawai'i Press.

Krauss, Ellis S., Thomas P. Rohlen, and Patricia G. Steinhoff, eds. 1984. *Conflict in Japan*. Honolulu: University of Hawai'i Press.

Krauss, Ellis S., and Bradford L. Simcock. 1980. "Citizen Movements: The Growth and Impact of Environmental Protest in Japan." In *Political Opposition and Local Politics in Japan*, ed. Kurt Steiner, Ellis S. Krauss, and Scott C. Flanagan, pp. 187–227. Princeton, N.J.: Princeton University Press.

Kroll, Robert J., and Ronald W. Stampfl. 1981. "The New Consumerism." In *The Consumer Movement As Related to Other Social Movements*, ed. Carol B. Meeks, pp. 97–100. Columbia, Mo: American Council on Consumer Interests.

Kurimoto, Akira. 1992. "Japan's Consumer Cooperative Movement: A Comparative Review." In *Robert Owen and the World of Cooperation*, ed. Tsuzuki Chushichi, pp. 223–37. Tōkyō: Robert Owen Association of Japan.

LeBlanc, Robin M. 1999. *Bicycle Citizens: The Political World of the Japanese Housewife*. Berkeley and Los Angeles: University of California Press.

Lee, Stuart M. 1981. "Consumer Issues in the '80s." In *The Consumer Movement As Related to Other Social Movements*, ed. Carol B. Meeks, pp. 112–16. Columbia, Mo: American Council on Consumer Interests.

Lewis, Michael. 1990. *Rioters and Citizens: Mass Protest in Imperial Japan*. Berkeley and Los Angeles: University of California Press.

Lipset, Seymour Martin, and William Schneider. 1979. "The Public View of Regulation." *Public Opinion* 2, no. 1: 6–13.

Lipsky, Michael. 1968. "Protest As a Political Resource." *American Political Science Review* 62, no. 4: 1144–58.

Lowi, Theodore. 1964. "American Business, Public Policy, Case Studies, and Political Theory." *World Politics* 16 (July): 677–715.

———. 1968. "The Public Philosophy: Interest Group Liberalism." In *Issues of American Public Policy*, ed. John H. Bunzel, pp. 19–47. Englewood-Cliffs, N.J.: Prentice-Hall.

Lucco, Joan. 1992. "Representing the Consumer Interest: Consumer Groups and the Presidency." In *The Politics of Interest: Interest Groups Transformed*, ed. Mark Petracca, pp. 242–62. Boulder, Colo.: Westview Press.

Maclachlan, Patricia L. 1995. "Consumer Groups and Regulatory Reform in the United States, Britain, and Japan." Paper presented to the annual meeting of the American Political Science Association, Chicago.

———. 1999. "Protecting Producers from Consumer Protection: The Politics of Products Liability Reform in Japan." *Social Science Japan Journal* 2, no. 2: 249–66.

———. 2000. "Information Disclosure and the Center-Local Relationship in Japan." In *Local Voices, National Issues: The Impact of Local Initiative in Japanese Policy-Making*, ed. Sheila A. Smith, pp. 9–30. Ann Arbor: Center for Japanese Studies, University of Michigan.

Madden, Thomas Leo. 1996. "An Explanation of Japan's Product Liability Law." *Pacific Rim Law and Policy Journal* 5, no. 2: 299–329.

Madge, Leila. 1999. "Japan's Emerging Civic Culture: A Product Liability Law Study Group." *JPRI Working Paper no. 54* (February).

Maier, Charles S. 1987. *Changing Boundaries of the Political: Essays on the Evolving Balance Between the State and Society, Public and Private in Europe*. Cambridge: Cambridge University Press.

Maki, Shōhei. 1976. "The Postwar Consumer Movement." *Japan Quarterly* 23, no. 2: 135–39.

———. 1979. "Shōhisha undō no ayumi to genjō" (The history and current conditions of the consumer movement). *Jurisuto zōkan sōgō tokushū* 13 (January): 44–48.

Maney, Ardith, and Loree Bykerk. 1994. *Consumer Politics: Protecting Public Interests on Capital Hill*. Westport, Conn.: Greenwood Press.

March, James G., and Johan P. Olsen. 1984. "The New Institutionalism: Organizational Factors in Political Life." *American Political Science Review* 78, no. 3: 734–49.

———. 1989. *Rediscovering Institutions: The Organizational Basis of Politics*. New York: Free Press.

Marcuse, Andrew. 1996. "Why Japan's New Products Liability Law Isn't." *Pacific Rim Law and Policy Journal* 5, no. 2: 365–98.

Masui Katsuyoshi. 1992. PLhō no susume (Recommendations for a product liability law). Tōkyō: Yōyōsha.

Matsubara, Haruō. 1977. "The Local Government and Citizens' Movements." *Local Government Review* 5: 52–69.

Matsushita, Mitsuō. 1978. "The Anti-Monopoly Law of Japan." *Law in Japan* 11: 57–75.

———. 1990. *Introduction to Japanese Antimonopoly Law*. Tōkyō: Yūhikaku.

———. 1993. *International Trade and Competition Law in Japan*. Oxford: Oxford University Press.

Mayer, Robert N. 1988. "Consumer Safety and the Issue Emergence Process." In *The Frontier of Research in the Consumer Interest*, ed. E. Scott Maynes and the ACCI Research Committee, pp. 82–96. Columbia, Mo.: ACCI.

———. 1989. *The Consumer Movement: Guardians of the Marketplace*. Boston: Twayne.

———. 1991. "Gone Yesterday, Here Today: Consumer Issues in the Agenda Setting Process." *Journal of Social Issues* 47, no. 1: 135–48.

Mayer, Robert N., and Stephen Brobeck. 1997. "Consumer Interest." In *Encyclopedia of the Consumer Movement*, ed. Stephen Brobeck, pp. 153–55. Santa Barbara, Calif.: ABC-Clio.

Maynes, E. Scott, and the ACCI Research Committee, eds. 1988. *The Frontier of Research in the Consumer Interest*. Columbia, Mo.: ACCI.

McAdam, Doug. 1982. *Political Process and the Development of Black Insurgency, 1930–1970*. Chicago: University of Chicago Press.

———. 1996. "Conceptual Origins, Current Problems, Future Directions." In *Comparative Perspectives on Social Movements: Political Opportunities, Mobilizing Structures, and Cultural Framings*, ed. Doug McAdam, John D. McCarthy, and Mayer N. Zald, pp. 23–40. Cambridge: Cambridge University Press.

McAdam, Doug, John D. McCarthy, and Mayer N. Zald, eds. 1996a. *Comparative*

Perspectives on Social Movements: Political Opportunities, Mobilizing Structures, and Cultural Framings. Cambridge, Mass.: Cambridge University Press.

McAdam, Doug, John D. McCarthy, and Mayer N. Zald. 1996b. Introduction to *Comparative Perspectives on Social Movements: Political Opportunities, Mobilizing Structures, and Cultural Framings,* ed. Doug McAdam, John D. McCarthy, and Mayer N. Zald, pp. 1–20. Cambridge: Cambridge University Press.

McCarthy, John D. 1996. "Constraints and Opportunities in Adopting, Adapting, and Inventing." In *Comparative Perspectives on Social Movements: Political Opportunities, Mobilizing Structures, and Cultural Framings,* ed. Doug McAdam, John D. McCarthy, and Mayer N. Zald, pp. 141–51. Cambridge: Cambridge University Press.

McCarthy, John D., and Mayer N. Zald. 1973. *The Trend of Social Movements in America: Professionalization and Resource Mobilization.* Morristown, N.J.: General Learning Press.

———. 1977. "Resource Mobilization and Social Movements: A Partial Theory." *American Journal of Sociology* 82, no. 6: 1212–41.

McConnell, Grant. 1966. *Private Power and American Democracy.* New York: Vintage Books.

McFarland, Andrew S. 1987. "Interest Groups and Theories of Power in America." *British Journal of Political Science* 17, no. 2: 129–47.

McKean, Margaret A. 1981. *Environmental Protest and Citizen Politics in Japan.* Berkeley and Los Angeles: University of California Press.

———. 1993. "State Strength and the Public Interest." In *Political Dynamics in Contemporary Japan,* ed. Gary D. Allinson and Yasunori Sone, pp. 72–104. Ithaca, N.Y.: Cornell University Press.

Meeks, Carol B., ed. 1981. *The Consumer Movement As Related to Other Social Movements.* Columbia, Mo.: American Council on Consumer Interests.

Middleton, Benet. 1998. "Consumerism: A Pragmatic Ideology." *Consumer Policy Review* 8, no. 6: 213–27.

Mierzwinski, Edmund. 1997. "Public Interest Research Groups." In *Encyclopedia of the Consumer Movement,* ed. Stephen Brobeck, pp. 467–73. Santa Barbara, Calif.: ABC-Clio.

Ministry of Health and Welfare. 1989. *Consumers' Livelihood Cooperative Society Law.* Tōkyō: Japan Consumer Cooperative Union.

Misono Hitoshi. 1987. *Nihon no dokusenkinshiseisaku to sangyō soshiki* (Japanese antitrust policy and industrial structure). Tōkyō: Kawade shōbo shinsha.

Mitchell, Jeremy. 1997. "The United Kingdom's Consumer Movement." In *Encyclopedia of the Consumer Movement,* ed. Stephen Brobeck, pp. 575–81. Santa Barbara, Calif.: ABC-Clio.

Mitchell, Robert Cameron. 1986. "Consumerism and Environmentalism in the 1980s: Competitive or Companionable Social Movements?" In *The Future of Consumerism,* ed. Paul N. Bloom and Ruth Bilk Smith, pp. 23–36. Lexington, Mass.: Lexington Books.

Miyachi, Shoshichi. 1984. "Food Should Not Be Compared with Industrial Products." *Japan Economic Journal*, May 22, pp. 20–21.

Miyagawa Kiyoshi. 1979. *Shimin undō no shiten* (The development of citizen movements). Tōkyō: Hōgaku shōin.

Miyasaka Tominosuke, Tanihara Osami, Uchida Kōsaku, and Suzuki Miyuki, eds. 1990a. *Gendai keizaihō kōza, 5: Shōhiseikatsu to hō* (Lectures on contemporary economic law, vol. 5: Consumer lifestyles and the law). Tōkyō: Sanseidō.

———. 1990b. "Gendai no shōhisha mondai to kenri" (Contemporary consumer issues and rights). In *Gendai keizaihō kōza, 5: Shōhiseikatsu to hō* (Lectures on contemporary economic law, vol. 5: Consumer lifestyles and the law), ed. Miyasaka et al. Tōkyō: Sanseidō.

Mochizuki, Toshiro M. 1999. "Baby Step or Giant Leap?: Parties' Expanded Access to Documentary Evidence Under the New Japanese Code of Civil Procedure." *Harvard International Law Journal* 40 (Winter): 285–312.

Morishima, Akio. 1993a. "The Japan Scene and the Present Product Liability Proposal." *University of Hawai'i Law Review* 15, no. 2: 717–27.

———. 1993b. "Kokuseishin ni okeru seizōbutsusekinin seido no kangaekata" (The Social Policy Council's position on product liability systems). *Kokumin seikatsu* 23, no. 3.

Morishima, Akio, and Malcolm Smith. 1986. "Accident Compensation Schemes in Japan: A Window on the Operation of Law in a Society." *University of British Columbia Law Review* 20, no. 2: 491–533.

Muramatsu, Michio. 1997. *Local Power in the Japanese State*. Berkeley and Los Angeles: University of California Press.

Muramatsu, Michio, and Ellis S. Krauss. 1984. "Bureaucrats and Politicians in Policymaking: The Case of Japan." *American Political Science Review* 78 (March): 126–46.

———. 1987. "The Conservative Policy Line and the Development of Patterned Pluralism." In *The Political Economy of Japan*. Vol. 1, *The Domestic Transformation*, ed. Kozo Yamamura and Yasuba Yasukichi, pp. 516–54. Stanford, Calif.: Stanford University Press.

Muramatsu Michio, Itō Mitsutoshi, and Tsujinaka Yutaka. 1986. *Sengo nihon no atsuryoku dantai* (Postwar Japanese pressure groups). Tōkyō: Toyo keizai shimbunsha.

Nadel, Mark V. 1971. *The Politics of Consumer Protection*. Indianapolis: Bobbs-Merrill.

———. 1974. "Representation and the Consumer Interest." In *Consumerism: Search for the Consumer Interest*. 2d ed., ed. David A. Aaker and George S. Day, pp. 64–73. New York: Free Press.

———. 1997. "Congress and Consumer Protection." In *Encyclopedia of the Consumer Movement*, ed. Stephen Brobeck, pp. 126–30. Santa Barbara, Calif.: ABC-Clio.

Nakakita Toru, ed. 1993. *Shōhisha no jidai* (The era of consumers). Tōkyō: Nihon hyōronsha.

Nakamura Kii. 1996. "'Furyō matchi taiji shufu taikai' no koro to" (The housewives' rally to suppress defective matches). In *Shōhisha undō 50 nen: 20 nin ga kataru sengo no ayumi* (Fifty years of the consumer movement: Postwar history as recounted by twenty individuals), ed. Kokumin seikatsu sentaa (KSS), pp. 8–13. Tōkyō: Domesu shuppansha.

Nakamura Masato. 1993. "PL rippō, kessen wa kono 1 nen" (Legislating PL, this year will be the decisive battle). *Shōhisha nettowaaku* 32 (January): 19–22.

Nakamura Masato, Tajima Junzō, and Yonekawa Chōhei. 1992. *Shoisha no tame no seizōbutsusekinin no hon* (A product liability book for consumers). Tōkyō: Nihon hyōronsha.

Nakano Minoru. 1992. *Gendai nihon no seisaku katei* (The policy process in contemporary Japan). Tōkyō: Tōkyō daigaku shuppankai.

Narita, Ryūichi. 1998. "Women in the Motherland: Oku Mumeo Through Wartime and Postwar." In *Total War and "Modernization,"* ed. Yasushi Yamanouchi, J. Victor Koschmann, and Ryūichi Narita, pp. 137–58. Ithaca, N.Y.: Cornell University East Asia Series.

National Consumer Council. 1979. *The Consumer and the State.* Amersham: National Consumer Council.

Nihon hōsō kyōkai (NHK). 1993. "Shingikai: 'Mini' wa kō tsukurareru" (Shingikai: This is how the 'public will' is conceived). *Kurashi no keizai*, January 16.

Nihon hōsō shuppan kyōkai (NHSK). 1980. *Nihon no shōhisha undō* (The Japanese consumer movement). Tōkyō: Nihon hōsō shuppan kyōkai.

Nihon keizai shimbunsha. 1991. PL no shōgeki: Seizōbutsusekinin ga kigyō wo kaeru (The PL shock: Product liability will change business). Tōkyō: Nihon keizai shimbunsha.

Nihon seikyōren. 1984. "Shokuten undō shiryōshū" (A collection of data on the food additives movement). Tōkyō: Nihon seikyōren.

Nihon shōhisha kyōiku gakkai. 1983. *Shōhisha hogoron* (Theories of consumer protection). Tōkyō: Nihon shōhisha kyōiku gakkai.

Nilles, Kathleen. 1985. "Defining the Limits of Liability: A Legal and Political Analysis of the European Community Products Liability Directive." *Virginia Journal of International Law* 25, no. 3: {{pages?}}.

National Institute for Research Advancement (NIRA). 1992. *Nihonteki seizōbutsusekininseido no arikata ni kansuru kenkyū* (Research on the nature of Japanese-style product liability systems). Tōkyō: NIRA.

———. 1994. *Saibangai funsō shōri kikan no arikata ni kansuru kenkyū* (Research on the establishment of an out-of-court system for product liability dispute resolution). Tōkyō: NIRA.

Nishijima Hidehisa. 1993. *Shōhisha no kenri to seizōbutsusekinin no kangaekata*

(Thoughts on consumer rights and product liability). Tōkyō: Koopu shuppansha.

Nishimura, Hiromichi, ed. 1992. *Cooperatives Today: Their Basic Problems.* Tōkyō: Keibunsha.

Nitagai Kamon, Kajita Takamichi, and Fukuoka Yasunori. 1986. *Shakai undō* (Social movements). Tōkyō: Tōkyō daigaku shuppankai.

Noll, Roger G., and Bruce M. Owen. 1983. *The Political Economy of Deregulation: Interest Groups in the Regulatory Process.* Washington, D.C.: American Enterprise Institute for Public Policy Research.

Nomura, Katsuko. 1973. "The Japanese Consumer Movement." Typescript.

————. 1990. *Nakineiri wa shinai—Kurashi wo mamoru shōhisha undō no chōryū* (Don't cry yourselves to sleep—Trends in the movement to protect livelihoods). Tōkyō: Komeitō kikanshi kyoku.

Nōrinsuisanshō. 1993. *Shokuhin ni kakaru shōhisha higai bōshi / kyūsai seisaku no arikata* (The nature of consumer protection and relief policy regarding food products). Tōkyō: Nōrinsuisanshō.

North, Douglass. 1990. *Institutions, Institutional Change, and Economic Performance.* Cambridge: Cambridge University Press.

Oberschall, Anthony. 1973. *Social Conflict and Social Movements.* Englewood Cliffs, N.J.: Prentice-Hall.

Ochiai Kenichi. 1999. "Shōhisha no jiko sekinin to kōseina shijō ruuru" (Consumer responsibility and fair market rules). *Kokumin seikatsu* 29, no. 5: 8–15.

O'Connor, Robert. 1998. "Litigation Agitation." *Best's Review* 99, no. 7: 67–68.

Oda, H. 1996. "Changes to the Code of Civil Procedure." In *Dispute Resolution in Japan,* ed. Joseph W. S. Davis, pp. 457–75. The Hague: Kluwer Law International.

Ohnuki-Tierny, Emiko. 1984. *Illness and Culture in Contemporary Japan: An Anthropological View.* Cambridge: Cambridge University Press.

Oikawa Shōgo. 1993. "Rippō e no shōhisha sankaku: Kihonhō nijūgo shūnen ni yosete" (Consumer participation in lawmaking: Facing the twenty-fifth anniversary of the basic law). *Kokumin seikatsu* 23, no. 5: 6–7.

————. 1999. "Kongo no shōhisha gyōsei no tenbō" (The outlook for consumer administration) *Kokumin seikatsu* 29, no. 1: 8–15.

Oku Mumeo. 1988. *Nobi akaaka to: Oku Mumeo jiden* (Brightly burning brush fires: The autobiography of Oku Mumeo). Tōkyō: Domesu shuppan.

Olson, Mancur. 1965. *The Logic of Collective Action.* Cambridge, Mass.: Harvard University Press.

Ono Shōji. 1994. "Waga kuni ni okeru shōhisha undō no seisei to keika" (The formation and development of our country's consumer movement). Tōkyō: Typescript.

————. 1996. "Keizai no minshuka mezashi kyōdō" (Activism toward the democratization of the economy). In *Shōhisha undō 50 nen: 20 nin ga kataru sengo no ayumi* (Fifty years of the consumer movement: Postwar history as recounted by twenty individuals), ed. Kokumin seikatsu sentaa (KSS), pp. 41–53. Tōkyō: Domesu shuppansha.

Osami, Marino. 1995. "Consumers of the World Unite." *Look Japan*, March, pp. 8–10.

Partner, Simon. 1999. *Assembled in Japan: Electrical Goods and the Making of the Japanese Consumer*. Berkeley and Los Angeles: University of California Press.

Pasch, Ursula. 1998. "Product Liability: Is It Strict Enough?" *Consumer Policy Review* 8, no. 5: 176–79.

Pekkanen, Robert. 2000. "Japan's New Politics: The Case of the NPO Law." *Journal of Japanese Studies* 26, no. 1: 111–48.

Pempel, T. J., ed. 1976. *Policymaking in Contemporary Japan*. Ithaca, N.Y.: Cornell University Press.

———. 1998. *Regime Shift: Comparative Dynamics of the Japanese Political Economy*. Ithaca, N.Y.: Cornell University Press.

Pempel, T. J., and Tsunekawa Keiichi. 1979. "Corporatism Without Labor? The Japanese Anomaly." In *Trends Toward Corporatist Intermediation*, ed. Philippe C. Schmitter and Gerhard Lehmbruch, pp. 231–70. Beverly Hills, Calif.: Sage.

Pertschuk, Michael. 1982. *Revolt Against Regulation: The Rise and Pause of the Consumer Movement*. Berkeley and Los Angeles: University of California Press.

Petracca, Mark P., ed. 1992. *The Politics of Interest: Interest Groups Transformed*. Boulder, Colo.: Westview Press.

Pharr, Susan J. 1981. *Political Women in Japan: The Search for a Place in Political Life*. Berkeley and Los Angeles: University of California Press.

———. 1990. *Losing Face: Status Politics in Japan*. Berkeley and Los Angeles: University of California Press.

Pharr, Susan J., and Ellis S. Krauss, eds. 1996. *Media and Politics in Japan*. Honolulu: University of Hawai'i Press.

Pierson, Paul. 1993. "When Effect Becomes Cause: Policy Feedback and Political Change." *World Politics* 45 (July): 595–628.

PL Kenkyūjo. 1991. *Seizōbutsusekinin nandemo jiten* (A comprehensive dictionary of product liability). Tōkyō: Daiyamondosha.

PL Renrakukai. 1997. "*Shōhisha no kenri" kakuritsu wo mezashite*: PLhō settei undō no kiroku (Toward the establishment of "consumer rights": A record of the movement to establish a PL law). Tōkyō: Shōhisha no tame no seizōbutsusekininhō no settei wo motomeru zenkoku renrakukai.

Port, Kenneth L. 1996. *Law and the Legal Process in Japan*. Durham, N.C.: Carolina Academic Press.

Potter, Jenny. 1988. "Consumerism and the Public Sector: How Well Does the Coat Fit?" *Public Administration* 66 (Summer): 149–64.

Powell, Walter W., and Paul J. DiMaggio, eds. 1991. *The New Institutionalism in Organizational Analysis*. Chicago: University of Chicago Press.

Pross, Paul. 1986. *Group Politics and Public Policy*. Toronto: Oxford University Press.

Putnam, Robert. 1993. *Making Democracy Work*. Princeton, N.J.: Princeton University Press.

Ramseyer, J. Mark. 1985. "The Costs of the Consensual Myth: Antitrust Enforcement and Institutional Barriers to Litigation in Japan." *Yale Law Journal* 94, no. 3: 604–45.

———. 1996. "Products Liability Through Private Ordering." *University of Pennsylvania Law Review* 144, no. 5: 1823–40.

Ramseyer, J. Mark, and Minoru Nakazato. 1989. "The Rational Litigant: Settlement Amounts and Verdict Rates in Japan." *Journal of Legal Studies* 18, no. 2: 263–90.

Reed, Steven R. 1981. "Is Japanese Government Really Centralized?" *Journal of Japanese Studies* 8 (Winter): 133–64.

———. 1986. *Japanese Prefectures and Policymaking*. Pittsburgh: University of Pittsburgh Press.

Reich, Michael. 1984. "Troubles, Issues, and Politics in Japan: The Case of Kanemi Yushō." In *Institutions for Change in Japanese Society*, ed. George DeVos. Berkeley, Calif.: Institute of East Asian Studies, University of California.

Richardson, Jeremy, ed. 1993. *Pressure Groups*. Oxford: Oxford University Press.

Rose, Lawrence E. 1981. "The Role of Interest Groups in Collective Interest Policy-Making: Consumer Protection in Norway and the United States." *European Journal of Political Research* 9 (March): 17–45.

Sacks, Paul M. 1980. "State Structure and the Asymmetrical Society: An Approach to Public Policy in Britain." *Comparative Politics* 12 (April): 349–76.

Sahara Yō. 1983. "Jijitai shōhisha gyōsei to shōhisha undō" (Local consumer administration and the consumer movement). *Toshi mondai* 74, no. 8: 3–13.

———. 1979. "Shōhisha gyōsei no ayumi to genjō" (The history and current state of consumer administration). *Jurisuto zōkan sōgō tokushū*, January, pp. 214–18.

Saito, Tadashi. 1994. "Product Liability Reform in Japan." JEI Report, January 21.

Sakamoto Jutoku. 1992. PL–seizōbutsusekinin–nyūmon (An introduction to PL-product liability). Tōkyō: Jitsugyō no Nihonsha.

Sakata, Tokio. 1978. "Citizen Movements and the Role of Local Assemblies." *Local Government Review* 6: 48–57.

Salisbury, Robert H. 1984. "Interest Representation: The Dominance of Institutions." *American Political Science Review* 78 (January): 64–76.

Samuels, Richard J. 1983. *The Politics of Regional Policy in Japan: Localities, Inc.?* Ithaca, N.Y.: Cornell University Press.

———. 1987. *The Business of the Japanese State: Energy Markets in Comparative and Historical Perspective*. Ithaca, N.Y.: Cornell University Press.

Sanekata, Kenji. 1986. "Antitrust in Japan: Recent Trends and Their Socio-Political Background." *University of British Columbia Law Review* 20, no. 2: 380–99.

Saxonhouse, Gary R., and Kozo Yamamura. 1986. *Law and Trade Issues of the Japanese Economy: American and Japanese Perspectives.* Seattle: University of Washington Press.

Schattschneider, E. E. 1935. *Politics, Pressures and the Tariff.* New York: Prentice-Hall.

Schoppa, Leonard J. 1997. *Bargaining with Japan: What American Pressure Can and Cannot Do.* New York: Columbia University Press.

Schwartz, Frank. 1993. "Fairy Cloaks and Familiar Talks: The Politics of Consultation." In *Political Dynamics in Contemporary Japan,* ed. Gary D. Allinson and Yasunori Sone, pp. 217–41. Ithaca, N.Y.: Cornell University Press.

———. 1998. *Advice and Consent: The Politics of Consultation in Japan.* Cambridge: Cambridge University Press.

Schweig, Barry B. 1980. "The Consumer As Plaintiff." *Current History* 78, no. 457: 197–200.

Seihin anzen kyōkai. 1995. *Shōhiseikatsuyō seihin* PL *sentaa no settchi ni tsuite* (Regarding the establishment of PL centers for consumer lifestyle products). Tōkyō: Seihin anzen kyōkai.

Seikyō sōgō kenkyūjo. 1993. *Shōhisha dantai, guruppu chōsa hōkokusho* (Report on a survey of consumer organizations and groups). Tōkyō: Seikyō sōgō kenkyūjo.

Shepsle, Kenneth A. 1989. "Studying Institutions: Some Lessons from the Rational Choice Approach." *Journal of Theoretical Politics* 1, no. 2: 131–47.

Shimada Kazuo. 1999. "Kore kara no chihō shōhisha gyōsei no arikata" (The future of regional consumer administration). *Kokumin seikatsu* 29, no. 1: 16–21.

Shimizu Makoto. 1994. "Shōhisha no kenri: Sono igi to jūyōsei" (Consumer rights: Their meaning and importance). *Hōritsu jihō* 66, no. 4: 14–18.

Shōda Akira. 1980. *Dokusenkinshihō* (The antimonopoly law). Tōkyō: Nihon hyōronsha.

———. 1982. "Dokusenkinshihō kaisei no keii to seikaku" (The details and character of antimonopoly law reform). In *Dokusenkinshihō kōza 4* (Lectures on the antimonopoly law 4), ed. Imamura Shigekazu, Kanazawa Yoshio, Shōda Akira, and Yoshinaga Eisuke, pp. 243–58. Tōkyō: Shōji hōmu kenkyūkai.

———. 1989. *Shōhisha undō to jijitai gyōsei* (The consumer movement and local administration). Tōkyō: Hoken shuppan.

Shōda Akira and Kanamori Fusako. 1991. *Shōhisha mondai wo manabu* (Learning about consumer issues). Tōkyō: Yūhikakusha.

Shōda Akira and Sanekata Kenji. 1976. *Dokusenkinshihō wo manabu* (Learning about the antimonopoly law). Tōkyō: Yūhikakusha.

Shōdanren. 1987a. *Kore kara no shōhisha no kenri* (The future of consumer rights). Tōkyō: Zenkoku shōhisha dantai renrakukai.

———. 1987b. *Shōhisha undō no 30 nen no ayumi* (A thirty-year history of the consumer movement). Tōkyō: Zenkoku shōhisha dantai renrakukai.

Shōhi kagaku sentaa. 1989. *Jūgonen purasu jūnen no kaikō to tenbō: 1979–89* (Fifteen years plus ten years of retrospection and prospects). Tōkyō: Shōhi kagaku sentaa, Shōhi kagaku rengōkai.

Shōhiseikatsu kenkyūjo. 1983. *Shōhisha undō nenpan, 1982: "Gyōsei kaikaku" to shōhisha undō* (Consumer movement yearbook, 1982: "Administrative reform" and the consumer movement). Tōkyō: Shōhiseikatsu kenkyūjo.

———. 1987. *Shōhisha undō nenpan, 1986: Shokuseikatsu no anzen to akushon puroguramu* (Consumer movement yearbook, 1986: Consumer lifestyle safety and action programs). Tōkyō: Shōhiseikatsu kenkyūjo.

Shufurengōkai. 1973. *Shufuren: 25 shūnen kinen ayumi* (Shufuren: History at the commemoration of the twenty-fifth anniversary). Tōkyō: Shufurengōkai.

———. 1978. *Shufuren: 30 shūnen kinen ayumi* (Shufuren: History at the commemoration of the thirtieth anniversary). Tōkyō: Shufurengōkai.

———. 1998. *Shufuren: 50 shūnen kinen ayumi* (Shufuren: History at the commemoration of the fiftieth anniversary). Tōkyō: Shufurengōkai.

Smelser, Neil J. 1959. *Social Change in the Industrial Revolution*. Chicago: University of Chicago Press.

Smith, George. 1982. *The Consumer Interest*. London: John Martin.

Smith, Martin. 1991. "Issue Advocacy in Parliament." In *Commercial Lobbyists: Politics for Profit in Britain*, ed. Grant Jordan, pp. 123–35. Aberdeen: Aberdeen University Press.

Smith, Martin J. 1993a. "Consumer Policy and the New Right." In *Public Policy and the Impact of the New Right*, ed. Nigel Ashford and Grant Jordan, pp. 145–64. London: Printer Publishers.

———. 1993b. *Pressure, Power, and Policy: State Autonomy and Policy Networks in Britain and the United States*. New York: Harvester Wheatsheaf.

Smith, Peter, and Dennis Swann. 1979. *Protecting the Consumer: An Economic and Legal Analysis*. Oxford: Martin Robinson.

Smith, Sheila A., ed. 2000. *Local Voices, National Issues: The Impact of Local Initiative in Japanese Policy-Making*. Ann Arbor: Center for Japanese Studies, University of Michigan.

Sommer, Robert. 1991. "Consciences in the Marketplace: The Role of Cooperatives in Consumer Protection." *Journal of Social Issues* 47, no. 1: 135–48.

Soranaka Seiji, Hasegawa Kōichi, Katagiri Shinji, and Terada Ryōichi. 1990. *Shakai undō ron no tōgō wo mezashite: Riron to bunseki* (Toward an integration of social movement discourse: Theory and analysis). Tōkyō: Seibundō.

Soranaka Seiji, Katagiri Shinji, Kurita Nobuyoshi, and Takata Akihiro. 1994. *Shakai undō no gendaiteki isō* (Contemporary phases of social movements). Tōkyō: Seibundō.

Steiner, Kurt, Ellis S. Krauss, and Scott C. Flanagan. 1980a. "Toward a Framework for the Study of Local Opposition." In *Political Opposition and Local Politics in Japan*, ed. Kurt Steiner, Ellis S. Krauss, and Scott C. Flanagan, pp. 3–32. Princeton, N.J.: Princeton University Press.

————, eds. 1980b. *Political Opposition and Local Politics in Japan*. Princeton, N.J.: Princeton University Press.

Steinmo, Sven. 1993. *Taxation and Democracy: Swedish, British and American Approaches to Financing the Modern State*. New Haven, Conn.: Yale University Press.

Steinmo, Sven, Kathleen Thelen, and Frank Longstreth, eds. 1992. *Structuring Politics: Historical Institutionalism in Comparative Analysis*. Cambridge: Cambridge University Press.

Steslick, William E. 1973. *Doctors in Politics: The Political Life of the Japan Medical Association*. New York: Praeger.

Stigler, George J. 1971. "The Theory of Economic Regulation." *Bell Journal of Economics* 2 (Spring): 3–19.

Stockwin, J. A. A. 1988. *Dynamic and Immobilist Politics in Japan*. London: Macmillan.

Suginamiku shōhisha no kai. 1982. *Daidokoro fusenki: Kawariyuku shufu no me* (A record of hard fighting from the kitchen: From the eyes of changing housewives). Tōkyō: San'ichi shōbo.

Sunada Jūmin. 1968. *Shōhisha hogo kihonhō ni tsuite* (On the consumer protection basic law). Tōkyō: Zennihon kokoku renmei.

Suzuki Miyuki. 1979. "Tōkyōto no shōhisha gyōsei" (Consumer administration in the Tōkyō metropolitan government). *Jurisuto zōkan sōgō tokushū* 13 (January): 260–64.

Swann, Dennis. 1979. *Competition and Consumer Protection*. New York: Penguin Books.

————. 1988. *The Retreat of the State: Deregulation and Privatization in the UK and U.S.* New York: Harvester Wheatsheaf.

————. 1989. "The Regulatory Scene: An Overview." In *The Age of Regulatory Reform*, ed. Kenneth Button and Dennis Swann, pp. 1–23. Oxford: Clarendon Press.

Swinbank, Alan. 1993. "The Economics of Food Safety." *Food Policy* 18, no. 2: 83–94.

"Symposium on Consumer Protection Policy: Introduction." 1983. *Policy Studies Review* 2, no. 3: 417–549.

Tada Kichisa. 1995. *Shōhisha mondai* (Consumer issues). Tōkyō: Kōyō shōbo.

Takada Yuri. 1979. "Shufuren no ayumi to kyō no kadai" (The history of Shufuren and the topics of today). *Jurisuto zōkan sōgō tokushū* 13 (January): 60–63.

————. 1996. "Shōhin tesuto wo moto ni rippō undō" (Legislative movements based on product testing). In *Shōhisha undō 50 nen: 20 nin ga kataru sengo no ayumi* (Fifty years of the consumer movement: Postwar history as recounted by twenty individuals), ed. Kokumin seikatsu sentaa (KSS), pp. 80–92. Tōkyō: Domesu shuppansha.

Takahashi, Fumitoshi. 1996. "Japan's Product Liability Law: Issues and Implications." *Journal of Japanese Studies* 22, no. 1: 105–28.

Takeuchi Haruo. 1990. *Waga kuni no seizōbutsusekininhō: Genjō to rippōron* (Our country's product liability law: The current situation and the debate over enactment). Tōkyō: Yūhikakusha.

Takeuchi Naokazu. 1990. *Nihon no shōhisha wa naze okoranai no ka* (Why don't Japanese consumers get mad?). Tōkyō: San'ichi shōbo.

Tanaka Satoko. 1996. "Chiiki fujin no pawaa ga dai kigyō wo ugokasu" (The power of regional women can move large companies). In *Shōhisha undō 50 nen: 20 nin ga kataru sengo no ayumi* (Fifty years of the consumer movement: Postwar history as recounted by twenty individuals), ed. Kokumin seikatsu sentaa (KSS), pp. 126–37. Tōkyō: Domesu shuppansha.

Tani Mitsuei. 1996. "'Shoku' de seimei to seikatsu kankyō wo sukoyakani" (Toward healthy lives and lifestyle environments through food). In *Shōhisha undō 50 nen: 20 nin ga kataru sengo no ayumi* (Fifty years of the consumer movement: Postwar history as recounted by twenty individuals), ed. Kokumin seikatsu sentaa (KSS), pp. 117–25. Tōkyō: Domesu shuppansha.

Taniguchi, Yasuhei. 1997. "The 1996 Code of Civil Procedure of Japan: A Procedure for the Coming Century?" *American Journal of Comparative Law* 45 (Fall): 767–91.

Tarrow, Sidney. 1994. *Power in Movement: Social Movements, Collective Action, and Politics.* Cambridge: Cambridge University Press.

———. 1996. "States and Opportunities: The Political Structuring of Social Movements." In *Comparative Perspectives on Social Movements: Political Opportunities, Mobilizing Structures, and Cultural Framings*, ed. Doug McAdam, John D. McCarthy, and Mayer N. Zald, pp. 41–61. Cambridge: Cambridge University Press.

Tejima, Yutaku. 1993. "Tort and Compensation in Japan: Medical Malpractice and Adverse Effects from Pharmaceuticals." *University of Hawai'i Law Review* 15, no. 2: 728–35.

Thelen, Kathleen, and Frank Longstreth. 1992. "Historical Institutionalism in Comparative Politics." In *Structuring Politics: Historical Institutionalism in Comparative Analysis*, ed. Sven Steinmo, Kathleen Thelen, and Frank Longstreth, pp. 1–32. Cambridge: Cambridge University Press.

Tilly, Charles. 1978. *From Mobilization to Revolution.* New York: Random House.

Tilton, Mark. 1996. *Restrained Trade: Cartels in Japan's Basic Materials Industries.* Ithaca, N.Y.: Cornell University Press.

Tivey, Leonard. 1974. "The Politics of the Consumer." In *Pressure Groups in Britain*, ed. Richard Kimber and J. J. Richardson, pp. 195–209. London: Dent.

Tokuza, Akiko. 1999. *The Rise of the Feminist Movement in Japan.* Tōkyō: Keiō University Press.

Tōkyō Initiative on International Cooperative Alliance. 1992. *Cooperative Action Based on "Han": A Study of Basic Cooperative Values Through Practices of the Seikatsu Club Consumers' Cooperative.* Tōkyō: Tōkyō Initiative on International Cooperative Alliance.

Tōkyōto seikatsu bunkakyoku. 1993. *Shōhiseikatsu jōrei to watashitachi* (Consumer lifestyles ordinances and us). Tōkyō: Tōkyōto seikatsu bunkakyoku.

———. 1994. *Tōkyōto shōhiseikatsu shingikai tōshin* (Report of the Tōkyō Consumer Lifestyle Policy Advisory Committee). Tōkyōto seikatsu bunkakyoku.

Tōkyōto shōhisha sentaa. 1994. *Kurashi no henkaku wo mezashite: Tenkanki no shōhisha* (Looking toward changing livelihoods: Consumers at a turning point). Tōkyō: Tōkyōto shōhisha sentaa.

"Tomorrow's 'Lifestyle Superpower,' or Just Another Pipedream?" 1992. *Tokyo Business Today*, August, pp. 14–16.

Trentmann, Frank. 2000. "Civil Society, Commerce, and the 'Citizen-Consumer': Popular Meanings of Free Trade in Modern Britain." In *Paradoxes of Civil Society: New Perspectives on Modern German and British History*, ed. Frank Trentmann, pp. 306–31. New York: Berghahn Books.

Tsujinaka Yutaka. 1988. *Rieki shūdan* (Interest groups). Tōkyō: Tōkyō daigaku shuppankai.

Tsuruoka Kenichi. 1996. "Minjisoshōhō kaisei wo megutte" (Concerning the amendments to the Code of Civil Procedure). *Kokumin seikatsu* 26, no. 10.

Tsūsanshō. 1993. *Sōgō seihin anzen taisaku no arikata ni tsuite: Sangyōkōzō shingikai sōgō seihin anzen bukai tōshin* (Final report of the General Product Safety Division of the Industrial Policy Council). Tōkyō: Tsūsanshō.

Turner, Ralph H. 1981. "Collective Behavior and Resource Mobilization As Approaches to Social Movements: Issues and Continuities." In *Research in Social Movements, Conflicts, and Change.* Vol. 4, ed. Louis Kriesberg, pp. 1–24. Greenwich, Conn.: JAI Press.

Turner, Ralph H., and Lewis M. Killian. 1987. *Collective Behavior.* 3rd ed. Englewood Cliffs, N.J.: Prentice-Hall.

Uchida, H. 1983. "The Progress and Current Activities of the Japanese Consumer Movement." *International Consumer Leader Forum*, June 21–22.

Uekusa, Masu. 1990. "Government Regulations in Japan: Toward Their International Harmonization and Integration." In *Japan's Economic Structure: Should It Change?* ed. Kozo Yamamura, pp. 237–69. Seattle: Society for Japanese Studies.

Upham, Frank K. 1987. *Law and Social Change in Postwar Japan.* Cambridge, Mass.: Harvard University Press.

———. 1993. "Privatizing Regulation: The Implementation of the Large-Scale Retail Store Law." In *Political Dynamics in Contemporary Japan*, ed. Gary D. Allinson and Yasunori Sone, pp. 264–94. Ithaca, N.Y.: Cornell University Press.

Urakawa Michitarō. 1993. "Nihon ni okeru seizōbutsusekinin no genjō to rippō no kadai" (Topics relating to the present state and enactment of product liability in Japan). Paper presented to the international symposium "Shōhisha hogo to hō" (Consumer protection and the law), Tōkyō, April 12.

———. 1995. "Seihin jiko ni kakaru genin kyūmei kikan no arikata ni tsuite" (Discovery services relating to product accidents). ESP, July, pp. 36–39.

van Staaveren, Jacob. 1994. *An American in Japan, 1945–1948: A Civilian View of the Occupation.* Seattle: University of Washington Press.

van Wolferen, Karel. 1990. *The Enigma of Japanese Power.* New York: Vintage Books.

Vogel, David. 1980/81. "The Public-Interest Movement and the American Reform Tradition." *Political Science Quarterly* 95, no. 4: 607–27.

———. 1989. *Fluctuating Fortunes: The Political Power of Business in American Politics.* New York: Basic Books.

———. 1992. "Consumer Protection and Protectionism in Japan." *Journal of Japanese Studies* 18, no. 1: 119–54.

———. 1995. *Trading Up: Consumer and Environmental Regulation in a Global Economy.* Cambridge, Mass.: Harvard University Press.

Vogel, David, and Mark V. Nadel. 1976. "The Consumer Coalition: Dimensions of Political Conflict." In *Protecting the Consumer: Private Initiative and Public Response*, ed. Robert M. Katz, pp. 7–28. Cambridge, Mass: Ballinger.

———. 1977. "Who Is a Consumer? An Analysis of the Politics of Consumer Conflict." *American Politics Quarterly* 5, no. 1: 27–55.

Vogel, Steven K. 1996. *Freer Markets, More Rules: Regulatory Reform in Advanced Industrial Countries.* Ithaca, N.Y.: Cornell University Press.

———. 1999. "When Interests Are Not Preferences: The Cautionary Tale of Japanese Consumers." *Comparative Politics*, January, pp. 187–207.

Walsh, Edward J. 1978. "Mobilization Theory vis-à-vis a Mobilization Process: The Case of the United Farm Workers Movement." In *Research in Social Movements, Conflict, and Change.* Vol. 1, ed. Louis Kriesberg, pp. 15–77. Greenwich, Conn.: JAI Press.

Weaver, R. Kent, and Bert A. Rockman. eds. 1993. *Do Institutions Matter? Government Capabilities in the United States and Abroad.* Washington, D.C.: Brookings Institution Press.

Wilson, Graham K. 1990. *Interest Groups.* Oxford: Blackwell.

Wilson, James Q. 1973. *Political Organizations.* New York: Basic Books.

———. 1980a. "The Politics of Regulation." In *The Politics of Regulation*, ed. James Q. Wilson, pp. 357–94. New York: Basic Books.

———, ed. 1980b. *The Politics of Regulation.* New York: Basic Books.

Wraith, Ronald. 1976. *The Consumer Cause: A Short Account of Its Organization, Power and Importance.* London: Royal Institute of Public Administration.

Yamamoto Akira. 1976. *Shōwa kome yokose undō no kiroku* (A record of the "give us back our rice" movement of the Shōwa period). Tōkyō: Hakuseki shoten.

———. 1982. *Nihon seikatsu kyōdō kumiai undōshi* (The history of Japan's lifestyle cooperative movement). Tōkyō: Nihon hyōronka.

Yamamura, Kozo. 1982a. "Success That Soured: Administrative Guidance and Cartels in Japan." In *Policy and Trade Issues of the Japanese Economy*, ed. Kozo Yamamura, pp. 77–112. Tōkyō: University of Tōkyō Press.

———, ed. 1982b. *Policy and Trade Issues of the Japanese Economy*. Tōkyō: University of Tōkyō Press.

Yamamura, Kozo, and Jan Vandenberg. 1986. "Japan's Rapid-Growth Policy on Trial: The Television Case." In *Law and Trade Issues of the Japanese Economy: American and Japanese Perspectives*, ed. Gary R. Saxonhouse and Kozo Yamamura, pp. 238–78. Seattle: University of Washington Press.

Yamamura, Kozo, and Yasuba Yasukichi, eds. 1987. *The Political Economy of Japan*. Vol. 1: *The Domestic Transformation*. Stanford, Calif.: Stanford University Press.

Yamane Hiroko, Seryō Shingo, and Mori Takashi. 1998. "Shōhisha dantai wa dokkinhō kanren jiken wo dō mita ka" (How have consumer organizations viewed incidents relating to the antimonopoly law?) *Toki no hōrei* 1579 (October): 67–82.

Yamanouchi, Nobutoshi, and Samuel J. Cohen. 1991. "Understanding the Incidence of Litigation in Japan: A Structural Analysis." *International Lawyer* 443: 443–54.

Yanagi Katsuki. 1995. "Kujō shōri iinkai no taisei seibi ni tsuite" (Managing the system of grievance consultation committees). ESP, July, pp. 27–31.

Yorimoto Katsumi. 1998. *Seisaku no keisei to kokumin* (Policymaking and the people). Tōkyō: Yūhikaku.

Zald, Mayer N., and John D. McCarthy. 1979. *The Dynamics of Social Movements*. Cambridge, Mass.: Winthrop Publishers.

———. 1980. "Social Movement Industries: Competition and Cooperation Among Movement Organizations." In *Research in Social Movements, Conflicts and Change*. Vol. 3, ed. Louis Kriesberg, pp. 1–20. Greenwich, Conn.: JAI Press.

Zenchifuren. 1973. *Zenchifuren no 20 nenshi* (A twenty-year history of Zenchifuren). Tōkyō: Zenkoku chiiki fujin dantai renraku kyōgikai.

———. 1986. *Zenchifuren: 30 nen no ayumi* (A thirty-year history of Zenchifuren). Tōkyō: Zenkoku chiiki fujin dantai renraku kyōgikai.

Interviews Cited

Andō Kyōji (general director, Tōkyō Consumer Group Liaison Committee), February 22, 1993; February 23, 1994; March 12, 1994; December 9, 1997.

Edano Yukio (Lower House Diet member, Japan New Party), March 1, 1994.

Fujimori Shinsei (executive councillor, Tōkyō Chamber of Commerce and Industry), June 8, 1993.

Hara Sanae (executive member, Shōkaren), February 4, 1993; April 12, 1994; July 9, 1999.

Haraguchi Kazuhiro (Lower House Diet member, Democratic Party), July 1, 1999.
Hikasa Katsuyuki (Lower House Diet member, Kōmeitō, and head of the party's product liability study group), March 11, 1993.
Hiwasa Nobuko (executive member, Tōkyō Consumer Cooperative Union), February 21, 1994.
Hosokawa Kōichi (Japan Consumer Information Center), February 25, 1994; July 9, 1999.
Ishige Eiko (Lower House Diet member, Democratic Party), July 2, 1999.
Itō Hideko (Lower House Diet member, Japan Social Democratic Party), February 24, 1994.
Itō Yasue (executive member, Shōkaren), April 5, 1994; December 18, 1997.
James, Reggie (director, Consumers Union, Southwest Regional Chapter), May 14, 1999.
Kanamori Fusako (social critic, consumer affairs writer), April 17, 1993.
Katsuyuki Hikasa (Lower House Diet member, Kōmeitō), March 11, 1993.
Kawaguchi Yasuhiro (deputy director, First Consumers' Affairs Division, Social Policy Bureau, Economic Planning Agency), June 2, 1993.
Kudō Hiroko (chief, Consumer Support Section, Tōkyō Consumer Center, Iidabashi branch), December 18, 1997.
Kumada Kazumitsu (deputy general manager, Legal Division, Toyota Motor Corporation), June 1, 1993.
Kurimoto Akira (International Department, Seikyōren), November 10, 1992; December 21, 1993.
Machimura Nobutaka (Lower House Diet member, Liberal Democratic Party, and chair of LDP subcommittee on product liability reform), June 7, 1993; April 13, 1994.
Matsuda Noriko (consumer affairs commentator), February 24, 1994.
Miyamoto Kazuko (executive member, Nippon Association of Consumer Specialists, NACS), February 1, 1994; December 12, 1997.
Nakamura Kii (president, Shufuren), April 11, 1994.
Nakamura Masato (Nichibenren), February 9, 1994.
Nishikawa Kazuko (member, Nihon shōhisha kyōkai), March 22, 1994.
Ohta Yoshiyasu (secretary-general, Shōdanren), November 10, 1992; December 21, 1993; (executive member, Seikyōren), June 29, 1999.
Ono Shōji (former chairman of Shōdanren), March 9, 1994.
Shimizu Hatoko (vice-president of Shufuren), February 15, 1993; July 8, 1999.
Shōda Akira (professor of law, Jōchi daigaku), December 8, 1993.
Tagaya Katsuhiko (staff writer, economic news section, *Asahi shimbun*), March 4, 1994.
Takada Yuri (vice-president, Shufuren), April 1 and 11, 1994.
Tanaka Satoko (secretary-general, Tōkyō Chifuren), May 6, 1993.
Tomiyama Yoko (chair, Shōhisha renmei), March 9, 1994.

Index

forming alliances, 28, 134–37
framing, 79
Friedman, Milton, 186–87
fujinkai, 65–67, 69, 74–75, 92–93,
    100, 263n11. *See also* Chifuren
Fukuda Takeo, 170–71, 173

gaiatsu. See foreign pressure
Gamson, William A., 22
Garon, Sheldon, 5, 66
Gelb, Joyce, 5
General Agreement on Tariffs and
    Trade (GATT), 55, 189
General Motors, 40
"Give us back our rice *furoshiki*
    movement," 62, 260n6, 261n7
Green Consumers Tōkyō Network,
    246

Hall, Peter, 23
han. See consumer cooperatives
Hani Motoko, 68
Haraguchi Kazuhiro, 244
Hart, Philip, 259n4
Hata Tsutomu, 243
Hatoyama Ichirō, 74, 77
Hayashi Yoshirō, 216
Higa Masako, 62, 73, 75, 77, 262n28.
    See also Kansai shufuren; Osaka
    shufu no kai
Hiratsuka Raichō, 68
historical institutionalism, 7, 23–30
Hiwasa Nobuko, 175
Home Ministry, 65
Hosokawa Morihiro, 131, 243; and
    product liability, 222, 224, 226,
    227; relations with movement, 135
House Committee on Un-American
    Activities. *See* Congress
housewives, 60–61, 63, 81, 86; and
    additives, 180; and antitrust, 164; as

consumer organization members,
    128. *See also* Chifuren; *fujinkai*;
    Shōkaren; Shufuren
housewives organizations. *See*
    Chifuren, *fujinkai*, Shōkaren,
    Shufuren
housewives' shops, 62–63, 65, 72
human rights movement, 16

Ichikawa Fusae, 60, 64, 66
Ikeda Hayato, 106, 264n21
ikensho. See opinion statements
Immergut, Ellen, 25
individual rights, 15–16, 101–2, 104,
    264nn17, 18; and duties, 264n19
Industrial Association Law, 69
Industrial Structure Council, 119,
    223; Committee on General
    Product Safety, 223
Information Disclosure Law, 244,
    245, 248, 250, 252; and citizen
    activism, 249, 253; exemptions to,
    274n6
institution: defined, 23; types of, 28–29.
    See also historical institutionalism
Ishige Eiko, 244
issue definition, 127–28, 129; and
    additives, 194; and antitrust, 147–
    49; in Britain, 128; and product
    liability, 206, 218; in the United
    States, 128
Itō Yasue, 199

Japan Automobile Users' Union,
    264n15
Japan Chamber of Commerce and
    Industry, and product liability, 213.
    See also business interests
Japan Communist Party, 165, 195–96;
    and product liability, 271n12. *See
    also* opposition parties

Nomura Katsuko, 68
Nonprofit Organization Law, 244, 253,
    274n9
North American Free Trade
    Agreement, consumer attitudes
    toward, 45, 259n11

Occupation, Allied, 29, 60, 78; and
    Antimonopoly Law, 144–45;
    democratic reforms of, 65–66, 71,
    83, 88; impact on consumer
    movement, 68–69, 73, 77, 83. *See
    also* Reverse Course
Office of Fair Trading, 51
Office of Telecommunications
    (OFTEL), 55
Ohnuki-Tierney, Emiko, 179
oil cartel, 157–60
oil shock, 143, 206; and antitrust, 159,
    164; impact on consumers, 157, 164
Oku Mumeo, 58, 63–65, 68, 80, 94,
    233, 262n28, 263n32, 267n9; as
    Upper House member, 64–65, 125.
    See also Shufuren
Olsen, Johan P., 258n22
Omnibus Trade and Competition Act,
    193
100,000,000 Guinea Pigs, 36
one-party dominance. *See* Liberal
    Democratic Party
opinion statements, 132–33; and AML
    reform, 167–68; impact on
    policymakers, 138; and product
    liability, 226
OPP, 188, 269n21
opposition parties, 113; and additives,
    192–93, 195–98; and antitrust, 165,
    169, 170–71; and product liability,
    209, 211; and relations with
    movement, 135–36, 168, 297;

weaknesses of, 117–18. *See also*
    names of individual parties
ordinances, local, 15, 120, 240; and
    additives, 194; and consumer
    rights, 124; impact on national
    policy, 124; Tōkyō Consumer
    Ordinance, 124, 265n11
Osaka shufu no kai, 62–63, 73–75, 77.
    See also Kansai shufuren
oshamoji. See rice paddle
Osugi Sakae, 64
Overseas Trade Ombudsman
    (OTO). *See* Economic Planning
    Agency

Parliament, 48, 49, 52, 237
Parliamentary Commissioner for
    Administration, 49
People's Cooperative Party, 64
Performance of Police Functions Act,
    150
"per se illegal" principle. *See*
    Antimonopoly Law
petitions, 132, 136; and additives, 194;
    impact on policymakers, 138; and
    product liability, 217, 226
Pharr, Susan, 61
Pierson, Paul, 25–26
PL project team, 224–26
PL promotion faction, 210–11, 217,
    221–22, 232
PL renrakukai, 217–18, 219, 222–26
policy-formulation process, 127; in
    Britain, 52, 57, 238; consumer
    influence on, 138–39, 238–39; in
    the United States, 36, 42, 56, 238
political entrepreneurs, 16, 117; in
    Britain, 48; in the United States, 39
political opportunity structures. *See*
    social movements theory

regulation (*Continued*)
and antitrust, 177; in Britain, 48,
54; capture theory of, 186–88; and
consumer rights, 17; consumer
support for, 187–88; criticisms of,
186–87; economic regulation, 176,
187; free-market model, 198;
public-interest model, 176, 199;
social regulation, 177, 178, 187,
188; in the United States, 33, 34,
38, 48. *See also* deregulation
renrakukai. See liaison committees
resale price maintenance, 146, 159,
267n8; reform of, 152–54, 160,
165, 166, 242, 273n1
Residents' Council to Protect
Livelihoods, 124
resource mobilization. *See* social
movements theory
Reverse Course, 59, 61, 69, 260n1;
and Antimonopoly Law, 145
Ribicoff, Abraham, 259n4
rice paddle, 65, 133, 261n11
Rice Price Advisory Council (Beka
shingikai), 96
rights. *See* consumer rights; individual
rights; women's rights
Rochdale Society of Equitable
Pioneers, 68
Roosevelt, Franklin D., and consumer
policy, 36, 38
Roosevelt, Theodore, and consumer
policy, 35
Rosenthal, Benjamin, 259n4
Roundtable on Citizen Policies, 244

Saitama Prefecture, and consumer
policy, 92
Samuels, Richard, 241
Sanbetsu kaigi, 73
savings, consumer, 65, 74, 262n24
Sawada Yasushi, 170

Schlink, F. J., 36, 258n3
Schoppa, Leonard, 193
seikatsu, 81, 262n31
Seikatsu Club, 5, 69, 70–71, 256–
57n10, 261n17
seikatsusha. See consumer identity
Seikatsusha Network, 256n10, 257n12
seikyō. See consumer cooperatives
Seikyōren, 68, 71, 99, 146; and color
TV boycott, 107–8; finances of,
261n16, 275n18; and food safety,
181. *See also* consumer
cooperatives
Sekki, 260n6
self-regulation, 187. *See also*
deregulation
self-responsibility, 187, 190, 199, 245,
246, 247. *See also* deregulation
SG Mark program. *See* mark programs
Shaminren, 191–92
shimin. See citizenship
shimin undō, see citizens' movement
Shimizu Hatoko, 233–34, 242, 253.
See also Shufuren
Shimizu Makoto, 262n30
shingikai, 29, 64, 125, 132, 192, 241–
42, 247; consumer-related, 119;
consumer representation in, 64, 91,
98, 121–22; local level, 123–24;
national level, 121–22; recent
changes in, 245. *See also* names of
individual councils
Shiseidō, 153–54
Shōdanren, 102, 126, 132, 175; and
AML reform, 143, 150–51, 168,
172; color TV boycott, 107–8;
Committee on Laws Relating to
Consumers, 247; expansion of,
252; finances of, 275n18; history of,
98–100; and labor, 136, 275n16;
and local government, 126;

Takahashi Toshihide, 153, 164, 159–
60, 168, 170. *See also* Japan Fair
Trade Commission
Takeuchi Naokazu, 97, 191, 268n1,
269n17. *See also* Japan Consumers
Union
takuan incident, 72, 180
Tanaka Kakuei, 162–63, 165–66
Tanaka Satoko, 166–67, 261n14. *See
also* Chifuren
Tani Mitsuei, 180
Tarrow, Sidney, 21
Taschner, Hans Claudius, 222
tatewari gyōsei. See vertical
administration
thalidomide incident, 87, 205
Thatcher, Margaret, and consumer
affairs, 53–55
Tōkyō bengōshikai, 210
Tōkyō Chamber of Commerce and
Industry, and AML reform, 162
Tōkyō Consumer Price Policy
Advisory Council, 88
Trade Association Law, 146
Tugwell, Rexford G., 37

Unfair Contract Terms Act, 53
United States Trade Representative,
193
Unsafe at Any Speed. See Nader,
Ralph
Unsolicited Goods and Services Act,
53
Upham, Frank, 121, 235, 258n20

van Wolferen, Karel, 2, 97
vertical administration, effects on
consumer policymaking, 90–91,
118
vertical cartel. *See* resale price
maintenance
Vogel, David, 4, 183, 268n9, 270n31
Vogel, Steven K., 4

Wagatsuma Sakae, 207, 210
War Ministry, 65
watchdog functions, consumer
advocates and, 249; in Britain, 55,
57; in the United States, 56
Which?, 51, 260n15
whistle-blowing. *See* watchdog
functions, consumer advocates and
white list. *See* Consumers League of
New York
White Paper on Citizen Affluence, 86
Wildavsky, Aaron, 178
women's movement. *See* feminist
movement
Women's Association for the Defense
of Japan, 65
Women's Patriotic Association, 65
women's rights, 64

yabumi. See Japan Consumers Union
Yamanaka Sadanori, 162
Yamataka Shigeri, 66

Zald, Mayer N., 21
Zenchū, *see* farmers

Tokugawa Confucian Education: The Kangien Academy of Hirose Tansō (1782–1856), by Marleen Kassel. State University of New York Press, 1996.

The Dilemma of the Modern in Japanese Fiction, by Dennis C. Washburn. Yale University Press, 1995.

The Final Confrontation: Japan's Negotiations with the United States, 1941, edited by James W. Morley. Columbia University Press, 1994.

Japan's Foreign Policy After the Cold War: Coping with Change, Gerald L. Curtis, ed. M.E. Sharpe, 1993.